Fourth Edition

PROBATION AND PAROLE
Theory and Practice

Howard Abadinsky

REGENTS/PRENTICE HALL
Englewood Cliffs, New Jersey 07632

Library of Congress Cataloging-in-Publication Data

Abadinsky, Howard
    Probation and parole : theory and practice/Howard Abadinsky. —
4th ed.
      p. cm.
    Includes bibliographical references and indexes.
    ISBN 0-13-717497-7
    1. Probation—United States. 2. Parole—United States.
I. Title.
HV9278.A2 1991
364.6'3'0973—dc20   90-39998
                                CIP

*Dedicated to the American Probation and Parole Association
and to dedicated probation and parole personnel everywhere*

Editorial/production supervision: Cyndy Lyle Rymer
Cover design: Lundgren Graphics
Prepress buyer: Mary McCartney
Manufacturing buyer: Ed O'Dougherty

 © 1991, 1987, 1982, 1977 by Prentice-Hall, Inc.
A Simon & Schuster Company
Englewood Cliffs, New Jersey 07632

Printed in the United States of America
10 9 8 7 6 5 4

ISBN 0-13-717497-7

Prentice-Hall International (UK) Limited, *London*
Prentice-Hall of Australia Pty. Limited, *Sydney*
Prentice-Hall Canada Inc., *Toronto*
Prentice-Hall Hispanoamericana, S.A., *Mexico*
Prentice-Hall of India Private Limited, *New Delhi*
Prentice-Hall of Japan, Inc., *Tokyo*
Simon & Schuster Asia Pte. Ltd., *Singapore*
Editora Prentice-Hall do Brasil, Ltda., *Rio de Janeiro*

Contents

Preface

The first edition of this book was written while I was a senior parole officer with the New York State Division of Parole. Since that time a great deal has changed — determinate sentencing gained popularity during the late 1970s and then waned as new realities began to set in. The political right and left fought it out over just deserts, and for the most part the right was victorious: The criminal justice system became less flexible and more punitive. Control models of offender supervision, long disparaged in the "progressive" corrections community, gained new adherents, particularly as the public attitude toward offenders hardened and the prison population surged to all-time highs. This edition reflects the swirling world of criminal justice of which probation, prisons, and parole are important parts.

Instead of merely depending on the scholarly literature, often written by researchers with little or no experience as probation and parole officers, this book continues to make extensive use of agency materials received from practitioners throughout the country. This edition has also retained the curriculum format with twelve chapters designed for the typical fifteen-week course. Chapters 1 through 8 and Chapters 11 and 12 should require about one week each; Chapters 9 and 10 should require about two weeks each. Review and examination should complete the course. (The instructor's guide available for this book provides a model curriculum.)

ABOUT THE AUTHOR

Howard Abadinsky is professor of criminal justice at Saint Xavier College, Chicago. He was an inspector for the Cook County Sheriff's Office for eight years, and a parole officer and senior parole officer in New York for fifteen years.

The author has a bachelor of arts degree from Queens College of the City University of New York, a master's degree in social work from Fordham University, and a Ph.D. in sociology from New York University. He is the author of several books in the field of crime and justice. Dr. Abadinsky encourages communication about his work and can be reached at Saint Xavier College, 3700 W. 103rd Street, Chicago, IL 60655.

Acknowledgments

Robert Altwies
(Arizona Department of Corrections/Adult Services)

Arthur C. Amann
(Erie County Adult Probation Department)

Bill Anderson
(Texas Juvenile Probation Commission)

Donald Atkinson
(Maryland Division of Parole and Probation)

Jack Barry
(New York State Division of Probation and Correctional Alternatives)

Deborah L. Bartles
(Texas Adult Probation Commission)

R. Barry Bollensen
(Illinois Probation Division)

Gerald S. Buck
(Contra Costa County, CA, Probation Department)

Julio Calderon
(California Youth Authority)

Joseph T. Carmichael
(Ohio Department of Youth Services)

G. Peter Chatfield
(Michigan Department of Correction)

Robert Corrado
(Municipal Court Probation, Little Rock, AK)

Welby A. Cramer
(California Youthful Offender Parole Board)

E. Robert Czaplicki
(Onondaga County, NY, Probation Department)

Ernest J. Dalton
(Grant County, IN, Probation Department)

Rev. Francis A. Davis
(Utah Board of Corrections)

Terry L. Davis
(Probation Department, Dauphin County, PA)

Albert Ding
(Probation Department, Santa Clara County, CA)

Victor D'Ilio
(New Jersey Department of Corrections/Bureau of Parole)

Harry Dodd
(Florida Probation and Parole Services)

Robert Dougherty
(St. Leonard's House/Chicago)

Nancy Downs
(Maine Department of Corrections/Probation and Parole)

Linda A. Druker
(Massachusetts Department of Correction)

Michael C. Dunston
(Virgin Islands Criminal and Family Law Division)

Robert M. Egles
(New Jersey State Parole Board)

William Elliott
(California Board of Prison Terms)

George W. Farmer
(Ohio Adult Parole Authority)

Tracy D. Fisk
(Nevada Department of Parole and Probation)

James P. Fogerty
(United States Probation)

Peter J. Fournier
(Probate Court, Juvenile Division, Wayne County, MI)

Mary C. Fry
(Juvenile Division of the Circuit Court of Jackson County, MO)

Richard M. George
(DuPage County, IL, Probation and Court Services)

James J. Goldbin
(Probation Department, Suffolk County, NY)

Leslie R. Green
(Minnesota Department of Corrections)

Jo Gustafson
(National Institute of Corrections)

Leo S. Hickie
(Probation Department, Dubuque County, IA)

Fred W. Hinickle
(Wisconsin Parole Board)

R. Barry Hollensen
(Illinois Probation Department)

Fred B. Holley
(New Jersey State Bureau of Parole)

Gail D. Hughes
(Missouri Board of Probation and Parole)

Christine Hunt
(Massachusetts Half-Way Houses, Inc.)

Robert Kaplan
(New York State Division of Parole)

Marcia Keesler
(Adult Probation Department, Allen County, IN)

William J. Kunkel
(Maryland Parole Commission)

Keith J. Leenhouts
(Volunteers in Prevention, Probation and Prisons, Inc.)

Dick Lewis
(Texas Adult Probation Commission)

Joseph M. Long
(Pennsylvania Board of Probation and Parole)

Arthur Lurigio
(Adult Probation Department, Cook County, IL)

Jacquelyn L. Manns
(Probation Department, Philadelphia, PA)

Sue Marquardt
(Utah Division of Youth Corrections)

Dennis R. Martin
(New Jersey Probation Services Division)

Kent W. Mason
(Montgomery County Pre-Release Center)

Steve McGuire
(Adult Probation Department, Cook County, IL)

Robert F. McManus
(South Carolina Department of Probation, Parole and Pardon Services)

Angelo R. Musto
(Massachusetts Probation Department)

Ted Nelson
(Oregon Corrections Division)

Jay M. Newberger
(South Dakota Unified Judicial System)

Barry J. Nidof
(Probation Department, Los Angeles County, CA)

Marc V. Oley
(Hawaii Paroling Authority)

Richard M. Ortiz
(Arizona Board of Pardons and Paroles)

Pledger W. Parker
(Probation Department, Bibb County, GA)

Robert L. Patterson
(California Board of Prison Terms)

Ross M. Peterson
(Washington Department of Corrections)

Donna L. Quirk
(N.Y. State Division for Youth)

Doreen Ranson
(Alaska Department of Corrections)

Nikki B. Reisen
(Nebraska Board of Pardons)

E. Guy Revell, Jr.
(Florida Parole Commission)

Carol Robinson
(Oklahoma Department of Corrections)

Toni L. Salazar
(Iowa Department of Corrections)

George Savastano
(New York State Division of Parole)

Linda Steadly Schwarb
(Michigan Youth Parole and Review Board)

Kenneth W. Simmons
(Florida Parole and Probation Commission)

Albert G. Smith
(California Department of Corrections/Parole)

Richard A. Smith
(Vermont Department of Corrections)

R. E. Smith
(Ohio Department of Rehabilitation and Correction)

Keith B. Snyder
(Juvenile Probation, Harrisburg, PA)

Beatrice A. Soman
(Nassau County, NY, Probation Department)

Vince Stinton
(BI Inc.)

Stephen J. Suknaic
(Juvenile Probation Department, Harrisburg, PA)

Patricia M. Sweeney
(Massachusetts Half-Way Houses, Inc.)

James P. Testani
(New York State Division of Probation)

Michael Van Winkle
(California Department of Corrections)

Larry Villnow
(Juvenile Court, Clark County, NE)

Marcia Wagner
(Allen County, IN, Adult Probation Department)

Jerome M. Wasson
(Washington Division of Juvenile Rehabilitation)

Paul J. Werrell
(Lehigh County, PA, Juvenile Probation Department)

James F. Wichtman
(Adult Probation Department, Montgomery County, OH)

Robert L. Williams
(Probation Department, Philadelphia, PA)

George W. Wilson
(Ohio Department of Rehabilitation and Correction)

Danny W. Yeary
(Kentucky Division of Probation and Parole)

Timothy Z. Zadai
(Massachusetts Parole Board)

ONE
Probation and Parole in Criminal Justice

Probation and parole are linked to particular segments of the criminal justice system, and criminal justice is tied to a system of laws most frequently invoked against a distinct type of offender. Law reflects the need to protect the person, the property, and the norms of those who have the power to enact laws — the criminal law reflects power relations in society. Thus, the harmful activities of those with power are often not even defined as criminal (for example, antitrust violations) but may instead constitute only a civil wrong. For example, the Eleventh District Court of Appeals overturned the fraud convictions of five Texas oilmen involved in a Florida fuel-oil pricing conspiracy that occurred in the mid-1970s. As a result of the scheme customers of the Florida Power Corporation paid as much as $7.5 million in overcharges. The court ruled that although the actions may have been "against the public interest," they were not illegal (*Chicago Tribune,* December 17, 1981: sec. 2: 3).

Marshall Clinard and his associates note that when the criminal law is invoked the results may represent distinctions in power; burglary prosecutions, for example, routinely invoke more significant penalties than business crime:

> A single case of corporate law violation may involve millions and even billions of dollars of losses. The injuries caused by product defects or impure or dangerous drugs can involve thousands of persons in a single case. For example, in the electrical price-fixing conspiracy of the 1960s [see R. A. Smith, 1961], losses amounted to over $2 billion, a sum far greater than the total losses from the 3 million burglaries in any given year. At the same time, the average loss from a larceny-theft is $165 and from a burglary $422, and the persons who commit

1

these offenses may receive sentences of as much as five to ten years, or even longer. For the crime committed by large corporations the sole punishment often consists of warnings, consent orders, or comparatively small fines. (1979: xix)

In 1980, for example, thirty-seven manufacturers were accused of being part of an eighteen-year nationwide conspiracy to fix the prices of corrugated containers and sheets, a multibillion-dollar scheme that defrauded American consumers. Thirty-four manufacturers merely settled "out of court," an option not available to most persons who become the clients of probation and parole agencies (*New York Times,* June 17, 1980: D1). In 1985 General Electric pleaded guilty to defrauding the Air Force by filing 108 false claims for payment, and E. F. Hutton pleaded guilty to 2,000 counts of wire and mail fraud. Ralph Nader states that these incidents constitute "crime without criminals" since not a single person was imprisoned (1985: 3F). In that same year, Eli Lilly and Company pleaded guilty to failing to report the dangers of the arthritis drug Oraflex which had been linked to at least twenty-six deaths — the company was fined $25,000 (*New York Times,* September 1, 1985: 6E). A similar situation involved the SmithKline Beckman Corporation, a drug company whose product was tied to the deaths of thirty-six persons — the firm was fined $100,000 (Shenon, 1985a, b).

Robert Lefcourt argues:

> The myth of "equality under law" would have us believe that everyone is subject to society's laws and those who violate laws are subject to prosecution. Yet in criminal courts across the country it can be easily observed that law enforcement affects most exclusively the working-man and the poor. . . . The other criminals, the extremely wealthy, the corporations, the landlords, and the middle-class white-collar workers are rarely prosecuted and almost never suffer the criminal court process as defendants. (1971: 22)

Or, as the title of a book by Jeffrey Reiman (1990) points out: *The Rich Get Richer and the Poor Get Prison.*

WHAT IS A CRIME? WHO IS A CRIMINAL?

Quite simply, a *crime* is any violation of the criminal law, and a *criminal* is a person convicted of a crime. This raises an important question: Is a person who violates the criminal law a "criminal" if he or she is not apprehended and/ or convicted? We need to consider that most reported crimes do not result in an arrest and conviction. Furthermore, studies indicate that most crimes simply are not reported to the police. Thus, has a probationer or parolee who is not arrested again been rehabilitated, or have they become more successful at avoiding detection?

Index Crimes

Crime Statistics are regularly compiled by the Federal Bureau of Investigation and divided into eight categories known as *The Uniform Crime Report*. The eight categories, or "index crimes," are those most likely to be reported by victims, that occur frequently, and that are serious by nature or as a result of their frequency of occurrence. They are divided into crimes against persons and crimes against property.

Crimes Against the Person

1. *Homicide.* Causing the death of another person without legal justification or excuse.
2. *Rape.* Unlawful sexual intercourse by force or without legal or factual consent.
3. *Robbery.* The unlawful taking or attempted taking of property that is in the immediate possession of another, by force or threat of force.
4. *Assault.* Unlawful intentional inflicting or attempted inflicting of injury upon the person of another.

Crimes Against Property

5. *Burglary.* Unlawful entry of any fixed structure, vehicle, or vessel used for regular residence, industry, or business, with or without force, with the intent to commit a felony or larceny.
6. *Larceny-Theft.* Unlawful taking or attempted taking of property other than a motor vehicle from the possession of another, by stealth, without force, and without deceit, with intent to permanently deprive the owner of the property.
7. *Motor Vehicle Theft.* Unlawful taking or attempted taking of a self-propelled road vehicle owned by another, with the intent of depriving him or her of it, permanently or temporarily.
8. *Arson.* The intentional damaging or destruction or attempted damaging or destruction by means of fire or explosion of property without the consent of the owner, or of one's own property with or without the intent to defraud.

Other relatively frequent (non-index) crimes include those that are *victimless,* referring to violations of the law unlikely to be reported by their victims, particularly drug offenses, prostitution, and gambling; *fraud:* using deceit or intentional misrepresentation of fact with the intent of unlawfully depriving a person of property; *driving under the influence* (DUI): operating any motor vehicle while drunk or under the influence of liquor or psychoactive substances; and *public order offenses:* violations of the peace or order of the community or threats to public health through unacceptable public conduct, interfering with governmental authority, violating civil rights or liberties, weapons offenses, bribery, and tax law violations. And there are also corporate crimes that include restraint of trade, securities violations, environmental pollution, and toxic waste-related offenses.

It is important for the study of probation and parole to consider who actually becomes identified as a criminal. We have already noted offenders who *do not* usually become identified as criminals. A composite sketch of the "average" offender convicted of a crime would reveal that he (more than 90 percent are male) is usually young (more than 40 percent are under age twenty; more than 70 percent are under age thirty), poor, and often from a minority group. Such persons tend to be clustered in particular sections of urban America, sections that are heavily policed, a fact which increases the likelihood of arrest and conviction. Persons who have already been arrested become part of the official records of law enforcement agencies. This increases their susceptibility to further arrests, a fact of life with which all probation and parole personnel must deal. However, on average only about one crime in four is cleared by an arrest.

Some offenders are given an opportunity to avoid being put through the criminal justice process. Later we will examine the use of programs that seek to "divert" offenders out of the criminal justice system and into some other method of being handled. Such programs easily can become another method for providing differential treatment whereby the middle class can avoid the stigma and severity of the criminal process, while the poor are made to face the full force and fury of criminal sanctions.

In response to the question of who is a criminal, some observers see the offender as *victim:* of poverty, discrimination, unequal and unjust laws and law enforcement. In 1902 Clarence Darrow, the famed trial lawyer, noted that "The people who go to jail are almost always poor people . . . " (1975: 29) and most persons on probation and parole come from an underclass.

RESPONDING TO CRIME

Early responses to deviant behavior ranged from the payment of fines to trial by combat, banishment, and death by torture. A primitive system of vengeance emerged, *lex talionis* — an eye for an eye — and was passed down from generation to generation as each family, tribe, or society sought to preserve its own existence without recourse to a written code of laws. About 4,000 years ago, Hammurabi, King of Babylonia, set down a code of laws. Although in written form, his laws continued the harsh tradition of *lex talionis*. Thirty-four crimes, including every form of theft, were punishable by death (Edmunds, 1959).

Later, the Hebrews adopted the concept of an eye for an eye, but under biblical law this meant financial compensation for the victim of crime or negligence (there was no compensation for murder, which carried the death penalty). A perpetrator who was unable to pay was placed in involuntary servitude, a precursor to the concept of probation. The servitude could not last more than six years, and masters had rehabilitative obligations and responsibilities toward their charges.

The Romans derided the use of fines for criminal offenses and utilized the death penalty extensively in ways that have become etched in history. The fall of the Roman Empire resulted in there being very little "rule of law" throughout Europe. When law was gradually restored, fines and restitution became an important form of punishment as those in power sought to increase their wealth. Offenders who were unable to pay, however, were often enslaved or subjected to mutilation or death. A parallel issue in contemporary criminal justice, the extensive use of restitution, will be discussed in later chapters.

Trial by combat also flourished, in part because of the difficulty of proving criminal allegations. With the spread of Christianity, trial by combat was reserved for private accusations, while crimes prosecuted by the crown called for trial by ordeal, an appeal to divine power. A defendant who survived the ordeal — passing through fire, for example — was ruled innocent. The unsuccessful defendant often received verdict and punishment simultaneously.

Trial by ordeal was eventually replaced with compurgation ("wager of law"). The accused was required to gather twelve reputable persons who would swear to the defendant's innocence. Reputable persons, it was believed, would not swear an oath for fear of divine retribution. Compurgation eventually evolved into testimony under oath and trial by jury (Vold and Bernard, 1986). Throughout the Middle Ages in Europe there was a continuation of the extensive use of torture to gain confessions, and public executions were often accompanied by torture, flaying, or the rack.

For many centuries there existed an extreme disparity in the manner in which punishment was meted out, with the rich and influential receiving little or no punishment for offenses which resulted in torture and death for the less fortunate. This was forcefully challenged in the eighteenth century with the advent of the *classical school*.

CLASSICAL SCHOOL

The classical school is an outgrowth of the European *Enlightenment* period of the eighteenth century (sometimes referred to as the "Age of Reason"). During this period philosophers such as Charles-Louis de Secondat, Baron de La Brede et de Montesquieu (1689–1755), usually referred to simply as Montesquieu, and Francois-Marie Arouet Voltaire (1694–1778), spoke out against the French penal code and punishments that were both inhumane and inequitable. Jean Jacques Rousseau (1712–78) and Cesare Bonesana marchese di Beccaria, usually referred to as Cesare Beccaria (1738–94), argued for a radical concept of justice based on *equality*. At a time when laws and law enforcement were unjust and disparate, and punishment often brutal, they demanded justice based on equality and punishment that was humane and proportionate to the offense. This revolutionary doctrine—*equality*—influenced the American Revolution with the declaration "that all men are created equal," and the French Revolution whose "Declaration of the Rights of Man and Citizen" (1791) emphasized the equality of all citizens.

Basic to classical thought is the notion of a *social contract,* a mythical state of affairs wherein each person agrees to a pact—social contract—whose basic stipulation is that, men being created equal, conditions of law are the same for all: "The social contract establishes among the citizens an equality of such character that each binds himself on the same terms as all the others, and is *thus* entitled to enjoy the same rights as all the others" (Rousseau, 1954: 45). Thus, Rousseau asserts, "One consents to die—if and when one becomes a murderer oneself—in order not to become a murderer's victim" (1954: 48). In order to be safe from crime, we have all consented to punishment if we resort to crime.

Contrary to the manner in which law was being enforced, the classical school argued that the law should respect neither rank nor station—all men are created equal—and punishment is to be meted out with a perfect uniformity. This premise was given impetus by Cesare Beccaria who, in *An Essay on Crimes and Punishments* (1764; English edition, 1867), states that laws should be drawn precisely and matched to punishment intended to be applied equally to all classes of men. The law, he argued, should stipulate a particular penalty for each specific crime, and judges should mete out identical sentences for each occurrence of the same offense. Punishment, he stated must be "the minimum possible in the given circumstances, proportionate to the crime, dictated by the laws" (Maestro, 1973: 33).

According to the classical position, punishment is justified because the offender who violates the social contract is rational and endowed with *free will.* This concept holds that every person has the ability to distinguish and choose between right and wrong, between being law-abiding or criminal. In other words, behavior that violates the law is a *rational choice* made by a person with free will—in legal terms, has *mens rea.* The classical school argues, however, that since human beings tend toward *hedonism*—that is, they seek pleasure and avoid pain—they must be restrained from pleasurable acts which are unlawful, by fear of punishment. Accordingly, the purpose of the criminal law is not simply *retribution,* but also *deterrence.* In sum, the "individual is responsible for his actions and is equal, no matter what his rank, in the eyes of the law" (Taylor, Walton, and Young, 1973: 2).

The approach of the classical school supported the interests of a rising eighteenth-century middle class which was demanding legal equality with the privileged noble class, as well as protection from the predations of the lower class. There remains, however, a contradiction between the defense of equality and the emphasis on maintaining an unequal distribution of wealth and property. Free will is an oversimplification, since one's position in society determines the degree of choice with respect to committing crimes: "A system of classical justice of this order could only operate in a society where property was distributed equally," where each person had an equal stake in the system (Taylor, Walton, and Young, 1973: 6). It is irrational for a society, which in too many instances does not offer a viable alternative to crime, to insist that criminal behavior is simply a matter of free will; the nature of our prison population for more than two hundred years belies this claim. Nevertheless, as noted by Anatole France (*Crainquebille*): "The law in its majestic equality, forbids the rich as well as the poor to sleep under bridges, to beg in the streets, and to steal."

The pictorial representation of the classical school appears on many courthouses and documents in the form of a woman—"Lady Justice"—carrying scales and wearing a blindfold. The classical view provides the basis for the *determinate sentence,* which will be discussed later. In sum, there are seven basic tenets of classicalism:

1. Human beings are rational.
2. All persons are created equal.
3. All persons have an equal stake in society and, thus, an equal stake in preventing crime.
4. Free will endows each person with the power to be law-abiding or criminal.
5. People tend toward hedonism.
6. The purpose of punishment is deterrence.
7. Punishment must be meted out fairly, with absolute equality, and in proportion to the offense.

POSITIVE SCHOOL

Positivism, as formulated by Auguste Comte (1798–1857), refers to a method for examining and understanding social behavior. Comte argued that the methods and logical form of the natural sciences—the *scientific method*—are applicable to the study of man as a social being, from whence we get the *social sciences.* Social phenomena, Comte stated, must be studied and understood by observation, hypothesis, and experimentation in a new discipline he called *sociology.* While the classical school is based on philosophy and law, the positive school is based on *empiricism.*

The positive approach to the study of crime became known as *criminology,* a discipline whose early efforts are identified with Cesare Lombroso (1835–1909), a Venetian physician. In his *L'uomo delinquente* ("The Criminal Man"), first published in 1876, Lombroso argued that the criminal is a "primitive throwback" to earlier developmental stages through which noncriminal man had already passed—the influence of *social Darwinism* is obvious. Lombroso's research centered on physiological characteristics believed indicative of criminality, although his later work (published in 1911) noted the importance of environmental factors in causing crime (see Lombroso, 1968).

Lombroso contributed to the study of crime by utilizing, in a rather imperfect way, the tools of science, shifting the field of inquiry from law and philosophy to empiricism. The positive school places emphasis not on the crime, but on the criminal. It contradicts the theory of free will for which positivists have substituted *a chain of interrelated causes* and, at its most extreme, a *deterministic* basis for criminal behavior: the criminal could not do otherwise. Since criminal behavior is the result of social and psychological, if not physiological, conditions over which the offender has little or no control, he or she is not culpable and, thus, punishment is inappropriate (in legal parlance, lacks *mens rea.*) However, since criminals do represent a threat to society, they must be "treated," "corrected," "rehabilitated" (or according to early Lombrosians, separated from society, perhaps castrated or executed). In practice, the change in emphasis from punishment to correction did not result in a less severe response to criminal offenders. Some modern critics contend that rehabilitation opened the door to a host of questionable schemes for dealing with offenders under the guise of "treatment" and "for their own good." The American Friends Service Committee notes: "Retribution and revenge necessarily imply punishment, but it does not necessarily follow that punishment is eliminated under rehabilitative regimes" (1971: 20). The positive view provides the basis for the *indeterminate sentence,* which will be discussed later.

The views of the classical and positive schools are important because they transcend their own time and continue to apply to contemporary issues in criminal justice. The question remains: *Do we judge the crime or the criminal?* This is a central question in the continuing debate over sentencing — determinate versus indeterminate — that will be discussed in later chapters. Probation and parole, it is often argued, emanate from a positivistic response to criminal behavior, a view that will be disputed later in this book.

This book is concerned with probation and parole as part of criminal justice. Let us locate these two services within the system of criminal justice.

PROBATION AND PAROLE IN CRIMINAL JUSTICE

American criminal justice is unique, the outgrowth of a fundamental distrust of government. Authority is divided between central (federal) and state governments, and at each level power is further diffused, shared by three branches — executive, legislative, judicial — in a system referred to as the "separation of powers." Furthermore, in each state authority is shared by governments at the municipal, county, and state levels. Thus, while policing is primarily a function of municipal government, jails are usually run by the county (often by the sheriff), prison and parole systems by the state — and

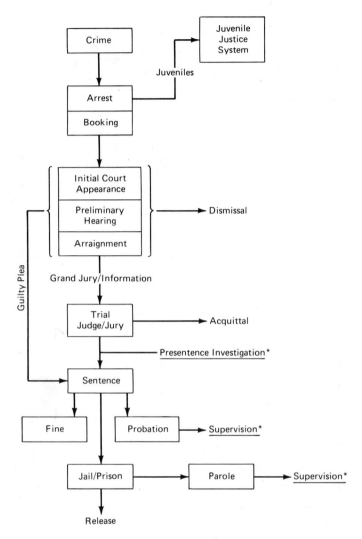

FIGURE 1.1 Probation and Parole in a State Criminal Justice System

there is a separate federal system of criminal justice. (Probation may be administered in a variety of ways discussed in Chapter 2.) As those who work in criminal justice recognize, there is a lack of joint planning and budgeting, or even systematic consultation, between the various agencies responsible for criminal justice. The result is *a system that is not systematic.*

While criminal justice agencies, from the police to parole, are interdependent, they do not, in toto, comprise a system: arranged so as to form a unity. While the operations of criminal justice agencies lack any significant level of coordination, each impacts on the other. A disproportionate share of

The Federal Criminal Justice Case Processing System

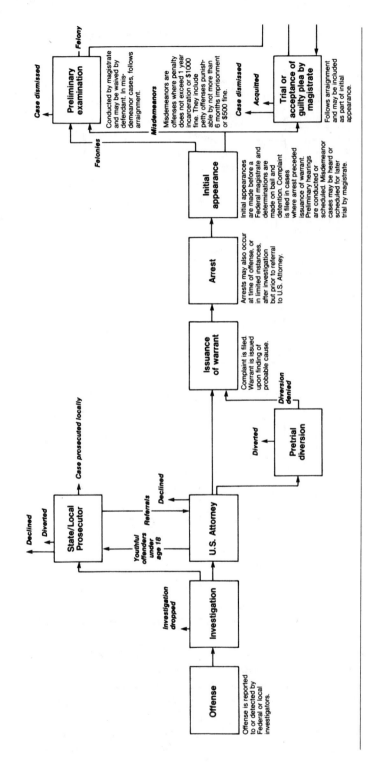

FIGURE 1.2 The Federal Criminal Justice Case Processing System. *Source:* U.S. Bureau of Justice Statistics. *Note:* The figure continues from top right to bottom left.

Felony

Information

Felony cases presented to Grand Jury may be reduced to misdemeanors. Grand Jury investigation may also precede arrest.

Case dropped

Grand Jury

Felony/Misdemeanor indictment

Misdemeanor information

Convictions or guilty pleas

New trial granted

Arraignment

Case dismissed

Pretrial hearing

Acquitted

Bench or Jury trial/Acceptance of guilty plea

Guilty plea may be entered at arraignment.

Pre-sentence investigation

Pre-sentence report is prepared unless waived by defendant or court finds sufficient data in case record to support sentencing decision.

Appeal granted

Post-trial procedures

New trial granted

Sentencing options:
Incarceration
Fines
Probation
Mixed sentence (fine and incarceration and/or probation)
Split sentence (incarceration followed by probation)
Youth Corrections Act (probation or treatment for persons under age 22)

Sentencing

Post-trial procedures

Appeal granted

Federal prison or jail

Discharge

Federal probation or parole

Discharge

Violations

Reincarceration, continued supervision, or trial as new crime

FIGURE 1.2 (Continued)

11

the criminal justice budget (about 42 percent) goes to that agency having the most public visibility, the police (plus 6 percent for federal law enforcement). The courts, prosecutors, and public defenders receive about 22 percent; corrections receives about 29 percent. (An additional one percent goes for miscellaneous functions.) As a result, more persons are brought into the system by the police than the rest of the system can adequately handle.

Because they are overburdened, judges and prosecutors tend to concentrate on the speedy processing of cases. This, in turn, encourages "bargain justice" that is frequently neither a bargain nor just. When a probation agency is understaffed, judges tend to send marginal cases to prison instead of using probation. Since prisons are underfunded and overcrowded, there is pressure on the parole board to accelerate the release of inmates, overburdening parole supervision that also is usually understaffed. In recent years some states have abolished their parole systems; while this may have made political sense, it does not respond to the problem of prison overcrowding. As pressure builds on prisons, usually the result of judicial scrutiny, prison officials are forced to release inmates without benefit of the type of analysis usually provided by a parole board. Prison overcrowding results in pressure on the judicial system; more persons are placed on probation and the revolving door of criminal justice continues to spin.

Entering the System

"Most crime is not responded to by the criminal justice system because it has not been discovered or reported to the police" and when reported most crimes are never solved *(American Response to Crime,* 1983: 1). When the police effect an arrest, the subject is transported to a holding facility, usually a police station equipped with cells—a "lockup." As opposed to jail, a lockup is used on a temporary basis from twenty-four to forty-eight hours. During this time the suspect will be booked, photographed, and fingerprinted, and the police will request that formal charges be instituted by the prosecutor's office. A fingerprint check reveals if the suspect has a previous arrest record, is wanted for other charges, or is on probation or parole.

Pretrial Court Appearances

Depending on what time of the day the arrest occurred and whether it happened on a weekday, weekend, or court holiday, the suspect may have to spend twenty-four hours or longer in the lockup before being transported to court. At the first appearance the primary question concerns bail, and the initial appearance may actually be a bond hearing at which bail is the only issue. If a defendant is under probation or parole supervision, this will affect the bail decision; for example, in some jurisdictions a probation or parole warrant will be filed to preclude release on bail. In some jurisdictions probation officers or other specialized court personnel will interview defendants with a view toward assisting the judge in making a bail decision. These *pretrial release* programs will be discussed in later chapters. If the subject is unable to provide bail, or a probation/parole warrant is filed as a detainer, he or she will be kept in jail pending further court action.

At pretrial hearings (sometimes referred to as an initial appearance, preliminary hearing, or arraignment) the official charges will be read, the need for counsel considered, and bail set or reviewed (if it has already been set at a bond hearing). Typically these hearings last only a few minutes. If the case is a misdemeanor it may be adjudicated at this time, often by a plea of guilty or dismissal of the charges on a motion by the prosecutor. If the charge(s) constitutes a felony, a *probable cause* hearing will be held to determine if the arresting officer had sufficient evidence, *probable cause,* to justify an arrest. This hearing takes the form of a short mini-trial at which the prosecutor calls witnesses and the defense may cross-examine and call its own witnesses.

If the judge finds probable cause—evidence sufficient to cause a reasonable person to believe that the suspect committed a crime—the prosecutor files an *information* (presents details of the charges), which has the effect of bringing the case to trial. In some states the prosecutor may avoid a probable cause hearing by presenting evidence directly to a *grand jury*—generally twenty-three citizens who hear charges in secret. If they vote a *true bill,* the defendant stands *indicted* and the case proceeds to trial.

Trial or Guilty Plea

Few cases entering the criminal justice system actually result in a jury trial, an expensive and time-consuming luxury most participants attempt to keep to a minimum; about 85 to 95 percent of all criminal convictions are the result of a guilty plea and most guilty pleas are the result of *plea bargaining*. This widely condemned practice for disposing of cases involves an *exchange*: the defendant agrees to waive his or her constitutional right to a jury trial, providing the prosecutor with a "win" and saving the court a great deal of time and effort; the defendant is rewarded for this behavior by receiving some form of sentencing leniency. If plea negotiations fail to result in an agreement, or if one or the other side refuses to bargain, the case is scheduled for trial. (For a discussion of plea bargaining, see Abadinsky, 1991).

The trial is an adversary proceeding in which both sides are represented by legal counsel. Each side can subpoena witnesses to present testimony and can cross-examine adverse witnesses. The defendant can take the stand on his or her own behalf or, if the defendant prefers not to testify, can maintain the Fifth Amendment privilege against self-incrimination. Defendants who are on probation or parole often decline to testify since this would subject them to cross-examination and result in a disclosure of their criminal record to the jury. After each side has introduced all of their evidence, the judge instructs the jury on the principles of law applicable to the case. Every jury is told (charged by the judge) that the facts pointing to the guilt of the defendant must be established *beyond a reasonable doubt,* as opposed to the *preponderance (greater weight) of the evidence* which is the standard in civil cases (and probation and parole violation hearings).

The jury now retires to deliberate in private; in most jurisdictions their decision for guilt or acquittal must be unanimous or the result is a *hung jury.* If the jury cannot reach a unanimous verdict the jurors will be discharged and, if the prosecutor decides, the case must be tried a second time before a different jury. Except in some relatively rare instances when there are violations of both federal and state law, the defendant who is acquitted cannot be tried again for the same charges since this would constitute *double jeopardy* (which is prohibited by the Fifth Amendment). If the jury finds the defendant guilty of one or more of the charges, the case moves to the sentencing stage and the probation officer enters the case, usually for the first time. (In some jurisdictions the probation officer is involved in gathering information—plea investigation—for the judge during plea bargaining.)

Sentencing

After a verdict or plea of guilty, the judge decides upon the sentence, although in some states the sentence is decided by the jury, particularly in cases of murder (Zawitz, 1988). The sentencing function reflects societal goals that may be in conflict:

1. *Retribution.* The punishment dimensions (*lex talionis,* an eye-for-an-eye, or just deserts) that expresses society's disapproval of criminal behavior.
2. *Incapacitation.* Reducing the opportunity for further criminal behavior by imprisonment.
3. *Deterrence.* A belief that punishment will reduce the likelihood of future criminal behavior by the particular offender *(individual/specific deterrence),* or by others in society who fear similar punishment *(general deterrence).*
4. *Rehabilitation.* A belief that by providing services—social, psychological, educational, vocational—an offender will be less likely to commit future crimes.
5. *Restitution.* Having an offender repay the victim or society in money or service for the harm committed.

Sentencing can be complicated further by concerns for:

proportionality: that punishment be commensurate with the seriousness of the crime;
equity: that similar crimes receive similar punishment;
social debt: that the severity of punishment should take into account the offender's prior criminal record (Zawitz, 1988).

These issues will be discussed in later chapters.

The trial judge sets a date for a sentencing hearing and in many jurisdictions will order a presentence investigation to be conducted by the probation department. A probation officer will search court records; examine other reports (such as psychiatric and school reports) and interview the defendant, spouse, employer, arresting officer and, sometimes, the victim. Information from the presentence investigation will be reduced to writing in the form of a presentence or probation report. It frequently contains the probation officer's sentencing recommendation. After reviewing the report the judge conducts a sentencing hearing at which both defense and prosecution are allowed to make statements. The judge then imposes a sentence: fine, suspended sentence, probation, incarceration, or any combination thereof.

A sentence of probation places the defendant, now a "convict," under the supervision of a probation officer. A sentence of incarceration results in the defendant being sent to jail (if convicted of a misdemeanor) for not more than one year, or to a state (or federal) prison if convicted of a felony. In most jurisdictions a parole board can release the defendant (now an "inmate") prior to the expiration of his or her sentence. In other states and the federal system, the inmate can be released early as the result of accumulating time off for "good behavior." Parolees and, in many states persons released for good behavior, come under the supervision of a parole officer.

Appeals

While the prosecutor cannot appeal a verdict of acquittal, the defendant is free to appeal a guilty verdict in hopes of obtaining a reversal. The defendant can ask an appellate court to review the proceedings that culminated in his or her conviction. In fact, American criminal justice is rather unique for the extensive post-conviction review procedures to which a defendant is entitled. A prison inmate may petition the trial court for a new trial, or take an appeal to the state's intermediate appellate court, and, if unsuccessful there, can still appeal to the state court of last resort. If unsuccessful in state court, he or she can petition the United States Supreme Court. The prisoner can also attack the conviction "collaterally," that is, using indirect means, by way of a writ of *habeas corpus,* claiming that his or her constitutional rights were violated in some way by the state court conviction. Having exhausted direct and indirect appeals in state courts, the inmate can move over to the federal courts, claiming again that the conviction was unconstitutional, usually on grounds of lack of due process.

The appellate court cannot act as a trial court; that is, receive new evidence concerning the facts already established at the original trial. It is limited to addressing new theories or legal arguments regarding the law applicable to these facts. The appellate court can uphold the verdict, overturn it, or order it reversed and remanded to the trial court for a new trial. The appellate court can also render decisions that impact on other cases by setting a precedent or handing down a ruling that governs the actions of criminal justice officials; for example, in *Morrissey v. Brewer* the United States Supreme

Court ruled that parolees are entitled some basic forms of due process before they can be returned to prison for violation of parole.

PROBATION AND PAROLE: WHY BOTHER?

Why are we concerned with probation or parole? Some say simply, "If you do the crime, do the time." While future chapters will elaborate on this issue, consider the following: The average yearly cost of supervising a person on parole is about $700; the annual cost of supervising a person on probation is about $600. The annual cost of housing an inmate in prison is about $12,000, although in some states, for example, New York, it is considerably higher (about $25,000). The cost of parole supervision in New York has been estimated at roughly 7 percent of the average per-capita cost of imprisonment. However, the cost of imprisonment is typically underestimated because it leaves out many actual expenses such as fringe benefits for employees that average more than 25 percent of salaries. And accurate cost estimates for probation and parole simply do not exist (McDonald, 1989). And the cost of building a maximum security prison averages over $70,000 per cell. Factors of cost, mediated by overcrowded prisons, have led to a dramatic expansion in the use of probation and parole. In 1979, for example, there were 1,086,535 persons on probation; in 1987 there were 2,242,053; an increase of more than 100 percent. In 1979, 218,690 persons were on parole from American prisons; in 1987, 362,192; an increase of more than 65 percent (U.S. Bureau of Justice Statistics).

Now that we have completed our overview of criminal justice, in the next chapter we will focus on the courts and probation.

REVIEW QUESTIONS

1. Why are the harmful activities of some persons not defined as "criminal?"
2. How does the definition of crime determine who is subjected to probation and parole?
3. How is the enforcement of the criminal law a factor in determining who is subjected to probation and parole?
4. What is the philosophy of law advocated by the Classical School?
5. What distinguishes the Positive School from the Classical School with respect to crime and criminal behavior?
6. Under a strictly positivistic view of criminal behavior, why is there an absence of culpability or *mens rea?*
7. Why is the system of criminal justice in America not systematic?
8. What are the effects of providing the police with an inordinate percentage of the allocations for criminal justice?
9. What are the five societal goals of sentencing?
10. What is the importance of probation and parole in criminal justice?

TWO
Probation and the Courts
History and Administration

A probation agency provides three basic services to the courts:

1. Juvenile services
2. Presentence investigation
3. Supervision of offenders

The administration of these services may be under the auspices of the judiciary, or of an agency in the executive branch of government; in either event, a probation agency provides services to the judicial branch of government. Before examining these services and their administration, it is necessary to look first at the court systems, federal and state.

COURT SYSTEMS: FEDERAL AND STATE

In both federal and state justice systems the four levels of courts are stratified by their jurisdiction:

1. lower court–limited jurisdiction
2. superior court–general trial jurisdiction
3. intermediate appeals court–appellate jurisdiction
4. supreme court–appellate jurisdiction

The Federal Courts

There is a *United States district court* in each of the ninety-four federal judicial districts (eighty-nine within the fifty states, and five for the U.S. territories and the District of Columbia); each state has at least one (only one district crosses a state line) and heavily populated states such as California, New York, and Texas have as many as four. There are about six hundred district court judges and a number of retired — or senior — judges who assist as trial judges. The number of judges assigned to each district varies with the size of the population, the largest being the Southern District of New York, located in Manhattan, which has twenty-seven. Each judicial district has a U.S. attorney (federal prosecutor), a U.S. marshal, and a chief probation officer; they are assisted by hundreds of employees: assistant U.S. attorneys, deputy U.S. marshals and U.S. probation officers. As opposed to most state judges, all federal judges are appointed to lifetime terms by the president (with the "advice and consent" of the Senate); lifetime tenure helps to insulate judges from both political pressures and popular sentiment.

In dealing with criminal cases, district courts employ *U.S. magistrates,* attorneys who are appointed by the district court judges for terms of eight years (or four years in the case of those who serve only part time). The magistrate, sometimes called "commissioner," is authorized to issue warrants and to conduct preliminary hearings and nonfelony trials held without a jury. A U.S. magistrate is usually the first judicial officer before whom a federal criminal defendant appears. Decisions of a magistrate can be appealed to a district court judge. District courts have *general jurisdiction* (meaning they can

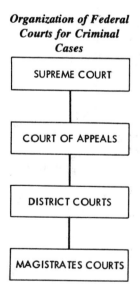

Organization of Federal Courts for Criminal Cases

FIGURE 2.1   Organization of Federal Courts for Criminal Cases

hold trials in any type of case), involving the violation of federal statutes. However, they actually have *exclusive jurisdiction* in only a relatively few types of criminal cases—most crimes involve violations of state law—and often their jurisdiction is shared with state courts. For example, drug trafficking and bank robbery are both federal *and* state crimes. As a result of efforts to deal with organized crime, many state crimes, if committed in a certain pattern, also violate the (federal) Racketeer Influenced and Corrupt Organizations (RICO) statute; for example, bribing a *state* judge (see Abadinsky, 1990 for more information).

The *United States Court of Appeals* (sometimes referred to as *circuit courts)* has jurisdiction over cases already decided in a federal district court—it does not act as a trial court. The country is divided into eleven circuits, each of which embraces several states, and a twelfth circuit which serves the District of Columbia. The Second Circuit, for example, serves New York, New Jersey, and Connecticut. Each circuit court has at least four judges, and a circuit with a great deal of litigation, such as the Second Circuit, will have more than twenty appellate judges. The chief judge (the most senior judge in terms of service in the circuit who has not reached seventy years of age) has supervisory responsibilities for the circuit. Court of appeals cases are usually considered in panels of three judges, although occasionally very important cases will be heard by the full court of the circuit (referred to as *en banc).* Judges of a court of appeals (appellate courts have no juries) review issues of law that have been applied by the district courts in their circuit, and the rulings of a court of appeals are binding only on the district courts in their circuit, although they may influence other circuits and even the Supreme Court. Each circuit has a Supreme Court justice assigned to it who is empowered to act in emergencies when the Supreme Court is not in session; this most often involves cases of capital punishment, and the justice can order a stay until the high court convenes.

The *United States Supreme Court,* the only court established by the Constitution, is unique—the least democratic of our governmental institutions. Whereas the president (executive branch) and the Congress (legislative branch) must, more or less, be responsive to the concerns of the voting public, the judicial branch can remain aloof. While the other branches of government reflect popular sentiment, the Supreme Court can render the decisions of elected executives and legislators null and void—*unconstitutional.* The Supreme Court can protect the rights and interests of persons who, in a democratic society, are very weak—who do not represent a significant block of votes or source of funds—and/or may be unpopular, such as accused criminal offenders. The Supreme Court decisions we will examine in this book, for example, have provided important rights to juveniles, prison inmates, probationers, and parolees—persons whose rights are not likely to be championed by elected officials.

As the highest court in the federal system, the Supreme Court is the *court of last resort*. The eight associate justices and the chief justice, who presides over the deliberations of the Supreme Court, are appointed for life by the president. Unlike the court of appeals, since 1914 (except in certain rare circumstances), the Supreme Court has had the power to decide which cases it will consider. Before the Court will consider an appeal a *writ of certiorari* is required—a minimum of four justices must agree to place the case on the court's calendar—and *certiorari* is granted in less than 4 percent of the cases appealed to the Supreme Court. The decisions of a state court of last resort are appealed directly to the Supreme Court.

In the federal system there are also specialized courts such as the court of claims, but only the court of military appeals handles criminal matters.

The State Courts

While there is one unitary federal court system, there are fifty state court systems and, while the system of each state resembles that of the others (see Figure 2.2), each has a distinct history and no two court systems are exactly alike. States present a confusing array of court systems with names that only add to the confusion. For example, in states with a *unified court system,* such as Illinois, there is no "lower court" (equivalent to the magistrate's court in the federal system). Thus, preliminary hearings and misdemeanors will all be heard in superior court (called the *circuit court* in Illinois, the *supreme court* in New York). In most states, however, there is a lower court which has limited jurisdiction. Sometimes referred to as magistrate's court, city or county court, police court, and, in some rural areas, justice of the peace court, a lower court has authority to try misdemeanors (crimes for which, in most states, the maximum penalty is one year of imprisonment), traffic offenses, sometimes juvenile cases; it is also the entry level for felony cases. This court will receive a defendant shortly (usually within twenty-four hours) after an arrest for an initial appearance that involves the formal reading of charges and setting of bail. In felony cases the lower court may arrange for counsel and conduct a preliminary (probable cause) hearing. Since this is a court of limited jurisdiction, if the charge(s) constitutes a felony, the case will be moved to the grand jury (in states that utilize this body for charging offenders) or directly to superior court (on the basis of a prosecutor's information).

The lower courts typically dispense what many observers refer to as *rough justice* (Robertson, 1974; Feeley, 1979). That is, they are characterized by heavy caseloads—about 90 percent of all criminal cases are disposed of at this level—and speed: justice dispensed very rapidly, often in a minute or less. Anything that tends to delay case processing is avoided. Under such circumstances very little attention may be paid to the niceties of individualized justice and due process, which serve to slow down the pace of case processing. The defendant who insists on his or her "rights" may be viewed as disruptive, and

*Organization of State
Courts for Criminal
Cases**

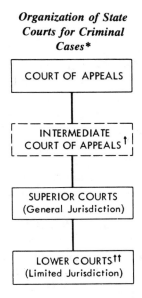

*Whereas there is only one federal system, each state has its own court structure. This diagram, although approximating all, does not necessarily reflect any single state court system.
†Some states have an intermediate court of appeals between the superior court and the court of last resort.
‡These would include county courts, magistrates courts, traffic courts, justices of the peace, and juvenile courts.

FIGURE 2.2   Organization of State Courts for Criminal Cases

this can entail costs. The defendant is likely to receive a higher bail or a more severe sentence than is the norm. On the other hand, the typical case adjudicated in lower court receives rather lenient treatment, a force for gaining the acquiescence of defendants. Persons on probation or parole are in a particularly disadvantageous position during this stage of criminal justice. A plea of guilty, although it may result in leniency from the lower court, can cause the defendant's probation or parole to be revoked.

A *superior court* has general jurisdiction, meaning that it can try any type of case: violations (for example, traffic offenses), misdemeanors, and felonies, although this court usually handles only felony cases. Most cases entering superior court have been transferred from a lower court (directly via a prosecutor's information or by way of the grand jury). Since the superior court receives only a small percentage of the cases that enter the criminal justice system, there is an absence of the hectic pace encountered in the lower court. Because of the seriousness of the charges — felonies — there is usually scrupulous concern for due process. There is also a lack of jury trials, most cases being adjudicated by a judge (in a "bench trial") or negotiations which end in a plea of guilty.

An *intermediate court of appeals* exists in about half the states; the courts are called "intermediate" because on the judicial organization chart they are situated between the superior court and the state's highest court. As is the case with all appellate courts, the intermediate court of appeals does not try cases; it receives cases on appeal from the superior court. An appeal from the decision of an intermediate court of appeals goes to the court of appeals. In states not having an intermediate court of appeals, an appeal from superior court goes directly to the *court of appeals,* the state *court of last resort.* Decisions of the court of appeals are binding on all of the courts in the state, unless overturned by the United States Supreme Court.

Most state court judges and justices (appeals court judges) are elected on a partisan (identified by political party—Republican, Democrat) or nonpartisan basis. In a single state some judges may be elected (on a partisan or nonpartisan basis) while others are appointed, usually by the governor. In some states, there is a so-called "merit system" for filling judicial vacancies: a gubernatorial commission nominates several persons for each judicial vacancy, and the governor must pick one of them. The judge serves for one year and his or her name is submitted to the voters for confirmation—or removal. (For the advantages and disadvantages of each of these systems, see Abadinsky, 1991.)

Juvenile Courts

The juvenile court system differs from state to state and even within states. Jurisdiction over juveniles may be located in a separate juvenile court, in a specialized branch of the superior court, or in various types of courts of limited jurisdiction. It is possible that within one state jurisdiction may be located in two or more different types of courts. Because the juvenile court differs so dramatically from the adult criminal court, it will be treated separately in Chapter 3.

PROBATION HISTORY AND ADMINISTRATION

While probation has antecedents that reach back to biblical times, its American history dates back to the nineteenth century.

Early Probation and John Augustus

In Chapter 1 we noted that the concept of probation has biblical roots. Another form of probation developed out of the practice of *judicial reprieve,* used in English courts to serve as a temporary suspension of sentence to allow a defendant to appeal to the crown for a pardon. Although originally intended to be only a temporary postponement of punishment, it eventually developed into a *suspended sentence* whereby punishment was never actually imposed. In the United States the suspended sentence was used as early as 1830 in Boston, and became widespread in U.S. courts, although there was no statutory authorization for such action. At first judges used "release on recognizance" or bail and simply failed to take further action. By the middle of the nineteenth century, however, many courts were using a judicial reprieve to suspend sentences and this posed a legal question.

A judge had always had the power to suspend a sentence, if he felt for some reason that the trial had miscarried. But could judges suspend sentences wholesale, after trials that were scrupulously fair, simply to give the defendant a second chance? (Friedman, 1973: 518) In 1894 this question was litigated in New York, and the court determined that the power to suspend sentence was inherent in criminal courts only when this right had been granted by the legislature. In 1916 the United States Supreme Court, in a case that affected only federal courts, ruled that judges did not have the discretionary authority to suspend a sentence. In its decision, however, the Court stated that Congress could authorize the temporary or indefinite suspension of sentence—a predecessor to probation statutes (Cromwell, Killinger, Kerper, and Walker, 1985).

The term *probation* was applied by John Augustus to the practice of bailing offenders out of court followed by a period of supervised living in the community. This pioneer of modern probation was born in Woburn, Massachusetts, and became a successful shoemaker in Boston. In 1852, a *Report of the Labors of John Augustus* was published at the request of his friends, and in it Augustus wrote:

> I was in court one morning . . . in which the man was charged with being a common drunkard. He told me that if he could be saved from the House of Correction, he never again would taste intoxicating liquors: I bailed him, by permission of the Court. (1972: 4–5)

Thus began the work of the nation's first probation officer, a volunteer who worked without pay.

Augustus's first experience with a drunkard led to an interest in helping others charged with the same offense. Augustus would appear in court and offer to bail a defendant. If the judge agreed, and they usually did, the defendant would become Augustus's charge. The shoemaker would assist the offender in finding work or a residence; Augustus's own house was filled with people he had bailed. When the defendant returned to court, Augustus would report on his progress toward rehabilitation and recommend a disposition of the case. These recommendations were usually accepted. During the first year of his efforts Augustus assisted ten drunkards who, because of his work, received small fines instead of imprisonment. He later helped other types of offenders, young and old, men and women, and was able to report only ten absconders (persons who jumped bail or probation) out of two thousand cases.

Augustus continued his work for eighteen years and generally received support from judges and newspapers which reported on his efforts. Prosecutors, however, viewed him as an interloper who kept court calendars crowded by preventing cases from being disposed of quickly. Policemen and court clerks opposed his work since they received a fee for each case disposed of by a commitment to the House of Correction. As a result of his probation work, Augustus neglected his business and eventually experienced financial ruin; he required the help of friends for his support.

Several aspects of the system used by Augustus remain a basic part of modern probation. Augustus thoroughly investigated each person he considered helping, taking account of "the previous character of the person, his age and the influences by which in the future he would likely be surrounded" (1972: 34). Augustus not only supervised each defendant, but kept a careful case record which he submitted to the court. Augustus died in 1859, and until 1878 probation work in Massachusetts was the work of volunteers.

Early Probation Statutes

In 1878, the Massachusetts legislature enacted the first probation statute, authorizing the mayor of Boston to hire a probation officer who would be supervised by the superintendent of police. For the first time the position of probation officer was given official recognition as an arm of the court. The law authorized a probation officer to investigate cases and recommend probation for "such persons as may reasonably be expected to be reformed without punishment." Probation was available in Boston to young and old, men and women, felons as well as misdemeanants. In 1880, the legislature granted to all municipalities the authority to employ probation officers, but few towns and villages did so. In 1891, the power to appoint probation officers was transferred to the lower courts, and each was required to employ a probation officer. In 1898, this requirement was extended to the superior courts as well. The second state to adopt a probation statute was Vermont, twenty years later—the lapse in time is attributable to the poor communications of that period. In 1898, Vermont authorized the appointment of a probation officer by the courts in each county, each officer serving all the courts in a particular county.

Another New England state, Rhode Island, soon followed Vermont with a probation law that was novel—it placed restrictions on who could be granted probation, excluding persons convicted of treason, murder, robbery, arson, rape, and burglary. This violated the basic tenet of the positive school: judge the offender, not just the offense. The restrictive aspects of Rhode Island's probation law, however, were copied by many other states. The Rhode Island probation law, which applied to children and adults, also introduced the concept of a state-administered probation system. A state agency, the Board of Charities and Correction, appointed a state probation officer and deputies, "at least one of whom should be a woman" (Glueck, 1933: 231).

In 1894, Maryland authorized its courts to suspend a sentence generally or for a specific time, and they could "make such order to enforce terms as to costs, recognizance for appearance, or matters relating to the residence or conduct of the convicts as may be deemed proper." The courts of Baltimore began using agents of the Prisoner's Aid Society and later appointed salaried probation officers. In 1897, Missouri enacted a "bench parole law" which authorized courts to suspend sentence under certain conditions. The courts also appointed probation officers, misnamed "parole officers," to carry out this probation ("bench parole") work (Glueck, 1933).

Probation at the Turn of the Century

The spread of probation was accelerated by the juvenile court movement, which started in the Midwest and developed quite rapidly. In 1899 Minnesota enacted a law that authorized the appointment of county probation officers, but the granting of probation was limited to those under eighteen. Four years later this was changed to twenty-one. In 1899 Illinois enacted the historic Juvenile Court Act which authorized the world's first juvenile court. The law also provided for the hiring of probation officers to investigate cases referred by the courts, but it made no provision for payment of the probation officers.

Charitable organizations and private philanthropists provided the funds for the Cook County juvenile court to hire probation officers. At the end of the first year there were six probation officers, supported by the Juvenile Court Committee of the Chicago Women's Club. In addition, in each police district a police officer spent part of his time out of uniform performing the duties of a probation officer. On July 1, 1899, Illinois's first juvenile court judge addressed the captains of Chicago's police districts:

> You are so situated that you, even more than the justices, can get at the underlying facts in each particular case brought before you by the officers of your command. I shall want you to select some good reliable officers from each district for the work of investigating juvenile cases. (Schultz, 1973: 465)

In 1899 Colorado enacted a compulsory education law that enabled the development of a juvenile court using truant officers as probation officers. By 1925, probation was available for juveniles in every state (Glueck, 1933).

In New York it was not until 1901 that legislation authorizing the appointment of probation officers was enacted—until that year they were volunteers (Lindner and Savarese, 1984). Probation for juveniles was authorized in Pennsylvania in 1903, and extended to adults in 1909: Except for the offenses of murder, administering poison, kidnapping, incest, sodomy, buggery, rape, assault with intent to rape, and arson or burglary of an inhabited dwelling, a judge could suspend the sentence and place the offender on probation. Although Texas enacted the Suspended Sentence Act in 1913 to provide an alternative to incarceration, probation supervision of the convicted offender was not required until 1947. Probation for adults in Alabama did not being until 1939, when the governor approved an enabling act giving the legislature power to authorize adult probation. Prior to that it had been held that courts did not have the inherent power to suspend sentences since it was held to be an encroachment on the executive power to pardon, commute, and reprieve. Probation was available for adults in every state by 1956 (Task Force on Corrections, 1966).

The first directory of probation officers in the United States, published in 1907, identified 795 probation officers working mainly in the juvenile courts. Like the first probation officer in Illinois, Alzina Stevens, many were volunteers, and some who were paid worked only part time. Training for probation officers was either limited or nonexistent; appointments were often based on considerations of political patronage, and salaries were typically low even when compared to those of unskilled laborers.

Administration of Probation

Probation in the United States is administered by more than two thousand separate agencies. Texas, for example, has more than one hundred county adult probation departments employing more than seventeen hundred probation officers. On the other hand, in about three-quarters of the states, adult probation is located in the executive branch of state government. For example, adult probation in Georgia is a division of the State Department of Offender Rehabilitation (see Figure 2.3) which also includes the state prison system and parole board (Board of Offender Rehabilitation). More than half of the agencies providing juvenile probation services, however, are administered on the local level. Juvenile probation may be provided by a separate juvenile agency or a (juvenile or family) division of the same agency that administers adult probation (see Figure 2.4). Fortunately, the administration of parole, which will be discussed in Chapter Eight, is much less complex: one agency per state and always in the executive branch. Even with parole, however, there is a slight deviation: in some states (Pennsylvania, for example) persons paroled from a local jail come under the supervision of a *county* probation and parole department.

The administration of probation systems can be separated into six categories, and a state may have more than one system in operation:

1. *Juvenile.* Separate probation services for juveniles are administered on a county or municipal level, or on a statewide basis.
2. *Municipal.* Independent probation units are administered by the lower courts under state laws and guidelines.

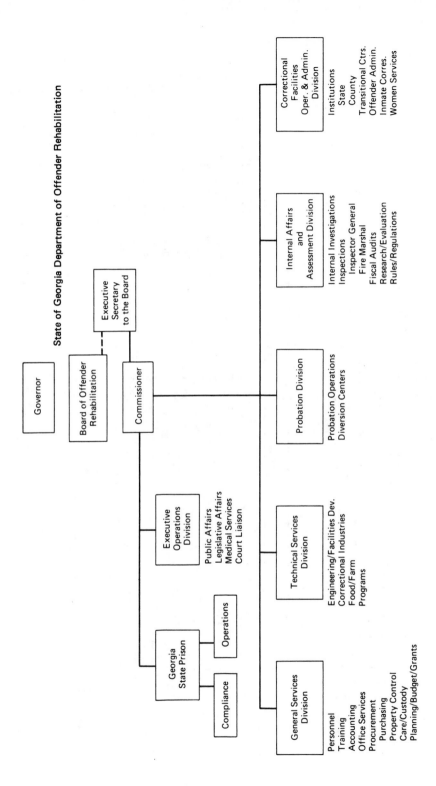

State of Georgia Department of Offender Rehabilitation

FIGURE 2.3   Organizational Chart for Georgia's Department of Offender Rehabilitation

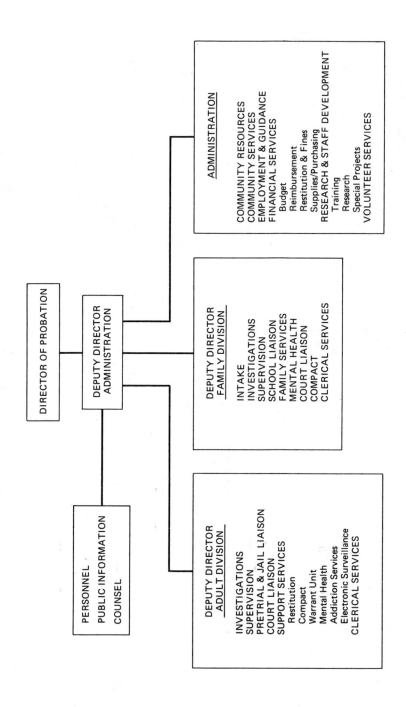

FIGURE 2.4 Nassau County, New York Probation Department

3. *County.* Under laws and guidelines established by the state, a county operates its own probation agency.
4. *State.* One agency administers a central probation system providing services throughout the state.
5. *State combined.* Probation and parole services are administered on a statewide basis by one agency.
6. *Federal.* Probation is administered nationally as an arm of the courts. Federal probation officers also supervise parolees.

Two basic issues arise in the administration of probation services. First: Should probation be part of the judicial or executive branch of government? Those who support placement of probation services into the judicial branch contend that (Nelson, Ohmart, and Harlow, 1978):

1. Probation is more responsive to the courts, to whom it provides services, when administered by the judiciary.
2. The relationship of probation staff to the courts creates an automatic feedback mechanism on the effectiveness of various dispositions.
3. Courts will have greater awareness of the resources needed by the probation agency.
4. Judges will have greater confidence in an agency for which they are responsible, allowing probation staff more discretion than they would allow members of an outside agency.
5. If probation is administered on a statewide basis, it is usually incorporated into a department of corrections. Under such circumstances, probation services might be assigned a lower priority than they would have as part of the court.

Those who oppose the placement of probation in the judiciary note the disadvantages:

1. Judges, trained in law, not administration, are not equipped to administer probation services.
2. Under judicial control, services to persons on probation may receive a lower priority than services to the judge, for example, presentence investigations.
3. Probation staff may be assigned duties unrelated to probation.
4. The courts are adjudicatory and regulative; they are not service-oriented bodies.

Placement in the *executive branch* (which means as part of the same agency that administers state parole), has these features to recommend it:

1. All other human service agencies are within the executive branch.
2. All other corrections subsystems are located in the executive branch.
3. With executive branch placement, program budgeting can be better coordinated and an increased ability to negotiate fully in the resource allocation process becomes possible.

4. A coordinated continuum of services to offenders and better utilization of probation manpower are facilitated.

E. Kim Nelson and her colleagues conclude:

> When compared, these arguments tend to support placing probation in the executive branch. The potential for increased coordination in planning, better utilization of manpower and improved services to offenders cannot be dismissed.
> A State administered probation system has decided advantages over local administration. A total system planning approach to probation as a subsystem of corrections is needed. Such planning requires state leadership. Furthermore, implementation of planning strategies requires uniformity of standards, reporting, and evaluation as well as resource allocation. (1978: 92)

Probation services as part of the executive branch means state government under the office of the governor. It may be as part of a larger department of corrections, as in Georgia, or as part of an independent probation and parole agency, as in Alabama. Probation services as part of the judicial branch of government usually places these services under the judges of the county. For example, in New Jersey:

> The judges of the County Court in each county, or a majority of them, acting jointly may appoint a *chief probation officer, [and] such men and women probation officers* as may be necessary. . . .
> *Probation officers* and *volunteers in probation* shall be appointed with standards fixed by the Supreme Court. All *probation officers* and *volunteers in probation* shall be responsible to and under the supervision of the *Chief Probation Officer* of the county who shall be responsible to and under the supervision of the judge of the county court or, in counties having more than one judge of the county court, the county court judge designated by the Assistant Judge to be responsible for the administration of the *probation department* in the county in accordance with the applicable statutes, rules of the Supreme Court, and directives of the Chief Justice, the Administrative Director of the Courts, and the Assignment Judge of the county.

Probation administered by the judiciary on a *county level* promotes diversity. Innovative programming can be implemented more easily in a county agency since it has a shorter line of bureaucratic control than would a statewide agency. A county agency can more easily adapt to change and the successful programs of one agency can more easily be adopted by probation departments in other counties, and unsuccessful programs avoided. Those most familiar with the local community — its resources, attitudes, and politics — will be responsible for providing probation services; this can increase public confidence in the services provided by the agency. While the judiciary is nominally responsible for the administration of probation, the day-to-day operations are in the hands of a professional administrator — the chief probation officer.

On the other hand, county-level administration results in a great deal of undesirable variance between agencies. For example, the ratio of probation officers to clients may differ dramatically from one county to the other — this would not be the case with a statewide agency. Because each county sets its own budget, probation staff cannot be shifted from a low-ratio county to a high-ratio county in order to equalize the services provided. In New Jersey, for example, the State Advisory Board for Probation in its 1985 report noted that while juvenile supervision caseloads statewide averaged about 80 per officer, in individual counties the range was between 35 and 145. For adult probation caseloads, the state average of 160 ranged from 71 to 284, amounting to a fourfold difference between the extremes.

The New Jersey board found variance with respect to the amount each county expended on probation services and "a great deal of variation in the way work is processed. Thus, the sequence of probation work from county to county is far from uniform" and the board noted:

> There is no accepted definition of what comprises quality probation services. Probation supervision, for example, suffers from a lack of definition and structure, making it difficult to determine what is high quality supervision.
>
> Finally, there is great variance from county to county in the environment which produces the need for probation services, creating large differences among counties in the work probation services must perform. The extent and seriousness of criminal, social, and economic problems has important implications for staffing, procedures, and resource requirements from county to county.

The latter finding, of course, can serve as an argument for county control of probation services. The board, however, raises a question: "Does the lack of uniformity in administering probation make justice less equitable statewide?"

This issue has led states with county-based probation systems to create statewide bodies for better coordination and uniformity of services. In Illinois, for example, the Probation Division of the Administrative Office of the Illinois Courts works to

> improve the quality and quantity of probation and related court services throughout Illinois, provide more uniformity of organization, structure, and services, and increase the use of probation as a meaningful alternative punishment for non-violent offenders. As part of these efforts, for example, the division promulgates regulations for the hiring and promotion of all probation personnel throughout the state.

The Texas Adult Probation Commission — by law, six district judges and three citizen members — is responsible for establishing statewide standards and providing state aid to those local adult probation departments which choose to participate and are in compliance with the standards. As part of these efforts the commission has supported research and experimental probation programs throughout Texas. The commission has promulgated a "Code of Ethics for Texas Adult Probation Officers" and publishes standards for all phases of adult probation in Texas. For example, caseload size:

> A caseload average within a department should be calculated by dividing the number of cases under direct supervision by the number of officers within the department devoting 80 percent or more of their time to direct case supervision. The average caseload of a probation officer in a department should not exceed 100 cases.

While commission standards are not mandatory, the failure of a probation department to maintain them can result in a loss of the considerable funding provided by the commission. For example, the commission provides $100 for each presentence investigation report completed by a probation department.

The New York State Division of Probation and Correctional Alternatives sets statewide standards for probation agencies. For example, "Requirements for training in fundamentals for new probation officers and probation officer trainees":

(a) All probation officers and probation officer trainees shall successfully complete, within the first four months of service, a basic program in the fundamentals of probation practice, which conforms to the guidelines as adapted by the State Director of Probation [who heads the Division of Probation].

(b) This program shall consist of a minimum of 70 hours of training.

(c) The training shall:
1. aid the probation officer and PO trainee in understanding the underlying philosophies and legal basis of the probation process;
2. provide him with an understanding of his role in the community and in the criminal justice system; and
3. introduce various principles, methods and techniques that will enable him to acquire knowledge and skills, and to develop attitudes which may be employed to accomplish the functions of the probation process.

(d) A basic program in the fundamentals of probation practice conducted by a local department shall be certified, in advance, by the State Director of Probation.

(e) A written examination shall be given at the conclusion of the basic program.

(f) Probation officers and PO trainees who fail the examination of the basic program, shall be required to pass a second examination within three months. Failure to pass the second examination shall require the officer to retake and complete the next available basic program. This subdivision shall not in any way impair, abridge or limit the exercise of any rights possessed by an employer of such an officer in accordance with applicable law governing his employment [read: his or her employment may be terminated].

(g) All new probation officers shall also comply with the peace officer training provisions of state law. The division also requires continuing in-service training for all probation officers on an annual basis.

Now that we have examined the history of probation and administration of probation agencies, in the next chapter we will turn to probation in the juvenile court.

REVIEW QUESTIONS

1. What are the three basic services provided by a probation agency?
2. What are the responsibilities of a U.S. magistrate?
3. Why do the federal courts have exclusive jurisdiction in relatively few criminal cases?
4. What is meant by a *court of limited jurisdiction?*
5. What category of courts do not try cases?
6. What is meant by a *court of general jurisdiction?*
7. What is the jurisdiction of a U.S. district court?
8. Why is the U.S. Supreme Court the least democratic part of our tripartite form of government?
9. Why do the lower courts often dispense what has been referred to as "rough justice"?
10. What is meant by a *court of last resort?*
11. What is the difference between a suspended sentence and probation?
12. What were the activities of John Augustus that are part of the services of a modern probation agency?
13. What led to the dramatic increase in the use of probation officers in the United States?
14. What are the six categories into which the administration of probation services can be placed?
15. What are the advantages and disadvantages of placing probation services in the judicial branch of government?
16. What are the advantages of placing probation services in the executive branch of government?
17. How can uniformity be encouraged in states where probation services are administered on a county level?

THREE
The Juvenile Court,
Juvenile Justice,
and Young Offenders

The system of justice used for juveniles in the United States is based on a philosophy radically different from the one on which the adult criminal justice system rests. Before we can examine the services provided by a probation agency to the juvenile court, it is necessary to understand the history and philosophy of this unique institution.

THE HISTORY OF THE JUVENILE COURT

In Europe, from Roman times to the late eighteenth century, children were routinely abandoned by their parents; the classical philosopher Rousseau, for example, abandoned five of his children to foundling homes. Most were subsequently subjected to extreme levels of deprivation and exploitation (Boswell, 1989). A rather indifferent attitude toward children became a characteristic of America, where children became creatures of exploitation with child labor remaining an important part of economic life into the twentieth century. Children of the poor labored in mines (where their size was an advantage), mills, and factories under unsanitary and unsafe conditions. Laws prohibiting children under twelve from employment and limiting the workday of those over twelve to ten hours were routinely disregarded. Increased industrialization and urbanization and the resulting ten- and twelve-hour workday left many children without parental supervision, and family disorganization became widespread. Many children took to living in the streets, where they became part of the rampant vice and disorder that permeated large parts of the urban environment.

In the early days of colonial America, the family remained the mainstay of social control, "although by 1700 the family's inability to accommodate and discipline its young was becoming more apparent" (Mennel, 1973: xxii). Numerous laws began to appear threatening parents for failing to properly discipline their children. Furthermore, the British practice of transporting wayward young to America for indenture—which often involved neglect, cruelty, and immorality—left many youngsters without supervision as they fled from these onerous circumstances. By the end of the eighteenth century it became obvious that a "system of social control would have to be developed apart from the family which would discipline homeless, vagrant, and destitute children—the offspring of the poor" (1973: xxvii). This need led to the rise of houses of refuge.

House of Refuge

In 1817 the Society for the Prevention of Pauperism was established in response to the problem of troubled and troublesome children; in 1824 it was renamed the Society for the Reformation of Juvenile Delinquency. The society conducted campaigns against the "corrupting" influence of taverns and theaters, and opposed the use of jails to house children. Their efforts led to the establishment of houses of refuge (Krisberg, 1988).

The first house of refuge opened in New York in 1825 and was quickly followed by one in Boston (1826) and another in Philadelphia (1828). These institutions provided housing and care for troublesome children who might otherwise be left in the streets or, if their behavior brought them into serious conflict with the law, sent to jail or prison. The house of refuge, LaMar Empey notes, was used "not only for the less serious juvenile criminal, but for runaways, disobedient children or vagrants" (1979: 25-26). Orphan asylums were used for abandoned or orphaned children, for the children of women without husbands or for children whose parents were deemed unfit. Robert Mennel points out that these institutions "were established to inculcate children with the values of hard work, orderliness, and subordination and thereby ensure their future good behavior" (1973: 8). To achieve these ends, however, discipline and punishments were often brutal, and the house of refuge in New York experienced group escapes and inmate uprisings.

Although these institutions were run by private charities, their public charters included the first statutory definitions of juvenile delinquency and provided the basis for the state to intervene in the lives of children who were neglected or in need of supervision, in addition to those youngsters who had committed crimes (Walker, 1980). In these charters was embodied a "medieval English doctrine of nebulous origin and meaning" (Schlossman, 1977: 8) known as *parens patriae,* originally referring to the feudal duties of the overlord to his vassals and later the legal duties of the king toward his subjects who were in need of care, particularly children and the mentally incompetent. In its original form *parens patriae* provided the Crown with authority to administer the estates of landed orphans (Sutton, 1988).

"With the independence of the American colonies and the transplanting of the English common-law system, the state in this country has taken the place of the crown as the *parens patriae* of all minors" (Lou, 1972: 4). This concept gave almost complete authority over children to the state—the Bill of Rights simply did not apply to children (*Ex parte Crouse* 4 Wharton 9, 1838)— and *parens patriae* became the legal basis for the juvenile court. While this concept has become identified with the rehabilitation of juvenile delinquents, it originally applied only to dependent children.

The Child-Savers

As immigration, industrialization, and urbanization continued, the fearful image of masses of undisciplined and uneducated children gave rise to the *child-saving movement.* Led by upper class women of earlier American stock, the child-savers were influenced by the nativist prejudices of their day as well as *social Darwinism:* natural selection resulted in an inferior underclass in need of control, but not aid in the sense of the modern social welfare state. Something had to be done to save these children from an environment which would only lead them into vice and crime and cause them to be the progenitors of the same. Reforming juvenile justice, notes Anthony Platt, became the task of women who "were generally well-educated, widely-traveled, and had access to political and financial resources" (1974: 77). The juvenile court was the result of their efforts, though controversy surrounds the interests and motivations of the child-savers.

Platt argues that these women, although they "viewed themselves as altruists and humanitarians dedicated to rescuing those who were less fortunately placed in the social order," were actually motivated by boredom and middle- and upper-class social, economic, and political interests (1974: 3). "The child-savers were concerned not with championing the rights of the poor against exploitation by the ruling class but rather integrating the poor into the established social order and protecting 'respectable' citizens from the 'dangerous classes' " who might otherwise be drawn into social revolution if not criminality (Platt quoted in Empey, 1979: 31). According to Platt, the juvenile court would serve to protect propertied and commercial interests from the predations of lower-class youngsters, while insuring an adequate supply of disciplined and vocationally-trained labor. In fact, however, many states had already separated juvenile cases from those of adults without establishing a distinct juvenile court. David Rothman (in Empey, 1979: 37) places the issue in perspective: the juvenile court movement "satisfied [both] the most humanitarian of impulses and the most crudely self-interested considerations."

THE JUVENILE COURT

Although a juvenile might be sent to the house of refuge, the orphan asylum, or the reformatory—there was confusion over which children should be relegated to which institution—they could be arrested, detained, and tried as would any adult accused of a crime. While some modifications of the trial process with respect to juveniles occurred as early as 1869, it was the *Illinois Juvenile Court Act of 1899* that established the first law creating a special comprehensive court for juveniles. Consistent with the concept of *parens patriae,* in addition to children who were delinquent—persons under sixteen who had violated the law—the juvenile court was given jurisdiction over neglected and dependent children:

> For the purposes of this act the words dependent child and neglected child shall mean any child who for any reason is destitute or homeless or abandoned; or has not proper parental care or guardianship; or who habitually begs or receives alms; or who is found living in any house of ill fame or with any vicious or disreputable person; or whose home, by reason of neglect, cruelty or depravity on the part of its parents, guardian or other person in whose care it may be, is an unfit place for such a child. . . .

Nondelinquents in whom the court was interested became known as *status offenders.* Within twenty-five years of the Illinois Juvenile Court Act every state but one had adopted legislation providing for one or all of the features of a juvenile court organization (Lenroot and Lundberg, 1925).

A book originally published in 1927 provides insight into the prevailing concepts of the juvenile court (Lou, 1972: 2):

> These principles upon which the juvenile court acts are radically different from those of the criminal courts. In place of judicial tribunals, restrained by antiquated procedure, saturated in an atmosphere of hostility, trying cases for determining guilt and inflicting punishment according to inflexible rules of law, we have now juvenile courts, in which the relations of the child to his parents or other adults and to the state or society are defined and are adjusted summarily according to the scientific findings about the child and his environments. In place of magistrates, limited by the outgrown custom and compelled to walk in the paths fixed by the law of the realm, we have now socially-minded judges, who hear and adjust cases according not to rigid rules of law but to what the interests of society and the interests of the child or good conscience demand. In the place of juries, prosecutors, and lawyers, trained in the old conception of law and staging dramatically, but often amusingly, legal battles, as the necessary paraphernalia of a criminal court, we have now probation officers, physicians, psychologists, and psychiatrists, who search for the social, physiological, psychological, and mental backgrounds of the child in order to arrive at reasonable and just solutions of individual cases.

This statement by Lou clearly embodies the position of the positive school—or, critics might say, the positive school run amok, with the child being denied the most basic due process rights. The unstructured and informal system of juvenile justice used in Illinois quickly became the standard as juvenile courts were established throughout the United States. The differences between the adult criminal court and the juvenile court even extended to the terminology used:

ADULT CRIMINAL COURT	JUVENILE COURT
defendent	respondent
charges/indictment	petition
arraignment	hearing
prosecution/trial	adjudication
verdict	finding
sentence	disposition

The terminology, consistent with the concept of *parens patriae,* reflects a nonpunitive approach to dealing with troubled and troublesome children. We often hear critics decry the lack of sufficient punishment inflicted in the juvenile court. Such comments indicate a complete misunderstanding of this court, which *should not punish.* While the concept of *parens patriae* is paternalistic and not inconsistent with the concept of punishment (Weisheit and Alexander, 1988), the use of a punitive approach in juvenile court would make it simply a *criminal court for children* and, therefore, without grounding as a separate system of justice. Thus, while one could logically argue for abolishing the juvenile court, a juvenile court that imposes punishment has no basis in American history or in logic.

However, because of the noncriminal approach, the usual safeguards of *due process* that were applicable in criminal courts were absent in juvenile court proceedings: the right to counsel, to confront and cross-examine adverse witnesses, to avoid self-incrimination. Because the focus of the juvenile court was on providing "treatment," procedures were often informal, if not vague, and the judge, with the assistance of the probation officer, was given broad powers over young persons. Platt argues:

> Granted the benign motives of the child savers, the programs they enthusi-astically supported diminished the civil liberties and privacy of youth. Adoles-cents were treated as though they were naturally dependent, requiring constant and pervasive supervision. Although the child savers were rhetorically concerned with protecting children from the physical and moral dangers of an increasingly industrialized and urban society, their remedies seemed to aggravate the prob-lem. (1974: 4)

The increasing concern over the operation of the juvenile court is reflected in the *Gault decision* (details appear later in this chapter), a 1967 case in which the Supreme Court ruled in favor of basic due process rights for persons adjudicated in juvenile court.

Procedures in Juvenile Court

The legal age of a juvenile varies from state to state from sixteen to eighteen (see Figure 3.1). In most jurisdictions a juvenile is not routinely fingerprinted or photographed by the police, and a juvenile's name usually is not printed in the newspapers. The juvenile court is often closed to the public and its records are kept confidential. In many states there are provisions for having a juvenile record sealed. The juvenile court typically handles four types of cases:

1. *Delinquency.* Behavior which if engaged in by an adult would constitute a crime.
2. *Status Offense.* Behavior which if engaged in by an adult would not constitute a crime, but which (in accord with *parens patriae*) provides the basis for governmental intervention: for example, chronic truancy, being beyond the control of parents or guardians, running away.
3. *Neglect or Abuse.* Children who are subjected to neglect or abuse by parents or guardians.
4. *Dependency.* Children who do not have parents or guardians available to provide proper care.

FIGURE 3.1   Age at which criminal courts gain jurisdiction of young offenders ranges from 16 to 19

AGE OF OFFENDER WHEN UNDER CRIMINAL COURT JURISDICTION	STATES
16 years	Connecticut, New York, North Carolina
17	Georgia, Illinois, Louisiana, Massachusetts, Missouri, South Carolina, Texas
18	Alabama, Alaska, Arizona, Arkansas, California, Colorado, Delaware, District of Columbia, Florida, Hawaii, Idaho, Indiana, Iowa, Kansas, Kentucky, Maine, Maryland, Michigan, Minnesota, Mississippi, Montana, Nebraska, Nevada, New Hampshire, New Jersey, New Mexico, North Dakota, Ohio, Oklahoma, Oregon, Pennsylvania, Rhode Island, South Dakota, Tennessee, Utah, Vermont, Virginia, Washington, West Virginia, Wisconsin, Federal districts
19	Wyoming

SOURCE: "Upper age of juvenile court jurisdiction statutes analysis," Linda A. Szymanski, National Center for Juvenile Justice, March 1987.

Instances of delinquency, status offense, neglect or abuse, or dependency which come to the attention of the authorities are often handled in a manner that does not involve the formal justice apparatus. School officials or the police, for example, may refer such cases directly to public or private social welfare or child protective agencies. Those situations which come to the attention of the juvenile court enter by way of the intake section, which is usually staffed by (juvenile) probation officers.

Intake   Children are referred to the juvenile court by the police, parents, school officials, or other public or private agency personnel. In some jurisdictions all cases are received by a probation officer (PO) assigned to the intake unit. In others, cases that involve criminal complaints are first sent to the

FIGURE 3.2   Juvenile Court Process

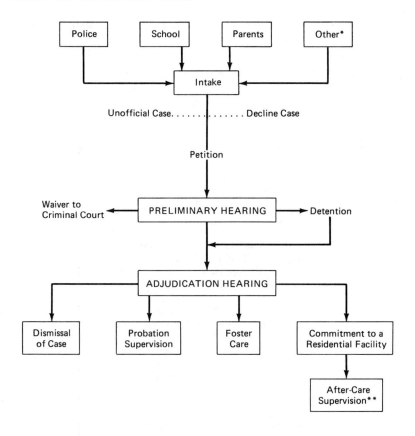

*Public and private agencies
**Supervision provided by the probation department or a juvenile after-care (Parole) agency

prosecutor's office. Intake in the juvenile court is unique; it permits the court to screen cases not only on jurisdictional and legal grounds, but on social dimensions as well. The PO interviews the presenting agent, the young person, and the child's parents or guardians. The officer then reviews court files for previous records concerning the child and, if the case involves a serious crime or child abuse, and has not been already screened by the prosecutor, consults with that office. At this stage the probation officer has a dual function: legal and social service.

The *legal function* requires that the PO determine if the juvenile court has jurisdiction and also requires that the child and parents be advised of the right to counsel and the right to remain silent during the intake conference. H. Ted Rubin argues that "defense attorney participation at a[n intake] conference is rare, waivers of rights tend to be finessed, and the norm is for parents to encourage the child to discuss his or her participation in the alleged offense with the intake officer" (1980: 304). In many states fewer than half of the juveniles adjudicated as delinquent receive the assistance of legal counsel (Feld, 1988). And when defense attorneys are present in juvenile court, there is tension inherent in their responsibilities to the client: "a choice between the traditional adversary role (or the procedural model that regulates professional behavior in the criminal court) and the historic treatment or rehabilitative concerns of the family [juvenile] court" (Fabricant, 1983: 41). Barry Feld reports that even when juveniles are represented by counsel, "attorneys may not be capable of or committed to representing their juvenile clients in an effective adversarial manner. Organizational pressures to cooperate, judicial hostility toward adversarial litigants, role ambiguity created by the dual goals of rehabilitation and punishment, reluctance to help juveniles 'beat a case,' or an internalization of a court's treatment philosophy may compromise the role of counsel in juvenile court" (1988: 395). Indeed, he notes, the presence of counsel may actually be disadvantageous to the juvenile — those represented by attorneys tending to receive more severe dispositions. Nevertheless, Feld, a law professor, advocates legislation that mandates counsel and does not permit a waiver of this important constitutional right.

The *social service function* involves an assessment of the child's situation — home, school, physical, and psychological — and can provide the basis for *adjusting* the case, handling it informally without the filing of a petition. This happens in about half the cases reaching the juvenile court — when the situation is not serious, when the matter can best be handled by the family, and when neither the child nor the public is in any danger (Zawitz, 1988). If the young person and parents agree to informal processing, the juvenile can be placed under supervision of a probation officer, usually for a period of ninety days. Although this may save the young person and his or her parents from the trauma of court action, unofficial handling has its critics. Informal processing requires an explicit or tacit admission of guilt. The substantial advantages that accrue from this admission (the avoidance of court action) also act as an incentive to confess. This casts doubt on the voluntariness and truthfulness of admissions of guilt.

Juvenile Intake in Grant County, Indiana

Most cases received by the probation department are referred by school officials and law enforcement officers after receiving and investigating complaints from private citizens. Referring agents complete an intake information form and upon receipt, the probation department orders the child and his or her parent(s)/guardian(s) to report to the probation department for a preliminary inquiry.

The preliminary inquiry is conducted by the intake PO for the purpose of determining whether the child committed a delinquent act and whether the interests of society or the child require further action. The PO advises the child and parents of the nature of the inquiry, the alleged offense, and their constitutional rights. If the child and parents choose to discuss the alleged offense, and if there is a determination of delinquency, the PO recommends to the court and to the prosecutor's office whether a formal petition alleging delinquency should be filed or whether the matter should be adjusted informally.

If the PO decides during the preliminary inquiry that an informal adjustment should be entered into, parent(s) and child must complete a preliminary investigation form which provides information about the child and the child's family: offense, education, siblings, employment, hobbies, recreation. An agreement is negotiated and the child and parents sign an informal agreement form describing the disposition agreed upon and the terms of that disposition. For example, driver's license restriction, curfew, sessions with a PO, referral to a community treatment — drug or alcohol — program, or for psychological treatment. An informal adjustment agreement cannot extend beyond six months. If at the end of that time the terms have not been followed, or if the child commits another offense, the original charges can be filed with the court as a petition. Should the PO recommend a petition instead of an informal adjustment, the prosecutor will file same with the court alleging delinquency.

The period of informal probation can be a crucial time in the life of a young person. If successful, the youngster may avoid further juvenile court processing; if unsuccessful, the child will face the labyrinth that is the juvenile court process and the serious consequences that can result. No one is more aware of this than the probation officer who, using all the skills and resources at the officer's command, attempts to assist the youngster and the youngster's parents through the crisis. Counseling, group therapy, tutoring, vocational guidance, psychiatric and psychological treatment, and recreational services, if they are available, will be put to use to help the young person. If informal efforts are unsuccessful, the PO can file a petition that will make the case an official one. The filing of a petition is made through the prosecutor or directly via the clerk of the court, who sets a date for the first of three types of juvenile court hearing.

In the Eighth Judicial District Court of the State of Nevada in and for the County of Clark Juvenile Division

Informal Supervision Agreement

In the matter of Michael Nelson.
Date of Birth: July 12, 1975.
Complaint: School Vandalism.

The minor admits the alleged offense as stated above.

The minor understands that an Informal Supervision period is an attempt by Clark County Juvenile Court Services, the minor, and his parents to resolve the alleged problems without formal judicial action.

The minor does hereby waive the right to a speedy trial and understands that he has the right to legal counsel and the right to remain silent throughout these proceedings and hereby waives these rights.

The minor understands that any information obtained during the supervision period will be admissible in evidence at any adjudicatory hearing and that the minor may withdraw from the Informal Supervision process at any time and demand an adjudicatory hearing.

The minor understands that the Clark County Juvenile Court Services or the District Attorney reserves the right to proceed on any petition heretofore filed against the undersigned and/or to proceed on other petitions for any new offense and may proceed to seek an adjudication on the pending matter in the event the minor fails to cooperate in the attempt at adjustment.

The minor and his parents further understand that the terms of this Informal Supervision Agreement are as follows:

1. That the minor will report in person to Probation Officer John Kerwin at the Clark County Juvenile Court Services, 3401 East Bonanza Road, Las Vegas, Nevada every Monday, on a weekly basis, until May 30, 1989.
2. That the minor will obey all laws of the City, County, State, and Federal governments.
3. That the minor will attend school, unless legally excused, and make every effort to maintain good conduct and an acceptable scholastic record.
4. That the minor will obey the reasonable and proper orders of his parents.
5. That the parents agree to make restitution for the damage caused by the minor to school property.

We agree to the terms and conditions of this Informal Supervision Agreement and waive the rights as stated above.

(Continued)

Signed _____ Date _____
       (Parent)

Signed _____ Date _____
       (Parent)

Signed _____ Date _____
       (Minor)

Order

Good cause appearing, therefore, the minor is placed under Supervision for a period of 90 days, reviewable (if a petition was filed) on the 30th Day of May, 1989, at the hour of 10:00 A.M.
    Dated this February 28, 1989.

_____
(Judge or Referee)

Preliminary hearing   Matters considered at preliminary hearings are those that must be dealt with before the case can proceed further. At the first hearing the judge (or in some jurisdictions a referee) informs the parties involved of the charges in the petition and of their rights in the proceeding. If the case involves an abused, neglected, or dependent child, a *guardian ad litem* is usually appointed to act as an advocate for the child. If appropriate, the hearing may be used to determine whether an alleged delinquent should remain in detention or shelter. If the judge determines, usually with the help of the probation officer, that the respondent's behavior makes him or her a danger to himself or herself or to the safety of others, or that he or she will probably not return to court voluntarily, the judge can order that the child remain in custody.

Kent County (Grand Rapids), Michigan Juvenile Detention

The facility, which was opened in 1963, provides secure custodial care for a maximum of forty-five youngsters, twelve to sixteen years of age, in three living units: two for boys and one co-ed. Forty-seven staff members are responsible for programmed activities in which the emphasis is on group living through a behavioral management program. A token economy (discussed in Chapter 9) is used permitting residents to earn points for engaging in positive behavior. These points are necessary for the youth to participate in various recreational activities and to purchase special snacks. Detention facility activities are designed to provide the staff with opportunities to better understand the youngsters, while at the same time providing outlets for active, healthy adolescents who are living under controlled conditions.

Individualized instruction is provided at each resident's actual functioning level, and there are volunteer tutors available for additional help in reading and math. Students earn credits toward a diploma and these are transferred to an appropriate school program when the resident leaves the facility. Daily use is made of the gymnasium and outdoor athletic fields. In addition, teams from other local juvenile facilities are invited to compete at the facility in various athletic events. Many college, civic, and other community groups provide special activities and seasonal parties for the residents. A dayroom within each living unit provides an area for a variety of leisure-time activities, such as ping pong and other table games, and television. A VCR is used for educational and entertaining movies. Adjoining the day rooms are quiet rooms that provide private space for letter writing and reading. A shop stocked with snacks, games, cards, and magazines provides an opportunity for youngsters to spend some of the points they have earned for good behavior. A separate game room with unique activities is also available on a privilege basis. Medical, dental, psychological, and religious services are available for each resident.

Detention facilities for juveniles have generally been inadequate. In some jurisdictions they are merely separate sections of an adult jail. Federal statutes required that states receiving funds under the 1974 Juvenile Justice and Delinquency Prevention Act eliminate the jailing of juveniles by 1988; in that year 22 of 52 states and territories receiving the funds were notified that they were not in compliance with this mandate (Schwartz, Harris, and Levi, 1988). Meda Chesney-Lind (1988) found that girls are often detained in jails for shoplifting and running away from home. California outlawed the practice of jailing of juveniles in 1986, and Utah makes the practice a misdemeanor. In New York City the primary detention facility for juveniles, Spoffard, was plagued with violence and other problems characteristic of adult jails.

In-Home Detention

In Dauphin County, Pennsylvania, the Juvenile Probation Department utilizes *In-Home Detention,* which provides supervision for juveniles who otherwise would be held in a detention facility. The program has two probation officers who share a caseload that does not exceed fourteen youngsters. The clients are visited once or twice a day at home, school, or place of employment. There is a rigidly enforced curfew set in cooperation with the youngster's parents. In-Home Detention is limited to sixty continuous days.

Candidates for the program are referred by the juvenile intake probation officer or juvenile "line" probation officer for juveniles who are awaiting a disposition based on allegations of delinquency. If the In-Home Detention Unit

(Continued)

has already screened the case, admittance occurs immediately following the detention hearing. Otherwise, admission takes place at the earliest possible time following a determination to accept. The criteria for a referral to the program include:

1. *Age:* the youngster must be between ages ten and seventeen.
2. *Home:* juvenile must have a home, real or surrogate, in which he or she may be placed, and its location must not offer a geographic impediment to daily supervision.
3. *Parents:* the youngster's parents, at the very least, must not be resistive to daily supervision of their child.
4. *Client:* the juvenile must not present a distinct, serious threat to the community, and must exhibit a cooperative attitude concerning the basic elements of the program including:
    (a) daily contacts by a probation officer;
    (b) daily school attendance/employment;
    (c) a curfew; and
    (d) compliance with other individualized guidelines as set forth by the PO.

Youngsters who become involved in delinquent activity, *persistent* evasion of supervision, and/or exhibit *persistent* uncooperative and belligerent behavior may be removed from the program by probation administrators. A youngster is terminated from the program when the court makes a disposition of the case. The day before a juvenile in the program is scheduled to appear in court, a written report on his or her attitude and adjustment while in the program is given to the judge, district attorney, and defense counsel. It can obviously influence the court's disposition.

In Cuyahoga County, (Cleveland) Ohio, the Home Detention Project has been in existence since 1981 and was established as an alternative to the "warehousing" of juveniles in the detention center. Youngsters referred to the juvenile court as delinquents or status offenders may be assigned to the program at intake, or at any time prior to disposition. In order to provide the program's staff with the legal authority to send a youth to the detention home if his or her behavior subsequently requires it, each juvenile is technically admitted to the detention center. Afterwards, youngsters and their parents or guardians meet with the program supervisor to discuss and sign a contract delineating the rules of home arrest, a violation of which can cause a referral to the detention center.

In-home detention usually lasts seventeen days and each youth is assigned to a caseworker who ensures that all court dates are met. The caseworker also works to keep the youngster out of any further trouble by counseling and spending time with him or her, having lunch together, attending sports events, and similar activities. Every day there are unscheduled daily face-to-face contacts with the youth, and the caseworker also contacts the parents daily. The caseworker maintains a log that documents compliance (or lack of it) with the program requirements. Teachers are asked to complete a daily school report form that verifies attendance and behavior. Prior to the court hearing, the caseworker provides the judge/referee with a report summarizing the youngster's history in the program (Ball, Huff, and Lilly, 1988).

Dependent, neglected, or abused children, and status offenders, may be placed in foster care or a residential shelter. Under such circumstances the judge will often appoint a temporary guardian for the child, a *guardian ad litem,* usually a representative of a child welfare agency, but sometimes a relative or friend of the family. The judge may also issue an order of protection containing specific restrictions on a potential abuser or assailant, a violation of which allows the penalties for contempt of court—summary imprisonment. Noting that most state prison inmates in California were physically or sexually abused as children and, furthermore, that most adult offenders at one time passed through the juvenile justice system, the Santa Clara County Probation Department screens each juvenile at intake to find out if they are or were the victims of physical or sexual abuse.

Adjudicatory hearing The adjudicatory hearing—"trial"—is for the purpose of deciding ("adjudge") whether the child should be made a ward of the juvenile court because he or she is delinquent, a status offender, abused, neglected, or dependent. If appropriate, the child (respondent) makes a plea, either an admission or denial of the allegations contained in the petition. If a denial is made, then evidence must be presented to prove "beyond a reasonable doubt" that a delinquent act occurred or, in the case of a status offender, with a simple "preponderance of evidence" that the child is in need of court supervision. If the allegations are sustained, the judge makes a *finding of fact* (that the child is delinquent, abused, neglected, or otherwise in need of supervision), sets a date for a dispositional hearing, and orders a social investigation or predisposition report.

Predisposition report The goal of the juvenile court is to provide services. In order to do so on the basis of the best available information, the judge orders a predispositional investigation. The probation officer who conducts the investigation will present his or her findings in a report that includes the sociocultural and psychodynamic factors that influenced the juvenile's behavior, providing a social history that is used by the judge to determine a disposition for the case. Since the judge's decision will often be influenced by the contents of the report, it must be factual and objective—a professional statement about the child's family, social and educational history, and any previous involvement with public or private agencies. It also indicates the physical and mental health of the child, as reported by a court psychologist or psychiatrist. The report will typically include the following:

1. A review of court records
2. A review of school records
3. A review of police records
4. Interviews with the respondent
5. Interviews with family members
6. Interviews with teachers and school officials

7. Interviews with employers, youth workers, and clergy whenever appropriate
8. Interviews with complainant, police officer, or witnesses
9. Results of any psychological or psychiatric exams
10. A recommendation, which should include the treatment alternatives available in the case

Probation officers must present their findings with supportive statements as to the actual situation found in the investigation. Other than a recommendation, suppositions or opinions are to be avoided. Sometimes the recommendation of the PO is not included in the report but is transmitted orally to the judge. The completed report should enable the judge to make the best disposition available based on the individual merits of the case and the service needs of the young person. One problem encountered at the disposition stage is the paucity of available alternatives for helping a youngster. This can be exacerbated by an (inexperienced) probation officer who recommends treatment that is simply not available. Quite often a youngster will be placed on probation because of a lack of viable alternatives.

Social Investigation in the Juvenile Court

The Juvenile Division of the Circuit Court
The City of St. Louis
Presiding Judge: Honorable Gary M. Gaertner

In the Interest of: *Date of Report:*
  Timothy Wells   June 17, 1989

Birthdate: *Case No.:* 50550
  July 22, 1975 (verified)

                              Juvenile Officer:
                                William Russell

Previous Police and/or Court History

5-26-87   Unauthorized Use of Fire Hydrant.   Worker Russell. Timothy Wells was taken into custody at 12:30 P.M. at 3124 Hoffman on 5-18-87 by Officer Purcell. The arrest occurred after the officer observed Timothy with a fire hydrant wrench in his hand, turning on the fire hydrant at 3124 Hoffman. The officer turned off the above hydrant and the one on the next corner east at Lake and 15th Avenues. Case serviced and closed on 7-29-87.

5-10-89   Trespassing and Peace Disturbance.   Worker Russell. Timothy Wells was taken into custody at his home, 3201 Octavia, at 8:30 A.M., on 4-17-89 by Officers Moore and Keller. The arrest occurred following a complaint filed on

4-15-89 by Bruce Kelly, Assistant Principal at Hawthorne School. Mr. Kelly reported that an ex-student at Hawthorne, Timothy Wells, came into the school yard and created a disturbance. When asked to leave, Timothy used profanity and threatened Mr. Kelly with bodily harm. Insufficient evidence, warrant refused; case referred to probation department for informal adjustment. The worker closed the case of 5-27-89 by referring the family to the St. Louis Speech and Hearing Center.

5-24-89 Common Assault. Worker Russell. Timothy Wells was taken into custody at 3038 Douglass at 6:45 P.M., on 5-21-89 by Officers Flynn and Burger. The arrest occurred following a complaint by one John Bullen of 3827 Broadway (on official court supervision on a suspended commitment to MSTS). Bullen reported that he was struck on the head with a baseball bat by Timothy Wells during a fight with Timothy and his brothers, Earl and William, and a sister Dolores.

Following an investigation, Timothy Wells, Earl Wells, and John Bullen were all conveyed to the Juvenile Court and booked for common assault. All warrants were refused for insufficient evidence, and the matter was referred to the probation department for an informal adjustment. The case was closed on 5-27-89 after enrolling Timothy (Earl and William) in the Work Restitution program for four weeks and referring Timothy to the St. Louis Speech and Hearing Center. On the following day, the worker learned of the petition for the present offense.

Reason for Hearing

On 5-10-89, Timothy allegedly attempted to steal three pairs of sunglasses from the Kresge's Store, 7800 Kingston Road in St. Louis, Missouri.

Timothy has remained in the home since the alleged offense on 5-10-89. He has since received one subsequent referral for common assault. He has also been present and worked well on three Saturday mornings of the Work Program for Probationers.

Collateral Contacts

Informants. The child's parents, Florence and Marvin Wells, were interviewed in their home on 6-5-89. Numerous other contacts have been made with them since two other children, Earl and William, were assigned to the supervision of this worker on 2-20-89. Both parents seem interested and have been cooperative with this court representative.

Contacts with Other Agencies

St. Louis Speech and Hearing Center. The Center was contacted by telephone on 6-8-89 to verify Timothy's appointment for a hearing evaluation. Timothy has such an appointment scheduled for 2:30 on 6-26-89. The Center is capable of providing diagnostic and treatment services for an apparent hearing and speech disorder.

(Continued)

Family History

Home.   Timothy resides with both parents, four sisters, two brothers, and a nephew at 3201 Octavia. The residence is a one-story brick home which includes three bedrooms, living room, kitchen, and an ample basement which has been partially converted for additional living quarters for Timothy, Earl, and William. A home visit made on 6-5-89 revealed that the residence is nicely furnished and was neat and orderly. Mr. and Mrs. Wells are purchasing the residence and make monthly installment payments of $312.00. The family moved to their present location in 1979.

Father.   Marvin Wells was born in St. Louis on 12-1-49. He was the youngest of eight children. Mr. Wells reports that he finished high school and two years of business college before beginning employment as a machinist at Weiss Welding Works. He was employed there between 1973 and 1984. With the promise of a higher salary, he worked for the Kramer Tool Co., from 1984 to 1987 but returned to his former employer. He currently works from 3:30 P.M. to midnight Monday through Friday and grosses approximately $2,200 per month.

Mother.   Florence Wells was born in St. Louis on 2-21-51. She was the fourth of eight children. She reports that she has completed high school and began work about three years ago when her youngest child, Christine, started school. Mrs. Wells has been working as a nurse's aid at the Laurel Heights Nursing Home. She works from 6:30 A.M. to 3:00 P.M. Sunday through Friday and earns approximately $1,100 per month. Mrs. Wells has stated that she has been suffering from hypertension for the past sixteen years.

Parents' Attitude.   Marvin and Florence Wells blame Timothy for the present offense. He has admitted that he tried to steal the sunglasses. His parents feel that they are capable of discipline supervision and care for Timothy but they also admit that he has problems for which they need assistance. They feel that Timothy is angry and depressed because of an apparent hearing handicap. They are willing to seek help with this problem.

Other Family Information

The other children are Andrea (BD: 9-2-70), Alicia (BD: 12-11-72), Dolores (BD: 1-14-73), Earl (BD: 8-15-75), William (BD: 12-1-78), and Christine (BD: 5-16-83). Dolores, Earl, and William are also known to the Court. Dolores received a referral on 9-6-88 for peace disturbance and loitering (a group demonstration at Westside High School), serviced and closed on 1-27-89. Dolores is a student at Westside High School, and has a pre-school-age son, Michael, who also lives with the family. Earl has three referrals and William has one referral. At a hearing held on 1-21-89, Earl and William were found to have committed a common assault and were both placed on official court supervision on a suspended commitment to Missouri Hills. They have been cooperative in keeping weekly appointments with the worker and following my instructions. There seem to be no special problems between Timothy and his siblings. However Timothy is most argumentative with William.

Personal History

Early Development. Timothy was a full-term baby born without complications. Mrs. Wells stated that Timothy was unusually prone to illness in his childhood. He seemed to catch everything. She went so far as to state that the family moved to their present home in 1979 because the family physician recommended gas heat for Timothy over the coal-burning furnace which they had in their last residence.

Health. Timothy is a black male who is 5 feet 4 inches tall and weighs 150 pounds. He is of medium complexion with brown eyes and black hair. Mrs. Wells reports that Timothy gets sick when he becomes overly excited.

Timothy has an apparent hearing and speech disorder. The problem reportedly was initially diagnosed by the school doctor at Northridge School who stated that Timothy would be totally deaf in his left ear by age seventeen.

School. No direct school contact can be made during the summer vacation. However, Mr. and Mrs. Wells stated that Timothy was suspended from Hawthorne School in 1988 for behavior problems. He began school at Northridge School in September 1988 and continued there until around January 1989. Mrs. Wells reported that Timothy enjoyed school there and did well because he liked his teacher, Sister Frances. However when Sister Frances left the school, Timothy's school problems resumed. Mrs. Wells stated that she then stopped sending Timothy to the school because they could no longer afford it. She attempted to enroll Timothy in the public schools but could not make the arrangements. Thus Timothy did not attend any school for the second semester of the past school year.

Employment. None.

Leisure-Time Activities. Timothy enjoys boxing, basketball, and football. However, his parents won't permit him to participate because of health reasons. Timothy and his parents report that he has no close friends.

Religion. Timothy is Baptist but is inactive in church.

General Personality. When asked, Timothy said he didn't think about himself. He said he has no problems and gets along with people. However, he also said that he has no friends, nor does he need them.

Child's Attitude. Timothy admits and accepts responsibility for his behavior. He stated that he doesn't know why he tried to steal the sunglasses. He said he had $6 in his pocket at the time.

(Continued)

Timothy has a very negative attitude. He appears sullen and angry and his verbal responses are generally short and gruff, especially if you must ask him to repeat himself. He also has a short temper.

Psychological or Psychiatric Evaluation

Timothy was given a psychological evaluation on 7-2-88 by the Rev. Raymond A. Hampe, Ph.D., associate director, Department of Special Education, Archdiocese of St. Louis. A battery of three tests was administered. Timothy was referred by Malcolm Bliss Mental Health Center for placement in special class because of behavior problems at school (Hawthorne).

Timothy was seen as functioning in the borderline to slow range of mental ability with probable higher potential which is unavailable due to emotional factors and major weakness in his grasp of language concepts. "Timothy is an immature, willful, anxious, sensitive boy who has strong achievement motivation and desires to be accepted. He does not see himself as being successful and accepted and therefore is greatly frustrated." Timothy projected hostility toward the examiner but cooperated. No obvious sensory or motor impairments were noted.

In summary, Timothy was seen as being anxious for success but expecting failure. Recommendations were for the parents to offer additional responsibilities and privileges marked by confidence in his ability to succeed. A special school placement was offered to eliminate the normal school's constant source of negative self-evaluation.

Summary and Evaluation

This is the matter of Timothy Wells, who will be fourteen years old on 7-22-89. Timothy is before the court for stealing three pairs of sunglasses from the Kresge's Store in St. Louis, Missouri, on 5-10-89. He admits doing so but offers no explanation. Timothy has a total of four referrals to the court, three of which occurred in May of this year.

Timothy's home situation is satisfactory. The parents are responsible working people who are purchasing a home. They express interest in their children and have demonstrated cooperation with this worker in connection with Earl and William, who are currently under supervision. The parents acknowledge that Timothy is a "problem child," and Mrs. Wells brought Timothy to my attention even before he officially came to the attention of the court.

Timothy is seen as an angry and frustrated youth. He has a low tolerance for frustration and a short temper which displays it. Timothy is sensitive to failure and has come to expect it of himself. He professes no problems which require correction but seems incapable of following advice and instructions.

Timothy apparently has some form of hearing and speech disorder. Mrs. Wells feels that his hearing is poor and speculates that Timothy has learned to compensate somewhat by learning to read lips. His speech is characterized by brief, to-the point statements which are rather unclear. Timothy is scheduled for a thorough hearing evaluation on 6-26-89.

Timothy is seen as an appropriate candidate for rehabilitation within the community. His three referrals in May 1989 seem to indicate that his need to act out has reached a peak level. Although angry and frustrated at the world around him, Timothy's referrals are not of a serious nature. He is therefore not regarded as a serious threat to persons or property although his unstable emotional characteristics might indicate some further form of striking back. However, a strong incentive can be offered to curb recidivism.

The plan for Timothy involves a thorough hearing and speech evaluation and follow-up on recommendations made for therapy. Timothy should also undergo psychiatric therapy, most realistically at the Child Guidance Center. Further, Timothy should be enrolled in a special school setting where teaching is individualized and tutorial in nature and where the program is stimulating and rewarding for appropriate behavior. Such programs are offered at Providence School and Project Door. No firm recommendation can be made in regard to a specific school, as the referral procedure is still under way. Furthermore, Timothy should have a regular weekly appointment with his Deputy Juvenile Officer for further counseling and to coordinate plans.

Alternative Plans

Placement in either a community group home or at Missouri Hills. Placement outside the home has been ruled out because Timothy's problems do not include poor parental supervision. Rather, his problem involves insecurity, which can best be treated in his home.

Restitution

The Victim Assistance Program report states that there was no loss suffered by the Kresge's Store, as the three pair of sunglasses involved were recovered. Furthermore, Timothy has worked well the past three Saturdays in the Work Program for Probationers. He has one more Saturday left in the original enrollment from the informal adjustment, so it is felt that he has made ample service restitution to the community.

Plan

It is therefore recommended that Timothy Wells be committed to the Division of Children's Services for placement at Missouri Hills. Further that the commitment be held in abeyance and said minor remain in the home of his parents on Official Court Supervision and subject to the following special rules. That said minor cooperate in prescribed hearing and speech therapy. To cooperate in prescribed psychiatric therapy. To keep a weekly appointment with the Deputy Juvenile

(Continued)

Officer through September 1989. And further that the Deputy Juvenile Officer investigate an appropriate school setting for said minor for the fall term of 1989.

Respectfully submitted,

_____
William Russell
Deputy Juvenile Officer

Approved by:

_____
Susan Davidson
Acting Supervisor

Dispositional hearing   Traditionally, the disposition stage of the juvenile court process has been based on the concept of *parens patriae*. Distinctions between dispositions were based on the *needs* of the children and not necessarily the behavior that brought a case to the attention of the juvenile court; dispositions were based, not on *justice* but on *rehabilitation*. Although the Supreme Court ruled that the juvenile court must adhere to due process, its *raison d'etre* as a separate court continued to be as a vehicle for providing social services to children in need. In some jurisdictions, however, the line between the adult criminal court and the juvenile court has become blurred as the latter moves toward a *justice model*—what the youngster *deserves*—rather than a *social service model*—what the youngster *needs*. (The *justice model* for adults is discussed in Chapter 7.) The state of Washington provides an example of this trend.

The state of Washington abrogated the doctrine of *parens patriae* in 1977 and in its place adopted a new philosophy based upon a *justice model* (Schram, et al., 1981: 65):

1. Make juvenile offenders accountable for their criminal behavior; and
2. Provide for punishment commensurate with age, crime, and criminal history. Nowhere is the rehabilitation of the juvenile offender mentioned as a purpose or intent [in the law].

As part of this approach the Washington Division of Juvenile Rehabilitation promulgated "Juvenile Disposition Sentencing Standards" to guide juvenile court judges in making uniform dispositions based, not upon the needs of the child but on the delinquent behavior—a classical school approach. This, of course, reduces the role of the probation officer in juvenile court. Colorado, Idaho, and New York have mandatory minimum periods of incarceration for juveniles—a clear distortion of the purposes of the juvenile court. But in Washington, and other states that have adopted a "hard line" on juvenile offenders, statutes enable reconsideration of severe sentences for a variety of mitigating circumstances including "manifest injustices" (Harris and Graff, 1988). In fact, write Patricia Harris and Lisa Graff (1988), the "hard line against juveniles" is often less than meets the eye: few of the harsher statutory provisions are mandatory. The state of Washington also relinquished juvenile court jurisdiction over status offenders.

Disposition Hearing*

William Price and his mother sat uneasily before the judge. The allegations of the amended petition had been sustained on the basis of a full admission. The judge was looking through the probation officer's report for information on which to base his disposition. His eye was drawn to the psychologist's report attached to the court report. The courtroom was silent, all eyes on the judge.

In the report William was described as "fairly handsome" and "athletically built." The judge glanced up and looked directly at the boy. William turned his eyes away. The judge decided that the boy might be called handsome despite his "waterfall" haircut and a slight case of acne, but he was certainly not sufficiently robust to be dubbed "athletic."

The psychologist's report indicated that William might or might not be aggressive to girls in the future. "That's not much help," the judge thought, "it could apply to most young men. Chances are the boy feels worse about the situation than the girl. At least he *looks* remorseful."

"William, do you realize you could have seriously injured that girl?"

"I didn't mean to hurt her. I thought it was what she wanted."

"That was a dangerous supposition, young man. I hope you realize by now that any use of violence in any circumstances can have the most serious consequences. Society doesn't regard such things lightly."

"Yes, sir."

"Besides the offense with the girl, you also ran away from the officer who was trying to arrest you."

"I'm sorry about that. I guess I lost my head."

"Are you in the habit of losing your head?"

"No, sir. I just wasn't thinking."

"William," the judge said sternly, "I have serious doubts about allowing you to remain in the community. How do I know you won't lose your head again and really hurt someone the next time?"

"I promise, Judge. I won't do anything foolish again."

The judge turned to Mrs. Price and said sympathetically, "I know it has been

*Source: Lawrence E. Cohen, *New Directions in Processing of Juvenile Offenders: The Denver Model* (Washington, D.C.: U.S. Government Printing Office, 1975).

(Continued)

very difficult for you to raise William by yourself. It would be a pity for all that effort to go to waste."

Tears welled up in Mrs. Price's eyes. "Yes, Your Honor. Please let William come home. I know he'll be good. And I've changed my job now so I can be with him more," she said in a trembling voice.

William's eyes were focused on his mother while she talked. The judge noted that concern for her was mirrored in his face.

"How has Bill been doing since he came home from Juvenile Hall, Mrs. Price?"

"Just like always, Judge. He's a good boy."

"William," the judge said, "what would you do with yourself if I allowed you to remain in your home?"

"Go to school."

"I see you are one year behind in your school grade. Do you plan to finish high school?"

"Yes, sir." William's face noticeably brightened.

"And then what do you plan to do?"

"I guess I'll go in the service."

The judge looked at the probation officer. "Mr. Clarke, I'm going to follow your recommendation and make William a ward of the court and place him on probation. If he stays out of trouble during the next year, I want him brought back to court so we can terminate his case. By my calculation he could be off probation about nine or ten months before he graduates. This should be long enough so that his record will not hinder him from entering the service."

The judge turned back to William. "I hope you've learned a lesson from this, Son. You stay out of trouble and you should have a good opportunity to make something of yourself. The burden is on you. Don't spoil your chances for a career and for a decent life for yourself and your mother."

"Thank you, Judge," Mrs. Price said. "William is a good boy. I don't think he'll make any more trouble for anyone."

She and her son left the room, the boy with his arm around her shoulders.

Status Offenders

As the juvenile court has moved closer to the adult criminal court in both the application of legal principles and use of punishment, there has been a corresponding shift away from exercising jurisdiction over status offenders. Official intervention by the legal system into the lives of children who have not been accused of criminal behavior — status offenders — has long been a center of controversy. Back in 1976 this writer argued:

> The juvenile court's continued use of coercion and the stigma it creates are grounds for serious concern. The "bottom line" of juvenile court authority is the policeman, ready to use his revolver, club and handcuffs to carry out the court's

orders. A society that considers preventive detention repulsive has, in some strange way, learned to tolerate the threat or the actual use of force against persons who have not been found guilty of a crime. (1976: 458)

Those who support continued jurisdiction of the juvenile court over status offenders (sometimes referred to as Minors in Need of Supervision, MINS; or Children in Need of Supervision, CHINS; or Persons in Need of Supervision, PINS) argue that status offenders are not essentially different from those youngsters committing delinquent acts—they are children in need of services, and without the intervention of the juvenile court these services would not be forthcoming. Opponents argue that juvenile court intervention does not help youngsters; the services are often inadequate and intervention intensifies existing problems by stigmatizing children. In other words, a juvenile may not be able to discern the subtle differences between the juvenile court and the criminal court—differences that are becoming vague (as in the *justice model*). Thus, the child, as well as the child's parents, friends, and community, may react to juvenile court intervention as if he or she were facing charges in criminal court. Edwin Schur warns that the "labeling" that results can set in motion "a complex process of response and counter-response with an initial act of rule-violation and developing into elaborated delinquent self-conceptions and a full-fledged delinquent career" (1973: 30). Randall Sheldon, John Horvath, and Sharon Tracy found, however, that "the majority of those whose first referral was a status offense did not become more serious delinquents. If anything, they became something considerably less than serious delinquents" (1989: 214).

Status offense (MINS, CHINS, PINS) petitions are most often filed on behalf of the children's parents, ostensibly because the youngsters are beyond their control. Quite often the child's behavior is merely a symptom of a wider problem. Children often become status offenders by running away from pathological family situations, alcoholic or abusing parents. Girls are often subjected to juvenile court for sexual behavior that goes unnoticed when committed by boys. Children who are found to be status offenders are usually warned or placed on probation in their initial encounter with the court. Probation can include placement in a shelter, group home, or foster care. If a youngster fails to cooperate with the treatment program, he or she can be returned to court for further disposition, which can lead to placement in a secure facility such as a training school. The Juvenile Justice and Delinquency Prevention Act of 1974 requires the deinstitutionalization of status offenders. Harvey Swanger reports that, although it sometimes required litigation to accomplish, "by 1986 all states seemingly met this laudable goal," although, he notes, "slippage has occurred and researchers have documented wholesale replacement of juvenile court institutionalization of status offenders with 'voluntary' mental health commitments in some states" (1988: 211).

CHINS in Clark County, Nevada

The most common status offenses involve youngsters who are unmanageable, runaways, or truants. Clark County responds by utilizing community-based shelter care, counseling, and a network of community resources.

Crisis Intervention

Families in need of immediate assistance may come to the Admissions/Intake Division at Juvenile Court, which operates on a twenty-four hour basis, and meet with an intake officer who is experienced in crisis management. The officer will conduct an intake interview to:

1. evaluate and assess the family situation and needs;
2. determine if alternative counseling or short-term emergency shelter care services are appropriate without further juvenile court intervention; and if applicable,
3. determine what services may be directly provided by the juvenile court — for example, information/referral, extended evaluation, psychological consultation, ninety-day probation supervision.

Diagnostic Interviews

The intake officer will consult with law enforcement and school officials and gather as much information as possible to assess thoroughly the family's situation. After completing the assessment, the officer develops a plan of action that requires continued parental involvement; the intent is to promote family unity. The officer will also explore parental rights and responsibilities regarding CHINS. Clark County Juvenile Services recognizes that CHINS' behaviors are difficult for everyone to deal with and that at times parents become extremely frustrated with their children and look to the court for quick and easy solutions — there are none. To help CHINS to grow up and behave better takes time, work, and patience. Court programs can be effective only if the parents and concerned others agree to address the problem.

Community Service Referrals

The community offers many excellent resources for families in need, and intake officers are aware of the various services of both public and private agencies. When a family's needs can best be met through a referral to one of them, we recommend such a plan of action. We rely on these agencies to divert CHINS from the court and into the most appropriate setting available within the community. Through such brokering we expect to put families in touch with the services they need.

Emergency Shelter Care

Some children are temporarily out of control. When the parent-child relationship has deteriorated to a point where temporary separation is necessary, the intake officer can arrange for the child to be placed in an emergency shelter care facility and refer the family to the Probation Division for continued supervision under a Family Services Agreement. The county has contracts with five emergency shelter care homes and CHINS are referred to these facilities rather than being confined in the court's secure Detention Center for delinquents.

Family Services Agreement

Some children continue to exhibit more severe and chronic CHINS behavior despite previous service attempts. For these CHINS the Probation Department has an ongoing supervision program. The Family Services Agreement is an informal voluntary contract between the family and the juvenile court which spells out mutual responsibilities and service expectations. Basically, it provides for three months of supervision by a probation officer and outlines what can be expected of the child, parents, and the court. Participation in individual or family counseling is usually indicated and, if the child is temporarily removed from the home and placed in shelter care, the agreement specifies the conditions for length of stay, reunification efforts, and financial obligations. Children are expected to obey reasonable and proper orders of their parents, attend school regularly, and participate in a treatment plan tailored to their individual needs. The PO monitors these expectations, coordinates interagency efforts, and participates in direct counseling with the child.

Mental Health Services

Psychological screenings and referrals for psychiatric services can be made in those instances where a severely emotionally disturbed child comes to the court's attention as a CHINS referral.

JUVENILES IN CRIMINAL COURT

At the other end of the juvenile justice spectrum are youngsters who can be tried as adults in criminal court (this action must be in accord with the *Breed* decision discussed later in this chapter). Every jurisdiction in the United States has one or more methods for transferring juvenile cases to the adult criminal court; there are three basic mechanisms to accomplish this:

1. *Legislative Exclusion.* Fourteen states have statutory provisions that exclude certain crimes from the jurisdiction of the juvenile court (White, 1987). Some states exclude only the most serious offenses against *persons;* in

Illinois, for example, juveniles fifteen years of age or older charged with murder, aggravated criminal sexual assault, or armed robbery with a firearm are automatically tried under criminal proceedings. Florida statutes mandate that juveniles charged with capital and life felonies be transferred to criminal court. In addition to the most serious crimes against persons, such as murder, New York excludes burglary, and some states exclude traffic, boating, fish and game and other minor violations (Wizner, 1984).

    2. *Judicial Waiver.* Forty-nine of fifty-two jurisdictions (fifty states, Washington, D.C., and the federal system) permit juvenile court judges to "waive" (transfer) their jurisdiction over certain juvenile offenders. This discretion is limited by statutory criteria with regard to such factors as age, type of offense, prior record, amenability to treatment, and dangerousness. Only Arkansas, Nebraska, and New York are without such provisions (White, 1987).

    3. *Prosecutorial Discretion.* Eight states empower prosecutors to charge juveniles in either juvenile or adult courts. This discretionary power may be limited by statutory criteria with regard to age and type of offense (White, 1987).

    The state of Florida, in a dramatic move toward a "justice" model, enacted legislation in 1981 that provides prosecutors with almost unlimited discretion—"when the public interest requires it"—to transfer sixteen- and seventeen-year-olds to criminal court. A study of transfer practices in Florida revealed that the direct transfer provisions have seldom been utilized for the serious and chronic offenders for whom transfer is arguably justified. In fact, the study found that relatively few cases are subjected to the direct transfer provisions and that "many of those who are transferred seem inappropriate" (Bishop, Frazier, and Henretta, 1989: 195).

Waiver of Jurisdiction, Maryland

(a) The Juvenile Court may waive the exclusive jurisdiction conferred by state law with respect to a petition alleging delinquency for:

1. A child who is fifteen years old or older, or
2. A child who has not reached his fifteenth birthday, but who is charged with committing an act which if committed by an adult, would be punishable by death or life imprisonment.

    (b) The court may not waive its jurisdiction until after it has conducted a waiver hearing, held prior to an adjudicatory hearing and after notice has been given to all parties as prescribed by the Maryland Rules. The waiver hearing is solely to determine whether the court should waive its jurisdiction.

(c) The court may not waive its jurisdiction unless it determines, based on the preponderance of the evidence presented at the hearing, that the child is an unfit subject for juvenile rehabilitative measures. For the purpose of determining whether to waive its jurisdiction, the court shall assume that the child committed the delinquent act alleged.

(d) In making its determination the court shall consider the following criteria individually and in relation to each other on the record:

1. Age of the child
2. Mental and physical condition of the child
3. The child's amenability to treatment in any institution, facility, or program available to delinquents
4. The nature of the offense and the child's alleged participation in it
5. The public safety

State of Indiana
County of Grant Juvenile Division

IN THE MATTER OF
  Michael Grant
DOB: 8/14/74
A CHILD ALLEGED TO BE DELINQUENT

Prosecutor's Motion for Waiver of Juvenile Jurisdiction

The State of Indiana, by the undersigned Deputy Prosecuting Attorney, hereby alleges and represents to the Court as follows:

1. That said child, Michael Grant, was born on the 14th day of August in the year 1974, and was fourteen (14) years of age or older, and under eighteen (18) years of age, at the time of the charged offense.
2. That said child is subject to the jurisdiction of the Juvenile Court herein by virtue of a Petition Alleging Delinquency having been filed on the 4th day of March in the year 1989.
3. That the act charged would be an offense if committed by an adult, to wit: ATTEMPTED MURDER.
4. That said offense charged is:
   (x) heinous or of an aggravated character;
   (x) an act against person;
   (x) part of a repetitive pattern of offenses (even though less serious in nature) in that the child has heretofore been arrested and/or adjudicated for: UNLAWFUL POSSESSION OF A FIREARM.
5. That there is probable cause to believe that said child committed the offense charged herein, and that said child is beyond rehabilitation under the juvenile justice system, and that it is in the best interest of the safety and welfare of the community that said child be required to stand trial as

(Continued)

an adult, and that a waiver of juvenile jurisdiction is sought under the provisions of I.C. 31-6-2-4(b).

WHEREFORE, your petitioner requests that a hearing be set by the Court to determine whether juvenile jurisdiction should be waived herein, and that after said hearing that the Court waive juvenile jurisdiction over the offense charged herein to the Criminal Court of Grant County, a Court that would have jurisdiction over the offense charged if that act were committed by an adult, and said waiver to be for the offense charged, and any lesser included offenses.
Dated this 6th day of April, 1989.

John L. Jamisen
Deputy Prosecuting Attorney

A youth tried in adult criminal court, depending on the state, may be sent to an institution operated by the same agency with responsibility for adults — department of corrections — or to a specialized agency that provides institutionalization for juveniles and young adults. For example, the Illinois Department of Corrections has a Juvenile Division that receives delinquents and juvenile offenders who have not reached their twenty-first birthday — at which time they may be transferred to an adult facility. In California, a judge has the option to sentence offenders aged sixteen to twenty to state prison but order them housed in a California Youth Authority (discussed below) facility until their twenty-fifth birthday or the expiration of their sentence, whichever is first. Offenders under the age of sixteen in New York are sent to a facility operated by the Division for Youth (discussed below), while those who have reached their sixteenth birthday are sent to a reformatory operated by the Department of Correctional Services.

Both conventional wisdom and research in corrections has revealed that juvenile offenders in adult facilities present a significant management problem for institutional officials. A study by Marilyn McShane and Frank Williams, for example, found that as compared to other young inmates, "imprisoned juvenile offenders exhibited significant adjustment problems in the institutional environment" (1989: 266).

Inger Sagatun, Loretta McCollum, and Leonard Edwards (1985) report a lack of significant difference in sentence outcome for youngsters adjudicated in juvenile court and those tried in criminal court, controlling for the severity of the offense. They note that the juvenile court is not as lenient as its critics would have it, and furthermore (1985: 87):

> minors are likely to be looked upon as special persons by prosecutors, probation officers, and judges in the criminal courts. They are younger than the main population of defendants before the criminal courts. Even jurors may view the

young person in criminal court differently. In the cases examined, there were more findings of "not guilty" in the criminal court than in the juvenile court. The labeling process may be different in the two courts. While a minor may be looked upon as a hardened criminal in the juvenile court, (s)he may be viewed as a mere innocent youngster in criminal court.

In another study, more than 90 percent of the judicial waiver or prosecutorial discretion cases tried in adult court resulted in guilty verdicts, with fines or probation imposed on half of the convicted juveniles. Those juveniles convicted of serious violent offenses, however, were likely to receive terms of incarceration: 14 percent to jail; 63 percent to prison with an average sentence of 6.8 years (Hamparian, et al., 1982). Carole Barnes and Randall Franz found that in the jurisdiction they studied

> Property offenders with a long history of property offenses tend to receive a substantially lighter sentence in adult court than they would have received when moving up the ladder in juvenile court. Conversely, personal and aggravated personal offenders with few prior offenses received significantly more punitive treatment in adult court than did comparable offenders in juvenile court. (1989: 133)

JUVENILE COURT JUDGES

Central to implementing the helping philosophy of the juvenile court is the juvenile court judge. However, the position presents an anomaly—while most judicial posts require only a knowledge of law and legal procedure, the juvenile court judge, in addition, needs a working knowledge of several disciplines: sociology, psychology, and social work. Were persons with such backgrounds readily available, the relatively low prestige of the juvenile court would make their recruitment difficult. In most states the juvenile court is located at the bottom of the judicial organizational chart (see Figure 3.3), and the position of juvenile court judge is often seen as the entry level for a future appointment to a more prestigious court.

In response to these difficulties, some states have mandated training for juvenile court judges, often provided by, or in conjunction with, the National Council of Juvenile Court Judges. The council sponsors a national college located on the campus of the University of Nevada at Reno. The college trains judges and holds periodic sessions throughout the year on topics designed to help juvenile court judges keep abreast of the laws and behavior approaches related to the problems of delinquency, neglect, and child abuse. Other topics include drug and alcohol abuse, juvenile institutions and their alternatives, and waiver of cases to the criminal court. Some jurisdictions use *referees* or *masters,* specialized attorneys who represent the judge and who are empowered to hold certain juvenile court hearings.

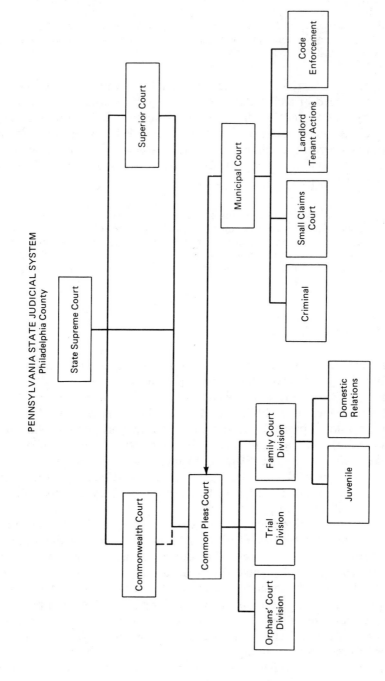

PENNSYLVANIA STATE JUDICIAL SYSTEM
Philadelphia County

FIGURE 3.3 Pennsylvania State Judicial System

JUVENILE COURT DISPOSITIONS

There is a wide variety of juvenile court dispositions:

- Reprimand with unsupervised probation
- Probation with supervision
- Foster care with or without probation
- Private school or residential treatment
- Training school
- Mental hospital
- Group home
- Community-based day treatment
- Community-based secure facility

Juveniles are sometimes released in the custody of their parents for placement in private boarding schools, military academies, sanitoria, and so on. This disposition is most often limited to children from at least middle-income status, and Dale Mann notes: "One obvious effect is to guarantee that public institutions for juvenile offenders serve an underclass population" (1976: 12).

Females often receive harsher treatment in juvenile court because of the lack of alternative programs for them: "Although a sentencing judge may be willing to consider a variety of dispositional alternatives, he or she is often faced with only one program possibility—the state training school or reformatory" (Female Offender Resource Center, 1978: 13). And

> once institutionalized, girls are afforded fewer services and program opportunities than boys. Boys, on the other hand, suffer from disadvantages which result from confinement in larger institutions which are filled to capacity.
>
> We can only speculate as to the reasons for these discrepancies. Some people in the juvenile justice system justify the differences in program and services available in girls' institutions by arguing that it is cost effective to spend the limited funds which do exist on boys who commit more serious crimes and who outnumber girls in the system nearly four to one.

Basic to dispositions in the juvenile court is the concept of *least restrictive alternative,* meaning that a disposition should not be more restrictive than that which will adequately serve the needs of the child. Our review of dispositions will generally follow this principle as we move from the less to the more restrictive.

PROBATION SUPERVISION

Probation supervision is used in about half the adjudicated delinquency cases. Probation supervision is appropriate for children who are not seriously delinquent or in obvious need of intensive services available only in a residential

SUPERIOR COURT OF THE STATE OF CALIFORNIA
IN AND FOR THE COUNTY OF SANTA CLARA
JUVENILE COURT

MINOR

No.

ORDER OF PROBATION

At a regular Hearing before the above-entitled Court on
the Court ordered that you were:

.... 1. Declared a Ward of the Court and permitted to return to your home on Probation and your care, custody, control and conduct to be under the supervision of the Probation Officer.

.... 2. Returned to your home on Probation under the supervision of the Probation Officer for a period not to exceed six months.

It is further ordered by the Court that you are required to:

1. Obey your parents or guardian.
2. Obey all laws of the community, including curfew, traffic and school laws.
3. Follow the school or work program approved by the Probation Officer.
4. Follow the instructions of the Probation Officer relating to your conduct at home, at school and in the community.
5. Report in person to the Probation Officer or the Court at such time and place as may be designated by the Probation Officer.
6. Comply with any special conditions of Probation and, if restitution has been ordered, you must make payment as promptly as possible and as directed by your Probation Officer.
7. Notify the Probation Officer of any anticipated change of address or other important changes.
8. Consult with the Probation Officer without hesitation when you are in need of further advice.

In addition to the above, the Court orders the following special conditions of your Probation:

This Order will remain in effect until further Order of the Court. Your case may be reviewed by the Court and your program modified, depending on the progress you made.

Failure to comply with any of the above instructions will be a violation of this Order and may result in a further Hearing before the Court.

Judge of the Juvenile Court

The foregoing Order has been read by me or read to me and I fully accept it and understand its contents.

---   ---
Signature of Ward or Probationer   Signature of Parent or Guardian

FIGURE 3.4   Juvenile Court Order of Probation, California Superior Court

setting. However, youngsters with severe behavior problems may be placed on probation, not because it is necessarily the most appropriate response, but because probation is the only response available.

As a condition of probation juveniles are usually required to obey their parents or guardians, attend school regularly, be home at an early hour in the evening, and avoid disreputable companions and places. The PO supervising the youngster works toward modifying some of the juvenile's attitudes in order to help the child relate to society in a law-abiding, prosocial manner. At the root of antisocial behavior in many juveniles is a difficulty in relating to authority and authority figures. Parents, school officials, and others who have represented authority to the young person have caused him or her to develop a negative, even hostile attitude toward authority in general. This leads to rebellion at home and at school, and/or against society in general. The probation officer must help the young person revise his or her ideas about people in authority by providing a role model as a healthy authority figure, or by helping the young person develop healthy attitudes toward others who can provide a desirable role model. These persons may be teachers, athletic coaches, or perhaps a recreation leader in the community.

The probation officer must be able to accept the young person and be able to demonstrate an attitude of respect and concern. At the same time the PO must be honest and firm with the youngster, setting realistic limits for him or her — something parents are often unable (or unwilling) to do. Misbehavior or antisocial activities cannot be accepted, but the client must be.

In the course of the helping process the probation officer will involve the family and meet with the young person on a regular basis. The PO will work with school officials, sometimes acting as an advocate for the child in order to secure for the client a public school placement. This is often a difficult task. The youngster has often exhibited disruptive behavior at school and officials are, understandably, resistive to his or her return. If necessary, the officer will seek placement in a foster home for the client (and in some circumstances, adoption).

Dauphin County, Pennsylvania
Adolescent Foster Home Care Program

Established in 1980, the Adolescent Foster Home Care Program (AFHC), in cooperation with the County Social Services and Youth Agency, recruits, screens, and trains foster parents and provides specialized services to both dependent and delinquent youth. It has long been established that one of the paramount contributing factors to juvenile delinquency is a dysfunctional home environment. Institutional placement for juveniles who need to be removed from their natural homes is not always in the best interest of a particular child. Therefore, the Dauphin County Probation Office views foster home care as a viable alternative living situation for certain adjudicated delinquent juveniles; those who have committed minor offenses usually stemming from inadequate parental supervision or conflict in the natural home. The purpose of the AFHC

(Continued)

Program is to provide carefully screened delinquent youth experiences in family living which are essential to positive and constructive growth and development.

The foster home care specialist is an experienced probation officer who works with the youth, his or her natural family, and the foster family toward the ultimate goal of reestablishing the youth in the natural home. If returning to the natural home is not deemed to be in the best interest of the youth, an alternative placement goal is established and worked toward (for example, independent living, armed services, job corps).

The Referral Process

1. A delinquent youth is referred to the Adolescent Foster Home Care Program by the active probation officer, whether it be an intake officer or line officer.

2. The foster home care specialist reviews all available information concerning the youth and the natural family. He or she interviews the youth and the natural family to explain the program and to determine the appropriateness of the referral.

3. If the foster home care specialist deems the child to be amenable to treatment in foster home care (rather than in some other modality of treatment) he or she schedules a placement planning conference with the child and Youth Agency to identify a prospective foster family for the youth.

4. A weekend preplacement visit for the prospective foster family and foster youth is arranged and implemented by the foster home care specialist. In this way, both the adolescent and the foster family have the opportunity to express any concerns they may have regarding the proposed placement. If a foster family does not feel that they can meet the needs of a particular youth, they may then disapprove the placement in their home.

5. Following a successful preplacement visit with the foster family, the youth is scheduled for a juvenile court dispositional hearing. The assigned probation officer recommends to the juvenile court judge that the youth be placed in the custody of the Dauphin County Social Services for Children and Youth Agency for placement in the AFHC Program. The youngster is also placed on strict probation under the supervision of the Juvenile Probation Office. The foster home specialist supervises all delinquent youth in foster home care. In most cases the youth is also placed on suspended commitment to an appropriate juvenile facility where the youth would go should he or she fail to comply with the terms of the AFHC Program. Only the juvenile court judge can commit juveniles to the program.

Program Description

Each youth in the AFHC Program is placed on strict probation supervision under the foster home care specialist who serves as both a probation officer and a caseworker for the foster youth and foster family. Probation rules include a curfew and mandatory school attendance or employment. The foster parents serve as important members of the treatment team; along with the foster care specialist and any other professional involved with the youth, they participate in defining the needs of the youth and his or her family and assist in implementing goals established for the youth during placement.

Within thirty days of a youth's placement, a Family and Placement Service Plan is developed based on the individualized needs and interests of the foster youth. It includes goals and objectives to be accomplished by the youth and natural family as well as specific actions to be taken by all parties to reach the stated objectives. The anticipated length of foster home care placement is also included in the plan. The plan is reviewed and updated every six months by means of a six-month review hearing held at the Juvenile Probation Office. The review is conducted by a juvenile master who is appointed by the juvenile court judge. The youth, foster parents, natural parents, and foster home care specialist are present at each six-month hearing. The juvenile court master ensures that the objectives of the Family and Placement Service Plan are being achieved and makes written recommendations to the court.

Initially, the foster home care specialist will have at least one personal contact each week with the youth and foster family to monitor the placement, to provide support services to foster parents, to assure the youth's compliance with the probation rules, and to assist the youth in the development and implementation of the placement objectives. As the needs of the client allow, supervision may be reduced to a minimum of two personal counseling contacts per month. The specialist will also meet with the natural family at least once per month for counseling and information sharing about the youth's progress, and will supervise all home visits made by the youth. The specialist maintains regular contact with school personnel and/or employer while the youth is in care.

When the goals of the Family and Placement Service Plan have been achieved and the foster home care specialist feels that the child can be successfully reunited with the natural family (or alternative placement goal), he or she will recommend to the juvenile court judge that the youth be released from the program. If the youth returns to the natural or surrogate home, he or she remains under probation supervision for approximately three months to assure continued successful community adjustment and to allow the foster home care specialist to provide continued support services to the reunited family unit.

Many orders of probation require restitution or community service. Restitution refers to the compensation provided by an offender to his or her victim; it can involve financial payments or a service alternative. An increasing interest in restitution as a condition of probation has been spurred by an increasing concern for the victims of crime. The service alternative is often imposed on youngsters who are unable to provide financial restitution, although it rarely means direct service to the victim. Instead, the juvenile usually is involved in unpaid work for a nonprofit community agency such as the Salvation Army or the Red Cross.

Juvenile Court Services

BLACK HAWK COUNTY — BUCHANAN COUNTY — GRUNDY COUNTY
P.O. Box 1468
312 East 6th Street
WATERLOO, IOWA 50704
Phone (319) 291-2506

RE: Restitution

This letter is in regard to restitution for damages brought about in the

which occurred on

If the offense is provable, our office will recommend reimbursement in your behalf. What we need is sufficient evidence of damages. Please fill out the enclosed restitution report. When the form has been completed, it should be signed and notarized on the backside. You may bring the form to Juvenile Court Services to get it notarized at no cost to you. Attach all supporting documentation to the report and return the information to Juvenile Court Services. If no restitution is involved, please write "none" on the form and return the form with any additional comments.

This information is needed immediately. If we do not receive it before

without an explanation of delay, our office cannot act in your behalf. You will have to take up the matter in Small Claims Court for reimbursement of your loss.

Please cooperate with us in this matter. We think it is important that juveniles be made responsible for their actions. Also, we feel victims should be reimbursed for their misfortune.

Sincerely,

Kathy L. Thompson
Restitution Assistant

Enclosure

FIGURE 3.5   Letter to a Victim, Waterloo, Iowa

If the youngster violates any of the conditions of probation, the PO prepares a violation of probation report and the youngster can then be subjected to a motion to revoke probation in favor of a more restrictive setting such as an institutional placement.

Superior Court of the District of Columbia

Social Services Division

Family Branch

Restitution Agreement
Juvenile Community Service Program

Superior Court of the District of Columbia
Social Services Division—Family Branch

I, _____, agree to participate in the Juvenile Restitution Program. I agree to all the requirements listed below under the checked paragraphs:

DIRECT SERVICE TO VICTIM. _____ was a victim of this offense. I will work directly for   him   her for a total of _____ hours in the following manner:

MONEY RESTITUTION. As a result of my offense _____ suffered monetary damages. I agree to repay   him   her for the total sum of $ _____, to be paid in the following manner:

COMMUNITY SERVICE. I agree to pay the community for my offense by performing _____ hours of community service. I will perform this service in the following manner:

_____
_____
_____
_____
_____
_____
_____

I agree that this agreement will become a condition of my probation and I further recognize that if I break this agreement, the Social Services Division may request that the Court revoke my probation and commit me to the Department of Human Services. I also recognize that I must fulfill other conditions in order to participate on probation in the Restitution Program. These conditions are:

_____
_____
_____
_____

PROBATIONER'S SIGNATURE: DATE:

ATTORNEY FOR DEFENDANT: DIVISION OF SOCIAL SERVICES:

COMMUNITY WORKER: VICTIM:

CORPORATION COUNSEL: MEDIATOR:

FIGURE 3.6   Restitution Agreement, Washington, D.C.

In the Circuit Court of Jackson County, Missouri Juvenile Division

IN THE INTEREST OF
James Matthews

M/DOB; 7/12/73

PETITION NO. JV87-10010

LIFE NO. 11326

Motion to Revoke Probation

COMES NOW the Juvenile Probation Officer and moves the Court to enter an order revoking the above-named juvenile's probation and, in support thereof, states to the Court:

1. On the 2nd day of November, 1987, the Court committed the above-named juvenile to the custody of the Juvenile Officer at McCune and suspended execution of said commitment and placed the juvenile in the custody of his mother, subject to rules of probation.
2. The juvenile has violated the following term of his probation:
   A.   To obey all law and ordinances.
3. The juvenile violated the aforesaid term of probation in that:
   On or about November 22, 1988, in Jackson County, Missouri, the juvenile knowingly altered and defaced a motor vehicle, a 1988 Nissan 300ZX automobile, without the consent of the owner thereof, in violation of Section 569.080 (Tampering, First Degree - Class C Felony), for which the juvenile would be criminally responsible if tried as an adult,

WHEREFORE, the Juvenile Officer prays the Court revoke the juvenile's probation and enter a dispositional order in the best interests of the juvenile.

_____

Forestal Lawton
Juvenile Officer

Community-Based Facility

There are a variety of noncustodial facilities which have been established to provide specialized services to youngsters referred by the juvenile court. Project New Pride and Project RISE provide examples.

Project New Pride[1]   New Pride was established in 1973 by the Denver, Colorado Anti-Crime Council. The target group for this nonresidential program is serious or violent youthful offenders from fourteen to seventeen years of age. They have at least two prior convictions for serious misdemeanors or felonies and are formally charged or convicted of another offense when referred to New Pride by the Juvenile Court Probation Placement Division:

> Mickey is sixteen and has been on probation for over a year. He lives with his mother and three sisters. Mickey doesn't know his father, and the family's only income is welfare assistance. Mickey has a history of violent outbursts—he has assaulted a teacher and a bus driver; he has now been arrested for attempting to rob a liquor store at knifepoint.

> Rosa is seventeen. Her parents threw her out of the house when she got pregnant. She dropped out of school and moved from place to place, staying with friends whenever she could. She snatched purses for money. She had to abandon her baby and was left with deep emotional scars. She has been arrested in the past for prostitution; she has now been arrested once more.

> John at seventeen had been in four different high schools throughout the country. His family moved constantly to avoid bill collectors. He finally dropped out of school and began driving the getaway car for a gang involved in a number of robberies. After another arrest he was sent to New Pride. Following several months in the program he received his high school diploma through the alternative school; he now drives a taxi. His family has been guided toward some financial assistance.

New Pride operates on the premise that individuals must confront their problems in their own environment—within the community. Youngsters receive a blend of counseling, alternative schooling, correction of learning disabilities, vocational training, job placement, recreation, and cultural activities. The goal is to create "new pride," thus enabling youngsters to adopt and maintain a conventional life-style. There is intensive supervision from the youth's intake through the end of his or her involvement with the program. The New Pride philosophy greets youngsters at the door:

> *If we fish for you,*
> *You will live for a day;*
> *If we teach you to fish,*
> *You will live for a lifetime.*

---

[1]Information from Carol Holliday Blew, Daniel McGillis, and Gerald Bryant, *Project New Pride* (Washington, D.C.: U.S. Government Printing Office, 1977); and Alfred S. Regnery, "Introducing New Pride," *NIJ Reports* 193 (September 1985): 9–12.

THE SERVICES

For the first three months, youngsters in the program receive intensive services. A nine-month follow-up period continues treatment geared to the youth's needs and interests. The follow-up may involve daily to weekly contact. And in some instances, clients have been served continuously since project inception.

The services provided include the following:

Education.   Based on test results, participants are assigned to classes in either the New Pride Alternative School (located at project headquarters) or the Learning Disabilities Center.

The *Alternative School* provides one-to-one tutoring with relatively little lecturing. Staff are strongly supportive of student efforts, encourage their strengths, and try especially to make academic work rewarding to students who have previously experienced repeated failures. Emphasis is on reintegrating students into the regular school system.

The staff of the *Learning Disabilities Center* works intensively with clients to correct their perceptual and cognitive disabilities. New Pride stresses the relationship between learning disabilities and juvenile delinquency. In the treatment approach, learning disability therapy and academic tutoring are equally important. Tests administered to project youth in the first two years of operations showed that 78 percent of the New Pride participants were found to have at least two learning disabilities.

> Shortly after Margaret entered the program, New Pride staff realized that she had poor sight and needed glasses. Her counselor helped her get a prescription and worked with her constantly. This disability corrected, Margaret displayed a notable improvement in her studies.

Counseling.   The project attempts to match clients with counselors who can best respond to their role model needs and personalities. Treatment is planned to enhance the youth's self-image and to help him/her cope with his/her environment. Counselors involve themselves in all aspects of their clients' lives and maintain frequent contact with family, teachers, social workers, and any others close to the youth. In the nine-month follow-up period, counselors continue to maintain a minimum of weekly contacts with a youth and his/her family.

> The Denver Juvenile Court Probation Placement Division referred Willy to New Pride. His counselor devoted most of the individual counseling sessions with Willy to the subject of alcoholism as a medical problem. He took Willy to an alcohol treatment center to talk to experts, and gave him literature on alcoholism. Once Willy accepted alcoholism as a medical problem, he began trying to overcome his alcohol problem.

Employment. Job preparation is a key part of the program. The employment component is designed to introduce clients to the working world and its expectations, and to provide employment experience along with much needed income. During their first month of project participation, youths attend a job skills workshop on such topics as filling out application forms and interviewing. The job placement specialist counsels each client individually to develop vocational interests and to provide realistic appraisals of career ambitions and requisite skills. Actual on-the-job training occurs in the second and third months of program participation.

Cultural Education. New Pride takes youngsters who have known little more than their immediate neighborhoods and exposes them to a range of experiences and activities in the Denver area. Extensive community contacts have created a rich variety of opportunities, including visits to a television station to watch the news hour being prepared, ski trips, an Outward Bound weekend, sports events, restaurant dinners, and many other educational and recreational events.

Traditionally, juvenile services have been highly specialized and fragmented. Coupled with this fragmentation was the inconsistency in the delivery of services, which consequently produced negative experiences for some youth. New Pride's approach is to integrate all services, providing comprehensive treatment to its clients, all of whom are "hard-core" delinquents — multiple offenders with a myriad of social adjustment problems. For example, a single youth may receive remedial treatment for a learning disability, take courses for high school credit, be placed in a part-time job, participate in family counseling, and experience cultural events at theaters and museums. The staff is familiar with the range of each client's activities and can reinforce gains in any one area. That is why New Pride is a concept rather than just a group of people each trying to answer one problem of a delinquent youth.

New Pride provides intensive services with limited caseloads afforded by a high staff-to-client ratio. In addition, a well-organized program draws a large, diverse group of volunteers from community organizations and local colleges and universities. Students receive credits for a semester's work at New Pride as counseling interns. Community volunteers may tutor clients, develop special activity programs such as a yoga course or mechanical shop, or provide administrative and clerical assistance.

In many instances New Pride youths are tutored by volunteers who are not of the same ethnic or racial group. The staff feel that bringing together inner-city, minority, delinquent youths, and volunteers from widely varied backgrounds is vital. This contact helps both groups learn to cope with differences and gives them the opportunity to develop more favorable attitudes toward each other.

Willy and his volunteer tutor have developed a very special relationship. That Willy is Chicano and his tutor is white is not what makes their relationship so special. His tutor is blind. In part to show how much he appreciates his help, and in part to impress him, Willy is learning how to read Braille.

Arrangements and relationships established with local court and probation officials have been integral to successful project operations. Furthermore, New Pride is involved with and derives support from numerous community and business organizations. With the support of both the legal and business communities, New Pride has succeeded in responding to the needs of the youths and of their communities.

Project RISE Pima County, Arizona, which includes the city of Tucson, provides another example of a community-based noncustodial response to troubled youth. Over the years, the Pima County Juvenile Court has found that there is a strong correlation between a child's school problems and delinquent behavior. All too often school officials and the juvenile court would work in isolation from each other. In 1982, a project at Howenstine School was begun to combine the treatments of the dual problems of delinquency and school failure. This program was a joint venture between the Tucson Unified School District and the Pima County Juvenile Court. Teachers, teacher aides, probation officers, and probation aides work side by side with a small number of juveniles to provide maximum supervision and a favorable environment for learning. The success of the Howenstine program was responsible for the Sunnyside School District inaugurating a similar program in 1983. Both programs are now known as Project RISE (Reentry Into Successful Education).

Project RISE is a full-time day program for about forty youngsters, combining the best of the educational and juvenile justice systems from which the project receives its clients. The goals of these programs are to reduce serious delinquent activity, improve school attendance, decrease school behavioral problems, raise the child's reading level by two years, and inculcate positive social values and survival skills in the youth. To accomplish these, Project RISE is housed in facilities separate from the mainstream high schools. Students are either transported to school or issued city bus passes. The staff to child ratio is extremely high, assuring intensive daily supervision in an innovative learning environment.

As children progress, their success is rewarded within the context of a behavior modification system. (Behavior modification is discussed in Chapter 9.) In this manner, undesirable activities and habits are eliminated while healthy, socially acceptable behaviors are reinforced. The child's self-image is bolstered by repeated successes in interpersonal as well as academic tasks. Emphasis is placed upon frequent organized outings in order to broaden the child's growing socialization.

Juveniles requiring residential care in a nonsecure setting may be sent to a "ranch" in jurisdictions that have such facilities available.

Log Cabin Ranch   The San Francisco Juvenile Court operates a county rehabilitation facility offering residential care for boys ranging in age from fifteen to eighteen years. The Log Cabin Ranch has a total capacity of eighty-six, and one-third of their overall school program is devoted to the appropriate vocational instruction. The ranch offers four vocational programs: auto mechanics, electronics, building maintenance, and culinary arts. Following four weeks of orientation and testing, qualified students are assigned to one of the programs. Successful graduates are assigned to job developers who are responsible for the placement of these youths in apprenticeship programs or part-time or full-time employment, depending on the age, skills, and needs of the particular youth.

Log Cabin provides a full range of counseling services to its students. Both individual and group counseling are prescribed, and reports detailing each student's progress are submitted every six weeks. Case conferences involving the student, his probation officer, the head teacher, and the assistant director are held at regular intervals and provide each student with individualized attention and feedback. The Forensic Health Services of the Department of Mental Health provides psychological services, crisis intervention, individual counseling, and consultation.

The School Department offers the necessary individualized remedial instruction in basic skill areas, while a learning specialist from the Court School provides individual assessments of each youth's learning abilities. Computer assisted instruction is available to the students on an individual basis. Log Cabin Ranch is an active member of the Central Coast Ranch League, fielding competitive teams in basketball, softball, volleyball, and cross-country.

The Group Home

Residential treatment can be classified according to the degree of custodial care provided. At the lower end of this scale is the group home. The group home may be privately operated under contract with the state (or other level of government), or it can be operated by the state. Generally, anywhere from six to fifteen youngsters live in the home at any one time. The typical home has several bedrooms, baths, large living room, dining area, and basement recreation area. The interior of the home approximates that of a large single-family dwelling. Group homes are usually located in residential areas that are in proximity to public transportation, public schools, and recreation facilities.

The group home is for youngsters who:

1. are in unresolvable conflict with their parents, but are not seriously disturbed or psychotic; and/or
2. have inadequate homes and need to develop skills for independent living; and/or
3. need to deal with community social adjustment problems in a therapeutic family environment; and/or
4. need to deal with individual adjustment problems and to learn about themselves in relation to others; and/or
5. need to develop self-confidence through successful experiences.

Each resident has daily chores, such as doing dishes, making the bed, or mowing the lawn. Houseparents, usually a married couple with graduate degrees in a therapeutic discipline such as social work or psychology, perform surrogate parent roles by preparing or overseeing the preparation of meals, enforcing a curfew, helping with homework, and other tasks usually handled by parents in healthy families. Youngsters attend local schools on a full-time basis, or they have a schedule that incorporates both school and employment.

There are group counseling sessions conducted by group workers geared to help the residents understand and overcome problems that have led to the placement, and to define goals consistent with their individual ability. Individual counseling programs are provided for those youngsters who need help in preparing for independent living, and for those who need assistance in improving their family relationships. Day-by-day counseling and conflict resolution are handled by the houseparents.

The most difficult aspects of the group home are relationships with the surrounding community—typically there is forceful neighborhood resistance to placing such a facility in most areas. While it is generally agreed by both professionals and lay persons that the group home concept is an excellent one for many youngsters coming to the attention of the juvenile court, this has not been translated into widespread acceptance of the reality. Group homes, not only for troubled youngsters, but also for the retarded and other handicapped persons, have been vigorously and all too often successfully resisted by local residents. This problem has become so severe, that in 1989 the United States Department of Justice brought suit against a Chicago suburb (Chicago Heights) because the municipality refused to permit the building of a group home for fifteen retarded adults (Johnson, 1989). While we may accept the moral imperative and recognize the value of helping the unfortunate, it is too often a concern for real estate values that prevails. *L'hypocrisie est un hommage que le vice rend a' la vertu.*

The Residential Treatment Center

The term residential treatment center (RTC) is being used to identify private institutions that provide residential care for youngsters with or without the intervention of the juvenile court. These institutions are often operated under the umbrella of a religious denomination—for example, Catholic Charities, or Protestant or Jewish welfare boards—although they are nondenominational insofar as clientele is concerned. Generally, the RTC provides a wide variety of enriched services; they also receive a great deal of public funding. Despite the fact almost all receive tax-levy money, the RTC retains the privilege of screening their residents—a luxury not afforded to public institutions. One study found, however, that in southern California there is considerable competition for residents between private facilities, and juveniles admitted to private institutions do not significantly differ from those sent to public facilities (Shichor and Bartollas, 1989). They can also mix adjudicated delinquents, status offenders, and voluntary clients in a manner that would not be permissible in a public institution, although the mixing of delinquent and nondelinquent children runs contrary to the prevailing wisdom in the field (Curran, 1988).

Highfields   On the former estate of Charles A. Lindbergh, near Hopewell, New Jersey, Highfields was established in 1950 under private auspices. Although it was taken over by the state of New Jersey in 1952, Highfields provides a prototype for many private juvenile facilities throughout the United States.

The treatment objective at Highfields is to give delinquent boys an opportunity for self-rehabilitation by achieving a series of preliminary and prerequisite goals. There are few formal rules, since the purpose is to enable the youngster to develop a nondelinquent orientation through *guided group interaction* (GGI).

Youngsters work or attend school during the day, and in the evening meet in groups of about ten for a daily therapy session lasting ninety minutes. The purpose is to assist residents to develop an understanding of their problems through unstructured interaction with others in similar circumstances (Finckenauer, 1984: 198).

> The subjects discussed in GGI revolve around the current problems of group members and the group itself. These problems emerge as a result of interaction with significant others, primarily peers, in a group setting. . . . The major emphasis in this technique is on the group and its development, rather than upon an exhaustive analysis of each individual group member. . . . Guided group interaction is considered to be most effective with adolescents because they seem to be more responsive to peer influences than any other age group.

Highfields has no guards or locked doors, and there is a deliberate absence of authoritarian leadership. The twenty residents, who have been adjudicated as delinquents and placed on probation, remain at Highfields for four months. Family and friends are encouraged to visit, and residents are given passes to visit nearby areas and sometimes go home on furlough. These privileges can be lost for misbehavior—the entire group is punished for the actions of any of its members. There have been a number of studies on the effectiveness of Highfields; claims and counterclaims abound.

A persistent problem for the juvenile court in providing alternative institutional care for youngsters is the ability of private treatment institutions to refuse to accept children who do not "fit in." Probation officers can be frustrated in their attempt to find suitable placement for certain youngsters because of this problem. The PO makes an evaluation based on professional judgment; this is transmitted to the judge in the form of a recommendation. However, in the final stage the private institution can decide that the youngster is "incompatible" with their program (read: "too delinquent" or "too disturbed"); the RTC often accepts only youngsters who are referred to by probation officers as "boy scouts." The court is then faced with the alternative of probation or a training school.

TRAINING SCHOOL

The training school is a public institution that accepts all youngsters committed by the courts. Each training school is usually set up to handle particular categories of juvenile. They may be assigned on the basis of age, aggressiveness, or delinquent history. This is done to avoid mixing older children with younger ones, adjudicated delinquents with status offenders, more disturbed youngsters with those having less serious problems. The training school usually provides a level of security not available in other types of juvenile institution (although less than that offered in a correctional facility). Juveniles are committed to training schools based on the following criteria:

1. There is a *finding of fact* that the child has committed an offense that would be punishable by imprisonment if committed by an adult.
2. The parents are unable to control their child or provide for his or her social, emotional, and educational needs.
3. There is no other child welfare service that is sufficient.
4. The child needs the services available at the training school.

Los Angeles County Probation Department
Residential Treatment Program

The Los Angeles County Probation Residential Treatment Program is divided into two age groupings: senior, sixteen through eighteen, and junior, thirteen through fifteen. One junior camp and two senior camps are secure (fenced); the remainder are open (not fenced) camps. The security camps are used to maintain those minors who represent a significant escape risk—essentially impulsive youngsters with a low degree of self-control. In these camps, emphasis is placed on developing self-control.

The system is composed of fifteen institutions; fourteen are located in mountain settings. An intake facility with sixty beds is maintained at San Fernando Valley Juvenile Hall. Almost all boys ordered to camp are screened here for medical or psychiatric problems and academic levels are established before the minor is assigned to a camp. Girls are processed directly from the juvenile hall in which they are detained. Deputy probation officers in all camps provide on-going individual and group counseling to all camp wards. Treatment programs are individual—the length of stay for each minor is dependent upon the minor's individual progress in the camp setting.

The principal objective of junior camps is to evaluate academic skills and achievement. These youngsters spend the bulk of the program day in school. Work is limited to in-camp maintenance and culinary assistance. The focus in senior camps is more oriented toward instilling work ethic disciplines. Senior youngsters ordinarily spend one-half of each day in school and one-half in parks and recreation work crews. A juvenile alternative work services program has been implemented whereby work crews are provided to public agencies on a contract basis. Extensive vocational training in such areas as welding, foundry work, and auto repair is available at one of the camps.

The establishment of the Lyman School for Boys in Massachusetts in 1847 began an era of providing separate facilities for juvenile offenders. The training, or reform, schools were patterned after adult prisons. They were regimented with large impersonal dormitories. Each provided some basic medical and dental treatment and limited educational and vocational training. Over the years there has been an increased emphasis on vocational training, remedial education, and rehabilitation through the use of social workers, teachers, psychiatrists, psychologists, and recreation workers. A training school, like a prison or hospital, operates 168 hours per week; this fact, combined with the level of security and services provided, makes the training school a very expensive institution where annual costs can easily run in excess of $30,000 per resident.

One training school, the Warwick School for Boys, is located fifty-five miles from New York City. It is one of the training schools operated by the New York State Division for Youth (DFY). The school is a pleasant-looking institution with seven hundred acres of lawns and trees; it houses about 170 residents in several dormitories. There are also some individual rooms assigned on a "merit" basis. The residents are adjudicated delinquents who have committed offenses ranging from petty larceny to serious felonies, all before their sixteenth birthday.

The school has about 180 staff members, and there are no walls or gates around the school—security is maintained through the use of supervised activities and a high staff to resident ratio. The daily schedule calls for two hours of compulsory academic instruction and two hours of physical education, with additional services for those who require more help. Both individual and group counseling are provided, as is vocational training in such areas as mechanical drawing, woodworking, electricity, and painting.

THE YOUTH AUTHORITY

Some states, for example, California, Ohio, and New York, have a state agency responsible for receiving cases from both juvenile and criminal courts. Typically, youngsters adjudicated delinquents in juvenile court; persons prosecuted and convicted under youthful or young offender statutes in criminal court; and juveniles prosecuted in criminal court under mandatory or optional waiver provisions, are remanded to the youth authority for a period of confinement and aftercare (parole) supervision.

California Youth Authority

The California Youth Authority (CYA) operates varied and specialized programs to provide care and custody for wards in institutions and on parole. After a ward is committed by the court and accepted by the authority, he or she is transferred to a reception center and clinic for about four weeks for evaluation and testing prior to making an appearance before the seven-member Youthful Offender Parole Board. Community assessment reports are generated by parole agents after visiting the ward's family and contacting appropriate local agencies. These reports add information about the ward's family and community relationships to information gathered by the clinic staff from the ward, probation reports, and from any psychological or educational testing done at the clinic. All of this information is compiled into a document called a *clinic study* and presented to the Youthful Offender Parole Board. The board uses this report in making decisions about the ward. Once the ward appears before the board and decisions about length of stay and program are made, the ward is transferred to his or her institution to begin programming.

The CYA has eleven institutions and six forestry camps located throughout the state. A youth is assigned to one based on age, maturity, delinquent sophistication, educational/vocational needs, security needs, and behavior. While in most cases wards are placed in an institution or conservation camp for a period of time and then released on parole, a few are placed on parole immediately after diagnostic studies. Under certain circumstances, a ward committed from a criminal court may be assigned to an institution of the Department of Corrections. Commitments from both criminal and juvenile courts may also be assigned to an institution of the Department of Mental Health.

While in a CYA institution, younger wards attend school all day, whereas older ones might be in school part-time and in vocational training part-time.

Many are assigned jobs within the institution, for example, working on the grounds or in food preparation. All wards are assigned a counselor and some are placed in psychiatric or psychological treatment. The CYA has special programs for drug and alcohol abusers, sex offenders, and the seriously mentally ill. Due to limited resources, not everyone needing specialized treatment can be assigned to these programs.

When the ward is considered ready for parole by the Youthful Offender Parole Board, the parole agent makes all the necessary arrangements for his or her return to the community. The agent contacts family members, law enforcement, and other agencies and assesses the need for special conditions of parole that the ward must adhere to. The agent then completes the re-entry report which includes a preliminary parole plan describing such things as employment, training, and school, and establishes goals to be achieved during the first thirty to ninety days. For the first ninety days on parole, intensive reentry services are provided. The parole agent has frequent contact with the ward and his or her family and provides needed brokerage with community agencies. The level and intensity of supervision gradually diminishes as the ward becomes increasingly self-sufficient. The decision to reduce the level of supervision, however, is based on a classification system which determines the level of control necessary based on the ward's potential risk score and his or her need for supportive services.

Ohio Department of Youth Services

The Ohio Department of Youth Services (DYS) is the state agency which provides a safe, secure environment, education, vocational guidance, and other developmental programs for young people aged twelve to eighteen, who have been charged with felony-level offenses and committed to the department by one of the state's eighty-eight county juvenile courts.

The department's philosophy emphasizes care which is aimed at ultimate reintegration of troubled youth into the community. Planning for this reintegration begins at the time of commitment to DYS. A team consisting of DYS staff, the youth, and his or her family, establishes a plan of development when the youth is committed to DYS. Obtainable goals, including educational goals, are established to help the youth develop self-control and discipline. The DYS Youth Recovery Program focuses on helping youth become free from chemical dependency, developing skills to avoid further contact with the juvenile justice system, and eliminating vocational handicaps as a result of being chemically dependent.

There are five institutions, two institutional complexes and eight regional offices within the jurisdiction of the Department of Youth Services. These regional offices are located in every major metropolitan center in the state. Youth assignments to DYS institutions are made on the basis of age, felony level of offense committed, and the proximity of the DYS institution to the youth's home. There are about 1,600 youngsters in DYS facilities and 1,800 in the aftercare program.

Each institution has a fully accredited school which all youth are required to

(Continued)

attend. Educational opportunities are available for all residents including those with learning disabilities and special needs. There are vocational programs in several of the DYS institutional high schools that offer youth a variety of possible career paths to choose from once they are reintegrated into their communities. These programs include auto mechanics, graphic arts, building maintenance, small engine repair, cosmetology, and barbering. There are a variety of recreational activities and extracurricular activities at each institution. At one location, youth have the chance to be on the award-winning DYS drill team or in the break-dancing group which gives public performances throughout the year at schools and community events. Youth at DYS make positive contributions to the community through the volunteer work they do in litter control programs and by working with elderly citizens.

New York State Division for Youth

Established in 1945, the Division for Youth (DFY) is the oldest comprehensive agency serving youth in the United States. The agency operates the state training schools and secure facilities for juveniles tried as adults, and regulates juvenile detention facilities. Youngsters are classified according to the level of security they require, and assigned to the appropriate DFY facility or program:

Secure Centers

Ranging in size from ten to one hundred beds, these facilities are characterized by physically restricting construction, hardware, and procedures, including security fencing and screens. The facility is either a single building or a small cluster of buildings in close proximity to each other, surrounded by a security fence. Most centers have single rooms which are locked at night. They are located in nonurban areas and virtually all services are provided on grounds—a "total institution." The secure center admits juvenile offenders tried in adult courts and serious delinquents adjudicated in family (juvenile) court. They typically have an extensive history of delinquent behavior and involvement with the juvenile justice system, including prior institutional commitments. Many exhibit serious psychological and emotional problems. Certain residents may be given the privilege of temporary release from facility grounds for carefully regulated periods of time for special reasons—for example, a death in the family, medical or dental treatment, community services program, industrial training, education leave, or work release.

One of these centers is located at Goshen, about seventy-five miles from New York City, and houses sixty residents who are serving criminal sentences for felonies committed before the age of sixteen, several for murder. Residents eighteen to twenty years old can be transferred to an adult facility, and at age twenty-one, all unexpired terms must be completed at an adult institution. At Goshen they receive vocational education, academic tutoring, counseling, and recreational services, all under strict discipline — the superintendent is a former marine sergeant with a master's degree in social work. And it is expensive: about $75,000 per year for each resident (Raab, 1989).

Limited Secure Centers

Ranging in size from 36-bed centers to 120-bed training schools, these facilities are located in rural areas and characterized by highly structured programs with virtually all services provided on-grounds. Residents are frequently transferred to less secure settings before returning to their home community. They are also used for certain youth previously placed in secure facilities as a first step in their transition back to the community.

Noncommunity-Based Families

These moderately structured and varied facilities are for youth who need to be removed from the community but are not high security risks. Limited trips for community activities, under close staff supervision, are an integral component of these programs. They are most often located in rural areas. These centers may admit only certain serious delinquents. Some of the residents have been previously placed in secure and limited secure facilities and are transferred as part of the transition back to their own communities. In other cases, youth who have been initially placed in community-based programs and have been unable to function there are transferred to these residential centers — they are in the middle of the DFY's continuum of residential services. These centers may admit all categories of delinquents, status offenders, and youths placed as a condition of probation, and cases placed through a bureau of child welfare (that is, without court intervention).

Youth Development Centers

These specialized community-based programs are configured and staffed to provide an entire array of services to youth within their community-based structure. These centers may admit delinquents, status offenders, youths placed as a condition of probation, and cases placed through a bureau of child welfare.

Group Homes / Centers

These are small residential units with seven to ten beds located in residential neighborhoods and which use community resources to provide many of the needs of the residents, education, medical/dental, recreation, etc. Residents are allowed frequent and unescorted access to the community. These centers may admit delinquents, status offenders, youths placed as a condition of probation, or those placed through a bureau of child welfare. One special center in Buffalo provides more structured and varied staffing than is normally found in a group residence.

(Continued)

Foster Homes / Alternative Programs

These programs serve youths who have been placed with the DFY but who can function in an alternative home situation, rather than in an institutional setting: delinquents, status offenders, and those placed as a condition of probation or through a bureau of child welfare.

Many of the (nonsecure) facilities used by the DFY are the result of contracts with private residential child care agencies.

Aftercare

Once a youth is in placement at either a DFY or private child care agency, a Youth Service Team counselor monitors his or her progress and serves as a liaison between the facility, the family, and the community. The counselor assists facility staff efforts to meet a youth's service needs as defined in the service plans and to modify such plans to meet developing needs. Aftercare services include a variety of counseling and brokering services for youth who have been released from facilities and are living at home. Individual advocacy is provided by aftercare staff to help youth obtain services for which they are eligible, such as schooling or medical help, and to help them take advantage of opportunities for which they must apply, such as jobs or scholarships. This frequently involves intervening directly on a youth's behalf to try to reduce the reluctance of some agencies to accept or serve youth with delinquent backgrounds.

AFTERCARE AND PAROLE

Aftercare is the planned release of a juvenile from a residential placement (group home, residential treatment center, training school, correctional institution) to supportive services in the community. The juvenile may be supervised by the juvenile probation agency or other aftercare (parole) worker. Aftercare services are often provided by the same agency that administers the juvenile institutions. For example, I worked for the New York State Department of Social Welfare which used to operate the state training schools. I had the title "Youth Parole Worker" and was responsible for supervising juveniles released from the boys training schools. In 1978, New York enacted the "Juvenile Offender Law" which mandates that thirteen-, fourteen-, and fifteen-year-olds who commit certain felonies be subjected to prosecution in adult criminal court. If convicted, the youngster can serve a term in a secure facility of the Division for Youth. During that term the juvenile becomes subject to the jurisdiction of the New York State Board of Parole for a release decision — parole — and eventual community supervision by a parole officer. Thus, the same agency that supervises adult felons in New York, the Division of Parole, also supervises juveniles convicted of certain violent felonies.

Jackson County Juvenile Court Services
McCune School for Boys

Request for Conditional Release / Aftercare

Name: Michael DeWitt
Birth Date: July 12, 1972
Address: 1900 West Briar Place
Enrollment: June 6, 1988
Date of Report: November 28, 1988

I REASON FOR PLACEMENT

Michael was committed to the McCune School for Boys on June 6, 1988, by Judge Harrison for Sexual Abuse.

II ADDITIONAL REFERRALS

There have been no additional referrals.

III ADJUSTMENT DURING PRESENT PERIOD OF SUPERVISION

While at McCune, Michael has made substantial advancement. Upon entrance into the program he was unable to work with his peers. Michael was often the target of harassment from other residents. He had told a story about his being offered chili to eat from resident Timothy Mordell working in the cafeteria. Michael asked if the meat in it was human flesh, and the incident became the source of ridicule during the remainder of his stay at McCune.

Over the past six months, Michael learned how to deal more appropriately with the harassment. He was also able to overcome racial problems that he had experienced since entering McCune. He has learned to deal with his prejudice in a fashion that permitted friendships to be established interracially.

He did so well in the McCune School that he was selected for Resident of the Week on three occasions. His grades reflect this:

English . . . . .B+
Science . . . . .A
Physical Ed . . . . .A
Vocational Preparation . . . . .A
Math . . . . .A
Social Studies . . . . .A
Citizenship . . . . .A

There were no problems in the community, and Michael spent almost all of his furlough time with his parents. On one occasion, his mother brought Michael back to McCune early because they saw and spoke with an individual who was associated with the victim. The resident and his mother were fearful that this

(Continued)

individual would accuse Michael of some indiscretion, so he wanted to check back in at McCune. No complaints were received.

The only medical problem was the result of Michael striking a glass hallway window and putting his hand through it on the weekend of June 26, 1988, following a verbal altercation with another resident. Michael was taken to the hospital where he received both stitches and a medical furlough.

IV FAMILY SITUATION AND RELATIONSHIPS

Michael is an only child and lives at the above address with his parents, Charles and Barbara DeWitt; his relationship with his parents has improved significantly while being at McCune. Barbara DeWitt has attended virtually every Family Group Therapy session. As a result, mother and child have moderated their interactions; previously, they were characterized by emotional exaggeration. Michael earned all but two possible home visits.

V DIAGNOSIS AND PLAN OF TREATMENT

Michael has completed all four of the four phases of the program. He has made great strides in the areas of authority, peer interaction, school, and family relationships. Possible problems in the future will involve his reputation for sexual acting out, although this has not yet been the case. He has been on furlough and attended Newtown High School.

VI SPECIFIC RECOMMENDATION

Michael has successfully completed his three-week furlough period. McCune staff, as well as his family, feel Michael is ready to return home. It is, therefore, recommended that Michael DeWitt be placed on Conditional Release and receive the services of an Aftercare Worker.

Carol Spalding
Social Worker

Similarly, in Minnesota parole agents of the Department of Corrections supervise juveniles who have been sentenced to a correctional facility. The release of a juvenile from a correctional institution in Minnesota is the responsibility of a juvenile hearing officer, who utilizes a scale that incorporates the severity of the offense and the delinquent history (see figure 3.7). Thus, for example, a juvenile who committed Burglary, 2nd Degree would have a *Severity Level* of II; if his or her *Delinquent History Factors* equalled "2" the inmate would normally be paroled sometime between the fifth and eighth month. The scale makes no reference to rehabilitation or prognosis—it is a "justice model" (discussed in Chapter 7).

In Michigan youngsters twelve to nineteen who have been adjudicated delinquent or found to be in need of supervision (status offenders) by the

Severity Level	Most Serious Current Offense[a]	Delinquent History Factors			
		0	1	2	3
I	Violation of Probation Contempt of Court Prostitution Assault—4th & 5th Degree Drivers Under Influence of Alcohol Negligent Fires Burglary—3rd & 4th Degree Damage to Property—$2,500 or less Forgery—$2,500 or less Possession of Controlled Substance Receiving Stolen Goods—$2,500 or less Theft—$2,500 or less Unauthorized Use of Motor Vehicle Dangerous Weapons Trespass All Other Misdemeanors and Gross Misdemeanors	4-3	5-3	6-4	7-5
II	Assault—2nd & 3rd Degree Burglary—2nd Degree Damage to Property—Over $2,500 Forgery—Over $2,500 False Imprisonment				
III	Receiving Stolen Goods—Over $2,500 Sale of Controlled Substance Theft From Person Theft—Over $2,500 Arson—3rd Degree Criminal Sexual Conduct—3rd & 4th Degree Simple Robbery Terroristic Threats Burglary—1st Degree Criminal Negligence Resulting in Death Aggravated Robbery Arson—1st & 2nd Degree	6-3	7-4	8-5	9-6
IV	Criminal Sexual Conduct—1st & 2nd Degree Kidnapping Manslaughter Assault—1st Degree	10-6	11-7	12-8	13-9
	Murder (all degrees)	b	b	b	b

[a]Commitment offenses not specifically listed shall be placed on the grid at the discretion of the hearing officer at the time of the initial institution review.

[b]Murder shall be dealt with on an individual basis.

FIGURE 3.7   Projected Institution Length of Stay, in Months

STATEMENT OF RULES, REGULATIONS, AND CONDITIONS
UNDER WHICH PAROLE IS GRANTED

In consideration of the parole granted to me by the Commissioner of Corrections I do hereby accept such parole and agree to abide by the following terms and conditions:

1. I will report immediately upon arrival at my destination, either by mail, telephone, or personal visit, as directed by my supervising agent, who is:

   Name: _____ Telephone No.: _____

   Address: _____

2. I recognize that my liberty on parole is conditional and that I am subject to supervision by an assigned agent. Therefore I will:

   a) Obey all federal, state, and local laws and ordinances;
   b) Obtain approval from my supervising agent before:
      1. Purchasing or using any motor vehicle;
      2. Borrowing money, going into debt or doing any credit or installment buying;
      3. Changing my residence, employment, vocational or school programs;
      4. Getting married;
   c) Obtain permission of my supervising agent before leaving the state for any reason:

   d) Abide by the following special terms and conditions: _____

   _____

   _____

   _____

   _____

   _____

   _____

3. I will keep in close contact with my supervising agent and seek his/her guidance and assistance on any problems I meet. I will at all times follow instructions and contact him/her in the event of any difficulty. I will submit such reports as may be required and will reply promptly to any communications.

4. I will be guided and abide by such specific instructions as may be issued by the Commissioner of Corrections and/or supervising agent with regard to companions, hours, intoxicants, medical attention, family responsibilities, support of self, and court obligations.

5. I shall not possess or use narcotics or other drugs or drug preparations, except those prescribed for me by a physician.

6. I will not purchase or otherwise obtain, or have in my possession, any type of firearm or dangerous weapon without expressed permission in writing by my supervising agent.

7. I understand that the Commissioner of Corrections has the authority to place me in custody at any time and to revoke my parole in the event that I violate any of the terms or conditions hereof.

   My present expiration date is _____ .

8. I agree that if I am returned to a state correctional institution on replacement or hold status, institutional rules constitute a condition of my parole agreement and a violation of these rules while on replacement on hold status may result in the revocation of my parole.

9. I hereby do waive extradition to the State of Minnesota from any jurisdiction in or outside the United States where I may be found and also agree that I will not contest any effort by any jurisdiction to return me to the State of Minnesota.

FIGURE 3.8 Juvenile Parole Agreement, Minnesota Department of Corrections

juvenile division of a probate court, can be committed to the Department of Social Services for placement in their own home, a foster home, group home, youth camp, diagnostic center, halfway house, residential treatment center, or state training school. In Michigan, status offenders are often committed to the Department of Social Services when the particular juvenile court has insufficient resources available for the youngster. The department offers secure juvenile residential treatment facilities which may be utilized as the "last resort" for the most seriously delinquent youth. Delinquent wards remain under state authority until discharged by the Youth Parole and Review Board (YPRB) or attainment of age nineteen. The YPRB is a three-member board within the Department of Social Services that conducts parole release, violation of parole, and discharge hearings for state delinquency wards.

Aftercare supervision is similar, if not identical, to probation supervision and, as noted above, is sometimes provided by a juvenile probation agency. The first responsibility of the aftercare worker is to plan for the release and placement of the young person. Placement plans include where the juvenile will live, whether he or she is to work or attend school or a training program, or both, and arrangements for any supportive services that may be needed by the client and which are available in the community. The young person released or paroled from a training school may be returned to his or her own home, if this is desirable, or be placed in an alternative setting such as foster care, a group home, or halfway house. (Halfway houses are discussed in Chapter 11.) The aftercare worker usually investigates placement alternatives and finalizes a program plan which is submitted to training school officials and those responsible for the release decision.

Once back in the community, the young person will be supervised by an aftercare worker, probation officer, or parole officer. The youngster will be required to abide by a set of rules and regulations, the violation of which can cause a return to a "secure setting." The worker will make regular visits to the youngster's residence, school and/or place of employment. The worker will involve family and school officials in an effort to facilitate the young person's reintegration and rehabilitation.

Aftercare in Dauphin County, Pennsylvania

Aftercare is the responsibility of juvenile aftercare workers who have caseloads of not more than twenty-five youngsters who are in placement or are receiving post-placement services. All delinquent and most dependent youths placed in a group home or institutional care by the juvenile court become clients of the program. The goals of aftercare are to reduce the amount of time that a youth spends in placement and to reduce the rate of recidivism experienced by youths returning from institutional care. The aftercare workers serve as case managers bridging the gap between the community and the placement resource, and serving as counselors helping the youth to improve decision-making ability. Each aftercare worker is assigned to specific placement resources so that all county youth at a particular placement have the same aftercare worker.

The aftercare worker begins involvement with the case during placement discussions prior to the dispositional hearing. The worker acts as an advisor during the placement planning process and, when possible, accompanies the intake worker and the client to the preplacement interview at the placement resource. Whenever possible the worker attends the court hearings for a client who is being recommended for a placement resource to which he or she is assigned.

(Continued)

The worker assists in the transportation of the client to the placement resource and insures that the child, parents, and institutional staff understand the role which the aftercare worker will play during and after placement. Within thirty days of the youth's placement, the worker prepares a written family service plan stating the short-term and long-term service objectives, the services to be provided, and the anticipated length of the placement. At least once each month the aftercare worker visits the youth and the staff at the placement resource, attends institutional meetings, and assists in the development of the treatment plan and monitors its implementation.

During placement the aftercare worker meets at least once a month with the youth's family for counseling and information sharing about the youth's progress, and supervises all home visits made by the youth. In the fifth month of the youth's continuous placement, the worker prepares a written review of the placement and family services plan in preparation for the six-month review-of-placement hearing before the juvenile court master. Prior to the youth's release, the aftercare worker coordinates the development of an aftercare plan which will be followed during post-placement supervision. To effectively implement these aftercare plans the worker must develop cooperative relationships with schools, employers, and local social service agencies.

After release from the placement resource, the aftercare worker supervises the client for three to six months. Initially, at least one personal contact is made each week to provide counseling and monitor the aftercare plan goals. As the needs of the client allow, supervision may subsequently be reduced to a minimum of two personal counseling contacts per month. Cases are reviewed with the aftercare supervisor at least once each month. Upon completion of the aftercare plan goals, the aftercare worker recommends to the juvenile court judge that supervision be terminated and the case closed.

THE JUVENILE COURT IN THE SUPREME COURT

Earlier in this chapter we noted that the juvenile court operated for many decades without attention or adherence to due process requirements or scrutiny by the judicial branch of government. This era of juvenile court history ended during the latter half of the 1960s, an era marked by the judicial activism of the Supreme Court with respect to issues involving civil liberties.

In 1966, the Supreme Court reviewed the operations of the juvenile court in *Kent* v. *United States* (383 U.S. 541). Morris Kent, age sixteen, was convicted in (adult) criminal court of raping a woman in her Washington, D.C., apartment and sentenced to a prison term of thirty to ninety years. In accord with existing federal statutes, the case had first been referred to the juvenile court where, over the objections of defense counsel, jurisdiction was waived to the criminal court. On appeal the Supreme Court ruled that before a juvenile can be tried in criminal court, he or she is entitled to a waiver hearing with counsel and, if jurisdiction is waived, the judge must state the reasons.

In *Kent* the Supreme Court also expressed concern over the lack of due process in the juvenile court:

> While there can be no doubt of the original laudable purpose of juvenile courts, studies and critiques in recent years raise serious questions as to whether actual performance measures well enough against theoretical purpose to make tolerable the immunity of the process from the reach of constitutional guarantees applicable to adults. There is much evidence that some juvenile courts, including that of the District of Columbia, lack the personnel, facilities and techniques to perform adequately as representatives of the State in a *parens patriae* capacity, at least with respect to children charged with law violation. There is evidence, in fact, that there may be grounds for concern that the child receives the worst of both worlds; that he gets neither the protections accorded to adults nor the solicitous care and regenerative treatment postulated for children.

The following year, 1967, the Supreme Court decided the case of Gerald Gault (*In Re Gault* 387 U.S. 1), a fifteen-year-old who had been arrested by the police on the complaint of a female neighbor that he and his friend had made lewd and indecent remarks over the telephone. Gerald's parents were not notified of their son's arrest and did not receive a copy of the juvenile court petition charging him with delinquency. Furthermore, Gerald was not advised of his right to remain silent or his right to counsel. The complainant was not present at the hearing, nor did the judge speak with her on any occasion. Instead, Gerald's mother and two probation officers appeared before the juvenile court judge in his chambers. No one was sworn and no transcript was made of the proceeding.

At a second hearing there was conflict over what had transpired at the first hearing. For the second time the complainant was not present; the judge ruled that her presence was not necessary. Gerald was declared to be a juvenile delinquent and committed to a state training school for a maximum of six years—until his twenty-first birthday. Had Gerald been an adult, above the age of eighteen, the maximum sentence would have been a fine of not more than $50 or imprisonment for not more than sixty days. Since no appeal in juvenile court cases was permitted under Arizona law, Gerald's parents filed a petition of *habeas corpus* (a legal challenge to custody) which, although it was dismissed by the state courts, was granted (*certiorari*) a hearing by the United States Supreme Court.

In its decision the Supreme Court acknowledged the helping—noncriminal—philosophy on which the juvenile court is based; but the decision also revealed a sense of outrage over what had transpired in the case of Gerald Gault: "Under our Constitution, the condition of being a boy does not justify a kangaroo court. . . ." The justices stated that *even* a child cannot be denied reasonable standards of due process; he or she is entitled to:

1. Written notice of the charges
2. Right to counsel

3. Protection against self-incrimination
4. Right to confront and cross-examine witnesses
5. Right to have written transcripts and appellate review

Because of the noncriminal nature of the juvenile court, instead of the *proof beyond a reasonable doubt* standard used in criminal trials, the level of evidence for a finding of delinquency was typically that used in a civil proceeding: *preponderance of the evidence.* In 1970, in the case of *In Re Winship* (397 U.S. 358), the Supreme Court noted: "The reasonable-doubt standard plays a vital role in the American scheme of criminal procedure. It is a prime instrument for reducing the risk of conviction resting on factual error." Accordingly, the Court ruled that "the constitutional safeguard of proof beyond a reasonable doubt is as much required during the adjudicatory stage of a delinquency proceeding as are those constitutional safeguards applied in *Gault. . . .*"

The right to an impartial jury in criminal trials is guaranteed by the Sixth Amendment, but the Supreme Court decided against this right in juvenile proceedings. In the 1971 decision of *McKeiver* v. *Pennsylvania* (403 U.S. 441) the Court ruled that a juvenile court proceeding is not a criminal prosecution within the meaning of the Sixth Amendment. Accordingly, the Court held: "The imposition of the jury trial on the juvenile court system would not strengthen greatly, if at all, the factfinding function. . . ." Nevertheless, sixteen states permit the use of juries in juvenile court (Zawitz, 1988).

In 1975 the Supreme Court was faced with the question of *double jeopardy*—which is prohibited by the Fifth Amendment—with respect to the juvenile court. *Breed* v. *Jones* (421 U.S. 519) concerned a seventeen-year-old who was the subject of a juvenile court petition alleging armed robbery. After taking testimony from two prosecution witnesses and the respondent, the juvenile court judge sustained the petition. At a subsequent disposition hearing the judge ruled that the respondent was "not . . . amenable to the care, treatment and training program available through the facilities of the juvenile court," and ordered that Breed be prosecuted as an adult. The youngster was subsequently found guilty of armed robbery in criminal (Superior) court, which led the Supreme Court to rule: "We hold that the prosecution of respondent in Superior Court, after an adjudicatory proceeding in Juvenile Court, violated that Double Jeopardy Clause of the Fifth Amendment, as applied to the States through the Fourteenth Amendment."

In 1984, the Supreme Court (*Schall* v. *Martin* No. 82-1248), in a strong affirmation of the concept of *parens patriae,* upheld the constitutionality of the preventive detention of juveniles. *Schall* involved a New York statute which authorizes the detention of juveniles arrested for an offense when there is "serious risk" that before trial, the juvenile may commit an act which if committed by an adult would constitute a crime. In this case Gregory Martin, fourteen, with two others, was accused of hitting a youth with a loaded gun and stealing his jacket and sneakers; when arrested he was in possession of the gun. The Court found that juveniles, unlike adults, "are always in some form of custody." That is, "by definition, [they] are not assumed to have the capacity to take care of themselves," but "are assumed to be subject to the control of their parents, and if parental control falters, the State may play its part as *parens patriae.*" The Court stipulated that the detention cannot be for purposes of punishment and must be strictly limited in time; the Court found that the maximum detention under the New York statute, seventeen days for serious crimes, six days for less serious crimes, was proper.

REVIEW QUESTIONS

1. What is the traditional philosophy of the system of justice used for juveniles in the United States?
2. What led to the establishment of the juvenile court?
3. What is meant by the "justice model" in juvenile court?
4. Why does the juvenile court represent a manifestation of the positive school?
5. How does the concept of *parens patriae* conflict with due process?
6. What are the different types of cases that may come under the jurisdiction of a juvenile court?
7. What are the responsibilities of a juvenile court intake officer?
8. What are the basic types of hearings in juvenile court?
9. What is meant by a "waiver" of juvenile court jurisdiction?
10. Why is it particularly difficult to be a judge in juvenile court?
11. Why are the juvenile services provided to females usually inferior to those provided to males?
12. What is the difference between a training school and residential treatment center?
13. What are the purposes of juvenile aftercare?
14. What did the Supreme Court rule in the case of *Kent* v. *United States?*
15. What rights did the *Gault* decision provide respondents accused of delinquency in juvenile court?
16. According to the *Winship* decision, what is the standard of proof required in a delinquency proceeding?
17. What did the *McKeiver* decision rule with respect to jury trials in juvenile court?
18. What was the issue in *Breed* v. *Jones,* and what did the court rule?

FOUR
Presentence Investigation

In the last chapter we looked at the variety of juvenile services provided by a probation agency. The second basic service provided by a probation agency is the presentence investigation (PSI) which is the basis for a presentence report (sometimes referred to as a "probation" report or simply a "PSI"). Following the conviction of a defendant and prior to a sentencing hearing a judge may (depending on the circumstances and the statutes of the jurisdiction) order a PSI which reflects positive school interest in the offender (not just the offense).

The report has five basic purposes:

1. The primary purpose is to help the court make an appropriate disposition of the case. The report should help in deciding for or against probation, and determining the conditions of probation; or in deciding among available institutions, and in determining the appropriate length of sentence. The American Bar Association (ABA) states that "the primary purpose of the presentence report is to provide the sentencing court with succinct and precise information upon which to base a rational sentencing decision" (1970: 11).

2. The PSI serves as the basis for a plan of probation or parole supervision and treatment. The report indicates problem areas in the defendant's life, his or her capacity for using help, and the opportunities available in the environment and community. During the investigation the defendant usually begins to relate to the probation department, learning how probation officers work and getting some understanding of the nature of the agency.

3. The PSI assists jail and prison personnel in their classification and treatment programs. Institutions are often quite dependent upon the report when the inmate is first received, a time when very little is known other than what is contained in commitment documents — conviction and sentence data. The PSI report helps institutional staff to understand and classify the offender; it can provide valuable information that will help in planning for the care, custody, and rehabilitation of the inmate. This includes everything from the type of custody required and the care of physical needs, to the planning of the various phases of the institutional program. Many institutions will have little, if any, background or social/medical/psychological information other than that provided by the PSI report. This means that the report will have a marked effect on the way in which an inmate is viewed and approached by institutional personnel, since they will take the word of the probation officer over that of the offender. The ideal report can give focus and initial direction to institutional authorities for treatment and training as well as care and management.

4. If the defendant is sentenced to a correctional institution, the report will eventually serve to furnish parole authorities with information pertinent to release planning and consideration for parole, and determination of any special conditions of supervision.

5. The report can serve as a source of information for research in criminal justice. Unfortunately, because of a lack of uniformity in form and content, not to mention quality, the usefulness of many or most presentence reports may be limited for research purposes.

In recent years determining the financial condition of defendants has become an important dimension in preparing a presentence report. In the 1984 Criminal Fine Enforcement Act, Congress cited the need to determine a defendant's ability to pay fines. Financial information is also necessary to assess the defendant's ability to make restitution and to pay any probation supervision fees that have become rather common in many jurisdictions. Some states include a separate victim impact statement (VIS) that is attached to the PSI, which usually includes a "description of the harm in terms of financial, social, psychological, and physical consequences of the crime. VIS also include a statement concerning the victim's feelings about the crime, the offender, and the proposed sentence" (Erez, 1990: 26).

In the report the probation officer (PO) attempts to "focus light on the character and personality of the defendant, and to offer insight into his problems and needs, to help understand the world in which he lives, to learn about his relationships with people, and to discover salient factors that underlie the specific offense and conduct in general," and to "suggest alternatives in the rehabilitation process" (Division of Probation, 1974: 48). The report is not expected to show guilt or innocence, only to relate the facts that the PO has been able to gather during the course of the PSI.

Content of the Presentence Investigation Report*

Presentence reports should be flexible in format, reflecting a difference in the background of different offenders and making the best use of available resources and probation department capabilities. A full report should normally contain the following items:

1. A complete description of the offense and circumstances surrounding it, not limited to the aspects developed for the record as part of the determination of guilt.
2. A statement from the victim and a description of the victim's status, the impact upon the victim, losses suffered by the victim, and restitution due the victim.
3. A full description of any prior criminal record of the offender.
4. A description of the educational background of the offender, present employment status, financial status, and capabilities.
5. A description of any military record.
6. The social history of the offender, including family relationships, marital status, dependents, interests and activities, residence history, and religious affiliations.
7. The offender's medical history and, if desirable, a psychological and/or psychiatric report.
8. Information about environments to which the offender might return or to which the defendant could be sent should probation be granted.
9. Supplementary reports from clinics, institutions, and other social agencies with which the offender has been involved.
10. Information about special resources which might be available to assist the offender, such as treatment centers, residential facilities, vocational training services, special educational facilities, rehabilitation programs of various institutions to which the offender might be committed, special programs in the probation department, and other similar programs which are particularly relevant to the offender's situation.
11. A summary and analysis of the most significant aspects of the report, including specific recommendations as to the sentence. A special effort should be made in the preparation of PSI reports not to burden the court with irrelevant and unconnected details.

Source: American Probation and Parole Association draft statement, 1985.

INTERVIEWS

In probation and parole, much of the necessary information is received directly from people. Thus report quality is often dependent on the interview skills of probation and parole personnel. In the PSI a great deal of information is gained by interviewing the defendant. "Interviews shall be directed toward obtaining and clarifying relevant information and making observations of the defendant's/respondent's behavior, attitudes and character" (N.Y. State *Code of Criminal Procedure,* 350.6-3ii). These interviews are conducted in all types of surroundings; from hot and noisy detention pens, where dozens of people may be awaiting a court hearing, to the relative quiet of the probation office.

Obviously, a quiet, comfortable setting with a maximum of privacy is the best environment for an interview. A place that lacks privacy or has numerous distractions will adversely affect the productivity of the interview. Sometimes interviews are conducted in the defendant's home. This provides an opportunity to observe the offender's home situation and adds an additional and sometimes vital dimension to the report. In New York, statutes advise:

> Whenever possible, interviews with the defendant/respondent shall be at the probation office; however, visits to the defendant's/respondent's residence may be made when there is an indication that additional information will be obtained that is likely to influence the recommendation or court disposition.

The interview is an anxiety-producing situation for the defendant. Previous experiences in similar situations, such as questioning by the police, may have been quite unpleasant. The PO tries to lower the anxiety level by cordially introducing him- or herself and explaining the purpose of the interview and the PSI report. This is especially important for the defendant who is not familiar with the criminal justice system in general, and the court process in particular.

The PO may try to deal with matters of concern to the defendant. A married male defendant may be engaged in a discussion of how his wife and children can secure public assistance in the event that he is imprisoned. The PO might offer to write a letter of referral for his wife to take with her to the welfare department or other social agency that can provide assistance. In some way the officer must show genuine concern and interest in the defendant, at the same time being realistic enough to expect many answers and statements that will be self-serving. Since the probation officer's contact with the defendant is limited, the officer cannot expect to probe deeply into the defendant's personality.

Some defendants will be overtly hostile, while others will mask their hostility or anxiety with "wisecrack" answers. The PO must control both

PROBATION DEPARTMENT
SOCIAL SERVICES BUILDING
COUNTY SEAT DRIVE & ELEVENTH STREET
P.O. BOX 189
MINEOLA, NEW YORK 11501

URGENT: Reply Needed By _____
Sentence Date:
Re:
Defendant:
Case #   Docket #:

Dear

This Department is conducting a court-ordered investigation of the defendant in the above-captioned offense. You may have suffered a loss, or otherwise be eligible to receive restitution. If this is the case, the court may order full or partial reimbursement of your losses.

In addition to specific losses or damages, you also may claim repayment for time lost from work due to injuries or court appearances, as well as materials used cleaning up premises or making repairs.

A Probation Officer may already have contacted you regarding your description of the crime, the impact it had on you, and any recommendation you may have regarding sentence. Please be advised that your Victim Impact Statement will be communicated to the court and that the District Attorney of the County of Nassau will make available to you a copy of that statement in the courtroom on the above-captioned sentence date.

It is important that you call the undersigned Restitution Investigator immediately. Your prompt return of the enclosed Statement of Losses, with copies of bills, receipts, appraisals, estimates, etc. will expedite our efforts on your behalf. We must hear from you by the reply date above or we will not be able to include your Statement of Losses in our report to the court. Please respond even if no restitution is desired, so that we may avoid inconveniencing you with any further contact.

Very truly yours,

_____
Restitution Investigator

_____
Tel. No.

Encl.

FIGURE 4.1   Letter from Nassau County Probation

temper and temperament. He or she is the professional and must never lose sight of that fact during an interview. In questioning, generalized queries ("What have you been doing?") should be avoided (lest the interviewer be told: "Nothin' much"). Questions should be specific but require an explanation rather than a simple yes or no answer. The PO must avoid putting answers into the defendant's mouth—for example, by asking "Did you quit that job because it was too hard?"

When the PSI is complete, the defendant should be reinterviewed in order to give him or her an opportunity to refute certain information, or clarify any aspect of the report which may be in conflict with other parts of the report.

In addition to the defendant, the PO may interview the arresting officer, the victim, employers, and significant others in the defendant's environment: spouse, parents, siblings, teachers, clergy.

REVIEW OF RECORDS AND REPORTS

The probation officer will be reviewing records and reports in the course of the presentence investigation. The first is the arrest record of the defendant, referred to as a "rap sheet." This record will take the form of an arrest sheet(s) of a law enforcement agency such as the state police. The form typically contains numerous abbreviations that must be deciphered by the PO if the record is to be useful—for example, *Att Burg* (attempted burglary) or *DWI* (driving while intoxicated). The arrest sheet does not describe the offense and may not even indicate if it is a felony or misdemeanor; it simply contains the official charge, for example, *Burg 2.* There is usually no mention of the premises that were burgled or what, if anything, was taken. In addition, the sheet often omits the disposition of the arrest. The officer may not be able to determine from the arrest report what happened to a particular case. Therefore, it if often necessary to check court records, or to contact out-of-state agencies, to determine the disposition of a case.

The nature of the defendant's prior record is extremely important. The law of many jurisdictions provides for a harsher sentence if the defendant has a prior felony conviction(s). In addition, the defendant's eligibility for probation and a variety of treatment programs, such as drug rehabilitation, may be affected by a prior criminal record.

The probation officer is particularly interested in any information that may influence the sentence but which was omitted during the trial, particularly any mitigating or aggravating circumstances, and information that can provide a different perspective on the case. The officer will review any previous PSI reports, as well as reports of other correctional agencies that have had contact with the defendant. These might include training schools or residential treatment centers, and prison and parole agencies. The PO may also be interested in reviewing the educational records of the defendant. With the increasing number of substance abusing defendants coming into the criminal justice system, probation officers must review this dimension of each defendant and explore the appropriateness of a recommendation for chemical abuse treatment.

If there are any psychiatric or psychological reports available, the PO will review and analyze them. To do this he or she must understand the nomenclature and the meaning of any tests used by mental health professionals. The PO should make a judgment as to whether a psychiatric and/or psychological referral should be made during the PSI. Indiscriminate referrals to mental health or court-based clinics are wasteful of resources—a crime may be quite rational, and criminal behavior is not generally symptomatic of an internalized conflict. In cases where symptoms of mental disorder are apparent, and in those situations where the offender may benefit from an exploration of his or her problems, a referral should be made. If no referral is made, and there is a lack of psychiatric and psychological information, the PO should present his or her own observations concerning the defendant's intellectual capacity and personality—for example, level of social functioning, contact with reality.

If the probation officer has received conflicting information about the defendant, and is unable to reconcile the discrepancies, this should be pointed out in the report and not left up to the reader to discover (or more likely, *not* discover).

Of crucial importance in any presentence report are the sections entitled *Evaluative Summary* and *Recommendation* (although in some jurisdictions a recommendation is not provided). Nothing should appear in either of these sections that is not supported by the rest of the report. The summary contains the highlights of the total report, and should serve as a reminder to the reader of the information that has already been presented. The recommendation is a carefully thought out statement, based on the officer's best professional judgment. It contains the alternatives that are available in the case and reflects the individualized attention that each case received (Carter, 1966).

Robert Carter (1966: 41) notes that the probation officer is in a unique position with respect to making a recommendation to the judge: "The officer has had an opportunity to observe the defendant in the community, not only from a legal-judicial, investigative perspective, but also from the viewpoint of a general life style." In order to present a meaningful recommendation, the PO must have knowledge of the resources and programs that are available. An inexperienced probation officer may submit a recommendation for a treatment program that is not available either in the community or at a correctional institution.

One question that the PO must decide in the recommendation is for or against a sentence of probation. In many jurisdictions a conviction for certain crimes, or a previous felony conviction, precludes a sentence of probation — the PO must know the statutes of the jurisdiction. The officer must also weigh the potential danger the defendant poses to the community; must evaluate the defendant's rehabilitative potential and ability to conform to probation regulations; and must consider whether probation will be construed by the community as too lenient in view of the offense, or by the defendant as "getting away with it."

Carter (1978: 15) recommends that the PSI report be "tailored to meet the needs of the individual criminal justice systems and be relatively short." He quotes John Hogarth:

> There is considerable research evidence suggesting that in human decision-making the capacity of individuals to use information effectively is limited to the use of not more than five or six items of information. In many cases, depending on the kind of information used, the purposes to which it is put, and the capacity of the individual concerned, the limit is much less. Despite this evidence there is a noticeable tendency for presentence reports to become longer. One of the most unfortunate myths in the folk-lore concerning sentencing, is the notion that the courts should know "all about the offender." Quite apart from whether much of the information is likely to be reliable, valid or even relevant to the decision possibilities open to the court, the burden of a mass of data can only result in information overload and the impairment of the efficiency in which relevant information is handled. This suggests that if probation officers wish to improve the effectiveness of their communications to magistrates they would be advised to shorten their reports.

This advice, and the overburdened nature of most probation agencies, has led to the popularity of the short-form PSI report.

SHORT- AND LONG-FORM PRESENTENCE INVESTIGATION REPORTS

There are two basic types of PSI report; the short form is usually less exhaustive and less time consuming. The N.Y. State *Code of Criminal Procedure* (350.6–2) states:

> The abbreviated investigation for short-form reports shall consist of the defendant's legal history and primarily current information with respect to: the circumstances attending the commission of the offense, family and social situation, employment and economic status, education and, when available, physical and mental conditions. Such investigation may also include any other matter which the probation department conducting the investigation deems relevant to the recommendation or court disposition and must include any matter directed by the court.

Following are examples of both forms, short form first.

Presentence Report*

United States District Court
Central District of New York

Name: John Jones

Address:
  1234 Astoria Blvd.
  New York City

Legal Residence:
  Same

Age: 33

Date of Birth: 2-8-55
  New York City

Sex: Male

Race: Caucasian

Citizenship: U.S. (birth)

Education: 10th grade

Marital Status: Married

Dependents: Three
  (wife and two children)

Soc. Sec. No.: 112-03-9559

FBI No.: 256 1126

Disposition:

Date:

Sentencing Judge:

Date: January 4, 1989

Docket No.: 89-103

Offense: Theft of Mail by Postal Employee
  (18 U.S.C. Sec. 1709) 2 cts.

Penalty: Ct. 2-5 years and/or $2,000 fine

Plea: Guilty on 12-16-88 to Ct. 2
  Ct. 1 pending

Verdict:

Custody: Released on own recognizance.
  No time in custody.

Asst. U.S. Attorney: Samuel Hayman

Defense Counsel: Thomas Lincoln, Federal
  Public Defender

Drug/Alcohol Involvement:
  Attributes offense to need for drinking
  money

Detainers or Charges Pending: None

Codefendants (Disposition): None

Offense: Official Version
Official sources revealed that during the course of routine observations on December 4, 1988 within the Postal Office Center, Long Island, New York,

*From Division of Probation: "The Selective Presentence Investigation Report," *Federal Probation,* 38 (December 1974), pp. 53-54.

postal inspectors observed the defendant paying particular attention to various packages. Since the defendant was seen to mishandle and tamper with several parcels, test parcels were prepared for his handling on December 5, 1988. The defendant was observed to mishandle one of the test parcels by tossing it to one side into a canvas tub. He then placed his jacket into the tub and leaned over the tub for a period of time. At this time the defendant left the area and went to the men's room. While he was gone the inspectors examined the mail tub and found that the test parcel had been rifled and that the contents, a watch, was missing.

The defendant returned to his work area and picked up his jacket. He then left the building. The defendant was stopped by the inspectors across the street from the post office. Hew was questioned about his activities and on his person he had the wristwatch from the test parcel. He was taken to the postal inspector's office, where he admitted the offense.

Defendant's Version of Offense

The defendant admits that he rifled the package in question and took the watch. He states that he intended to sell the watch at a later date. He admits that he has been drinking too much lately and needed extra cash for "drinking money." He exhibits remorse and is concerned about the possibility of incarceration and the effect that it would have on his family.

Prior Record

Date	Offense	Place	Disposition
5-7-81 (age 26)	Possession of Policy Slips	Manhattan CR. CT. N.Y., N.Y.	$100.00 Fine 7-11-81
3-21-87 (age 32)	Intoxication	Manhattan CR. CT. N.Y., N.Y.	4-17-87 Nolle

Personal History

The defendant was born in New York City on February 8, 1955, the oldest of three children. He attended the public school, completed the 10th grade, and left school to go to work. He was rated as an average student and was active in sports, especially basketball and baseball.

The defendant's father, John, died of a heart attack in 1982, at the age of fifty-three years. He had an elementary school education and worked as a construction laborer most of his life.

The defendant's mother, Mary Smith Jones, is fifty-five years of age and is employed as a seamstress. She has an elementary school education and married defendant's father when she was twenty years of age. Three sons were issue of the marriage. She presently resides in New York City, and is in good health.

Defendant's brother, Paul, age thirty-two years, completed two and a half

(Continued)

years of high school. He is employed as a bus driver and resides with his wife and two children in New York City.

Defendant's brother, Lawrence, age thirty years, completed three semesters of college. He is employed as a New York City firefighter. He resides with his wife and one child in Dutch Point, Long Island.

The defendant after leaving high school worked as a delivery boy for a retail supermarket chain, then served two years in the U.S. Army as an infantryman (ASN 123 45678). He received an honorable discharge and attained the rank of corporal serving from 2-10-73 to 2-1-75. After service he held a number of jobs of the laboring type.

The defendant was employed as a truck driver for the City of New York when he married Ann Sweeny on 6-15-78. Two children were issue of this marriage, John, age eight, and Mary, age six. The family has resided at the same address (which is a four-room apartment) since their marriage.

The defendant has been in good health all of his life but he admits he has been drinking to excess the past eighteen months, which has resulted in some domestic strife. The wife stated that she loved her husband and will stand by him. She is amenable to a referral for family counseling.

Defendant has worked for the Postal Service since 12-1-80 and resigned on 12-5-88 as a result of the present arrest. His work ratings by his supervisors were always "excellent."

Evaluative Summary

The defendant is a thirty-three-year-old male who entered a plea of guilty to mail theft. While an employee of the U.S. Postal Service he rifled and stole a watch from a test package. He admitted that he planned on selling the watch to finance his drinking, which has become a problem, resulting in domestic strife.

Defendant is a married man with two children with no prior serious record. He completed 10 years of school, has an honorable military record, and has a good work history. He expresses remorse for his present offense and is concerned over the loss of his job and the shame to his family.

Recommendation

It is respectfully recommended that the defendant be admitted to probation. If placed on probation the defendant expresses willingness to seek counseling for his domestic problems. He will require increased motivation if there is to be significant change in his drinking pattern.

Respectfully submitted,

_____

Donald M. Fredericks
U.S. Probation Officer

The Montgomery County Common Pleas Court, Adult Probation Department Presentence Report

Case Number: 79–CR–321

Name: Willy Marx

Address:
25 Rose Court
Dayton, Ohio 12354

Adjudicted Charge/O.R.C./
Penalty: Guilty Plea — As Charged

Drug Abuse (Count 8) 2925.02 (F-4)
$1/2$, 1 $1^1/2$ years C.C.I. (Definite)
$2,500 Fine

Counts 1 thru 7 nolled

Other Pending Cases/Detainers

Parole detainer #77–CR–564
Judicial Notice Taken #78–CR–125

Prior Felonies:

None

Repeat Offender Status:
Yes, 2929.01
(A) (3) (5) (6)

Codefendant — Status:

Cathy Minor — Disposition
pending 1/24/89

Judge: Honorable Frederick F. Smith

Prosecutor: James Harris

Attorney: Richard Morris
Status: Retained

Amount of   *Posted:*
Bond: $5,000 Cash   *Jail:* XX

Days in Custody: 2

Original Jurisdiction: Direct

Indicted Charge: Drug Abuse (8 cts.)
2925.02

Probation Officer:
Laurence Nelson
Central I (br)

Restitution: None

Referred: 1/17/89
Disposition: 2/24/89

AGE __32__ SEX Male _____
LAST GRADE COMPLETED __10th__
YEARS OF WORK RECORD __2__
years _____
EMPLOYMENT STATUS _____
Unemployed _____

(Continued)

MARITAL STATUS ___Divorced___
NUMBER OF DEPENDENTS ___2___
DOES DEF. PROVIDE SUPPORT _   NO PHOTO ABAILABLE
No _____
INVOLVEMENT WITH SOCIAL
SERVICES AGENCIES:
  PAST ___Ohio Adult Parole_____

_____
  PRESENT ___Adult Parole; Adult___

  Probation _____
LIMITATIONS: Drug addiction
Rec. Bailiff _____ Date/Time _____

Client Identification Data

NAME	Marx, Willy (NMN)
ALIASES	"Swifty," John Q. Dunn
F.B.I. NO.	163–541–M5
B.C.I. NO.	A600–531
D.P.D. NO.	76543
RACE	White
SEX	Male
HEIGHT	73″
WEIGHT	185 lbs.
EYES	Hazel
HAIR	Red
SCARS	Appendectomy
TATTOOS	Love between knuckles on left hand
DATE OF BIRTH	3/13/52
PLACE OF BIRTH	Gary, Indiana
SOCIAL SECURITY NO.	065–43–2130
TELEPHONE NO.	276–1111

WILLY (NMN) MARX   **CASE NUMBER 84–CR–321**

Summary of the Offense:
On November 7, 1984, at 10:30 P.M., Officer Jim Harris of the Dayton Police Department responded to a complaint of a disturbance at the Lucky Lady Lounge, 111 Moose Lane, Dayton, Ohio. Upon investigation, the defendant was identified as one of the individuals involved in the disturbance. The defendant appeared to be intoxicated and was abusive to the investigating officer. Due to his behavior, he was arrested for Public Intoxication. However, upon booking him in the City Jail, a search found a medicine vial containing eight barbiturates. Thus, the defendant was charged with Drug Abuse.

WILLY (NMN) MARX   CASE NUMBER 84–CR–321

Prosecutor's Statement:

Mr. James Harris reports that he is concerned about the fact that this is the defendant's second appearance before the Court, but recognizes that the defendant does have a drug abuse problem that may be able to be treated. He has no strong feelings if the defendant should be resentenced to the state institution.

Defendant's Statement:

Mr. Marx stated that he was with some friends in a local bar where he had been drinking beer after having taken some barbiturates. He indicated that an argument ensued which he was not personally responsible for. However, he did admit to having been abusive with the police officer investigating the offense. Mr. Marx further stated that the drugs found on his person were for his personal use. He indicated that he was concerned about his use of these drugs, but had been using them since 1978.

Defense Attorney's Statement:

On January 10, 1985, I forwarded a standard form probation letter to Mr. Richard Morris soliciting his comments regarding the defendant. As of this time Mr. Morris has not returned the form that I forwarded to him, nor has he returned my telephone calls, which were made on January 16 and January 17, 1985. Therefore, there will be no input from him regarding his client.

Prior Record:

Verification Sources: Gary Indiana, Juvenile Court; Montgomery County, Ohio, Juvenile Court; City of Dayton, Ohio, Police Department; Montogomery County, Ohio, Sheriff's Department, Ohio BCI

Date	Convicted Offense	Disposition
Juvenile		
10/1/68	Possession of Marijuana	10/20/68 — Probation
5/6/69	Purse Snatching	5/9/69 — Committed to Ohio Youth Commission
Adult:		
6/16/82	Forgery (#77-CR-564)	6/25/82 — 1-5 years Columbus Correctional Facility
12/4/83	Carrying a Concealed Weapon (#83–CR–125)	12/27/83 — Probation 5 years
11/7/84	Drug Abuse	Instant offense

Additional Data:

A review of Mr. Marx's record reveals three traffic-related offenses with three convictions for Driving While Intoxicated, two of which resulted in time committed to the Dayton Human Rehabilitation Center. His record also reveals two

(Continued)

WILLY (NMN) MARX   **CASE NUMBER 84–CR–321**

offenses of Petty Theft, one of which resulted in a 60-day commitment to the Dayton Human Rehabilitation Center. In 1980, Mr. Marx was charged with Passing Bad Checks and was placed on probation supervision with the Dayton, Ohio Municipal Probation Department. In 1981, Mr. Marx was further charged with Carrying a Concealed Weapon and was placed on probation in Case No. 81–CR–125.

It should be noted that Mr. Marx is presently on parole with the Ohio Adult Parole Authority in Case No. 82–CR–564 for the offense of Forgery. A parole detainer has been placed on him at the Montgomery County Jail and according to his parole officer, Henry Hardcore, Mr. Marx's parole will be revoked at the time of his first parole hearing if he is sentenced for this offense.

Family History:
List of Immediate

Members	Relationship	Age	Address
Frank Marx	Father	66	23 Rose Court, Dayton, Ohio
Marie Marx	Mother	62	23 Rose Court, Dayton, Ohio
Mike Marx	Brother	28	23 Rose Court, Dayton, Ohio
Susie Marx	Ex-wife	26	20 Somewhere Place, Tampa, Florida
Sonny Marx	Son	3	20 Somewhere Place, Tampa, Florida
Sally Marx	Daughter	1	20 Somewhere Place, Tampa, Florida

Reared by: Parents and maternal grandmother

Comments: At the age of 14, the defendant's parents had marital problems which resulted in the defendant's father's move to Dayton, Ohio. The defendant's mother later moved to Dayton for the purposes of reconciliation. However, in view of the tenuousness of their relationship, the defendant did not move to Dayton, but remained under the care of his maternal grandmother until the age of 17. At that time, he joined his parents. A review of the defendant's record with the juvenile authorities during that time would indicate some concern for the defendant's ability to deal with his family situation. A home visit was made on January 20, 1989, to his parents' home at 23 Rose Court, Dayton, Ohio, to verify his residence.

Living with: Frank and Marie Marx, 23 Rose Court, Dayton, Ohio 12354 (Parents)

Name and Address of Nearest Other Relative: Rosa Flowers, 12 Lonesome Road, Gary, Indiana (Maternal grandmother)

WILLY (NMN) MARX   CASE NUMBER 84-CR-321

EDUCATION
Highest grade completed: 10th
Name and address of school: Montgomery County Joint Vocational School
Last date attended: 6/2/71
Verified: Montgomery County Joint Vocational School, Mrs. Jane Knox
Comments: While in attendance at the joint vocational school, Mr. Marx was involved in classes in Auto Mechanics. He has never used those skills gained through that education in an employment opportunity. It should be noted that Mr. Marx has no future plans to continue his education.

TRAINING
Type(s):   Food preparation
Verified: Unverifiable
Comments: On January 20, 1989, I attempted to contact the Garfield Training Center to verify Mr. Marx's training in food preparation. At that time, I was told that Mrs. Joan Klein would be returning my call. As of this date, Mrs. Klein has not attempted to return my call; therefore, I made another attempt to contact her without success on January 25, 1989

EMPLOYMENT HISTORY

Employed By	Job Title	Dates	Wage	Verified
1. Dayton Holiday Inn	Porter	4/18/80–5/16/81	$3.90/hr.	Personnel, Holiday Inn
2. Big Burger	Cook	8/10/79–4/15/80	$3.65/hr.	Manager, Mr. Al Jackson
3. Brussel Up Restaurant	Busboy	5/15/79 8/1/79	Unknown	Unverifiable

Comments: The sum total of Mr. Marx's employment is in the area of fast food restaurants totals approximately two full years. It should be noted that I was unable to verify his employment at the Brussel Up Restaurant due to the fact that it is no longer in business.

MEANS OF SUPPORT IF UNEMPLOYED
Source: Parents
Amount: Room and Board

MILITARY
Branch: United States Army
Dates: 2/4/75–10/4/75
Type Discharge: General — Medical
Verified: DD214

(Continued)

WILLY (NMN) MARX   **CASE NUMBER 84–CR–321**

HEALTH

Physical or Mental Disabilities: At the present time, Mr. Marx states that he is in very good physical and mental health. He is not currently on any medication nor is he under any doctor's care. Mr. Marx has not attended any mental health counseling nor has he received drug or alcohol treatment.

Assaultive Behavior: Yes _____ No __x_____
Known Alcohol Involvement: No __x_____ Occasional _____ Frequent
_____

Known Drug Involvement: No _____ Occasional _____ Frequent
__x_____

Mr Marx has stated that he is presently involved in the use of Dilaudids. He has expressed some desire for treatment as shown by his inpatient treatment at NOVA House. He entered treatment on January 18, 1985.

Eligibility of Conditional Probation:
Motion not filed.

Evaluative Summary:

The defendant is an individual who is well known to the criminal justice system as a juvenile and as an adult. While under community supervision, he has done well in responding to a supervising officer. Mr. Marx has many problem areas in his life that may directly or indirectly have had a bearing upon his involvement in criminal behavior. He seems to frequently run with the wrong crowd, lacks employment knowhow, has limited family identity, and as a result suffers from some emotional instability. He has not responded well to structured treatment offered him in the past through the relations established under parole and probation. This may be the first time that Mr. Marx's real problem has been identified: i.e., drug abuse. It should be noted that Mr. Marx is presently on parole with the Ohio Parole Authority as well as probation with Montgomery County Adult Probation Department.

Mr. Marx's life has been rather chaotic to say the least. His unstable family environment in the past and his abuse of drugs would point to this fact. It would appear that his family environment has stabilized to some extent as indicated in his present living situation. It would appear that his life has further potential for stabilization in that he has established a relationship with an individual named Reah Winter, whom he intends to marry.

The defendant is presently a resident of NOVA House, Residential Treatment Facility for drug abuse. He entered this facility on 1/18/85, and reports from that treatment facility indicate that the defendant is responding very well. In fact, a report from Mr. Jack Silver from the NOVA House revealed that the defendant is a model resident. He further states that Mr. Marx's potential for success in the program is the best he has seen in a long time. Any effort to work with the defendant will be contingent upon his commitment to a sustained drug-free

WILLY (NMN) MARX   **CASE NUMBER 84-CR-321**

existence. A stabilized employment record is also important for Mr. Marx, as is his stabilization in his personal life and family relationships.

Recommendation:

In view of Mr. Marx's positive commitment to the NOVA House Residential Treatment Facility, wherein the defendant's fundamental personal problem has finally been addressed, it is felt that he is a viable candidate for probation. This recommendation is being made in spite of the fact that the defendant has previously spent time in a penal institution and the fact that he is currently on probation and parole. It is felt that this is the first time that a basic problem previously possessed by the defendant has been identified.

Respectfully submitted,

_____

Samuel Stuart
Probation Officer
Ext. 4303

_____

Rober Kaplan
Division Manager
Ext. 6017

SS/br

Victim Impact Statement

Judge: Frederick F. Smith

Case No.:   79-CR-321

Name of Victim: Officer Jim Harris
                                 Dayton Police Department
                                 316 East 5th Lane
                                 Dayton, Ohio 45444

Name of Defendant: Willy Marx

Disposition Date: February 24, 1989

A. *Economic Loss:*
   Due to the nature of the offense, there was no economic loss suffered.

B. *Physical Injury:*
   There was no physical injury suffered, according to Officer Harris.

C. *Change in Personal Welfare for Familial Relationships:*
   None noted.

(Continued)

WILLY (NMN) MARX   **CASE NUMBER 84–CR–321**

D. *Psychological Impact:*
   None noted.

E. *Comments:*
   Officer Jim Harris was contacted on January 24, 1989, regarding the defendant. Officer Harris feels that the defendant deserves to go back to prison. He is very well known on the streets and he feels his whole department would be happier if he were behind bars. He feels his cry for help with his drug addiction is his way of avoiding another jail term.

Requiring a Presentence Investigation Report

In some states the law requires a PSI report for crimes punishable by more than one year of imprisonment; in others the judge retains the discretion to order the report. In New York and Michigan, for example, a long-form report is required in all felony cases; in misdemeanor cases the report is discretionary and, when done, is usually in the short form. In Missouri, a PSI is mandatory in all felony cases unless the defendant waives the requirement — in which case, at the judge's discretion, a PSI may still be compiled. In Texas, there is no legal requirement that a PSI be prepared in each felony case; the trial judge has discretion to order a report or to sentence without one. In Illinois (Chapter 38, 1005–3–1) "A defendant shall not be sentenced for a felony before a written presentence report of investigation is presented to and considered by the court," although this right is frequently waived by the defense counsel because a plea agreement has already been arranged.

PLEA BARGAINING AND SENTENCING GUIDELINES

In many jurisdictions, the extensive use of *plea bargaining* has reduced the need for a PSI. A plea bargain requires that the defendant enter a plea of guilty in return for some form of sentence leniency. In many jurisdictions the plea agreement actually specifies the sentence that the defendant will receive. Under such conditions a presentence report would not serve any useful purpose at a sentencing hearing. Plea bargaining, however, has resulted in the use of a *pretrial/plea investigation report*.

If prosecutor and defense counsel negotiate a plea agreement, and the judge retains a great deal of discretion over the sentence to be imposed (which is the case in many states), the judge may request a pretrial investigation before agreeing to the negotiated plea. In Illinois, for example, for a simple burglary as a first offense, the judge has the discretion to sentence an offender to a term of three years, or four years or five years, all the way up to fourteen years. In Cook County, which includes the city of Chicago, judges often require a

Presumptive Sentence Lengths in Months

Italicized numbers within the grid denote the range within which a judge may sentence without the sentence being deemed a departure.

CRIMINAL HISTORY SCORE

SEVERITY LEVELS OF CONVICTION OFFENSE		0	1	2	3	4	5	6 or more
Unauthorized Use of Motor Vehicle Possession of Marijuana	I	12*	12*	12*	15	18	21	24 23-25
Theft Related Crimes ($150 - $2500) Sale of Marijuana	II	12*	12*	14	17	20	23	27 25-29
Theft Crimes ($150 - $2500)	III	12*	13	16	19	22 21-23	27 25-29	32 30-34
Burglary - Felony Intent Receiving Stolen Goods ($150 - $2500)	IV	12*	15	18	21	25 24-26	32 30-34	41 37-45
Simple Robbery	V	18	23	27	30 29-31	38 36-40	46 43-49	54 50-58
Assault, 2nd Degree	VI	21	26	30	34 33-35	44 42-46	54 50-58	65 60-70
Aggravated Robbery	VII	24 23-25	32 30-34	41 38-44	49 45-53	65 60-70	81 75-87	97 90-104
Assault, 1st Degree Criminal Sexual Conduct, 1st Degree	VIII	43 41-45	54 50-58	65 60-70	76 71-81	95 89-101	113 106-120	132 124-140
Murder, 3rd Degree	IX	97 94-100	119 116-122	127 124-130	149 143-155	176 168-184	205 192-215	230 218-242
Murder, 2nd Degree	X	116 111-121	140 133-147	162 153-171	203 192-214	243 231-255	284 270-298	324 309-339

First degree murder is excluded from the guidelines by law and continues to have a mandatory life sentence.

*One year and one day

FIGURE 4.2 Minnesota Sentencing Guidelines Grid

pretrial/plea investigation report before confirming a plea agreement; in fact, pretrial reports, which are shortform, are more frequent than PSI reports.

The practice of using a pre-plea report requires that the defendant agree to the investigation; in New York (*Code of Criminal Procedure,* 350.10):

> The probation department shall conduct a pre-plea investigation only upon a court order and written authorization by the defendant, his attorney, the prosecuting attorney and the judge ordering the investigation. Such written authorization shall include statements that no probation department personnel will be

called to testify regarding information acquired by the probation department, that information obtained by the probation department may not be used in a subsequent trial, and that this exemption does not apply to defense or prosecution material which may be included in the plea report.

Sentencing guidelines have also reduced, and in some cases obviated, the need for a PSI. A number of states and the federal government use sentencing guidelines in an attempt to limit judicial discretion and reduce sentence disparity—a turn toward the classical school. In Minnesota, for example, sentencing guidelines were instituted in 1980, and are changed periodically. A judge is provided with a sentencing grid that considers only the severity of the instant offense and the offender's prior criminal history. Departures from mandatory sentences derived from the grid are permitted only under limited circumstances. Probation officers (state parole and probation agents) are responsible for completing the sentencing guidelines worksheet and calculating the presumed sentence; they no longer write PSI reports (Doom, Roerich, and Zoey, 1988).

CONFIDENTIALITY OF THE PRESENTENCE INVESTIGATION REPORT

There is some controversy over whether the contents of the PSI report should be disclosed to the defendant or his or her attorney. The basic argument against disclosure is that sources of information must be protected or they will hesitate to provide information. Family members or employers may fear retribution from the defendant if they provide negative information. In addition, law enforcement agencies may be reluctant to provide confidential information if the defendant or the defendant's attorney will be privy to it.

The basic argument in favor of disclosure is to enable the defendant to contest information that he or she considers unfair, and to be protected from the effects of unfounded information. Norm Larkins (1972: 59) states: "Disclosure of information has led probation officers [in Alberta, Canada] to develop techniques whereby the information obtained by them and presented in the report is more objective and accurate (with less reliance on hearsay information)." Before the initial interview with the defendant is conducted, "it is explained that a copy of the report will be made available to the offender or his legal counselor prior to sentencing. It is the duty of the offender to bring to the judge's attention any mistakes or omissions which he feels would be important in influencing the sentencing."

The American Bar Association recommends that all information that adversely affects the defendant be discussed with the defendant or his or her attorney. The President's Commission stated that "in the absence of impelling reasons for non-disclosure of specific information, the defendant and his counsel should be permitted to examine the entire presentence report" (1972: 356). The National Advisory Commission recommended that the PSI be made available to the defense and the prosecution. The commission rejected the argument that sources of information will dry up: "(1) those jurisdictions which have required disclosure have not experienced this phenomenon; and (2) more importantly, if the same evidence were given as testimony at trial, there would be no protection or confidentiality" (1973: 189).

The U.S. Supreme Court has consistently upheld the confidentiality of the presentence investigation report. This has been based on the (presumed) neutrality/objectivity of the probation officer—he or she has no interest in punishment; by disposition and training the PO is a helping, not a prosecutorial, agent. Thus, in the 1949 case of *Williams* v. *New York* (337 U.S. 241) the judge imposed a sentence of death based on information contained in the PSI report. The defendant had been convicted of murder but the jury recommended life imprisonment. The PSI—to which the jury was not privy—revealed that Williams was a suspect in thirty burglaries. Although he had not been convicted of these crimes, the report indicated that he had confessed to some and had been identified as the perpetrator of some of the others. The judge had referred to parts of the report which indicated that the defendant was a "menace to society."

Williams appealed the death sentence, arguing that the procedure violated due process of law "in that the sentence of death was based upon information supplied by witnesses with whom the accused had not been confronted and as to whom he had no opportunity for cross examination or rebuttal." The Supreme Court rejected this argument, stating:

> Under the practice of individualizing punishments, investigational techniques have been given an important role. Probation workers making reports of their investigations have not been trained to prosecute but to aid offenders. Their reports have been given high value by conscientious judges who want to sentence persons on the best available information rather than on guesswork and inadequate information. To deprive sentencing judges of this kind of information would undermine modern procedural policies that have been cautiously adopted throughout the nation after careful consideration and experimentation. We must recognize that most of the information now relied upon by judges to guide them in the intelligent imposition of sentences would be unavailable if information were restricted to that given in open court by witnesses subject to cross-examination. And the modern probation report draws on information concerning every aspect of a defendant's life. The types and extent of this information make totally impractical if not impossible open court testimony with cross-examination. Such procedure could endlessly delay criminal administration in a re-trial of collateral issues.

Williams was executed.

In some jurisdictions law or custom allows the defendant access to the report, while some states give the judge the option of disclosing the contents of the report. In Texas the statutes require that the entire contents of the report be revealed to the defendant. However, there is a trend toward adopting the position of the federal system: the PSI can be revealed to the defendant and/or counsel, *but* the *Rules of Criminal Procedure* exclude the probation officer's recommendation and any

> diagnostic opinion which may seriously disrupt a program of rehabilitation, sources of information obtained upon a promise of confidentiality, or any other information which, if disclosed, might result in harm, physical or otherwise, to the defendant or other persons. . . .

In Michigan, while the court must permit the prosecutor, the defendant's attorney, and the defendant an opportunity to review the report prior to sentencing:

> . . . the court may exempt from disclosure information or a diagnostic opinion which might seriously disrupt a program of rehabilitation or sources of information obtained on a promise of confidentiality. . . . Any information exempted from disclosure by the court must be specifically noted in the PSI and is subject to appellate review ("Procedure of the Michigan Department of Corrections" No. OP-BFS-71.01).

CRITICISM OF THE PSI REPORT

Abraham Blumberg (1970) maintains that some judges do not read the presentence report, while others carefully select passages condemning the defendant to read aloud in the courtroom in order to justify their sentences. He argues that many judges discount the report because of the hearsay nature of the information. Walter Dickey (1979: 33–34) reports on the types of inaccurate or misleading information he found in the PSI reports of one state:

> (1) rumors and suspicions that are reported without any factual explanations; (2) incomplete explanations of events that leave a misleading impression; (3) factual errors relating, usually, to the criminal record of the offender.
>
> Rumors and suspicions are often reported in presentence reports and identified as such. The report that the rumor exists may be accurate. What is objectionable is the fact that the subject of the rumor may cause the reader to give more weight to the rumor than it deserves, if any. If the rumor is without foundation, reference to it is particularly troubling.
>
> It is difficult to assess the impact of rumors, although they sometimes seem to directly affect correctional decisions. For example, one sex offender's presentence report contained the statement that the offender "was rumored to have killed his mother." This was referred to in several parole decisions before it was investigated. Upon inquiry, it was determined to the satisfaction of the parole board that the offender had been confined in another state at the time of his mother's death and had no connection to it.

Some reports do not contain complete information and are therefore misleading. One inmate's report contained the statement that he "had been arrested for attempted first degree murder after a bar fight. The charges were later dropped." Investigation showed that the reason the charges were dropped was that the inmate was actually the victim of an attack and not the aggressor. The other person involved was later charged with a crime for the attack.

The most frequently recurring factual problem with the reports is related to past offenses. The so-called "FBI Rap Sheet" or "Yellow Sheet" is part of the report. It contains a confounding listing of past offenses that is frequently repetitious, i.e., it reports the same offense more than once. The repetitions are not so identified. Past charges do not always contain their disposition, so the reader is never sure how many offenses there actually were which were dropped and why, what the facts underlying the charges and offenses are, and what the outcome was.

Willard Gaylin (1974) is concerned with the enormous dependence on the PSI that he argues tends to make the probation officer, rather than the judge, the sentencer. Numerous studies have indicated a high correlation between the recommendation of the PO and the judge's sentence. Research by the American Justice Institute (1981), for example, using samples from representative probation departments throughout the United States, found that recommendations for probation were adopted by the sentencing judge between 66 and 95 percent of the time (see Table 4.1).

Rodney Kingsnorth and Louis Rizzo (1979) investigated the relationship between plea bargaining, the probation officer's recommendation, and the final disposition of the case in a large western county.

In this county, after the defendant has accepted a "bargain" in exchange for a plea of guilty, the case is sent to the probation department for a PSI report. Kingsnorth and Rizzo found a very high correlation (93 percent) between the recommendation and the sentence. However, Robert Dawson (1969) states that the probation officer may write into the PSI the recommendation that the PO believes will be well-received by the judge. Eugene Czajkoski (1973) suggests that the prosecutor often finds a way of communicating the plea bargain agreement to the probation department and the latter responds with a conforming recommendation. On the other hand, Dickey (1979: 30) found that in Wisconsin:

> The prosecutor is often influenced by the recommendation in the report and the information underlying it. Some prosecutors frequently adopt the report's recommendations as their own recommendation to the court or use it as a benchmark in deciding on their recommendation. Sometimes a plea agreement will include the condition that the prosecutor will adopt the report's recommendation as his own.

Kingsnorth and Rizzo point out that in the county they studied the minutes of the plea bargaining session, including the details of the negotiated agreement, are sent to the probation department prior to the submission of the

TABLE 4.1 Levels of Agreement between Recommendations and Sentences.

RECOMMENDATION AND SENTENCE	DISTRICT OF COLUMBIA	STATE OF CONNECTICUT	COUNTY OF DELAWARE	COUNTY OF LOS ANGELES	COUNTY OF MULTNOMAH	STATE OF NEW JERSEY	COUNTY OF SANTA CLARA	STATE OF TEXAS
For or against probation	83%	82%	86%	87%	87%	66%	91%	95%
Probation/ incarceration (unspecified)	79	74	78	72	63	63	83	93
Probation/ incarceration (specified)	73	72	78	61	60	62	73	93
Treatment	91	86	NA	95	77	82	88	92
Financial obligation	85	85	NA	95	68	67	95	98
Surveillance	NA	NA	NA	99	92	NA	97	NA

The offender random sample established a high correlation between probation officers' recommendations and judicial sentencing. Levels of agreement between recommendations and sentences were measured in three different ways. The first measure shows the level of agreement between recommendations and sentences "for or against probation." The second measure examined probation/incarceration combinations. The third measure takes into consideration specified forms of probation/incarceration (e.g., supervised probation with jail on weekends).

Levels of agreement between recommended and court-ordered treatment (alcohol, drug, psychiatric); financial obligation (fine, restitution, community service work); and surveillance (search and seizure, chemical testing); have also been ascertained. Level of agreement is defined narrowly. If, for example, alcohol and drug treatment were recommended, and only alcohol treatment was ordered by the court, the recommendation and court order were not found in agreement.

SOURCE: American Justice Institute, 1981: 165

presentence report. They conclude that "probation officer concurrence with previously negotiated sentence agreements is a consequence, not of case characteristics, but of pressures emanating from the organizational structure of which the probation department is a part, namely the court system itself" (1979: 9). These and other studies serve to remind us that the probation officer is simply one actor in a rather complex setting. How much influence the PO can exert may often depend on procedural or structural variables, or perhaps the officer's force of personality.

In many jurisdictions the PO is overburdened with presentence investigations and does not have the time to do an adequate investigation and prepare a (potentially) useful report. In courts where the judge usually pays little or no attention to the contents of the report, the PO will not be inclined to pursue the necessary information and prepare well-written reports. Jonas Robitscher (1980: 35), an attorney and psychiatrist, states that while psychiatric reports and evaluations contained in the PSI often make the difference between probation, a short sentence, or a long sentence: "Many of these reports and evaluations contain dynamic formulations about the cause of behavior based on as little as twenty minutes spent with the subject of the report."

Dickey found a most distressing problem related to the issue of erroneous information in the report:

> Even when an alleged error is challenged at sentencing and a contrary finding made, it does not necessarily follow that the report will be corrected. When a judge makes a finding of fact that is inconsistent with the presentence report, he usually states the finding in the record of the sentencing hearing. Without more, this leaves the report itself uncorrected. The sentencing transcript is not made a part of the report; it is not attached to it. The oral finding does not signal anyone to amend the report or any of the copies of it. Subsequent users of the report, correctional and parole authorities, rely on the uncorrected report. Rarely is the report amended to reflect additional information or findings of fact inconsistent with it at sentencing. (1979: 35)

In Michigan, however, state law requires that if the court finds that challenged information is inaccurate or irrelevant, that finding will be made part of the court record, *and the inaccurate or irrelevant information must be stricken from the report prior to distribution.*

In order to improve the reliability of the report, the Massachusetts Commissioner of Probation provides the following standards:

1. The probation officer should identify the sources of information in the report.
2. The PO should make personal contact with informants or sources of information, when practicable, who can substantiate information. The PO should clearly state in the report those instances in which information has not been substantiated.
3. The PO should obtain pertinent documentation such as letters, clinical reports,

school reports, certified statements, when practicable. The PO should indicate when information in the report is supported by such documentation.

4. Sources of information should be identified in most instances; however, this does not exclude from a report relevant information from unnamed sources or informants with whom the PO has had personal contact. If a probation officer includes such information in an investigative report, the PO shall clearly indicate in the report that the information was obtained from sources or informants not being identified in this report.

Dickey (1979) points out that defendants are often quite dissatisfied with the role of their attorneys in the sentencing process. Federal District Court Judge Irving Cooper (1977: 101) has stated:

It is particularly distressing that many attorneys for the defense, who have proven themselves competent as to the facts and law in the case at trial . . . display on sentence hardly more than a faint glimmer as to who their clients really are as human beings.

Dickey adds (1979: 36):

Another source of the sense of injustice is the belief that lawyers do not provide the court with positive information about the offender to supplement the presentence report which, it is frequently asserted, is incomplete. Sophisticated defendants realize that even the most forceful statements, if they are general, are of little value to their case. They recognize the importance of presenting the court with alternatives to confinement (i.e., job or school plan, place to live) if probation is sought or a specific statement of plans after release if a short period of confinement is the goal. These defendants are usually dissatisfied because they feel the court is forced to rely on an incomplete report because their lawyers did not provide the additional information.

In response to this problem, in New York City the Legal Aid Society has used social workers to prepare sentencing memoranda for use by defense counsel at the sentencing hearing. In Buncombe County, North Carolina, I set up a similar effort using senior undergraduate students from Western Carolina University. The students worked for the Public Defender, providing presentence reports for use by defense counsel. There are other profit and nonprofit agencies that prepare presentence reports and there has also been a proliferation of privately for-profit commissioned PSI reports, and this raises a serious question of *equal justice,* since only those with the necessary financial resources can commission such a report.

REVIEW QUESTIONS

1. Why is the presentence report a manifestation of the positive school?
2. What is the primary purpose of a presentence investigation (PSI) report?
3. What are the other purposes to which the PSI report can be put?

4. What are the categories of information contained in a PSI report?
5. What are the sources of information for a PSI?
6. Why is the nature of a defendant's prior criminal record important for a probation officer to determine?
7. What are the variables that are considered in making a recommendation for or against a sentence of probation?
8. What is the law and practice with respect to requiring a PSI report?
9. How has plea bargaining affected the PSI report?
10. What are the arguments for and against the contents of a PSI report being disclosed to a defendant or defense counsel?
11. What is the basis of the Supreme Court's determination that a PSI report is confidential?
12. What are the various criticisms of the PSI report?
13. What has led to the use of the privately commissioned PSI report?
14. Why does the privately commissioned PSI report raise a question of equal justice?

FIVE
Supervision of Probationers

The dynamics of probation (and parole) supervision are discussed at length in Part Three. In this chapter we will look at the granting of probation, conditions of probation, length of supervision, violation of probation, and the legal decisions affecting probation.

GRANTING PROBATION

Most states have statutory restrictions on who may be granted probation in felony cases. Crimes such as murder, kidnaping, and rape often preclude a sentence of probation, as do second or third felony convictions. In Texas, a defendant may elect to be sentenced by a jury, but can thereby receive probation only if it is proven that he or she "has never before been convicted of a felony in this or any other State." In any event, in the Lone Star State no person is eligible to receive probation for a felony unless assessed a sentence of ten years or fewer by a judge or jury. In Georgia, a defendant who pleads guilty (or *nolo contendere* — "no contest") and who has never before been convicted of a felony can be placed on probation without the court entering a judgment of *guilty*. If the person successfully completes the terms of probation, he or she "shall not be considered to have a criminal conviction." In Arizona, only first-time nondangerous offenders are eligible for probation (Kennedy, 1988).

When probation is a statutory alternative, judges (and, in some cases, juries) differ in their approach to granting it. Although the recommendation of the probation department would be of obvious importance—it is difficult to envision cases where a judge would grant probation against the recommendation of the probation officer—judges may also seek advice from the police and prosecutor. The geographic area where the court is situated may also affect the granting of probation. Social and political attitudes in rural and urban jurisdictions can differ and, thus, affect the process. When court calendars are crowded, as they are in many urban areas, plea bargaining is more likely to result in probation being granted. And there is the pressing problem of jail and prison overcrowding. Dean Champion (1988) found that in the rural districts he studied, many felons are placed on probation as the result of a plea bargain. In Tennessee this appears to be directly related to the severe prison overcrowding experienced by that state. The judge's feelings toward the particular offense or the offender may also enter into the sentencing decision. The many factors that determine if a defendant is granted probation contribute to the continuing controversy over "differential punishment," a challenge to the classical approach to criminal justice.

However, there are factors which, to a greater or lesser extent, are considered in all cases relative to the granting of probation: the age and rehabilitation potential of the defendant; the defendant's criminal record, including indications of professional criminality, organized crime (see Abadinsky, 1990), and crimes of violence; the defendant's relationship with his or her family; evidence of any deviant behavior such as drug abuse or sex offenses; and the attitude of the community toward the particular offense and the particular offender. There are also other questions which may be considered: Does the defendant's attitude toward the offense indicate genuine remorse? Was probation promised to the defendant to induce him or her to plead guilty? Will being placed on probation enable the defendant to provide the victim with restitution? Will being placed on probation enable the defendant to provide support and care for his or her family?

The quality of service provided by a probation agency must also be considered by the sentencing judge. Unfortunately, in too many jurisdictions probation is nothing more than a suspending of sentence, since little or no supervision is actually provided. Under such circumstances a judge who might otherwise be inclined to place an offender on probation may, instead, impose a sentence of imprisonment. The cost to both the offender and the taxpayer is obvious—according to most estimates imprisonment costs from ten to thirteen times as much as probation. In many jurisdictions there is actually a built-in incentive for sentences of imprisonment, even when probation is a viable alternative. If probation services are funded by the county, and the cost of prisons are always borne by the state, each defendant sent to prison instead of being placed on probation, represents a savings to county government. This can be overcome with a *probation subsidy* through which the state reimburses the county for offenders placed on probation instead of being sentenced to a state prison.

The American Bar Association (ABA) presents the advantages of probation rather than imprisonment (1970: 3–4):

1. The liberty of the individual is maximized by such a sentence; at the same time the authority of the law is vindicated and the public effectively protected from further violations of the law.
2. The rehabilitation of the offender is affirmatively promoted by continuing normal community contacts.
3. The negative and frequently stultifying effects of confinement are avoided, thus removing a factor that often complicates the reintegration of the offender into the community.
4. The financial costs of crime control to the public treasury are greatly reduced by reliance on probation as an important part of the correctional system.
5. Probation minimizes the impact on innocent dependents of the offender.

The ABA sets forth three conditions for a sentence of imprisonment rather than probation (1970: 3–4):

1. When confinement is necessary to protect the public from further criminal activity by the defendant.
2. When the offender is in need of correctional treatment which can effectively be provided if he or she is confined.
3. When the seriousness of the offense would be unduly depreciated if a sentence of probation were imposed.

CONDITIONS OF PROBATION

Although the Task Force on Corrections (1966: 34) observed more than two decades ago that "differential treatment requires that the rules [of probation] be tailored to the needs of the case and of the individual offender," this suggestion is often not put into practice. Probation agencies require a defendant to sign a standard form which usually contains a variety of regulations that may or may not reflect the client's individual needs. There are also special conditions that can be imposed by the judge or the probation department, such as ordering a child molester to avoid places frequented by children.

Edwin Sutherland and Donald Cressey (1966) state that when conditions of probation are too restrictive, the probation officer is inclined to overlook their violation. This can result in the PO losing the respect of the probationer, making the supervision process quite difficult. The ABA (1970: 9) recommends that the conditions of probation be spelled out by the court at the time of sentencing, and emphasizes that they should be appropriate for the offender.

The American Probation and Parole Association (APPA) recommends that the only condition that should be imposed on every person sentenced to probation is that the probationer lead a law-abiding life during the period of probation. "No other conditions should be required by statute, but the probation officer in making recommendations [in the PSI report] should recommend additional conditions to fit the circumstances of each case." In a draft of a position statement the APPA recommends that conditions "be reasonably related to the avoidance of further criminal behavior and not unduly restrictive of the probationer's liberty or incompatible with his freedom of religion. They should not be so vague or ambitious as to give no real guidance."

The APPA draft states: "Conditions may appropriately include, but not be necessarily limited to, matters such as the following:

1. Cooperating with the program of supervision.
2. Meeting family responsibilities.
3. Maintaining steady employment or engaging or refraining from engaging in a specific employment or occupation (for example, a drug abuser prohibited from employment in a medical setting).
4. Pursuing prescribed educational or vocational training.
5. Undergoing medical or psychiatric treatment.
6. Maintaining residence in a prescribed area or in a prescribed facility established for, or available to, persons on probation.

FIGURE 5.1   Conditions of Probation, Oregon Corrections Division

Oregon Corrections Division—Marion County Department of Community Corrections
Conditions of Probation

NAME: _____ COUNTY: _____ DOCKET #: _____

I. *GENERAL:*

The Court places the defendant on probation, who shall be subject to the following General Conditions unless specifically deleted by the Court (ORS 137.540). The Probationer shall:

1. Remain under the supervision and control of the Probation Department.
2. Abide by the direction of the Probation Department and its representatives.
3. Promptly and truthfully answer all reasonable inquiries of the Probation Officer relating to probation performance.
4. Truthfully report monthly at times and in a manner specified by the Probation Department or its representative.
5. Remain in the State of Oregon until written permission to leave is granted by the Probation Department or its representatives.
6. Find and maintain gainful full-time employment, approved schooling, or a full-time combination of both. Any waiver of this requirement must be based on a finding by the Court stating the reasons for the waiver.
7. Change neither employment nor residence without promptly informing the Probation Department or its representatives.

FIGURE 5.1 *Continued*

8. Permit the Probation Officer to visit the probationer or the probationer's residence or worksite.
9. Submit to fingerprinting or photographing, or both, when requested by the Probation Department for supervision purposes.
10. Obey all laws, municipal, county, state and federal. (The Federal Gun Law of 1968 prohibits any person convicted of a crime punishable as a felony the use or possession of a firearm.)
11. Pay fines, costs including probation costs, attorney fees or restitution or any combination thereof ordered by the Court on a schedule of payments determined by the Court.

II. *STANDARD CONDITIONS:*

In addition, the following Standard Conditions of the Marion County Department of Community Corrections are imposed for the protection of the public or reformation of the offender. The Probationer shall:

1. Not use alcoholic beverages to excess. The excessive use of alcoholic beverage is understood to mean that the effects disrupt or interfere with my domestic life, employment, or community conduct.
2. Not possess or be in control of a concealable weapon.
3. Pay a monthly supervision fee of $15 unless otherwise ordered.
4. Not knowingly associate with any person with a criminal record without prior approval of his/her Probation Officer.
5. Not knowingly associate with persons who use or possess narcotics or dangerous drugs illegally.
6. Shall report to his/her Probation Officer as directed.

III. *SPECIAL CONDITIONS:*

The following Special Conditions of probation and any other special conditions as set out in the Judgment Order are imposed for the protection of the public or reformation of the offender (ORS 137.540(2)). The Probationer shall:

—— 1. Be confined in the Marion County Jail for a period not to exceed _____ commencing _____.
—— 2. Be confined to the Marion County Probation Center for a period not to exceed _____ and shall abide by all Center rules and regulations. The probationer shall immediately report to the Marion County Department of Community Corrections and shall commence serving the sentence as soon as space is available.

Failure to abide by all General, Standard, and Special Conditions imposed by the Court and supervised by the Probation Department and its representatives may result in arrest and revocation of probation and will result in notification of the violation to the sentencing Court. The Court may at any time modify the Conditions of Probation.

_____ _____
Date   Judge

I understand and accept the Conditions of Probation under which I have been released by the sentencing Court. I agree to abide by and conform to them and fully understand my failure to do so may result in the revocation of my probation by the Court.

_____ _____
Date   Person Under Probation

7. Refraining from consorting with certain types of people or frequenting certain types of places.
8. Making restitution for the fruits of the crime or reparation for losses or damages caused thereby.
9. Paying fines, restitution, reparation or family support.
10. Requiring the probationer to submit to search and seizure.
11. Requiring the probationer to submit to drug tests; i.e., urine test for analysis as directed by the probation officer.

Probation regulations in different probation agencies tend to be markedly similar. They typically exhort the probationer to live a law-abiding life, to work, and to support dependents. They require that the offender inform the PO of his or her residence and that permission be secured before leaving the jurisdiction of the court. Some require that the probationer obtain permission before getting married, applying for a motor vehicle license, or contracting any indebtedness. Many probation departments require that the offender pay a "supervision fee."

Restitution, Community Service, and Fees

Restitution   Res-ti-tu-tion—*n.:* an act of restoring or a condition of being restored; a making good or giving an equivalent for some injury—has become a very popular condition of probation. In addition to being required to pay for court costs, fines, and fees, a probationer may be required to make restitution; paying a percentage of his or her income, as determined by the court, to the victim of the offense for any property damage or medical expenses sustained as a direct result of the commission of the offense. This concept has an ancient history: the Bible (*Exodus* 21, 22; *Leviticus* 5) orders restitution for theft, burglary, or robbery, and a form of "community service"—indentured servitude—in the event the criminal has no means of providing restitution. Restitution fell out of favor when kings, seeking to centralize power, made crime a public (state) matter and directed payments (fines) away from the victim or his or her kin, in favor of the crown. (Personal claims had to be brought in civil court.) Community service emerged as a modern sentencing option in Alameda County, California, in 1966, and the Minnesota Restitution Program was established in 1972. Persons convicted of property offenses were given the opportunity to reduce their jail sentence or avoid incarceration altogether if they secured employment and provided restitution to their victims. The idea soon spread to other states (McDonald, 1988).

Douglas McDonald notes that one impulse animating restitution

> has been the hope and belief that both may contribute to the rehabilitation of offenders. Disciplined work has long been considered reformative. In addition, offenders performing community service may acquire some employable skills, improved work habits, and a record of quasi-employment that may be longer than any job they've held before. Victim restitution, when it brings offenders and

PHILADELPHIA COURT OF COMMON PLEAS
OFFICE OF COURT ADMINISTRATION
ADULT PROBATION DEPARTMENT

RULES OF PROBATION AND PAROLE

_____

NAME OF PROBATIONER/PAROLEE   POLICE PHOTO NUMBER

_____

BILL AND TERM NUMBER   SUPERVISING DISTRICT

The Honorable Judge _____ has placed you on probation and/or parole and expec
you to comply with the following Rules of Probation/Parole:

1. Report to the Probation/Parole Officer as directed and permit the Officer to visit you at your hom
   or place of employment when necessary.

2. Respond promptly to any summons to appear in court.

3. Report any change of address to your Probation/Parole Officer within 72 hours, and do not lea
   Philadelphia without permission from your Probation/Parole Officer.

4. Make every effort to seek and maintain employment, and promptly inform your Probation/Paro
   Officer of any change in your employment status.

5. Obey all federal, state, county criminal laws and city ordinances.

6. You may not unlawfully possess, use, sell or distribute controlled substances of any kind.

7. You may not possess firearms or any other deadly weapons.

8. Notify your Probation/Parole Officer within 72 hours of any new arrest.

   You will also comply with the following special conditions of Probation/Parol

   _____

   _____

   _____

ACKNOWLEDGEMENT OF PROBATIONER/PAROLEE

I have read, or have had read to me, the foregoing rules and conditions of my Probation/Parole; I ful
understand them and agree to follow them.

_____   _____
WITNESS   *SIGNATURE OF PROBATIONER/PAROLEE*
                                          (NOTE: If signed by a mark, two witnesses must
                                          execute this instrument.)

_____   _____
WITNESS   *DATE*
30-806

PROBATIONER/PAROLEE

FIGURE 5.2 Rules of Probation and Parole, Adult Probation Department,
Philadelphia Court of Common Pleas

victims face to face, also forces offenders to see firsthand the consequences of
their deeds and thus may encourage the development of greater social responsibility and maturity. (1988: 2)

Texas is so committed to the concept of restitution, that since 1983, based on models established in Georgia and Mississippi, it has operated "restitution centers" throughout the state. As a condition of probation, non-violent, employable felony offenders who would have otherwise been imprisoned, can be sent to a restitution center for between six to twelve months, during which time the restitution center director attempts to secure employment for each resident. The director also attempts to place each probationer as a worker in a community-service project either during off-work hours if the probationer is employed, or full-time if the probationer is unable to find employment. The restitution facility, which is operated by probation staff, accommodates between thirty to sixty persons and is usually located in light industrial areas for access to employment.

The probationer's salary is submitted by the employer directly to the director of the restitution center. The director deducts the cost of food, housing and supervision, support for the probationer's dependents, and restitution to the victim(s)—the remainder, if any, going to the probationer upon release from the center. However,

> If a restitution center director determines that the probationer is knowingly or intentionally failing to seek employment, the director shall request the court having jurisdiction of the case to revoke the probationer's probation and transfer the probationer to the custody of the Texas Department of Corrections. If the judge determines that a resident has demonstrated an acceptance of responsibility, the court may order the resident released from the center. The first two months following release, the former resident will be intensely supervised before being transferred to a regular probation caseload.

Steven L. Chesney studied the use of restitution in Minnesota and reports (n.d.: 158):

> It is clear that the most important determinant of whether an otherwise eligible defendant was to be ordered to make restitution was his supposed "ability to pay." As evident from both interviews with judges and from the cases themselves, this criterion was generally operationalized by choosing offenders who were white, well-educated, and from the working and middle classes. This contrasted markedly with what is known about the criminal justice system in general. Those caught up in the system are overwhelmingly the poor, the lower class, and members of minority groups.

Chesney raises some issues with respect to the use of restitution:

1. Perhaps the relatively well-educated and well-employed group of offenders that is able to pay restitution is the group of offenders for whom restitution has the least meaning; and
2. Restitution may be one way that members of the more affluent social classes can avoid incarceration.

Chesney concludes:

Restitution is not addressed to a rehabilitative or a victim compensatory need; instead, it answers a moral need. It reflects the way we feel that people should treat other people. As such, the evaluations of the effects of restitution may need to show only that it is no worse than other rehabilitative alternatives and that it does compensate some victims. Any effects beyond these are serendipitous because the primary goal of restitution is the elimination of the contradictions between our systems of morality and our criminal justice system. (n.d.: 169)

Community service   Because relatively few offenders coming into the criminal justice system are in a position to provide meaningful financial restitution, the alternative of community service has gained in popularity.

The State of New Jersey (Administrative Office of the Courts, n.d.: 11) points out:

Community service by offenders is being utilized as a sentencing alternative with ever increasing frequency. Offenders are sentenced to community service work without monetary compensation at public or private non-profit agencies in the community. These offenders usually perform their community service during the evenings and on weekends to complete their sentences. The punitive aspect of a community service order is reflected in the imposition upon the time and freedom of offenders. While functioning in the traditional role as punishment, a community service order also directly benefits the public through the performance of services that may otherwise not be available.

Community service in Georgia is seen as "an alternative sentencing option which is definitely punitive, yet is not perceived as being as harsh as incarceration, nor as lenient as regular probation." In the state of Washington compulsory service without compensation performed for the benefit of the community is available as an alternative to incarceration for certain nonviolent crimes. The Department of Corrections Division of Community Services solicits requests for manpower services from nonprofit or governmental agencies. Community service has included chore service, work in food banks, park and street cleanup, milloil removal, and recycling. The requesting agency is expected:

1. Not to displace a paid worker with an offender.
2. Supply a description of the work site and tasks.
3. Assign a supervisor for training and supervision of the offender.
4. Provide working conditions for the offender equal to that of paid staff.
5. Provide written verification of offender performance.

There are similar programs in a number of states including: Georgia, Indiana, Kansas, Louisiana, Maryland, Minnesota, Ohio, Oregon, and Virginia. In Illinois and New Jersey community service is used as an alternative for persons convicted of driving while intoxicated. In New Jersey the community service program is the responsibility of the county probation department. While no offender is automatically disqualified for the community service alternative in New Jersey, the Administrative Office of the Courts recommends that persons suffering from chronic alcohol or drug abuse problems, persons convicted of arson or assaultive offenses, and those with previous convictions for certain sex offenses, be excluded. In Georgia, community service is recommended for, but not limited to, persons convicted of traffic and ordinance violations, and nonviolent, nondestructive misdemeanors and felonies. In other cases: "The judge may confer with the prosecutor, defense attorney, probation supervisor, community service officer, or other interested persons to determine if the community service program is appropriate for an offender." Typical placements in Georgia have included hospitals, Red Cross, parks and recreation systems, senior citizen centers, associations for the blind and deaf, and humane societies.

The Dauphin County (PA) Adult Probation/Parole Department has a Community Resource Program in conjunction with the Harrisburg Chapter of the American Red Cross. Clients placed at the Red Cross are regarded as volunteers (even though participation is a mandatory condition of the sentence of probation or county parole) and are provided with the same training, expectations, and benefits that any Red Cross volunteer receives. The Red Cross provides monthly evaluation reports. If work is satisfactory, a completion letter is given to the client and a copy to the probation/parole officer; unsatisfactory work results in a termination letter. Clients have served as first aid aides, assisting an instructor in providing courses in first aid, and have conducted their own courses in first aid utilizing multimedia systems; others serve in clerical, public relations, custodial, and research positions. While there are no restrictions on who may enter the program, clients have been nonviolent offenders.

Fees   The imposition of "user" fees has grown in popularity, with about two-thirds of the probation agencies imposing them as a condition of supervision. These fees frequently account for a significant portion of the probation budget, twenty percent for county departments and ten percent for state probation/parole agencies (Wheeler, et al., 1989), while in Texas they provide more than half of the cost of basic probation services. Although Texas has had a great deal of success in imposing and collecting fees, the use of probation violation as a compliance mechanism has been rare; in fact, states Dale Parent (1989), prison overcrowding has made judges reluctant to revoke probation even for willful failure to pay. Instead, intermediate punishments such as a short jail stay or several weeks of community service are imposed. Parent noted that in Texas there is considerable pressure on probation officers for successful collection of fees.

_____ COUNTY PROBATION DEPARTMENT
COMMUNITY SERVICE PROGRAM

Community Service Conditions and Release of Information

I, _____, having been (convicted of) (charged with)
_____ in _____ Court, understand that
I am required to perform _____ days, or _____ hours, of Community Service work.

I understand that as a participant in the Community Service Program, I am not an employee of the County and, therefore, am not entitled to employee benefits including Workmen's Compensation Coverage. I am covered by an accident/medical expense insurance policy. Notice of injury must be given to Community Service staff within 24 hours of the accident. I must provide verification that the injury was related to the performance of Community Service.

I agree to give the Community Service staff permission to release information about me to participating agencies. Community Service staff employees have the authority to assign me to a work site and to supervise the work performed. Community Service staff will be notified immediately of any change of job, residence, telephone number, or health condition. Inquiries from Community Service staff will be answered promptly and truthfully.

I am expected to perform a minimum of _____ hours of Community Service per week. I must report at the time assigned and notify the agency in advance whenever I am unable to appear for work. Any extended absence for illness will be documented by a physician's note.

While at the work site, I will be cooperative, courteous and reliable, and obey all rules and directions. I understand that I am not to report to a work site having consumed alcohol or used illegal drugs. I am responsible for ensuring that a record of Community Service hours is accurately maintained. Agencies will report my work progress to the Community Service Program and this information will be made available to the court.

I understand that failure to comply with the rules and procedures of the program and participating agencies may be cause for returning my case to court for another disposition that may include sentence to a period of incarceration.

The above has been explained to me and I have been provided with a copy of this document.

_____
DEFENDANT

_____
PROBATION OFFICER

_____
DATE

FIGURE 5.3   Community Service Conditions and Release of Information

The use of these fees raises important questions:

1. Will persons who can pay fees be more likely to be granted probation?
2. Will the need to collect fees change the focus of probation supervision away from providing services?
3. Will the failure to pay fees result in probation revocation?
4. Will persons be kept under supervision longer because of their ability to pay fees or a need to collect unpaid fees?
5. Will the imposition of fees cause an increase in absconding from supervision?

COMMUNITY SERVICE REPORT

TO: _____
FROM:_____ County Community Service Program
DATE:_____

                                    RE:_____
                             Docket No.:_____
                                Charge:_____
                            Court Date:_____

PLEASE BE INFORMED THAT: (Check appropriate lines and fill in the blanks.)

_____Client has completed the community service requirement of _____ hours
       at:_____
       Client's performance was rated:

_____Client's performance in community service has been unsatisfactory because:

_____Client is inappropriate for community service because:

THEREFORE WE:

_____Are closing our interest in this case.
_____Recommend returning the client to court.
_____Recommend the following action:_____
_____
_____Other_____

PLEASE ADVISE THIS OFFICE OF COURT ACTION.

                                    Respectfully submitted,

FIGURE 5.4 Community Service Report

In 1983 the Supreme Court (*Beardon* v. *Georgia* 461 U.S. 660) ruled that probation cannot be revoked because of an inability to pay a fine and restitution as a condition of probation, as a result of indigence and not a refusal to pay. This would appear to apply to supervision fees.

Objectives of Probation Supervision*

(a)   To provide public protection in keeping with the special duties of a probation officer.

Source: N.Y. State *Code of Criminal Procedure,* 351.2.

(Continued)

(b)   To prepare the probationer for independent, law-abiding living.
(c)   To provide an opportunity for full participation of the probationer in planning his or her activities in the community.
(d)   To identify, utilize and create resources in the community to fulfill program needs of probationers.
(e)   To provide a system of differential supervision based on the classification and program needs of all probationers.
(f)   To conduct a cost effective supervision program.
(g)   To provide restitution and/or reparation to victims of criminal acts whenever applicable.

Probation Supervision/Philadelphia

Once a person has been sentenced to probation, a probation officer is assigned who conducts an orientation to the rules of supervision and assesses the needs and risks of the offender. The PO then works with the offender to insure that special conditions which have been stipulated by the judge are met. This department has placed a high priority on the collection of restitution which is a frequent stipulation imposed by judges. A probation plan is developed then which will aid the offender in successfully completing his or her term.

When necessary, referrals are made to community based agencies to help clients who require intensive and special treatment for severe drug, alcohol, and mental health problems. These clients may have the option of remaining in a treatment facility, if necessary, even when their probation has expired. Offenders who are poly-drug abusers or who have obvious psychiatric problems are evaluated by the department's Assessment Team composed of psychologists and a psychiatric social worker. A supervision plan is then developed to assist the PO in supervising the case.

If it is found to be appropriate, some clients are referred to a residential drug treatment program at the Philadelphia State Hospital which provides group and individual counseling to drug abusers and is administered by a staff person from this department. The department also has a special unit that provides group counseling to clients who cannot or will not take advantage of community mental health services. This unit operates under the supervision of a trained psychologist, and serves primarily psychiatric and sex offenders. Offenders charged with driving under the influence are supervised within a special unit called the Alcohol Highway Safety Unit. This unit handles cases that are both within a pretrial as well as posttrial status. The unit monitors the offender's attendance in safe-driving school and in the specified treatment facility.

The Victim Services Unit provides appropriate direct and referral services to victims; helps coordinate victim services among providers so that resources can be provided efficiently and effectively; and increases victim input at sentencing and prior to an inmate's release on parole.

LENGTH OF SUPERVISION

The length of probation terms vary from state to state. The American Bar Association recommends that the term should be two years for a misdemeanor conviction and five years for a felony. In Illinois it is four years for the more serious felonies, thirty months for other felonies; for a misdemeanor it is one year. In Texas, "the court may fix the period of probation without regard to the term of punishment assessed, but in no event may the period of probation be greater than 10 years or less than the minimum prescribed for the offense for which the defendant was convicted."

Some states authorize early termination of probation without actually having statutory guidelines as to when it is to be exercised. In most states, however, probation statutes provide for the termination of probation and the discharge of the offender from supervision prior to the end of the term. This allows the judge some needed flexibility since it is difficult to determine, at the time of sentencing, how long the term should actually be. In Texas, for example:

> At any time, after the defendant has satisfactorily completed one-third of the original probationary period or two years of probation, whichever is the lesser, the period of probation may be reduced or terminated by the court.

In Illinois, "The court may at any time terminate probation . . . if warranted by the conduct of the offender and the ends of justice. . . ." In Oklahoma, probation supervision "shall not normally exceed two years unless it is determined the interests of the public and the probationer would be best served by an extended period of supervision not to exceed the length of the original sentence."

The decision to terminate probation early and discharge the offender from supervision should be based on exemplary conduct. Unfortunately, the termination decision may not have any direct relationship to the merits of the case, but is often a reflection of the need to keep caseloads down to a manageable size. This means that probationers may be discharged even though they are in need of further supervision.

VIOLATION OF PROBATION

The New York State *Code of Criminal Procedure* (352.3) states:

> Probation as a sentence or disposition is a means of offering the offender the opportunity for law-abiding adjustment in the community. Although the proba-

ALLEN COUNTY PROBATION DEPARTMENT

Violation Notice No:

You are hereby given notice that on or about the _____ day of
_____ , 19____ , you violated Rule No. _____ of the
Allen County Probation Department Rules and Regulations.

By signing/initialing this notice, you are hereby stating that your Probation
Officer, _____ has discussed the
violation with you.   Further, you are informed that although no action may
be taken at this time, should further violations occur warranting a Probable
Cause Hearing, this violation may and can be included in same.

Be advised a copy of this notice will be retained in your probation file.

_____
Date Notice Served

_____   _____
Probationer   Cause

_____
Probation Officer

FIGURE 5.5   Probation Violation Report

tioner is not deprived of his liberty, his life situation is circumscribed by the
conditions which are intended to ensure protection of the community and adjustment of the probationer through effective supervision. It is the Probation Department's responsibility to see that the conditions of probation are properly
enforced and to inform the court of any significant deviation.

There are two types of probation violation:

1. *Technical.* When any of the conditions of probation have been violated, there
   exists a technical violation of probation.

2. *New Offense*. When a violation involves a new crime, it is a nontechnical or new offense violation.

The probation response to a violation is a matter of considerable discretion. For example, in Philadelphia the Adult Probation Department advises its probation officers:

> Minor violations of probation/[county]parole do not necessarily need to be brought to the attention of the sentencing Judge, but may be handled between the P.O. and the p/p [probationer/parolee] if such violations are not repeated and do not develop into a pattern.

In many jurisdictions—Allen County, Pennsylvania and New York, for example—the PO has the authority to "discuss the alleged violation(s) with the probationer and inform him that repeated or more serious violation(s) will be dealt with by the court." (See Figure 5.5.) If the behavior continues, but a formal violation of probation is not necessary, in New York "the court shall be informed of the alleged violation(s) and the department's action to date . . . [and] a recommendation may be made to the court requesting that the court require that the probationer appear before it . . . for a judicial reprimand."

Eugene Czajkoski is critical of the discretionary powers exercised by probation departments; he maintains that technical violations—for example, changing residence without immediately notifying the PO—are often ignored until it is believed that the probationer has committed a new crime.

> Invoking the technical violation thus becomes the result of the probation officer making the adjudication that a crime has been committed. The probationer has a hearing on the technical violation, but is denied a trial on the suspected crime which triggered the technical violation (1973: 13).

As we shall see, it is easier to find a person "guilty" of a violation of probation than it is to prove criminal charges.

Court Notification of a Technical Violation of Probation

STATE OF NEW JERSEY	SUPERIOR COURT OF NEW JERSEY
	Bergen County
—VS—	Indictment No. S-584-88-01
MICHAEL JOHNSON	BEFORE THE HONORABLE
	Alfred D. Schiaffo

(Continued)

I, RICHARD L. ALBERA, Chief Probation Officer of the County of Bergen, aforesaid, do hereby charge that MICHAEL JOHNSON late of the Borough of Totowa, County of Passaic was on the 28th day of September, 1988, convicted in the above-entitled Court on a charge of Possession of a Controlled Dangerous Substance (Cocaine) With the Intent to Distribute and that upon said conviction the Court rendered the following judgment: On December 2, 1988;
COUNT 1 – $3000.00 Fine and three (3) years Probation.
July 20, 1989 – Violation of Probation: Probation continued with added condition of serving sixty (60) days in Bergen County Jail.
That the said MICHAEL JOHNSON did violate the terms and conditions of said probation in the following respects:

1. Violated Rule No. 2 by failing to report on December 6, 1987, December 13, 1989, December 20, 1989, December 27, 1989, January 17, 1990, January 24, 1990, January 31, 1990, February 28, 1990, or any date subsequent to March 4, 1990, although directed to report on a once per week basis.
2. Violated Rule No. 1, by being under the influence of Controlled Dangerous Substance, to wit: Cocaine on November 8, 1989, November 29, 1989, January 3, 1990, January 11, 1990, and February 21, 1990, as witnessed by abnormal results of urinalysis submitted on those dates.

Dated: March 21, 1990

Chief Probation Officer

The revocation process originates with probation officers who exercise what Czajkoski (1973) refers to as a "quasi-judicial role" in that they decide whether or not to seek revocation. The probation officer's attitude toward the probationer and the violation will influence whether revocation action is initiated. Although the actual procedures differ from jurisdiction to jurisdiction, typically the PO confers with his or her superiors and, if a violation is considered serious enough, a notice will be filed with the court. The case will then be placed on the court calendar and the probationer will be given a copy of the alleged violations and directed to appear for a preliminary or *probable cause hearing* (see Figure 5.6). In some jurisdictions, the preliminary hearing is conducted by an official other than a judge, and in some jurisdictions, for example, Texas: "A probationer is not entitled to a preliminary hearing or examining trial to determine whether there is probable cause to proceed to a revocation hearing." In Texas, in cases of violation the case goes directly before a judge for a revocation hearing. (A probable cause hearing is necessary only if the probationer is to be held in custody pending the revocation hearing.) In any event, if a probationer fails to respond to a notice or summons to appear for a hearing, the judge will usually issue a warrant (see Figure 5.7). A probationer may also waive the right to a preliminary hearing (see Figure 5.8).

CAUSE NO.:_____

__NOTICE OF PROBABLE CAUSE HEARING__

DATE FILED:_____

TO:_____

ADDRESS:_____

You are hereby given notice of a Probable Cause Probation Violation Hearing to be

conducted _____ , 19_____ , at _____ a.m. p.m.

at the_____ ,

It is alleged you have violated your probation in the following manner to-wit:

Violation of any one of the above conditions of probation and suspended sentence could cause you to be returned to the Judge of original jurisdiction and thus result in the revocation of your suspended sentence and probation and commitment to the institution as the Court originally sentenced you to.

You are entitled to have witnesses to present evidence in your behalf and to challenge or question these allegations at the time of the Probable Cause Hearing.

_____

HEARING JUDGE or OFFICER

NOTICE SERVED BY: _____   *Date:* _____   *Time:* _____

WITNESS: _____

FIGURE 5.6   Notice of Probable Cause Hearing

```
┌────────────────────────────────────────────────────────────────┐
│                                                                  │
│           WARRANT FOR ARREST OF PROBATIONER                      │
│                                                                  │
│        STATE OF GEORGIA      ) COUNTY OF _____         │
│                vs.           )                                   │
│   _____     ) NO. _____            │
│                                                                  │
│   TO THE SHERIFF OF THE ABOVE NAMED COUNTY OR                    │
│   OTHER LAW ENFORCEMENT OFFICER OF THE STATE:                    │
│                                                                  │
│   Under authority of the Georgia Statewide Probation Act you are hereby commanded to take the body of │
│                                                                  │
│   _____   │
│                                                                  │
│   of the following address _____     │
│                                                                  │
│   _____   │
│                                                                  │
│   and safely keep _____until _____ may be returned to this Court, there to answer │
│   to a charge of violation of the following conditions of probation: │
│                                                                  │
│   _____   │
│                                                                  │
│   _____   │
│                                                                  │
│   Probationer is charged with violation of said conditions, in willful disregard of a Court Order, specifically │
│   as follows:                                                    │
│                                                                  │
│   _____   │
│                                                                  │
│   _____   │
│                                                                  │
│   Issued this _____ day of _____ 19 _____ │
│                                                                  │
│   Sworn to and subscribed before me                              │
│                                                                  │
│   This _____ day of                                       │
│                                                                  │
│   _____, 19 ____.        Probation/Parole Supervisor    │
│                                                                  │
│   _____      _____ │
│   Notary Public                   Judge                          │
│   (SEAL)                                                          │
│                                                                  │
└────────────────────────────────────────────────────────────────┘
```

FIGURE 5.7   Warrant for Arrest of Probationer, Georgia

Preliminary Hearing

The accompanying flow chart (Figure 5.9 on p. 144) indicates the possibilities presented at each stage of the probation revocation process. At the preliminary hearing the probationer can deny the charges of probation violation or plead guilty to them. If the plea is "guilty," the judge may deal with the case at once. If the probationer denies the charges, the judge will decide if there is sufficient (probable) cause to believe that probation was violated (in order to remand the probationer to custody), and a revocation hearing is scheduled. The judge may remand the probationer to custody pending the hearing, or can release him or her on bail or on his or her own recognizance.

COMMONWEALTH OF PENNSYLVANIA   :   IN THE COURT OF COMMON PLEAS
:   DAUPHIN COUNTY, PENNSYLVANIA

V.

:   NO(S):
:   CHARGE(S):   CD 19——

Waiver of Prerevocation Preliminary Hearing

I hereby waive (give up) my right to have a prerevocation preliminary hearing in the above captioned case. I understand that I have been accused of committing certain violations of my probation/parole as set forth on the notice of alleged violations dated

——————————.

I understand and it has been explained to me that:

——   1. I am not required to waive (give up) my right to have a prerevocation preliminary hearing.

——   2. The prerevocation preliminary hearing (sometimes called a "Gagnon 1 hearing") is held for the purpose of having a neutral (impartial) hearing officer determine whether there is probable (reasonable) cause to believe that I have committed acts which would constitute a violation of my probation/parole conditions.

——   3. At such prerevocation preliminary hearing I would have an opportunity to speak in person, present witnesses and documentary evidence and confront and cross-examine adverse witnesses (unless the hearing officer specifically finds good cause for not allowing confrontation.)

——   4. At such prerevocation hearing, the hearing officer may also make a determination as to probable cause to detain me pending a revocation hearing to be scheduled before the Dauphin County Court of Common Pleas.

——   5. At such prerevocation hearing, I would be able to have the evidence against me disclosed and obtain a written summary of the hearing from the hearing officer.

——   6. After having all of the above explained to me, and being given a chance to read this document and ask questions, I was further advised that I could have a lawyer represent me at such prerevocation hearing and that if I could not afford to pay for a lawyer for this hearing that the Court would appoint a lawyer free of cost to me.

Understanding all of the above, I still give up my right to have a prerevocation preliminary hearing.

DATE: _____   _____
                                       PROBATIONER/PAROLEE

_____   _____
WITNESS   PROBATION/PAROLE OFFICER

FIGURE 5.8   Waiver of Prerevocation Preliminary Hearing, Pennsylvania

Probation Violation Flowchart

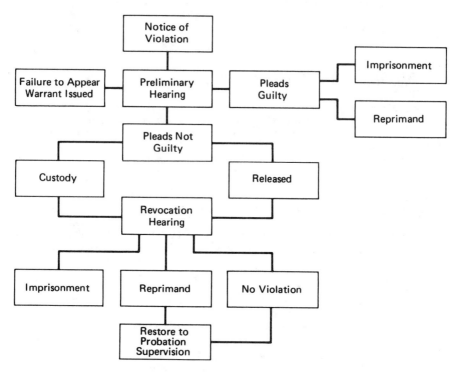

FIGURE 5.9   Probation Violation Flowchart

The probation department will subsequently prepare a violation of probation report: "The report shall contain a summary of the probationer's supervision activities to date, and the alleged facts which would be sufficient, if proven, to establish any violation(s) of probation occurred" (N.Y. State *Code of Criminal Procedure,* 352.6). As opposed to a narrow legal document, the violation of probation report contains information about the probationer's behavior under supervision — for example, employment record — and is presented to the judge prior to the revocation hearing.

State of Alabama
Board of Pardons and Paroles

Officer's Report on Delinquent Probationer

Probationary Judge: William H. Gordon, Montgomery Circuit Court
Probationer: Louis Merchant

Race, Sex, Age: W/M — 30
Offense: Theft of Property 1st degree
Date of Conviction: 2-17-88
Sentence: 2 years suspended; 2 years probation
Date of Probation: 2-17-88 EXPIRES: 4-10-89
Restitution Paid: $249.00
Supervision Fee Paid: 3 months arrears

DELINQUENT CHARGES

Charge No. 1.

New Offense — Burglary III

Legal Facts

Subject was arrested on 12/24/88 by the Montgomery Police Department for the offense of Burglary 3rd degree. Bond was set at $2,000. A preliminary hearing was held 1/5/89, and the case was bound to the Grand Jury. Indictment was returned, arraignment held, and case set for trial 2/17/89. A Probation Officer's Authorization of Arrest was issued on 12/25/88.

Details

Police reports reflect that at 2 a.m. on 12/24/88, Officer M. D. Jones with the Montgomery Police Department, while on routine patrol, observed a W/M subject exit Ace Hardware, 4240 Ames Road, Montgomery, Alabama, by way of a back window in possession of a box. The subject fled on foot but was caught by Officer Jones about three hundred feet from the building. The person was identified as Louis Merchant. He had in his possession property identified as having come from Ace Hardware by the Manager, A. L. Pope. It was determined that the hardware store had been entered by forcing open an air conditioning vent at the rear of the store.

Charge No. 2

Failure to Report.

Legal Facts
A probation warrant was issued and given to the Sheriff's Office on 12/25/88, to prevent the subject's release pending court action.

Details

According to the records of the supervising officer, on 2/17/88, subject was instructed by Officer Dan Jones regarding probation rules and regulations and specially that he must report to the Probation Office each month by the third. He stated that he understood all rules and regulations.

    Subject failed to report or have any contact with the probation officer for months of October, November, and December 1988.

    On 9/19/88, he reported for the month of September. He stated he forgot to

(Continued)

report by the third. He was reprimanded and encouraged to report in accordance with instructions.

On 10/10/88, I visited his residence. He was not present. His mother, Mae Merchant, said she had not seen him in three days. I asked that she have him report. On 10/15/88, I wrote subject a letter to report and received no response. On 10/25/88, I visited his home, his mother said he had received my letter. He was not present. I requested she attempt to have him report and advised of consequences if he failed.

On 11/15/88, a letter was written to subject reminding him and instructing that he make contact with his probation officer. On 11/10/88, I called his residence and spoke with his 17-year-old sister, Sue Merchant, and requested that she tell him to report. On 11/20/88, I visited his father, Joseph Merchant, at their residence and requested to have the subject report.

On 12/6/88, I visited the subject's residence and talked to his parents. They stated he had been told to report but refused. On 12/10/88, I wrote him a letter instructing that he report within 7 days or I would file a report of Probation Violation, which would cause him to be arrested as a probation violator. He failed to contact the Probation Office thereafter.

Supervision Summary

The probationer resided with his parents until September, 1988. He worked steadily with Biloxi Industries until July, 1988. There was a reduction in the work force which caused subject to be laid off. He reported regularly until September. During this period he reported and his attitude was satisfactory. Law enforcement officers suspected he was involved with persons using drugs. There was no evidence of his using or selling drugs.

Recommendation

I recommend revocation.

Signed and dated at Montgomery, Alabama, this 5th day of January, 1989.

Dan Jones
Probation and Parole Officer

Revocation Hearing

At the revocation hearing the probationer will have an opportunity to testify and present witnesses. In Texas and other jurisdictions, "It is quite common for the defense attorney and the prosecutor to plea bargain in probation revocation proceedings as they do when new criminal charges are filed" (Dawson, 1983: 61). There may be an attorney present to represent the probationer (as per the provisions outlined in the *Mempa* and *Gagnon* decisions discussed later in this chapter). If the judge finds no violations, the probationer is restored to supervision. If the judge sustains any of the charges brought by the probation department, the probationer can be reprimanded and restored to supervision, or probation can be revoked and imprisonment ordered. In some cases the defendant is actually sentenced at the time of conviction, but the imposition of sentence is suspended in favor of probation. Less frequently, the defendant is placed directly on probation without being sentenced. In the latter case, if the violation charge(s) is sustained, the judge can revoke probation and sentence the probationer to a term of imprisonment. The sentence, however, must be in accord with the penalty provided by law for the crime for which the probationer was originally convicted.

Proof of guilt in a criminal trial must be *beyond a reasonable doubt* but, at a probation revocation hearing, need not be greater than by a *preponderance of the evidence,* a lower standard used in civil cases. In a criminal trial the testimony of an accomplice usually has to be corroborated, but there is no such requirement for revocation hearings. Evidence that would not ordinarily be admitted in a criminal trial, such as hearsay testimony, can be entered into evidence at a revocation hearing. When the judge renders a decision on the charges, he or she can only consider the evidence presented at the hearing. When making a decision as to the disposition of a probationer found in violation, the judge can consider many items, such as employment record, relationship to spouse and children, and efforts at drug treatment.

Street Time

A defendant is convicted of burglary and sentenced to three and one-half years' imprisonment (written 3–6–0: three years, six months, zero days). The probationer spends one year (1–0–0) under supervision and then violates the conditions of probation in an important respect. After a revocation hearing the judge revokes probation and orders the probationer to begin serving the 3–6–0 sentence in prison. *Question:* Must the offender serve a maximum of 3–6–0 in prison, or is the 1–0–0 year of probation supervision ("street") time to be subtracted from the 3–6–0 sentence?

The answer to this question varies from state to state. Some states do not recognize the time spent under supervision as time served against the sentence unless the full probationary term is successfully completed. A minority of states provide street-time credit for probation violations not involving the commission of a new crime; others leave it to the discretion of the judge.

LEGAL DECISIONS AFFECTING PROBATION

Legal decisions that affect probation usually affect parole, and vice-versa. For example, the *Gagnon* decision to be discussed in this section used the *Morrissey* decision (discussed in Chapter 8), which concerned parole violation, as a precedent. However, for purposes of study the significant decisions in probation and parole have been divided according to the primary thrust of the case.

THREE THEORIES OF PROBATION

Traditionally, an individual on probation has not been considered a free person, despite the fact that the probationer is not incarcerated. The basis for imposing restrictions (conditions) on a probationer's liberty—and for punishing violations—is contained in three theories.

    1. *Grace theory.* Probation is a conditional privilege; an act of mercy by the judge which has not been earned by the defendant. As such, probation can simply be withdrawn if any condition of the privilege is violated.

    2. *Contract theory.* Each probationer is required to sign a *contract*—a stipulation agreeing to certain terms in return for conditional liberty. As in any contractual situation, a breach of contract can result in penalties, in this case revocation of probation.

    3. *Custody theory.* Persons placed on probation in lieu of imprisonment are in the legal custody of the court and, therefore, quasi-prisoners with their constitutional rights being abridged accordingly. Under such conditions, the court has the authority to move the convict from a community setting to a prison setting in the event of a violation of the conditions of supervision.

Legal decisions discussed in this chapter have challenged these theories.

    As the least democratic of our three branches of government, the judiciary—particularly the federal courts and, especially, the Supreme Court—can decide cases in a manner that may be politically unpopular. It can champion the legal rights of persons who: (1) do not represent a significant block of votes; (2) are not a source of campaign funding; (3) or cannot generate a great deal of media attention and sympathy or public support. Thus in 1966 the Supreme Court rendered the famous *Miranda* decision (*Miranda* v. *Arizona* 384 U.S. 436) which mandated that police suspects be informed of certain rights (to remain silent, to have counsel) prior to any questioning. The following year, in another Arizona case, the Supreme Court rendered the *Gault* decision which gave important rights to juveniles (discussed in Chapter 3). In that same year the *Mempa* decision gave probationers the right to counsel in certain instances of probation violation. The Court continued to show an interest in persons with a "disadvantaged status"—juveniles, probationers, welfare recipients, prison inmates, the mentally ill, parolees—in the many cases that will be discussed in this section and in Chapter 8.

    The basis for these decisions has been the constitutional concern for *due process* contained in Amendments Four through Eight. The Fourteenth

Amendment, which was adopted in 1868 to protect newly freed slaves, applied these amendments to the states: "No state shall make or enforce any law which shall abridge the privileges or immunities of citizens of the United States; nor shall any State deprive any person of life, liberty, or property, without due process of law. . . ." However, the courts did not uniformly apply the Fourteenth Amendment to all constitutional guarantees until 1961. In that year the Supreme Court decided the case of *Mapp* v. *Ohio* (367 U.S. 643). In *Mapp* the Court ruled that evidence (pornographic materials) seized by the police in violation of the Fourth Amendment could not be admitted to evidence in a *state* trial (such evidence was already inadmissible in federal trials). This decision provided a basis for the so-called *exclusionary rule,* which *does not* apply to probation (or parole) violation proceedings — evidence seized by the police in violation of the Fourth Amendment, can generally be used in a probation (or parole) violation hearing.

CONDITIONS OF PROBATION

In general, the courts can impose any conditions of probation that are reasonably related to the rehabilitation of the offender (for example, to undergo treatment for drug addiction) or the protection of community (for example, to avoid the possession of any weapons). The state has a compelling interest in setting limits upon the behavior of probationers and, the Fourth Amendment notwithstanding, probationers enjoy a diminished expectation of privacy. Thus, an offender with a history of drug addiction can be required to submit to periodic urinalysis; as a condition of probation a warrantless search by a probation officer is permitted, although the same search by a police officer would constitute a violation of the Fourth Amendment. Probationers can be required to report in person and to answer all reasonable inquiries by the PO, the Fifth Amendment right to remain silent notwithstanding, although the probationer need not incriminate him- or herself (*Minnesota* v. *Murphy* 104 S. Ct. (1984)). Probationers can be required to avoid bars or "notorious" parts of a city (for example, areas where a great deal of drug trafficking is known to occur).

In 1982 the United States Court of Appeals for the Fifth Circuit reviewed a case involving the First Amendment (*Owens* v. *Kelley* 681 F.2d 1362). The plaintiff (probationer) claimed that a probation condition requiring him to participate in a program called "Emotional Maturity Instruction" violated his First Amendment freedom of religion because of the religious content of the course. The court stated that a

> condition of probation which requires the probationer to adopt religion or to adopt any particular religion would be unconstitutional. . . . It follows that a condition of probation which requires the probationer to submit himself to a

course advocating the adoption of religion or a particular religion also transgresses the First Amendment.

Owens also challenged a probation condition that required him to "submit to and cooperate with a lie detector test . . . whenever so directed by the Probation Supervisor [title of probation officers in Georgia] or any other law enforcement officer." The probationer claimed this condition violated his Fifth Amendment privilege against compelled self-incrimination. The court of appeals rejected this claim:

> The condition on its face does not impinge upon Owens' Fifth Amendment rights. The condition does not stipulate that Owens must answer incriminating questions. If any question is asked during [the lie detector] examination which Owens believes requires an incriminating answer he is free to assert his Fifth Amendment privilege, and nothing in the probation condition suggests otherwise.

PROBATION REVOCATION

In 1967, the Supreme Court ruled (*Mempa* v. *Rhay* 389 U.S. 128) that under certain conditions a probationer is entitled to be represented by counsel at a revocation hearing. In 1959, Jerry Mempa entered a plea of guilty to the charge of "joyriding" in a stolen car in the state of Washington. Imposition of sentence was deferred and Mempa was placed on probation for two years on the condition that he spend thirty days in the county jail. About four months later, the Spokane County prosecutor moved to have Mempa's probation revoked on the ground that he had been involved in a burglary while on probation. Mempa, who was seventeen years old at the time, was not represented by counsel at his revocation hearing, nor was he asked whether he wished to have counsel appointed for him.

At the hearing Mempa was asked if it was true that he had been involved in the alleged burglary, and he answered in the affirmative. A probation officer testified without cross-examination that according to his information Mempa had been involved in the burglary and had previously denied participation in it. Without asking the probationer if he had any evidence to present or any statement to make, Mempa's probation was revoked and he was sentenced to ten years imprisonment. The judge added that he would recommend to the parole board that Mempa be required to serve only one year.

In a companion case considered by the Court, William Earl Walkling was placed on probation (for burglary) with imposition of sentence deferred. At a subsequent revocation hearing, Walkling informed the court that he had retained an attorney. When the attorney did not arrive on time, the court proceeded with the hearing at which a probation officer presented hearsay testimony to the effect that the probationer had committed fourteen separate acts of forgery and grand larceny. The court revoked probation and imposed a sentence of fifteen years. No record was kept of the proceeding. The *Walkling* case was consolidated with the *Mempa* case by the Supreme Court.

The Supreme Court noted that previously it had held that the right to counsel is not confined merely to representation during a trial. The Court stated that counsel is required at *every* stage of a criminal proceeding where substantial rights of an accused criminal may be affected, and sentencing is one of these critical stages. In *Mempa* the Court stated that counsel could aid in marshalling facts, introducing evidence of mitigating circumstances, and in general assist the defendant in presenting his or her case with respect to sentence. The Court ruled that some rights could be lost if counsel were not present at a sentencing hearing and "we decide here that a lawyer must be afforded at this proceeding whether it is labeled a revocation of probation or a deferred sentencing. . . ." The importance of the *Mempa* case goes beyond the limited finding made by the Court—it was the first time that the Supreme Court had ruled in favor of the rights of a person on probation.

In the next important probation/parole case, the Supreme Court stipulated that the amount of due process rights to which a person is constitutionally entitled, is directly related to the potential loss that can result. The greatest amount of potential loss is clearly in a criminal case—total liberty and, at times, life itself—may be forfeited. Thus, the criminal process represents the extreme end of the due process continuum: right to counsel, to remain silent, to a jury trial, to cross examine adverse witnesses. Located somewhere at the other extreme would be the due process rights of a student to challenge a course grade. Where are probation and parole located along this due process continuum?

In 1972, the Supreme Court ruled (in *Morrissey* v. *Brewer,* to be discussed in Chapter 8) that parolees accused of violating the conditions of parole are entitled to certain due process rights, including a preliminary and revocation hearing. In 1973, the Court rendered a similar decision in the case of a probation violation, *Gagnon* v. *Scarpelli* (411 U.S. 778). In 1965, Gerald Scarpelli pleaded guilty to a charge of armed robbery and was sentenced to fifteen years imprisonment, but the sentence was suspended and he was placed on probation for seven years. The probationer was given permission to reside in Illinois (under the Interstate Compact discussed in Chapter 11), where he was placed under the supervision of the Cook County Adult Probation Department. Shortly afterwards, Scarpelli was arrested in a Chicago suburb with a codefendant and charged with burglary. The following month his probation was revoked and Scarpelli was incarcerated in the Wisconsin Reformatory to begin serving the fifteen years to which he had originally been sentenced. At no time was he afforded a hearing; Scarpelli appealed.

Scarpelli was released on parole in Wisconsin, at which time his appeal reached the United States Supreme Court. He claimed that revocation of probation without a hearing and counsel was a denial of due process. The Court ruled:

> Probation revocation, like parole revocation, is not a stage of a criminal prosecution, but does result in a loss of liberty. Accordingly, we hold that a probationer, like a parolee, is entitled to a preliminary and a final revocation hearing under the conditions specified in *Morrissey* v. *Brewer, supra.*

In other words, as noted in a 1982 state of Texas decision (*Rogers* v. *State* 640 S.W.2d 248), liberty on probation, although indeterminate, "includes many of the core values of unqualified liberty, such as freedom to be with family and friends, freedom to form other enduring attachments of normal life, freedom to be gainfully employed, and freedom to function as a responsible and self-reliant person." In *Gagnon* the Supreme Court held that a probationer is entitled to:

1. A notice of the alleged violations;
2. A preliminary hearing to decide if there is sufficient (probable) cause to believe that probation was violated (in order to remand the probationer to custody); and
3. A revocation hearing, which is "a somewhat more comprehensive hearing prior to the making of the final revocation decision." At these hearings, the Court ruled, the probationer will have the opportunity to appear and present witnesses and evidence on his or her own behalf, and a conditional right to confront adverse witnesses.

With respect to the right to counsel, the Court was ambiguous: "We . . . find no justification for a new inflexible constitutional rule with respect to the requirement of counsel. We think, rather, that the decision as to the need for counsel must be made on a case-by-case basis." In practice, however, probationers have been afforded the right to privately-engaged or appointed counsel at probation revocation hearings.

Now that we have completed our examination of the courts and probation, the next section will examine prisons and parole.

REVIEW QUESTIONS

1. What are the variables that can affect the granting of probation?
2. Why, in some jurisdictions, is there a built-in incentive to sentence a defendant to a prison instead of probation?
3. What are the advantages of a sentence of probation?
4. Under what conditions is a sentence of imprisonment to be preferred over a sentence of probation?
5. What are the advantages and shortcomings of requiring restitution as a condition of probation?

6. Why has community service as a condition of probation become very popular?

7. Why would offenders be discharged from probation when their behavior did not justify early termination of supervision?

8. What are the three theories that have formed the basis for imposing restrictions on a probationer's liberty?

9. Why is the judiciary in a better position to guarantee the rights of probationers and parolees (and others) than the other branches of government?

10. What have the courts ruled with respect to conditions of probation?

11. What was the issue decided in the case of *Mempa* v. *Rhay?* What was the real significance of the *Mempa* case?

12. What rights were provided to persons accused of violating probation in the case of *Gagnon* v. *Scarpelli?*

SIX
A History of Prisons and Parole

The degree of civilization in a society is revealed by entering its prisons.
                                    —Dostoevsky, *The House of the Dead*

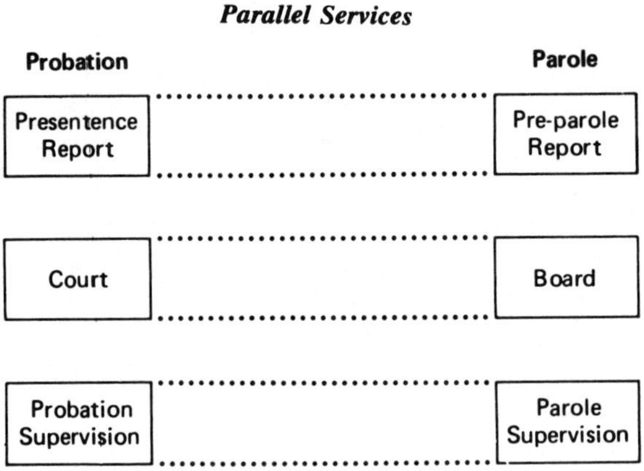

Parallel Services

FIGURE 6.1   Parallel Services

Whom will we find upon entering America's prisons? Almost one-half million persons, 95 percent of whom are male;[1] almost half are black; about 10

---

[1] For a concise and informative examination of the history and contemporary state of women's prisons, see Pollock-Byrne (1990).

percent are Hispanic; more than 60 percent are under thirty years of age; and most have not completed high school. About half grew up primarily in one-parent households and many have been victims of child abuse.[2] About half were unemployed or employed only part-time at the time of their arrest (Zawitz, 1988). In America's prisons are persons who are poorer, darker,[3] younger, and less educated than the rest of the population.

What will we find upon entering America's prisons? In one word: *overcrowding*. More than 675,000 inmates are in a system not capable of managing such a large population in a manner that meets constitutional standards. Conditions were so bad in Alabama, that in 1976 (when it had only about 4,500 inmates) a federal judge placed that state's entire prison system in a receivership that was not relinquished until the end of 1988. In that year Alabama had more than 11,000 inmates, and ten other prison systems were operating under court orders to improve conditions, with at least one major institution in forty additional jurisdictions, including the District of Columbia, Puerto Rico, and the Virgin Islands, under court orders to alleviate overcrowding or other unconstitutional conditions.

In New York from 1976 to 1987 the prison population increased from 20,000 to 40,842. Between 1980 and 1986, New Jersey's prison population increased by 136 percent; Virginia's by 111 percent; and California's by 127 percent. In Illinois in 1989 more than 21,000 inmates inhabited state correctional facilities designed for 16,492; and the state's four maximum-security institutions were 54 percent over the designed capacity. In Connecticut, six of the state's fifteen prisons are under court orders to reduce overcrowding (Malcolm, 1989). In 1985, the state of Texas signed an agreement to end overcrowding in its prison system; Texas had been under federal supervision since a judge ruled that conditions in its prisons violated constitutional guarantees against cruel and unusual punishment. In order to meet constitutional standards, Texas has been granting time off for good behavior at the rate of up to ninety days for every thirty days served.

And none of these states are in the "Top Ten" when it comes to rates of incarceration per 100,000 residents (National Institute of Justice statistics). That dubious honor goes to:

Nevada   −432
Louisiana   −346
South Carolina −344
Alaska   −339

[2]Matthew Zingraff and Michael Belyea (1986) found, however, that inmates who had been victims of child abuse were not more likely to have engaged in crimes of violence than their nonabused counterparts. Child abuse is more heavily concentrated in areas of poverty, the same neighborhoods in which certain types of crime are most prevalent.

[3]This is so even in Hawaii, where the Hawaii Paroling Authority (1987) reports that persons of Hawaiian and part-Hawaiian ancestry are grossly overrepresented in the state's prisons in comparison with the general population.

Delaware	− 327
Alabama	− 307
Arizona	− 307
Oklahoma	− 296
Maryland	− 282
Georgia	− 274

In Michigan the legislature had to enact the "Prison Overcrowding Powers Act of 1983" to allow for the automatic release of inmates as new commitments were received. In Oklahoma whenever the prison population exceeds 95 percent of capacity, inmates who have served at least 15 percent of their sentence and are within one year of their parole consideration date can be released. Legislation to accomplish this was necessary due to the severity of overcrowding — previously the state was simply releasing inmates without benefit of parole supervision. Absconding from this preparole conditional supervision is considered an escape from prison. In Florida, if the prison population reaches 98 percent for a period of seven consecutive days, the Department of Corrections has the authority to release certain inmates that meet established criteria. In Connecticut, a state law mandates the immediate release of 10 percent of the prison population if the number of male prisoners exceeds 110 percent of capacity for thirty consecutive days. In both Florida and Connecticut these inmates are released without supervision (since there is no parole board nor any post-prison supervision of offenders in either state). Connecticut, however, has "reinvented" parole through its supervised home release program in which correction officers are now playing the role normally filled by parole officers (Johnson, 1989b).

And a tremendous increase in the number of prison facilities and expansion of existing facilities during the last few years — in excess of 30,000 beds — has not had a significant impact. At any one time there are between ten and twenty thousand inmates being housed in local jails because of a lack of prison space. Many jails are also under court order to reduce overcrowding, and the federal prison system is operating at 162 percent capacity. In 1988, 130 facilities or additions were under construction at a cost of more than $2.5 billion (Durham, 1989b).

The United States has the "distinction" of being third when it comes to incarcerating citizenry; only the Soviet Union and South Africa imprison a higher percentage of their populations. How did we reach this crisis? The historical review in Chapters 6 and 7 is designed to help answer this question.

ORIGINS OF THE AMERICAN SYSTEM OF PRISONS

The American colonies inherited an English approach to crime and punishment, and the English system of laws into the eighteenth century impresses one with the extent to which the death penalty was used, often for seemingly minor offenses. Jerome Hall states: "Thus it was believed that Henry VIII [1491-1457] executed 72,000 thieves and vagabonds during his reign"; and under George III (1738-1820) as many as 220 offenses were punishable by death (1952: 116). Robert Lilly and Richard Ball (1987) state that by 1780 there were 350 capital crimes, most of which were for property offenses. (In practice, however, there was extensive use of pardons and the dismissal of indictments for technical reasons (Kelman, 1987).) At the same time, England established institutional approaches to the old and the infirm, vagrants, beggars, homeless children, as well as certain criminals: gaols, bridewells, and houses of correction. Local jails emerged throughout the American colonies usually under management of a sheriff. These poorly constructed institutions, David Rothman notes, "were not only unlikely places for intimidating the criminal, but even ill-suited for confining him"—escapes were frequent (1971: 56).

Dramatically different conditions in England and the colonies resulted in differing needs, and this impacted on the response to criminals. In England land was scarce and an excess labor supply had the potential for political and social unrest. "As a matter of policy," notes Bradley Chapin, "it must have seemed that no great harm was done if the hangman thinned the horde of vagrant Englishmen. In the colonies, the need for labor urged the use of penalties that might bring redemption" (1983: 9). Consequently, beginning with William Penn in 1682 (Melossi and Pavarini, 1981), the use of capital punishment in the American colonies was severely restricted and virtually banned for property crimes.

In Pennsylvania, however, the Quakers were in an economic bind: because British law was so severe, colonial juries would often find defendants not guilty rather than subject them to the extreme punishments in place for property offenses. "In this way, criminals had escaped all discipline, and the community had allowed, even encouraged, them to persist in their ways" (Rothman, 1971: 60). And it was Quaker property that was often at risk in Philadelphia where their Calvinist urgings—honesty, thrift, and hard work—resulted in economic success as a rising commercial class. (For the relationship between Calvinism and economic success, see Weber, 1958.) The use of imprisonment provided a way to mete out punishment in a manner that was proportionate to the severity of the offense and appealed to both the humanitarian and economic concerns of the Quakers.

Three intertwined developments led to the establishment of the American system of prisons: Calvinism, the American Revolution, and the classical school: Thorsten Sellin states, "The credit for the gradual substitution of imprisonment for corporal and capital punishments must go to the philosophers of the 18th century" (1967: 19). Following the revolution, a repugnance for things British inspired Americans to discard corporal punishment in favor of imprisonment, a process that was complete at about the time of the Civil War. The type of imprisonment that resulted had its origins in Calvinist socio-religious doctrine, which can be seen in the life of John Howard (1726-1790), and the work of Quaker reformers in Philadelphia and New York; Howard coined the term *penitentiary* as a place to do penance (Teeters, 1970).

Walnut Street and Other Early Prisons

The first prison in the United States was authorized by the Connecticut legislature in 1773, and that same year the colony converted an abandoned copper mine into a prison for serious offenders (Durham, 1989c). Newgate (not to be confused with a New York prison by the same name) consisted of a wood lodging house for communal habitation built about twenty feet below the surface. The first keeper, a retired military officer, lived across the road, and there was a lack of security personnel. Within three weeks of receiving its first prisoner, he managed to escape, and escapes continued to plague New-gate. As opposed to early prisons established elsewhere, there was an absence of any reformative or rehabilitative agenda, and it was expected that the prison would be self-supporting. In the early days of the prison, miners were hired to provide inmate instruction, but mining failed to achieve a profit. Other trades were initiated, but they too failed to achieve any level of economic success. The Revolutionary War and a rash of violent incidents led to the closing of Newgate in 1782; it reopened in 1790 as a Connecticut state prison (Durham, 1989c).

In Philadelphia, by 1762 Quaker reformers were successful in having the list of capital offenses limited and substituting fines and imprisonment for torture and execution for many offenses; and in 1786 the Pennsylvania legislature enacted penal reform to replace capital punishment for certain crimes. The law called for convicted felons who were lodged in the Walnut Street Jail to be subjected to hard labor "publicly and disgracefully imposed . . . in streets of cities and towns, and upon the highways of the open country and other public works" (Atherton, 1987: 1). With shaved heads, bizarre dress, and wearing balls and chains riveted to their ankles, the convicts working in the streets drew the ridicule and abuse of passing crowds—the work was both onerous and humiliating. However, Paul Takagi (1975) states that convicts working in the city streets drew large crowds of sympathetic people, including friends and relatives of the prisoners. They made contact and, at times, liquor and other goods were given to the convicts. In any event, at the urging of Benjamin Rush, the Philadelphia Society for Alleviating the Miseries of the Public Prisons (later renamed the Philadelphia Prison Society and then the Pennsylvania Prison Society) was formed at the home of Benjamin Franklin in 1787. In 1789 the society succeeded in having the 1786 law repealed.

John Howard, the son of a Calvinist merchant, was born in England in 1726. His interest in penal reform led him to publish *The State of the Prisons* a year after the American Declaration of Independence. Working out of a strong religious commitment, Howard influenced other religiously endowed reformers, Quakers of the Philadelphia Society for Alleviating the Miseries of the Public Prisons, with whom he was in contact. As a result, in 1790 a law was enacted creating a penitentiary in a portion of the Walnut Street Jail (Atherton, 1987); the Walnut Street Jail became a state prison based on a Calvinist model of hard labor and religious study. Takagi (1975) argues, however, that it was the Episcopalians of the Philadelphia Society who argued for hard labor, while solitary confinement was stressed by the Quakers.

At Walnut Street most inmates were confined in separate cells and released to work in a courtyard during the day at a variety of tasks: handicrafts such as weaving and shoemaking, and routine labor such as beating hemp and sawing logwood, all in total silence. The "hardened and atrocious offenders," persons who formerly would have been whipped, mutilated, or executed, were confined in isolation and almost total darkness with nothing but a Bible: "The old Quakers, sensitive as they were to the inflicting of bodily pain, seem to have been unable to form in their minds an image of the fearful mental torture of solitude in idleness" (Wines, 1975: 152). These convicts were blindfolded upon arrival and remained in their cells until released; they never saw another inmate. Inspectors from the Prison Society provided oversight at Walnut Street, and had the authority to hire and fire penitentiary officials.

Solitary confinement was seen as a way of preventing fraternization between prisoners, behavior that would only lead to the spread of evil inclinations among inmates. Gustave de Beaumont and Alexis de Tocqueville, who visited the United States in 1831 to research the American prison system, reported:

> If it is true that in establishments of this nature, all evil originates from the intercourse of the prisoners among themselves, we are obliged to acknowledge that nowhere is this vice avoided with greater safety than at Philadelphia, where the prisoners find themselves utterly unable to communicate with each other; and it is incontestable that this perfect isolation secures the prison from all fatal contamination. (1964: 57)

Michael Ignatieff notes that John Howard and the Quakers shared a common religious lifestyle that led them to favor imprisonment as a form of purgatory, "a forced withdrawal from the distractions of the senses into silent and solitary confrontation with the self" (1978: 58). It was out of solitude and silence that the convict "would begin to hear the inner voice of conscience and feel the transforming of God's love" (1978: 58). News of the "success" of Walnut Street attracted many persons from other states and countries. One of these visitors was a Quaker from New York, Thomas Eddy (1758–1827), who had been briefly imprisoned as a Tory during the Revolutionary War.

Eddy was influenced by what he saw in Philadelphia, and as a result of his efforts New York constructed its first penitentiary in Greenwich Village. Newgate was named after the famous British prison, and Eddy became its first agent. Consistent with the prevailing belief of prison reformers, Eddy maintained that the goal of deterrence required inflicting pain on criminal offenders

(Lewis, 1965). However, he discarded the idea that it was necessary to keep inmates in solitary all day and, instead, convicts slept in congregate rooms measuring twelve feet by eighteen feet and housing eight inmates. There were also fourteen cells for solitary confinement which were used as punishment for violating prison rules. Eddy encouraged religious worship, established a night school, and approved of provisions in the law that prohibited corporal punishment at Newgate. Despite improvements in treatment at the prison, in 1802 there was a bloody riot and a mass-escape attempt that required calling in the military. In response to these developments, Eddy recommended that future penitentiaries utilize single cells for all inmates at night, and shops where they could work in strict silence during the day. His suggestions were incorporated into a new prison that was built in Auburn, New York.

Eddy was eventually removed because of political considerations (Lewis, 1965) or resigned in protest when, in 1803, the state turned the prison industries over to a private contractor (McKelvey, 1972). In either event, difficulties increased at Newgate, and a return to flogging was legislated in 1819 (Lewis, 1965). In 1828, the penitentiary was abandoned in favor of a newly completed prison at Sing Sing (Department of Correctional Services, 1970). In Philadelphia, overcrowding caused the demise of Walnut Street; industry and isolation became unworkable in the congested prison; discipline lapsed and riots ensued (McKelvey, 1972).

> While the original inspectors were still active in the oversight of the prison, thus preventing rampant corruption of guards and overseers, there was little they could do to prevent the decline of the conditions of the jail. The funds needed to create a system of solitary confinement were simply greater than had been anticipated. (Dumm, 1987: 105)

Pennsylvania After Walnut Street

The Pennsylvania Prison Society succeeded in having prisons built at Pittsburgh (Western State Penitentiary opened in 1826) and (Cherry Hill) Philadelphia (Eastern State Penitentiary opened in 1829). These institutions featured massive stone walls around a building that branched out from a central rotunda like the spokes of a wheel—architecture influenced by the *Panopticon* penitentiary advanced by the British classical philosopher Jeremy Bentham (1748–1832). The design prevented prisoner contact, and inmates remained in their cells except for one hour of exercise in a yard also designed to prevent inmate contact. The Pennsylvania system

> isolated each prisoner for the entire period of his confinement. According to its blueprint, convicts were to eat, work, and sleep in individual cells, seeing and talking with only a handful of responsible guards and selected visitors. They were to leave the institution as ignorant of the identity of other convicts as on the day they entered. (Rothman, 1971: 82)

The guiding principles were punishment and reformation through penitence:

> The convicted prisoner was to be kept totally separated from other prisoners, but not from human contact. The avenue to reform was through repentance—the true and deep recognition of one's "sins" and acceptance of God's leadership in one's life. It was obvious that prisoners left totally alone would be unable to follow this path; for this, guidance was needed, good examples, people who could help the convict accept responsibility for his/her crimes and embark on the difficult path of repentance and redemption. (Atherton, 1987: 7)

Guidance and role models were provided by four groups of people who visited prisoners: prison staff, chaplains, officials of the Prison Society, and the Board of Inspectors.

The Pennsylvania system proved quite expensive—the cost of constructing an institution for solitary confinement was staggering, and there could be little profitable exploitation of inmate labor under such conditions (McKelvey, 1972). And at the beginning of the nineteenth century, the need for labor was increasing: new legislation made slave trading more difficult, new territories were settled, and there was rapid industrialization with a corresponding increase in wages. Prisons with solitary confinement deprived the market of needed labor (Melossi and Pavarini, 1981). As a result, most states patterned their prisons after the next great milestone in American prison history, an institution suggested by Thomas Eddy, which became the world's most frequently copied prison. Beginning in the 1860s, the isolation of prisoners at Eastern State Penitentiary began to break down, and inmates began sharing cells. "In 1913 the system, which had become so diluted as to be unrecognizable, was officially abolished and from then on, it became just another Auburn-type prison" (Teeters, 1970: 11).

Auburn Prison

Auburn Prison opened in 1819 and, as designed by its first agent, William Brittin, featured a center that was comprised of tiers of cellblocks surrounded by a vacant area—the yard—with a high wall encircling the entire institution. Each cell measured 7 by 3.5 feet and was 7 feet high.

> It was designed for separation by night only; the convicts were employed during the day in large workshops, in which, under the superintendency of Elam Lynds, formerly a captain in the army, the rule of absolute silence was enforced with unflinching sternness. Captain Lynds said that he regarded flogging as the most effective, and at the same time the most humane, of all punishments, since it did no injury to the prisoner's health and in no wise impaired his physical strength; he did not believe that a large prison could be governed without it. (Wines, 1975: 154)

Instead of replacing corporal punishment with imprisonment, as was advocated by the religious reformers, the practice of flogging became widespread in the penitentiary system—criminals were punished with imprisonment, and prisoners were punished with flogging and other forms of corporal punishment. And there were no written regulations governing the use of the whip; guards were simply authorized to impose flogging when "absolutely necessary."

Auburn divided its inmates into three classes. The most difficult inmates were placed in solitary; a less dangerous group spent part of the day in solitude and worked the rest of the time in groups; the "least guilty" worked together throughout the day and were separated only at night when they returned to their individual cells. As in Walnut Street, solitary confinement played havoc on the psyche—inmates jumped off tiers, cut their veins, smashed their heads against walls. Solitary confinement in Auburn was discontinued except as punishment for violations of prison rules (Lewis, 1965).

> New Yorkers felt that the complete isolation of prisoners from arrival to release was too inhumane; it was both unnatural and cruel. Far from reforming men, they felt such absolute solitude resulted in insanity and despair. In addition, there was the issue, perhaps more pressing, of expense to the state. Inmates restricted to their cells 24 hours a day contributed nothing to the cost of their own confinement. The state had to provide all food, clothing, supplies, and materials to its prisoners.
>
> If the prisoners were to learn the advantages and satisfactions of hard work and thrift, New York authorities believed, there could be no better way than to be compelled to work together in harmony. If such a system also offered the potential for inmates to grow and harvest their own vegetables, raise and butcher their own meat, make their own clothes, and manufacture other items for use or sale by the state, such a boon to the state's budget could not be reasonably ignored (New York State Special Commission on Attica, 1972: 8; hereafter, Attica Commission).

Under the system developed by Lynds, who became warden when William Brittin died in 1821, prisoners worked in small, strictly supervised units in workshops and out-of-doors during the daytime, and returned to individual cells at night. They dressed in grotesque and ridiculous-looking black and white striped uniforms and caps; they marched in complete silence, worked in complete silence, and ate in complete silence. "A breach of this rule was punished by flogging. Discipline was extremely strict in all other respects. Inmates were required to keep their eyes downcast when walking" (Eriksson, 1976: 50). Auburn developed the infamous lockstep shuffle: inmates stood in line with the right foot slightly behind the left and the right arm outstretched with the hand on the right shoulder of the man in front of him; they moved together in a shuffle, sliding the left foot forward, then bringing the right foot to its position just behind the left, then the left again, then the right. Free citizens were encouraged to visit the prison where for a small fee they could view the inmates, an act that was designed to cause further degradation.

Beaumont and Tocqueville reported on their visit to Auburn where

> nothing is heard in the whole prison but the steps of those who march, or the sounds proceeding from the workshops. But when the day is finished, and the prisoners have retired to their cells, the silence within these vast walls, which contain so many prisoners, is like that of death. We have often trod during night those monotonous and dumb galleries, where a lamp is always burning: we felt as if we traversed catacombs; there were a thousand living beings, and yet it was a desert solitude. (1964: 65)

The administrators of Auburn believed that their most important task was the breaking of an inmates's spirit in order to drive him into a state of submission. There was some difference of opinion about what to do after the "breaking" process. One school of thought stressed deterrence as its goal and was determined to derive as much economic benefit from inmate labor as possible. In fact, in the early years, Auburn actually made a net profit for the state. Another school of thought held that rehabilitation was the ultimate goal and that, after breaking, inmates should be helped through education and religion so that they could return to society better persons (Lewis, 1965).

The Auburn system consisted of an unrelenting routine of silence, hard labor, moderate meals, and solitary evenings in individual cells six days a week: "Their labor is not interrupted until the hour of taking food. There is not a single instant given to recreation" (Beaumont and Tocqueville, 1964: 65). On Sundays, when there was no work, inmates attended church — in silence — where they were addressed by the prison chaplain who stressed the American virtues of simple faith and hard work (Attica Commission, 1972). The Auburn-style prison became the prototype for American prisons; it was cheaper to construct than those of Pennsylvania, and allowed for a factory system that could make profitable use of inmate labor. The concept of reformation gradually declined and by the end of the nineteenth century rehabilitation had virtually disappeared — prisons were viewed simply as places to keep criminals incarcerated as cheaply as possible. This was reflected even in the name of the warden's first assistant, the "principal keeper" (Attica Commission, 1972). Prisons became bleak and silent factories with labor pools of broken people.

Convict Labor

Sellin notes that imprisonment has its roots in penal servitude:

> The prisons operated on the Auburn plan, in particular, were, most of them, notorious for the maltreatment of prisoners and for the excessive labor required of them in an attempt to meet the demand of legislators that prisons be self-supporting and even show a profit if possible. (1967: 21)

The use of convict labor often made American prisons not only self-supporting institutions, but also profit-making enterprises throughout the nineteenth and well into the twentieth century. Auburn Penitentiary balanced its books in 1829, and produced a profit of $1,800 in 1831, and Sing Sing netted $29,000 in 1835 (Melossi and Pavarini, 1981). In Alabama, prison labor netted the state profits of almost $1 million annually, and just one prison industry manufacturing shirts in Florida netted that state almost $150,000 annually (Gillin, 1931). Minnesota's Stillwater Prison netted $25,000 annually as late as 1930, and served as a model for other northern prisons (Hagerty, 1934). In 1964, the Arkansas state penitentiary showed a net profit of nearly half a million dollars—it also gave rise to the scandalous conditions uncovered at the Tucker Prison Farm which were portrayed in the motion picture *Brubaker*. However, prison industries also prevented the forced idleness that plagues many contemporary correctional institutions and helped maintain discipline.

There were three systems used to exploit convict labor:

1. *Contract system.* Convict labor was sold to private entrepreneurs who provided the necessary machinery, tools, raw materials and, in some cases, the supervisory staff. In many cases the prison was built as a factory with walls around it. "As late as 1919 a committee of the American Prison Association reported, after a national survey, that most prisons worked their prisoners in a manner reminiscent of the early forms of penal servitude and that reformation was an empty word" (Sellin, 1967: 21).

2. *Lease system.* Prisoners were leased out to private business interests for a fixed fee. This system was used extensively in agriculture and mining, particularly in the South. In Florida, for example, in 1877 the state "transferred the control and custody of prisoners to private contractors who could now employ them anywhere in the State. Prisoners were leased to individuals and corporations and set to work in phosphate mines and in turpentine camps in the forests" (Sellin, 1967: 22).

3. *State-use system.* Prison inmates produce goods for use or sale by state agencies, for example, office furniture and license plates. Other than that necessary for prison maintenance, this is the most frequent form of prison labor in use today.

By 1874 the contract system was used in twenty state prisons, the lease system in six, and a mixed system in seven (Mohler, 1925). For wardens of the convict labor era, notes Alexis Durham, the ability to turn a profit was the determining factor in whether he kept his job: "The nineteenth century's most famous wardens first gained recognition because of their fiscal success: (1989: 127). Wardens unable to run self-sufficient institutions were replaced by legislators forced to appropriate funds to maintain the prison.

During the latter part of the nineteenth and into the twentieth century there were numerous scandals involving the use of inmate labor. The growing labor union movement in the United States saw inmate labor undermining employee leverage for increased wages and improvements in working conditions. At times, inmate labor was leased out to break strikes. The National Anti-Contract Association, a manufacturers group whose members suffered from having to compete with goods produced by cheap convict labor, campaigned against the contract system. These activities resulted in laws curbing convict labor in several industrial states: Massachusetts, New York, and Pennsylvania; the federal government enacted legislation in 1887 that forbid the contracting of any federal prisoners (McKelvey, 1977).

In the states of the Confederacy the lease system continued to be widespread into the twentieth century, when southern states slowly began to abolish the practice, the last to do so being Alabama in 1928 (Sellin, 1967). The contract system remained widespread until the Great Depression and the passage of the Hawes-Cooper Act in 1929 and the Ashurst-Sumners Act in 1935. These federal statutes eventually curtailed the interstate commerce in goods produced with convict labor, and their constitutionality was upheld by the Supreme Court in 1936 (*Whitfield* v. *Ohio* 297 U.S. 439).

The curtailing of convict labor had two long-ranging effects:

1. It increased the cost of imprisonment and, thus, encouraged the development of parole; and
2. It forced prison officials to find other ways to deal with prison idleness. As a result, many prisons initiated programs to train and educate their inmates.

In 1979 Congress enacted the Percy Amendment, which removed the blanket federal restrictions on the sale of prisoner-made goods in interstate commerce. Instead, the amendment sets forth minimum conditions under which such sales can take place, including consultation with labor unions, the need to avoid impacting on local industries, and a requirement that inmates be paid the prevailing local wage for work of a similar nature. The law also permits the establishment of pilot projects utilizing prison labor by private enterprise. By 1987 there were thirty-eight such projects employing over 1,000 inmates (Auerbach, et al., 1988).

In response to prison overcrowding and prison construction costs, some states now utilize inmate labor to build correctional facilities. These states are typically those where organized labor is relatively weak, such as South Carolina where inmates have been constructing new correctional facilities, and expanding and renovating existing facilities. "With the exception of installing locks and ordering supplies, inmates work in all phases of construction in the field and in the office" (Carter and Humphries, 1987: 3). An audit of inmate construction projects revealed that they took twice as long to build, but labor costs were 50 percent less than private contracting. And inmates received valuable training and work experience. Inmates are volunteers from medium and minimum security institutions; they are paid thirty-five cents an hour and become eligible for salary increases and bonuses. They also receive additional days off their sentences depending on their level of skill; this serves as an incentive for them to improve their skills through available training programs. Unsatisfactory performance or rule violations result in being dropped from the program. In other states inmates are not paid, but receive time off their sentences while learning employment skills. Inmate-worker turnover and the need to take counts of inmates several times a day, reduce the efficiency of these construction projects.

The state of California utilizes more than three thousand inmates in its Conservation Camp Program. In thirty-eight conservation camps run by the Department of Corrections in cooperation with the Department of Forestry and Fire Protection, inmates fight fires that periodically threaten the state's forests. They also clear streams, plant trees, and do flood control work and other community service projects. The inmates are carefully screened volunteers; those with histories of violent crimes, sex offenses, arson, or escape are excluded. The inmates receive two weeks of training and are paid $1.45 to $3.90 a day, and $1.00 an hour during firefighting assignments.

The "Big House"

The construction of Auburn-type prisons ceased with the onset of the depression in 1929; in its place emerged what John Irwin (1980) refers to as the "Big House." Architecturally it is an Auburn-style prison: one or two-man cells clustered in cellblocks on tiers surrounded by a high stone wall with guard towers, and often holding in excess of two thousand inmates. Unlike Auburn, however, silence, hard labor, the lockstep shuffle, and official use of corporal punishment were absent. The cells had toilets and sinks, were ventilated and heated, and had more space than the typical Auburn cell. In the Big House inmates were frequently permitted to furnish and decorate their own cells. The better equipped institutions had recreational facilities, baseball diamonds, basketball and handball courts. Many prisoners were black, but in most Big Houses outside of the South, the inmates were mostly white. There was a great deal of idleness and an absence of rehabilitative programming.

Scholarly studies of the prison environment, such as the one by Donald Clemmer (1958) during the 1930s, reported a phenomenon which became known as *prisonization* and the existence of an *inmate subculture*. Prisonization refers to the process by which an inmate is socialized into the prison environment. Although they may arrive with varied backgrounds, prisoners share a common suspicion and fear of other inmates and guards. In response, they tend to align themselves into cliques which serve to counter, if not subvert, the power of prison officials. These cliques form the basis of a prison subculture that emerged in the less rigid environment of the Big House. This subculture developed and enforced its own rules. A number of contemporary scholars argue, however, that the subculture found in the Big House by earlier researchers did not develop in prison, but was actually brought into the Big House by inmates who shared a common subcultural orientation. In either event, the guards faced a terrifying problem.

Big House guards were vastly outnumbered by inmates who were organized into cliques and who formed a distinct subculture in opposition to the prison administration. While prison officials could rely on help from outside forces, the state police and National Guard, there was insufficient coercive force immediately available for them to be routinely in effective control of the institution. Corporal punishment was no longer (officially) permitted, and loss of "good time" (time off for "good behavior") or solitary confinement often proved ineffective in controlling behavior in the volatile atmosphere of a prison. As a result, Irwin (1980) states, guards developed effective informal control strategies involving personal agreements and corrupt favoritism:

(a) *Personal agreements* between guards and inmates were implicit or tacit exchange relationships in which an inmate would refrain from rule-violative behavior in return for some favor or special consideration from a guard.

(b) *Corrupt favoritism* involved guards who granted special privileges to key prisoners who served as inmate leaders, in return for their support in maintaining order.

The Big House inmate leaders helped to maintain order:

1. By keeping their own violations within acceptable limits, and by supporting the prevailing prison norm which required inmates to "do your own time"; that is, mind your own business and "don't make no waves" (which encouraged conformity); and

2. By threatening or actually using violence against prisoners who disrupted the prison routine and thereby endangered the privileged inmates' special arrangements with the guards.

After World War II, a changing philosophy led to the widespread use of the indeterminate sentence, parole release, and the replacement of the Big House with the "correctional institution," the subjects of Chapter 7.

ORIGINS OF THE AMERICAN SYSTEM OF PAROLE

Parole, from the French *parol,* referring to "word of honor," was a means of releasing prisoners of war who promised not to resume arms in a current conflict. Modern parole, the conditional release of convicts prior to the expiration of their sentence, has a number of antecedents.

Transportation to America

In colonial America early in the seventeenth century, a shortage of labor led to the transporting of children—the indentured poor and delinquents—and the pardoning of criminals from England. In the beginning no specific conditions were imposed upon those who received these pardons. However, after a number of those pardoned evaded transportation or returned to England prior to the expiration of their term, it was found necessary to impose certain restrictions. Around 1655 the form of pardons was amended to include specific conditions and provide for the nullification of the pardon if the recipient failed to abide by the conditions imposed.

During the early days of transportation, the government paid a fee to contractors for each prisoner transported. Subsequently, this was changed and the contractor was given "property in service"—custody of the prisoner until the expiration of his full term. Once prisoners were delivered to the contractor, the government took no further interest in their welfare or behavior unless they violated the conditions of the pardon by returning to England prior to the expiration of their sentences.

Upon the arrival of pardoned felons in the colonies, their services were sold to the highest bidder. The contractor then transferred the "property in service" agreement to the new master and the felon was no longer referred to as a criminal but became an *indentured servant*. These indentures bear a similarity to the procedure now followed by parole boards. Like the criminal *qua* indentured servant, a prisoner released on parole agrees in writing to accept certain conditions. A release form is signed by the prisoner and the parole board, and some of the conditions imposed today on parolees are similar to those included on the indenture agreement (*Parole Officer's Manual,* 1953). The termination of the Revolutionary War ended transportation to America, and England then sent her convicts to Australia until 1879 (Hughes, 1987).

Maconochie and Norfolk Island

Torsten Eriksson refers to the year 1840 as one in which "one of the most remarkable experiments in the history of penology was initiated" (1976: 81). In that year, Alexander Maconochie (1787–1860) became superintendent of the British penal colony on Norfolk Island, about 930 miles northeast of Sidney, Australia. He set out a philosophy of punishment based on reforming the individual criminal: the convict was to be punished for the past and trained for the future. Since the amount of time needed to instill self-discipline and train a criminal could not be estimated in advance of sentencing, Maconochie advocated sentences that were open-ended, what is known today as an *indeterminate sentence*. He set up a system of *marks* to be earned by each inmate based on good behavior; a sentence could not be terminated until a certain amount of marks had been achieved.

Norfolk housed the most dangerous felons, and riots occurred both before Maconochie's arrival and after he left the island. His system, however, brought tranquility to the colony. Convicts passed through three stages on the way to release, each with an increasing amount of personal liberty; misbehavior moved an offender back to an earlier stage. Although Maconochie's experiment at Norfolk was successful from the standpoint of penology, it was opposed by authorities back in Australia who viewed it as "coddling criminals," while also incurring extra costs on the government. Maconochie was relieved of his position in 1844 and returned to England where he campaigned for penal reforms as a writer and speaker. One of those he influenced was Walter Crofton.

Crofton and the Irish System

In 1853, Parliament enacted the "Penal Servitude Act" which enabled prisoners to be released — paroled — on a *Ticket of Leave* and supervised by the police. That same year, Sir Walter Crofton (1815–97) was commissioned to investigate conditions in Irish prisons, and in 1854 became director of the Irish prison system. Crofton was familiar with the work of Alexander Maconochie, and their views on the reformation of criminals were similar. The *Irish System* that Crofton established was based on Maconochie's work at Norfolk Island, and consisted of four stages:

1. The first stage involved solitary confinement for nine months; during the first three months the inmate was on reduced rations and was allowed no labor whatsoever. It was reasoned that after three months of forced idleness, even the laziest prisoner would long for something to do. He would then be given full rations, instructed in useful skills, and exposed to religious influences.

2. In the second stage, the convict was placed in a special prison to work with other inmates, during which time he could earn marks to qualify for a transfer to the third stage.

3. Stage three involved transportation to an open institution where the convict, by evidencing signs of reformation, could earn release on a Ticket of Leave.

4. Ticket of Leave men were conditionally released and, in rural districts, supervised by the police; those residing in Dublin, however, were supervised by a civilian employee who had the title of Inspector of Released Prisoners. He worked cooperatively with the police, but it was his responsibility to secure employment for Ticket of Leave men. He required them to report at stated intervals, visited their homes every two weeks, and verified their employment — he was the forerunner of a modern parole officer.

Developments in the United States

A modified version of the Irish System was adopted in England, and Crofton's work was widely publicized in the United States. American supporters of the Irish System, however, did not believe that the adoption of the

Ticket of Leave would ever be accepted in the United States. Their attitude was apparently based on the belief that it would be un-American to place any individual under the supervision of the police, and they did not believe that any other form of supervision would be effective. A letter written by Crofton in 1874, in reply to an inquiry sent to him by the secretary of the New York Prison Association, stressed that the police of Ireland were permitted to delegate competent individuals in the community to act as custodians for Ticket of Leave men, and he suggested a similar system for the United States (*Parole Officer's Manual,* 1953). These principles were first implemented in the Elmira Reformatory.

Elmira Reformatory   In 1869 a reformatory was authorized for Elmira, New York to receive male offenders between the ages of sixteen and thirty. The following year, the first convention of the American Prison Association met in Cincinnati. A paper based on the Irish System and dealing with the idea of an indeterminate sentence and the possibilities of a system of parole, was presented by the noted Michigan penologist, Zebulon R. Brockway. The prison reformers meeting in Cincinnati urged New York to adopt Brockway's proposal at Elmira. When the Elmira Reformatory opened in 1876, Brockway was appointed superintendent.

Brockway drafted a statute directing the sending of young first offenders to Elmira under an indeterminate sentence not to exceed the maximum term which was already in place for nonreformatory offenders. The actual release date was set by the Board of Managers based on institutional behavior: "After the inmate accumulated a certain number of marks based on institutional conduct and progress in academic or vocational training, and if the investigation of his assurance of employment was positive, he could be released" (Division of Parole, 1984: 6).

Frederick Wines, a colleague of Brockway, described the principles on which the Elmira system was based, a clear manifestation of the positive school:

> . . . criminals can be reformed; that reformation is the right of the convict and the duty of the State; that every prisoner must be individualized and given special treatment adapted to develop him to the point in which he is weak — physical, intellectual, or moral culture, in combination, but in varying proportions, according to the diagnosis of each case; that time must be given for the reformatory process to take effect, before allowing him to be sent away, uncured; that his cure is always facilitated by his cooperation, and often impossible without it. (1975: 230)

Cooperation was fostered by corporal punishment and the use of inmate classifications, according to which privileges were dispensed. Behavior judged to be "reformative" was rewarded by reclassification which meant increased privileges, eventually leading to release on parole. Upon being admitted to

Elmira each inmate was placed in the second grade (of classification). Six months of good conduct meant promotion to the first grade—misbehavior could result in being placed in the third grade from which the inmate would have to work his way back up. Continued good behavior in the first grade resulted in release—America's first parole system.

Paroled inmates remained under the jurisdiction of reformatory authorities for an additional six months, during which the parolee was required to report on the first day of every month to his appointed guardian (from which parole officers evolved) and provide an account of his situation and conduct. It was believed that a longer period under supervision would be discouraging to the average parolee. "Inmates were released conditionally, subject to return if the Board believed there was actual or potential reversion to criminal behavior" (Division of Parole, 1984: 6).

However, there was no real attention given to the training of prisoners toward their future adjustment in the community, and both prison administrators and inmates soon accepted the idea that reformed or unreformed, allowance of time for good behavior was automatic and release at the earliest possible date was a right rather than a privilege. After release, supervision was either nonexistent or totally inadequate.

The Elmira system was copied by reformatories in other states such as the Massachusetts Reformatory at Concord, and made applicable to all or part of the prison population in states such as Pennsylvania, Michigan, and Illinois (Wines, 1975). Ohio and California had parole release statutes in place before the turn of the twentieth century (Zevitz and Takata, 1988). In 1907, New York extended indeterminate sentencing and parole release to all first offenders except those convicted of murder. Margaret Cahalan (1986) reports that by 1922, parole was used in forty-four states, and by 1939 only three states (Florida, Mississippi, and Virginia) did not have provisions for parole. (According to the South Carolina Parole board, however, that state did not begin to use parole until 1941.) The great impetus for the expansion of the use of parole release, however, had to wait until the Great Depression, as these statistics for parole release indicate (Cahalan, 1986):

1923—21,632
1926—19,917
1930—29,509
1936—37,794

The Great Depression, which began in 1929 and ended only with the onset of World War II, resulted in large numbers of unemployed workers and led to legislation which effectively abolished the economic exploitation of convict labor. This was accompanied by the prohibitive cost of constructing prisons, prison overcrowding, and an outbreak of prison riots. A 1931 report (National Commission on Law Observance and Law Enforcement) described the overcrowding of America's prisons as "incredible"; Michigan, for example, had 78.6 percent more inmates than its original capacity; California, 62.2 percent; Ohio, 54.1 percent; and Oklahoma 56.7 percent. In 1923 there were 81,959 prison inmates (74 per 100,000 population); in 1930 there were 120,496 (98 per 100,000 population); on the eve of World War II, 1940, there were 165,585 (125 per 100,000 population) (Cahalan, 1986). Pressing economic conditions, and not the press of prison reform, led to the popularity of parole release: by 1935 there were more than sixty thousand persons on parole in the United States, although only six states had what was described as "suitable" parole systems (Prison Association of New York, 1936).

In the next chapter we will look at prison—nee correctional institutions—and parole in the decades following World War II.

REVIEW QUESTIONS

1. How does the prison population differ from the rest of the population in the United States?
2. Why were colonial juries often unwilling to find defendants guilty?
3. What were the three intertwined developments that led to the establishment of the American system of prisons?
4. What was the Quaker approach to punishment?
5. What led to the demise of the Walnut Street Jail?
6. What are the characteristics of the Pennsylvania system?
7. Why did most states pattern themselves after the Auburn, rather than Pennsylvania, system?
8. What are the characteristics of the Auburn System?
9. What are the three categories of convict labor?
10. What factors led to the demise of most forms of convict labor?
11. What were the long-range effects of the curtailing of convict labor?
12. What is meant by a "Big House" prison?
13. What is meant by prisonization and inmate subcultures?
14. How did guards maintain control of the Big House despite being vastly outnumbered by inmates?
15. What is the connection between the system employed by Alexander Maconochie at Norfolk Island and the indeterminate sentence?
16. What was the Irish System established by Walter Crofton?
17. What is meant by the Elmira system?
18. What conditions led to the popularity of parole release in the United States?

SEVEN
Corrections and the Indeterminate Sentence

War, despite its ravaging consequences, can also provide the impetus for many long-lasting social and scientific advances: an end to unemployment, improvements in manufacturing, communication, transportation, and medicine. During World War II we experienced such important developments as the jet plane and the rocket, streptomycin, radar, sonar, and atomic energy. By the end of the war the horizons of science appeared to be unlimited, and the influence of the positive school and positivism reemerged in penology.

CORRECTIONAL INSTITUTIONS

The great faith in science was occurring during a period of concern over the apparent rise in (statistical) crime. The war had kept the wheels of industry spinning; unemployment did not exist. Suddenly, wartime production had ceased and millions of young men who had been trained to kill and destroy, and who had done little else for several years, were returning from overseas. The vast allocation of societal resources in wartime had proven successful in the area of science; could not a corresponding commitment of resources prove successful in dealing with the problem of crime? The state of California provided an answer.

Toward the end of the war, a penological revolution occurred in California where Earl Warren (1891–1974) had been elected governor in the wake of a prison scandal. Under Warren's leadership, California reorganized its prison system according to the positivistic ideal of individual reformation. The system was organized, not for punishment, but around rehabilitation. California would apply the methods of the behavioral sciences to *correct* criminal behavior.

In order to operationalize the new approach to penology, California implemented an extreme version of the *indeterminate sentence.* Judges would remand a criminal with an indefinite sentence to the California Adult (or Youth) Authority, which would determine his or her *treatment* needs through a process of classification and assign the *convict-client* to an appropriate facility—not a prison, but a correctional institution. A convict would remain "under treatment"—incarcerated—until the Adult Authority determined that the client had been rehabilitated, at which time he or she would be paroled to a community-based treatment program—that is, supervised by a parole agent.

There were no longer prisons in California, they became "correctional institutions"; there were no longer any guards, they became "correction officers"; there were no longer any wardens, they became "superintendents." New institutions were built—medium and minimum security correctional facilities. Adult Authority clients could be moved from maximum, to medium, to minimum security facilities, and to parole. Or, if their behavior required, they could be moved from parole supervision back into the institution for further "treatment in a secure setting."

Into these correctional institutions came the *treaters;* new superintendents often had extensive education in the behavioral sciences, and their institutions employed teachers, social workers, psychologists, and psychiatrists to implement a rehabilitative regimen. Very slowly, but steadily, the California system was copied, at least in part, by all of the other states— prisons virtually disappeared from America. Parole and the indeterminate sentence became intertwined with the idea of corrections and a medical model approach to dealing with criminal behavior.

THE MEDICAL MODEL

The positivistic approach to crime and criminals seeks to explain and respond to criminal behavior in a manner that is not dependent on issues of law, philosophy, or theology. Instead, criminal behavior is to be examined using the principles and methods of science, much as physical illness is subjected to examination by the physician (Robitscher, 1980: 44):

> This new approach to criminal behavior stressed deviance as pathology. The criminal was not seen as "bad" but as "mad," and he was to be given the benefit of the medical approach to madness. He should be helped to understand his unconscious motivation and to go through a process of psychoanalytic change.

Donal MacNamara states: "In its simplest (perhaps oversimplified) terms, the medical model as applied to corrections assumed the offender to be 'sick' (physically, mentally, and/or socially); his offense to be a manifestation or symptom of his illness, a cry for help" (1977: 439). The medical metaphor extended to the post-conviction process:

1. *examination* — presentence investigation report
2. *diagnosis* — classification
3. *treatment* — correctional program

According to the medical model, as applied to corrections, the effects of a treatment program are subjected to review by the parole board, which determines if the offender is sufficiently rehabilitated to be discharged from the correctional institution. A positive response means that treatment will continue on an out-patient basis in the form of parole supervision. The American Friends' Service Committee sums up the rationale for this approach:

> It rejects inherited concepts of criminal punishment as the payment of a debt owed to society, a debt proportioned to the magnitude of the offender's wrong. Instead it would save the offender through constructive measures of reformation, [and] protect society by keeping the offender locked up until the reformation is accomplished. . . . (1971: 37)

The medical model is based on two very questionable assumptions:

1. Criminals are "sick" and can thus benefit from treatment/therapy; and
2. The behavioral sciences can provide the necessary treatment/therapeutic methods.

Although there was a paucity of systematic research to support this approach to criminal behavior, the medical/corrections model was adopted in most states, in theory, if not practice. William Parker argues that the theory never actually matched the practice:

> The theory of rehabilitation has made some changes in the prison: terminology has changed, there are more programs, sweeping floors is now work therapy. . . . The theory of rehabilitation has merely been imposed upon the theories of punishment and control. (1975: 26)

The corrections approach continued without serious opposition into the 1970s. Whatever opposition there was came primarily from the right of the political spectrum as exemplified by the attacks of John Edgar Hoover; he saw parole as "coddling" criminals, releasing them before they completed their sentence. During the 1970s, however, the attack on the corrections approach shifted to the political left.

In 1971, the (Quaker sponsored) American Friends' Service Committee (AFSC) published the first comprehensive attack on the indeterminate sentence and parole. The committee noted that the indeterminate sentence and parole rest on a view of crime as a result of individual pathology that can best be "cured" by treating *individual* criminals. Such an approach, the AFSC noted, downgrades environmental factors such as poverty, discrimination, and lack of employment opportunities. Furthermore, the committee argued, even if the medical model approach is valid, the achievement level of the behavioral sciences does not offer a scientific basis for treatment.

The work of the AFSC had only limited impact and no practical effect until 1974. In that year Robert Martinson published a review of correctional treatment efforts—"What Works?" (1974), to which he answered: virtually nothing! "What Works?" was actually a synopsis of the research findings of Martinson, Douglas Lipton, and Judith Wilks; the complete work was published the following year (Lipton, et al., 1975). It surveyed 231 studies of correctional programs up until 1968 about which Martinson (1974: 25) concluded: "With few and isolated exceptions, the rehabilitative efforts that have been reported so far have had no appreciable effect on recidivism." While the Martinson summary is more critical than the larger report, both lent credence to the arguments of the AFSC. In a review of the Lipton, Martinson, and Wilks research, a panel of the National Research Council concluded that it was "reasonably accurate and fair in the appraisal of the rehabilitation literature." In fact, the panel concluded, Lipton, et al., "were, if anything, more likely to accept evidence in favor of rehabilitation than was justified" (Sechrest, et al., 1979: 31).

Paul Gendreau and Robert Ross argue that the research examined by Martinson was dated and, furthermore, there was substantial literature since 1968 (Martinson's cut-off date) demonstrating "that successful rehabilitation of offenders had been accomplished, and continued to be accomplished quite well" (1987: 350). In fact,

> between 1973 and 1980 reductions in recidivism, sometimes as substantial as 80 percent, had been achieved in a considerable number of well-controlled studies. Effective programs were conducted in a variety of community and (to a lesser degree) institutional settings, involving predelinquents, hard-core adolescent offenders, and recidivistic adult offenders, including heroin addicts. (1987: 350–351)

And these results were not short-lived: "follow-up periods of at least two years were not uncommon, and several studies reported longer followups" (1987: 351; see Gendreau and Ross for a review of this literature).

Nevertheless, criticism of the indeterminate sentence, corrections, and parole increased. David Fogel presented a *justice model* in which he criticized the unbridled discretion exercised by correctional officials, particularly parole boards, under the guise of "treatment:"

> It is evident that correctional administrators have for too long operated with practical immunity in the backwashes of administrative law. They have been

unmindful that the process of justice more strictly observed by the visible police and courts in relation to rights due the accused before and through adjudication must not stop when the convicted person is sentenced. The justice perspective demands accountability from all processors, even the "pure of heart." (1975: 192)

Instead of the often hidden discretion exercised by parole boards, Fogel recommended:

(a) A return to flat time/determinate sentences with procedural rules in law limiting sentencing discretion; and

(b) The elimination of parole boards and parole agencies.

Furthermore, Fogel argued, whatever "treatment" is offered in a prison should be voluntary and should in no way affect the release date of an inmate.

Andrew von Hirsch (1976) offered the concept of *just deserts,* according to which the punishment is to be commensurate with the seriousness of the crime — a return to the classical approach: "A specific penalty level must apply in all instances of law-breaking which involves a given degree of harmfulness and culpability" (von Hirsch and Hanrahan, 1978: 4). Indeterminacy and parole are to be replaced with a specific penalty for a specific offense.

The Twentieth Century Fund Task Force on Sentencing offered the *presumptive sentencing system:* each category of crime would have a presumptive sentence "that should generally be imposed on typical first offenders who have committed the crime in the typical fashion" (1976: 20; italics deleted). For succeeding convictions or other aggravating circumstances, the judge could increase the presumptive sentence by a specific, albeit limited, percentage. Mitigating circumstances could, similarly, reduce the presumptive sentence.

In sum, the basic thrust of these criticisms and proposals was to limit judicial discretion, eliminate the indeterminate sentence, and abolish the parole board. Here was an issue on which both the political left and right could agree — but for different reasons. Alfred Blumenstein notes:

In the mid-1970s a striking consensus of the political left and the political right emerged in opposition to the indeterminate sentence. The political left was concerned over the excess of discretion in decisions about individual's liberty and the excessive disparity that appeared in sentences in presumably similar cases. The political right appeared to be far more concerned about "leniency" than about disparity. They viewed the parole boards as excessively ready to release prisoners early, and expressed shock that prisoners were back on the street on parole well before the maximum sentence. (1984: 130; edited)

In at least nine states, prosecutors were active in leading the fight for abolishing the indeterminate sentence and parole. "Clearly, parole was an easy target for those looking for political opportunities," notes Barbara Krauth, and "the emotional appeal of an attack on the system that released criminals to the streets may have benefitted some political careers more than it actually addressed any of the complex problems of criminal justice" (1987: 52). By 1980 eight states had already adopted some form of determinate sentencing, including the pioneering state of California; the federal government and several other states have abolished the indeterminate sentence and parole release since that time, although at least one (Colorado) restored its parole board in response to the early release of an inmate (who probably would have been denied parole) on "good time." The federal Sentencing Reform Act of 1984 was designed to reduce sentence disparity and phase out parole release; the federal parole board is scheduled for abolition in 1992. The statute also generated a great deal of confusion and litigation — many sentencing judges contested the legislation's removal of judicial discretion. On January 18, 1989, however, the Supreme Court ruled that the sentencing rules established by a commission created under the 1984 statute were constitutional.

The commission established forty-three offense levels and assigned each federal offense to one of the levels. Judges must impose sentences according to these levels, adding to or subtracting from them based on factors such as the offender's age, prior record, or use of a firearm. Any deviation from the guidelines requires a written explanation. And inmates can earn a maximum of only fifty-four days off their sentence per year for good behavior. This has significantly changed the role of federal probation officers. Instead of preparing presentence investigations based on a positivistic approach to the offender, the PO must now focus on the details of the offense and prior criminal history. Franklin Marshall, a federal PO in Philadelphia, points out that it has become imperative "that every detail about offense and offenders be included when these reports are prepared. Otherwise, minor point fluctuations on either offense level or criminal history can make a significant difference of several years in time to be served by convicted offenders" (1989: 10).

INDETERMINATE AND DETERMINATE SENTENCING

The indeterminate sentence was established as part of the Elmira system discussed in the last chapter. Under this form of sentencing, a judge imposes a prison term that has both a minimum and a maximum. For example, a defendant convicted of a Class 3 felony could receive a sentence with a minimum of three years (written 3-0-0) and a maximum of nine years (written 9-0-0); the actual release of the inmate (between 3-0-0 and 9-0-0) is determined by a parole board. There is also a provision for *good time* which is deducted from the maximum sentence because of good institutional behavior, typically one-third. Thus, for example, an inmate with a maximum sentence of 9-0-0 could accumulate up to 3-0-0 years of good time, thus being released after 6-0-0 years without the intervention of the parole board.

Under a system of indeterminate sentencing, persons convicted for the same class of offense could receive different sentences; and even those who receive the same sentence, for example, 3-0-0 to 9-0-0 for a Class 3 felony, can be released (paroled) at different times: 3-0-0, or 4-0-0, or 5-0-0, or . . . all the way up to 9-0-0 (minus "good time"). Criticism of the indeterminate sentence has involved this differential treatment of persons convicted of similar crimes, which is contrary to the classical approach to criminal behavior:

> critics of the indeterminate sentence argued that the treatment model has never realized its lofty objectives in practice and that, given the nature of the correctional system, these goals never will be realized. Furthermore, they maintained that the indeterminate sentence has created a situation of gross sentencing disparity that no longer can be justified by referring to treatment goals. (Goodstein and Hepburn, 1985: 17)

In response to criticism of indeterminate sentencing and parole boards, a variety of so-called flat or definite sentence schemes have been adopted. While each requires the setting of a *specific* sentence — no minimum and maximum — they differ according to the amount of discretion left to the judge:

1. *Definite Sentence/No Discretion.* The legislature provides for a specific sentence for each level of offense. For example, all crimes that constitute a Class 2 felony would require the judge to impose a specific sentence — no deviations permitted. If a Class 2 felony was punishable by imprisonment for seven years, all judges would be required to sentence all defendants convicted of a Class 2 felony to 7-0-0.

2. *Definite Sentence/Wide Discretion.* The legislature provides for a range of sentences for each level of offense. For example, a Class 2 felony would be punishable with a sentence of between 3-0-0 to 7-0-0. Under this system the judge retains discretion to sentence a Class 2 offender to 3-0-0, or 4-0-0, . . . all the way up to 7-0-0. The sentence imposed is definite — for a specific number of years — but the judge's discretion is quite wide.

3. *Presumptive/Narrow Discretion.* The legislature limits discretion to a narrow range of sentences for each level of offense; and for each level there is a presumed sentence from which the judge cannot deviate except if there are aggravating or mitigating circumstances, and then only in a very limited manner. In other words, if a defendant is convicted of a Class 2 felony, the judge would be required to set a sentence of (for example) 5-0-0. Upon a showing of *aggravation* by the prosecutor, however, the judge could increase the presumptive sentence to (for example) 6-0-0; upon a showing of mitigation by the defense, the judge could decrease the presumptive sentence to (for example) 4-0-0. In some states, such as Minnesota, the presumed sentence is increased by a fixed amount based on the severity of any prior convictions (see Figure 4.2 in Chapter 4).

4. *Presumptive/Wide Discretion.* As in the presumptive sentence with narrow discretion, the legislature provides three possible terms for each class of felony. However, while each class has a presumptive sentence, the judge may decrease (for mitigation) or increase (for aggravation) by significant amounts: for example, in Arizona, for mitigation the judge can lower the sentence by a few months or as much as three years (depending on the class of offense); for aggravation the judge can increase the sentence by as much as 100 percent. A departure from the presumptive sentence, however, requires a "written statement of factual findings and reasons for the departure" (Kennedy, 1988: 8).

Determinate sentencing systems usually include a provision for "good time," in order to promote prison discipline, and it generally consists of one day for every day served — fifty percent of the sentence. Thus, for example, a defendant sentenced to a determinate sentence of 5-0-0 would be released (presuming good behavior) after 2-6-0. In practice, good time is deducted in advance, when the offender is first received at the institution; misbehavior results in time being added. In some states an inmate may be entitled to additional time off the sentence for exemplary performance: "meritorious good time" or "industrial good time." These grants of additional time off are usually the result of prison overcrowding in states without parole release.

In Florida, for example, one-third is taken off the sentence when the inmate is received at a correctional institution, called Basic Gaintime. On the first day of each month an inmate can receive an additional twenty days off, Incentive Goodtime, as a reward for attending classes, satisfactory work performance, and general good behavior. Then there is Oneshot Meritorious Gaintime, up to sixty days for exemplary performance. And, as a result of critical overcrowding, in 1987 the legislature provided for Provisional Release Credit, an additional sixty days per month whenever the prison system is over 97.5 percent of capacity. As a result of these schemes, the average Florida inmate serves a little over one-third of his or her sentence (Malcolm, 1989). Florida's experience reveals the often poor fit between theory and practice when it comes to "getting tough on criminals." While sentencing guidelines imposed more severe sentences, "inmates may actually serve shorter and shorter sentences and also serve smaller proportions of their sentences than they did prior to the implementation of the guidelines" (Griswold, 1989: 49).

In many states without parole, an inmate released under good time ("mandatory release") provisions is placed under the supervision of a parole officer. In the absence of discretionary release, however, the incentive to adequately fund offender supervision is often absent — there is no one (governor, parole board) to hold accountable for the serious misconduct of mandatory releasees. In Illinois, for example, a budget crisis in 1987 led to the laying off of 98 of the state's 159 parole agents. Most were reinstated at the beginning of 1989, because of a substantial increase in new arrests among releases against whom no delinquency action was taken because parole agents were not available.

Although in theory the determinate or definite sentence was supposed to reduce unwarranted variation in sentencing and amount of time served in prison, the practice has been otherwise. No state, for example, has adopted a determinate sentence with no discretion, while a number have adopted schemes with wide discretion. Thus, in Illinois, a defendant convicted of selling narcotics as a first offense can receive a *determinate* sentence of anywhere from 4-0-0 all the way up to 30-0-0; Illinois has no parole board. Herbert Covey and Mary Mande found that in Colorado determinate sentencing did not reduce unwarranted variation, "but it may have enhanced the discretionary powers of prosecutors" (1985: 270).

It is the issue of discretion that presents the most obvious deficiency in the proposals set out by Fogel, von Hirsch, et al. Although they propose to deal with discretion exercised by judges and parole boards, they fail to deal with *prosecutorial discretion*. This discretion is typically exercised privately, outside of the scrutiny of official review; and prosecutorial discretion affects sentencing more often and more significantly than does judicial discretion. While a judge, acting under a definite system with narrow discretion, or a presumptive system with narrow discretion, must apply a specific sentence for a particular class of crime (in the absence of mitigation or aggravation), it is the prosecutor using charging powers that determines the particular class of crime and whether to move for aggravation or oppose a motion for mitigation. In return for cooperation—a plea of guilty—the prosecutor can reduce the class of crime for which the offender will be charged; agree not to move for mitigation; and/or agree to accept mitigation offered by defense counsel. By manipulating the charging decision, the prosecutor, not the judge, can often determine the actual sentence. Thus, determinate sentencing can increase the ability of a prosecutor to engage in plea bargaining. In many instances determinate sentencing merely shifts discretion away from judges and parole boards and toward the prosecution end of criminal justice.

Furthermore, the abolition of parole boards, a practical accomplishment of determinate sentencing schemes, ignores the role of the board in reducing the very sentence disparity that the "classicalists" decry. Since the parole board reviews the sentences of all state prisoners, it is in a position to act as a panel for mediating disparate sentences for similar criminal behavior. In Nebraska, for example, the Board of Parole "serves as an 'equalizer.' Within the framework of the law, it attempts to produce equity and uniformity in the sentencing structure caused by the inherent disparity which understandably results from having ninety-three prosecuting offices and multiple judicial districts." The Georgia Board of Pardons and Paroles states that "the board's unique central position and authority allow it to reduce sentencing disparity. Excessive harshness is more readily reduced, but excessive leniency in the form of a too light confinement sentence may be corrected partially by parole denial." Let us look at a hypothetical example of the parole board as sentencing review panel (see Figure 7.1).

A second issue with respect to parole has been given scant attention.

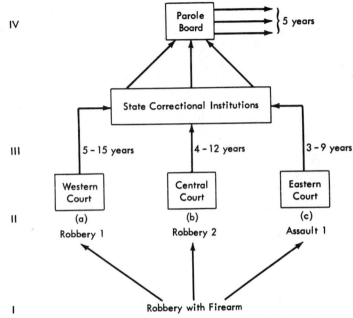

I   Three offenders, (a) (b) (c), each enter stores in different counties within the same state. They each brandish loaded revolvers and rob several hundred dollars.

II   Defendant (a) is processed in Western Court. Attempts at plea bargaining fail, he stands trial and is convicted of First Degree Robbery.
Defendant (b) is processed in Central Court. He is allowed to plead guilty to Second Degree Robbery.
Defendant (c) is processed in Eastern Court. He is allowed to plead guilty to First Degree Assault.

III Defendant (a) is sentenced to a minimum of 5 years and a maximum of 15 years in state prison.
Defendant (b) is sentenced to a minimum of 4 years and a maximum of 12 years in state prison.
Defendant (c) is sentenced to a minimum of 3 years and a maximum of 9 years in state prison.

IV   The parole board, recognizing that the three defendants have committed the same criminal acts and despite variations in the legal category of conviction (Robbery 1, Robbery 2, Assault 1), requires that each serve 5 years before being paroled.

Under a determinate sentencing scheme devoid of a parole board, the sentences for this hypothetical example would be:

defendant (a) would serve 8 years;
defendant (b) would serve 6 years;
defendant (c) would serve 4 years.

FIGURE 7.1   The Parole Board as Sentencing Review Panel

There is a presumption (for example, AFSC, 1971; Fogel, 1975; MacNamara, 1977) that parole is based on a medical model or some humanitarian effort gone astray. However, the history of prisons and parole in the United States underscores the fact that parole release has been used, possibly abused, as a mechanism for maintaining prison discipline and reducing prison overcrowding. The parole board evolved out of the power of governors to issue pardons to selected convicts. Prior to the creation of parole boards governors often used their pardoning powers to relieve prison overcrowding. In Florida, for example, the Pardon Board often presided over as many as two hundred pardon applications a day until the Parole and Probation Commission was established in 1941. In Utah, the Board of Pardons continues to have parole responsibilities and the Alabama Board of Pardons and Paroles, established in 1939, has final authority on all pardons. The Vermont Parole Board was created in 1968; until that time, release from prison was by conditional pardon granted by the governor.

That parole release is a response to prison overcrowding can be seen by a 12.5 percent increase in the number of prisoners paroled in 1988 (when there were 627,402 prisoners), the largest since 1983 when the number increased by 12.06 percent (when there were 437,248 prisoners); while there were 251,708 offenders on parole in 1983, there were 407,977 in 1988 (National Institute of Justice).

Blumenstein (1984: 131) points out:

> One of the functions the parole agencies carried out during the period of indeterminate sentencing was serving as a "safety valve" for crowded prisons. As prison populations began to approach or exceed the prison capacity, the parole board could simply lower the threshold of the degree of rehabilitation that warranted release.

In many states with determinate sentences the same function is being carried out using good time provisions by prison authorities who lack the information, time, and/or expertise to make rational release decisions. Those who see parole as simply a rehabilitative device have bought the *rhetoric,* but not the *reality.* Corrections officials in several states that have abolished the indeterminate sentence have, by necessity—read: overcrowding—become de facto parole boards.

In Maine, the first state to abandon parole release, along with parole supervision, a clemency board assists the governor in making commutation decisions whose purpose is to relieve prison overcrowding (Burke, 1988). Furthermore, post-release supervision was reestablished by judges in the form of split sentences—"judicial parole"—whereby offenders are sentenced to imprisonment followed by a period of probation supervision (Anspach and Monsen, 1989).

David Greenberg and Drew Humphries (1980) argue that the forces of the political right coopted the issue of sentencing reform and abolition of parole and were successful in implementing changes that are increasing the length of time served by offenders, now without the possibility of parole release, in a prison atmosphere devoid of any rehabilitative component. In a strong defense of the correctional/rehabilitative model, Francis Cullen and Karen Gilbert (1982: xxix) state: "Whatever its failings, criminal justice rehabilitation has thus persisted as a rationale for caring for offender needs and not for making the wayward suffer. Without its humanizing influence, the history of American corrections would be even bleaker than is now the case."

The relevant question is now at issue: Do we entrust the role of reducing prison populations and the "risk management" of criminal offenders to judges, institutional officials, or parole boards? A review of the history that led to parole in the first instance argues for this discretion to be the responsibility of a professional parole board.

COMMUNITY-BASED CORRECTIONS

By the 1960s it was becoming increasingly apparent that the "correctional" expectations of prisons were not being fulfilled: "The spending of years in confined quarters, perhaps as small as eight by ten feet, in a setting dominated by a toilet and a possibly criminally-aggressive cellmate, can hardly be considered conducive to encourage socially acceptable behavior upon release" (Hahn, 1976: 6). The prison is what Erving Goffman (1961: xiii) refers to as a *total institution:* "a place of residence and work where a large number of like-situated individuals, cut off from the wider society for an appreciable period of time, together lead an enclosed, formally administered round of life." As such, these institutions have a tendency to mold persons into compliant and often shapeless forms in order to maintain discipline and a sound working order, or for less utilitarian reasons. The prison provides a dreary uniformity that leaves little room for self-assertion and decision making, the requisites for living in the free community.

"Even the most well-developed treatment program," notes Paul Cromwell "if totally contained within the institution, will lack one ingredient essential to an inmates's success after release. The missing factor is contact with the community and family" (1978: 68). In place of these "rehabilitative" factors, the inmate is exposed to the counterproductive influences of the prison subculture. Instead of abandoning the rehabilitative ideal, supporters of the corrections approach in the late 1960s and early 1970s argued for a new approach they referred to as *community-based corrections.*

Belinda and Bernard McCarthy trace the concept of community-based corrections "back to the years following World War II, when returning veterans encountered adjustment problems as they attempted to reenter civilian life" (1984: 9). The successful integration of many servicemen was accomplished with assistance ranging from informal outpatient counseling, to education, job preparation and, in some cases, intensive therapy in residential settings. In 1967, the President's Commission on Law Enforcement and Administration of Justice stated:

> Institutions tend to isolate offenders from society, both physically and psychologically, cutting them off from schools, jobs, families, and other supportive influences and increasing the probability that the label of criminal will be indelibly impressed upon them. The goal of reintegration is likely to be furthered much more readily by working with offenders in the community than by incarceration. (1972: 398)

The commission added that the high cost of incarceration also served to make community-based corrections attractive.

In 1965, the Federal Rehabilitative Act authorized programs designed to aid in the rehabilitation of offenders while holding down the number of persons in prison. In 1968, Congress enacted the Omnibus Crime Control and Safe Streets Act which led to the establishment of the Law Enforcement Assistance Administration (LEAA). With encouragement and funding from LEAA, state correctional officials began to look outside of the prison for ways to rehabilitate offenders. The approach they adopted centered on reintegrating the offender back into the community, and it became known as "community-based corrections." Vernon Fox states that community-based corrections refers to that part of corrections, other than traditional probation, prison, and parole, which makes use of community resources to assist the more traditional functions. The purposes are the

1. "mobilization and management of community resources to assist in the rehabilitation of offenders;" and
2. "provision of alternatives to incarceration in a way that is compatible with the public interest and safety." (1977:1)

There are a number of programs that are generally offered as being a part of community-based corrections, including diversion, pretrial release, deferred sentencing, halfway houses, and work-release. In this chapter we will summarize these programs, while in Chapter 11 we will include a more in-depth review.

1. *Diversion.* The President's Commission (1972) noted that for many persons who come to the attention of the criminal justice system, criminal sanctions would be excessive; but these persons are often in need of treatment or supervision. Since the courts are overburdened with cases, programs that provide needed services for nonserious offenders, while easing court congestion, proved quite attractive. Diversion programs were operated by or in conjunction with police and prosecutor's offices; they dealt with adults and juveniles. Instead of being arrested and/or prosecuted, these offenders were sent for "treatment." Criticism of diversion centered on research which indicated that persons who are diverted would often not have been arrested or prosecuted in the first place—diversion programs frequently *increased* ("net widening") the number of persons involved in criminal justice.

2. *Pretrial release.* Persons who lack the funds necessary to be released on bail, who are detained pending trial, suffer from significant disadvantages. The jail experience itself is punishing, but the person is also separated from the community: family, friends, employment. While it handicaps the defendant, it also burdens the criminal justice system, which must provide for the pretrial detention. Pretrial release programs utilize investigators—sometimes probation officers—to screen persons after they have entered the criminal justice system and before bail has been set. This enables the judge to make an informed bail decision, particularly in cases where the investigator indicates that the defendant is a good candidate for release on his or her own recognizance (ROR). Some programs expanded to include supervision and a variety of services to persons on ROR.

3. *Deferred sentencing.* A program of deferred sentencing usually involves a plea of guilty followed by either restitution or some form of community service instead of a sentence. Satisfactory completion of the conditions of the deferred sentence results in the charges being dropped; on the other hand, a failure can result in incarceration. Some programs use probation officers to supervise deferred offenders.

4. *Halfway houses.* This type of facility may be operated by a public or private agency. Some provide room and board and help with employment, while others, in addition provide a whole range of social services. It may be used to place probationers in lieu of prison (halfway in), or for parolees in need of supportive services when they are released from prison (halfway out).

5. *Work release.* Like the halfway house, work release is designed to prepare inmates for the freedom of community living. Typically an inmate leaves the institution or work-release center during the day for employment and returns at the end of the work day. Work release may also be granted to secure employment or to attend job training or educational programs.

Greenberg questions some of the basic assumptions of community-based corrections:

> One might ask why, if the community is so therapeutic, the offender got into trouble there in the first place? Indeed, an offender's home community, where he is already known as a delinquent or criminal, might pose more obstacles to the abandonment of criminal activity than some new residential location. (1975: 4)

Furthermore, Greenberg argues, to the extent that criminal behavior is a rational response to the lack of lawful employment opportunity, it is beyond the ability of community-based corrections to correct.

The impetus for the expansion of community-based corrections was the availability of federal funding; Andrew Scull notes that "since the creation of the Law Enforcement Assistance Administration, efforts have been under way to manipulate federal funding and support for state and local law enforcement so as to provide sizable financial incentives for the development of community corrections' programs." (1977: 45) During the early 1980s, however, funding through LEAA dried up and the agency was dismantled. State and local governments, already severely pressed for services while trying to hold the line on taxes, slowly abandoned the often costly programming that adequate community-based corrections required.

CORRECTIONAL INSTITUTIONS: DIVISIONS, REBELLIONS, RIOTS

Despite the corrections revolution, prison officials remained preoccupied with management and security issues; most of the allocations for correctional institutions were for administration and security, leaving about 5 percent for items that could reasonably be labeled "rehabilitative." Providing such services has always been problematic. Correctional salaries are relatively low and most prisons are located in rural areas not particularly attractive to urban graduates trained in therapeutic disciplines. Inadequate funding results in vocational training that is badly out of date and often of little use to inmates seeking employment based on skills developed in the correctional institution.

The problems encountered by the corrections approach were compounded by differences between correction officers and the "treaters." Older members of staff, particularly those responsible for prison security, were often resistant to the changes brought in by the treaters. This could be expected from an examination of their differing backgrounds. Correction officers were typically rural, white Protestants, socially and politically conservative with, at best, a high school education; they tended to be poorly trained. The treaters tended to be reform-minded urban college graduates, many of whom were Catholics and Jews—and women.

Furthermore, the rhetoric did not match the reality, and prisoners soured on rehabilitative programs which raised unrealistic expectations (Irwin, 1980: 63): "After prisoners were convinced that treatment programs did not work (by the appearance of persons who had participated fully in treatment programs streaming back to prison with new crimes or violations of parole), hope shaded to cynicism and then turned to bitterness."

Blake McKelvey points out that during the 1950s prisoners were usually divided to the point of impotence:

> The prisonization process, which had aligned the great majority of inmates against their keepers, had also divided them from one another, making effective collaboration extremely difficult. Only a rumor of an excessively brutal incident

or a report of revolts elsewhere could arouse a sense of community sufficient to support a riotous outbreak. (1977: 323)

And, McKelvey adds, there were such outbreaks during the 1950s in California, Louisiana, Massachusetts, Michigan, Missouri, New Jersey, Ohio, Pennsylvania, and Washington.

Into this environment came thousands of new black and Hispanic inmates. During the 1950s the number of blacks and other nonwhites committed annually to adult federal and state prisons increased from 17,200 to 28,500 (McKelvey, 1977)—and it continued to grow during the 1960s and 1970s. While the predominantly white inmates of the Big House could relate to their keepers, the young urban black and Hispanic found no such comfort. In 1954 the Supreme Court handed down its decision in *Brown* v. *Board of Education of Topeka, Kansas* (347 U.S. 483) and set off the civil rights revolution in the United States.

Rising black consciousness occurring in the wider community took on more radical dimensions inside the prison. The Black Muslims emerged as a major separatist organization and confronted prison officials with demands based on religious freedom. The antiwar movement and activities of radical groups such as the Black Panthers and Students for a Democratic Society (SDS) stirred and politicized inmates, black and white. These inmates confronted correctional officials with demands often couched in Marxist terminology.

The traditional relationship between inmates and correction officers— *rapprochement* based on private agreements or corrupt favoritism—started to come apart. Inmates became increasingly militant in their refusal to cooperate with their keepers. Correctional officials responded in the best tradition of the Big House—with repression that touched off violence in institutions throughout the country. Correctional institutions simmered throughout the 1960s and into 1971 when in the month of September the focus of attention shifted to a small upstate New York town where the last of the Auburn-style prisons was built.

Attica

The state prison at Attica (a town which in 1971 had a population of less than three thousand) was completed in 1931 and boasted of being the most secure, escape-proof prison ever built; at the time, it was also the most expensive prison ever built. Attica was a response to an outbreak of prison riots throughout the United States in the late 1920s. In 1929, Clinton Prison in Dannemora, New York, experienced a riot protesting overcrowded conditions; three inmates were killed. In that same year, the prison at Auburn experienced a general riot in which inmates used firearms; the assistant warden was killed and four inmates escaped before the prison was brought back under control.

Typical of prisons in New York and elsewhere, Attica was placed in a rural area where residents would accept the institution as a basis for employment and other economic benefits. On July 8, 1970, Attica, and the other state prisons in New York, received a name change:

> On that date the names of all the state's maximum security prisons were changed. There were no more prisons; in their places, instead, stood six maximum security "correctional facilities." The prison wardens became "institutional superintendents"; the former principal keepers became "deputy superintendents"; and the old-line prison guards awakened that morning to find themselves suddenly "correction officers." No one's job or essential duties changed, only his title. (Attica Commission, 1972: 18)

Fourteen months later Attica Correctional Facility had more than two thousand inmates who were locked in their cells for twelve to sixteen hours a day being "rehabilitated," and who spent the remainder of the day with very little to occupy their time. There was no gymnasium and recreational opportunities were limited. There was almost a total absence of any meaningful rehabilitation programs. Showers were available for most inmates — once a week.

Most inmates were black and Hispanic from the downstate New York area, or upstate cities such as Buffalo, Syracuse, and Rochester. All but one (he was Puerto Rican) of the fewer than 400 correction officers were non-Hispanic whites drawn primarily from the communities surrounding Attica. While the superintendent had a master's degree in correctional administration, correction officers who began their jobs between World War II and the late 1950s received no formal training. Those who started after that were given two weeks training. They were expected to enforce the dozens of petty rules typical of correctional institutions and to relate in a meaningful way to inmates with whom they had little in common.

Attica had a large number of Black Muslims (members of the Nation of Islam) who had difficulty with a prison diet that was heavy with pork. Muslims also objected to the lack of ministers. Correctional officials would not allow the ministers, many of whom had prison records, into Attica. Black Muslims spent their recreation time in the yard engaging in worship and highly disciplined physical exercise. The correctional staff, which never understood Black Muslims, was quite fearful of this group, who exhibited military-type discipline and remained aloof from both staff and other inmates.

Typical of large correctional institutions, in Attica "popular conceptions of homosexual advances and assaults in prison were not exaggerated" (Attica Commission, 1972: 78). Correction officers were unable to protect inmates who were forced to resort to forms of self-protection, such as carrying a "shiv" (homemade knife), in violation of prison rules (1972: 79):

> The irony was not lost on the inmates. They perceived themselves surrounded by high walls and gates, and tightly regimented by a myriad of written and unwritten

rules; but when they needed protection, they often had to resort to the same skills that had brought many of them to Attica in the first place.

The Riot   During the summer of 1971 there were a number of peaceful protests by inmates over conditions at Attica. Leaders of previously antagonistic inmate groups such as the Young Lords, a Puerto Rican group, and the Black Panthers and Black Muslims, gained greater political awareness, submerged their differences, and joined with white inmates in a peaceful effort to effect changes at Attica. The new solidarity among inmates frightened officials. The superintendent responded by attempting to transfer the leaders as "troublemakers." He was prevented from doing so by the new Commissioner of the Department of Correctional Services, Russell G. Oswald. Oswald, who had been Chairman of the New York State Board of Parole, met with inmate representatives at the prison, but was called away on a personal emergency — his wife was seriously ill — before any agreement could be arranged.

On September 8, 1971, when a correction officer attempted to discipline two inmates who appeared to be sparring, a confrontation ensued. The incident passed without any action on the part of the outnumbered staff. That evening officers appeared and took the inmates from their cells. A noisy protest ensued during the evening, and it was renewed when inmates gathered for breakfast on the morning of September 9. A melee broke out, correction officers were taken hostage, and a riot quickly developed. Prison officials had no plan, nor had they been trained to deal with such an emergency. As a result, within twenty minutes inmates secured control of the four main cellblocks and seized forty hostages. Correction officers were beaten and one died later as a result of his wounds. The Black Muslims, who had not taken part in the initial uprising, moved to protect the hostages, who were used as a basis for negotiations. An inmate committee for that purpose was formed.

Commissioner Oswald found that when he arrived at Attica the police were not prepared to immediately retake the prison. By the time sufficient forces had gathered, negotiations were already underway and Oswald chose to continue them in an effort to avoid more bloodshed. At the request of the inmate committee a number of outside observers were permitted to enter Attica, including reporters, lawyers, and politicians. Although the negotiations were quite disorganized, Oswald agreed to most of the inmate demands for improved conditions at Attica. The negotiations broke down, however, over the issue of complete amnesty because of the injured officer who had died after the negotiations began.

On the morning of September 13, in a poorly planned and uncoordinated nine-minute assault, heavily armed state police and correction officers retook the prison: two hostages were seriously injured by the inmates, and ten hostages and twenty-nine inmates were killed by state troopers and correction officers (Wicker, 1975). In 1989, the New York State Court of Claims awarded

$1.3 million to seven inmates who, although they had not participated in the uprising, had been injured at Attica by state police gunfire (Kolbert, 1989).

A number of official investigations occurred in the aftermath of the rebellion at Attica. In particular, rehabilitation, the parole board, and the indeterminate sentence came in for severe criticism. Cullen and Gilbert point out that

> Americans in the first half of the 1970's were faced with the prospect of an intractable crime rate and confronted with the reality—powerfully symbolized by Attica—that their prisons were both inhumane and grossly ineffective. In this context, a culprit was needed to take the blame, and a candidate was readily found. Rehabilitation would take the rap. (1982: 6)

MODERN CORRECTIONAL INSTITUTIONS

Did the events at Attica result in any lasting changes? Observers of the current state of our prisons would be hard-pressed to document any positive changes of substance. A distinct political turn to the right has increased the number of prison commitments and lengthened the terms of imprisonment in many states which now have no parole system with which to deal with overcrowding. During an era when crime, as measured by the National Crime Survey, has been declining, the prison population increased dramatically. In fact, it is difficult to posit a relationship between increased imprisonment and the rate of crime. Lester Velie and Jerome Miller point out, for example, that while Texas and Pennsylvania have similar sized populations:

> Texas imprisons three times as many offenders as Pennsylvania, yet crime in Texas grew 2 percent from 1983 through 1984; crime in Pennsylvania declined 1.9 percent. The Washington, D.C., incarceration rate is three and one-third that of the country. Yet while crime declined nationally 3 percent from 1983 through 1984, in Washington it dropped 0.7 percent. (1985: 31).

And during the 1980s, adding to the numerous safety and health problems endemic to prisons, is that presented by Acquired Immunodeficiency Syndrome (AIDS), first identified in the United States in 1981. Intravenous drug users and male homosexuals have been identified as primary groups at risk from the disease, and prisons house many intravenous drug users and inmates who resort to homosexual practices in the absence of available female partners. (See Hammett, 1989 for a review of this issue.) Prison officials are also acknowledging the difficulties created by the widespread use of drugs in their institutions: "Drug use has become a major problem with a variety of ramifications, including threats to prison order, violence among inmates, and corruption of guards and other employees" (Malcolm, 1989c: 1). The dramatic increase in convicted drug offenders has been a driving force behind prison overcrowding and the smuggling of drugs into correctional institutions.

Prison violence, mostly inmate against inmate, is widespread. In 1985, for example, dozens of inmates were murdered by other inmates in Texas prisons—until recent years Texas boasted of having the most orderly and peaceful prison system in the United States. A particularly grisly outbreak occurred at the New Mexico State Penitentiary, which was built in 1957 to house 850 inmates. On February 1, 1980, the prison had nearly one thousand inmates and was badly understaffed; there were only eighteen correction officers on duty when prisoners took over the institution. Although the prison was quickly retaken by police and National Guard, it was only after inmates had systematically slaughtered thirty-three of their fellow prisoners—many of whom were tortured to death.

Overcrowding was seen as a major reason for the 1989 two-day prison riot at the Correctional Institution at Camp Hill, Pennsylvania which, although it was built to house 1,826, had 2,607 inmates. More than 118 persons were injured and half of the facility's thirty-one buildings destroyed. Prison overcrowding has been exacerbated by a substantial increase in drug prosecutions. In Illinois, for example, in 1989 the number of convictions for drug offenses increased by 50 percent, driving up the prison population to nearly 32 percent over capacity ("Drug Offenders Push Population Estimates Higher," 1989). The number of inmates imprisoned in Illinois for drug offenses between 1985 and 1989 increased more than 300 percent. According to the Department of Corrections, the number of inmates over capacity in Illinois has reached the equivalent of eight new prisons. In New York, the number of New York inmates serving time for drug-related offenses has surpassed those imprisoned for any other type of crime. In addition to overcrowding, the perennial problem of prison discipline and violence has been exacerbated by gangs and court orders limiting the authority of correctional officials.

Prison Gangs

Some gangs develop in prison while others are brought into the institution by convicted gang members. In either case, the contemporary prison has provided fertile soil for the proliferation and growth of these often dangerous entities. In most instances gangs are organized along racial or ethnic lines. Instead of the politicized groups of the 1960s, there is an array of gangs with exotic-sounding names. So extensive is gang membership, that a U.S. court of appeals in Illinois concluded that 90 percent of Pontiac Correctional Center's inmates are gang members, and that they were running much of prison life (Crawford, 1988). The gangs have increased the potential for violence with members using the power of their gang affiliations for various extortionate practices. Inmates without the protection of the gang are quite vulnerable and often easy prey for the violence-prone gang members. Attempts by correctional officials to dissipate the power of the gangs by transferring their leadership to other institutions, has often served only to spread the phenomenon. The gangs often transcend the prison, with members active inside and outside the institution. This has obvious implications for parole officers.

Gang members engage in extortion, drug, and weapons trafficking.

> Many prison gangs have a 'blood-in-blood-out' policy, meaning that an inmate may become a member only after killing or assaulting another prisoner or staffer and that his blood will be spilled before he is allowed to quit the gang. Members released from prison remain in the gang, often providing support and enforcement for the organization outside. (President's Commission on Organized Crime; hereafter PCOC, 1986: 75)

The Department of Justice has identified 114 different gangs with greatly varying structures, some of whom appear to meet the criteria of an organized crime group: the Mexican Mafia, Aryan Brotherhood, Black Guerilla Family, and Texas Syndicate. Some sources add La Nuestra Familia. In all five, either murder or the drawing of blood are prerequisites for membership.

Mexican Mafia Reputed to be the most powerful of the prison-organized groups, the Mexican Mafia is comprised primarily of Mexican-American convicts and ex-convicts from the barrios of East Los Angeles. Its origins are traced to the Deuel Vocational Institute in Tracy, California, where the Mexican Mafia began as a self-protective group by twenty young Mexican-Americans from the Maravilla area of East Los Angeles in 1957. But, notes the President's Commission, they soon "began to control such illicit activities as homosexual prostitution, gambling, and narcotics. They called themselves the Mexican Mafia out of admiration for *La Cosa Nostra*" (1986: 73). Attempts by the Department of Corrections to diminish gang power by transferring members to other institutions only helped to spread their influence. Vigorous recruiting occurs among the most violent Mexican-American inmates, particularly those housed in adjustment centers for the most dangerous and incorrigible.

By the mid-1960s the Mexican Mafia had assumed control over prison heroin trafficking and numerous other inmate activities. In 1966 they started to move their operations outside the prison. By 1967 their influence and reliance on wholesale violence increased, and in that year they attacked the first Mexican-American outside their group. This attack on an inmate from rural Northern California led to the formation of a second Mexican-American gang, *La Nuestra Familia,* with whom the Mexican Mafia has been feuding since 1968.

La Nuestra Familia   "Originally founded in 1967 as a Latin cultural organization in Soledad Prison, *La Nuestra Familia* began to sell protection to others who had been victimized by the Mexican Mafia," and the two groups have been feuding since then. "Soon the group moved into the extortion rackets that their rivals had monopolized. In 1975, the gang began establishing 'regiments' outside prison, using Fresno County, California, as a home base" (PCOC, 1986: 77). The group operates with a constitution regulating prison and nonprison members, most of whom are Mexican-Americans from rural areas in California. The structure consists of a single "general" with supreme power, captains, lieutenants, and *soldados*. "Rank is usually achieved by the number of 'hits' in which a member is involved" (1986: 77). In its struggle with the Mexican Mafia, La Nuestra Familia has been allied with the white supremacist group known as the Aryan Brotherhood, and the Black Guerilla Family.

Aryan Brotherhood   The Aryan Brotherhood originated in the early 1960s San Quentin Prison as the "Diamond Tooth Gang"—members had a piece of glass embedded in one of their front teeth—and developed into a Nazi-oriented, white-supremacist group dominated by members and associates of outlaw motorcycle gangs. The present name dates back to 1968, and the gang has branches in prisons around the country, but is particularly active in California, Arizona, Wisconsin, Idaho, and the federal prison system. The gang insignia is a three-leafed shamrock, three sixes (666), and the letters "AB."

The Aryan Brotherhood, which engages in extortion and protection schemes, is ruled by a commission and a governing council, and members advance in the ranks through acts of violence. Leadership is by a commission of three, but gang members as a group do not usually relate to any one leader. Internal discipline and control has been lax, and there has been a great deal of internal conflict and violence within the Aryan Brotherhood. Upon leaving prison, members often become part of outlaw motorcycle clubs or street gangs.

Black Guerilla Family   The Black Guerilla Family was established by George Jackson of the Black Panther Party when he was in San Quentin in 1966; in accord with its founder, it is the most politically oriented of the five major prison gangs, generally following a Maoist philosophy. Many of its members were formerly part of the Black Liberation Army and various street gangs. The motivation of its membership—political action and pecuniary profit—has led to a split between those favoring one or the other goal. The ruling structure consists of a single leader known as the Chairman or Supreme Commander, a central committee, and a very loose ranking of soldiers (PCOC, 1986: 79).

Texas Syndicate This third major Mexican-American prison gang originated in California's Folsom Prison, although the founders were all from Texas. They banded together for mutual protection and soon became known for their swift retaliation against any opposition. As gang members were released from California, they returned to their home state. Many were soon rearrested and imprisoned in Texas (PCOC, 1986). Members take a life oath, and the group is more secretive than most prison gangs; they are also known to be exceptionally violent, frequently assaulting or killing nonmembers and prison staff. In Texas and California members participate in drug trafficking, contract assaults and murders, and extortion (Fong, 1990).

PRISONS AND THE COURTS

Throughout most of our history the courts have been unwilling to intervene in matters pertaining to prisons "out of concern for federalism and separation of powers and a fear that judicial review of administrative decisions would undermine prison security and discipline" (Jacobs, 1980: 433). Once the requirements of due process had been met leading to conviction and sentencing, the judiciary had taken a "hands off" policy. Prisons are obviously difficult to manage, and this made judges reluctant to impose their legal standards in place of the expertise of prison administrators. In 1961, however, the Black Muslims began to litigate their First Amendment claims in New York, California, and the District of Columbia. As Claire Cripe (1977), points out, these cases served to "open the floodgates" of prison litigation. Once the courts became involved in prisons there was no easy way to withdraw.

In 1968, fourteen years after segregation in public schools was declared unconstitutional, the Supreme Court ruled that the racial segregation of prisoners violated the Fourth Amendment (*Lee* v. *Washington* 390 U.S. 333). The following year the Court ruled that prison officials must permit prisoners ("jail-house lawyers") to assist their fellow inmates with legal questions (*Johnson* v. *Avery* 393 U.S. 483). In 1971 the court expanded this right by requiring prison officials to provide legal materials, law books, legal forms, etc., for inmates (*Younger* v. *Gilmore* 404 U.S. 15). In 1974 the Court extended its previous decisions by requiring correctional officials to provide either adequate law libraries or adequate legal assistance (*Bounds* v. *Smith* 430 U.S. 817). That same year, the Court limited the power of prison officials to censor inmate letters (*Procunier* v. *Martinez* 417 U.S. 817). In 1989, however, the Court (*Thornburgh* v. *Abbott,* No. 87–1344) limited the *Procunier* decision to *outgoing* mail and held that incoming items can quickly circulate throughout the institution and be a source of disorder. Accordingly, the Court gave prison officials greater flexibility in censoring publications that inmates may receive: "In the volatile prison environment, it is essential that prison officials be given discretion to prevent such disorder."

In 1974 the Supreme Court ruled that prisoners are entitled to minimal due process protections whenever disciplinary action threatens their "liberty" by imposing solitary confinement and loss of privileges of good time (*Wolf* v. *McDonnell* 418 U.S. 817):

> . . . though his rights may be diminished by the needs and exigencies of the institutional environment, a prisoner is not wholly stripped of constitutional protections when he is imprisoned for a crime. There is no iron curtain drawn between the Constitution and the prisons of this country.

In 1977, however, the Court apparently decided to draw a line between the prison and the Constitution: it rejected the notion that prisoners had the right under the First Amendment to organize an inmate union (*Jones* v. *North Carolina Prisoners' Union* 433 U.S. 119). In 1978 the court ruled that solitary confinement in a harsh setting for more than thirty days constitutes cruel and unusual punishment (*Hutto* v. *Finney* 437 U.S. 678).

There has been a great deal of litigation over prison conditions, particularly with respect to overcrowding. Federal and state courts in many jurisdictions have ordered prison officials to reduce inmate populations and to take other corrective steps to bring their institutions into line with constitutional requirements. In 1979 (*Bell* v. *Wolfish* 441 U.S. 520) and 1981 (*Chapman* v. *Rhodes* 101 S. Ct. 2392), however, the Supreme Court overturned lower court decisions that found overcrowding per se, to be unconstitutional. The Court ruled that the Constitution does not require inmates to be housed in single cells; double-bunking is permitted even for those prisoners legally innocent — in jail awaiting trial. In *Chapman* the Court ruled that prison conditions were constitutional as long as the totality of the conditions does not "involve the wanton and unnecessary infliction of pain."

In 1984 (*Hudson* v. *Palmer* No. 1630) the Supreme Court ruled that the Fourth Amendment's protection against unreasonable search and seizure does not apply to prison cells. In a five to four decision the court held: "The recognition of privacy rights for prisoners in their individual cells simply cannot be reconciled with the concept of incarceration and the needs and objectives of penal institutions." In *Hudson* the court overturned a U.S. court of appeals decision which had upheld the right of a convicted bank robber in Virginia to sue prison officials for the destruction of his property resulting from a search of his cell by correction officers.

PRISONS FOR PROFIT

While prisons have proven to be a costly liability for state governments since the Great Depression, some localities and private entrepreneurs view them as a source of potential income. For example, the town of Horton in northeastern

Kansas, population 2,100, is planning to build a one-thousand-cell prison which, for a fee, will house inmates from jurisdictions experiencing prison overcrowding problems (Robbins, 1989). And one of the more recent responses to the problem of an increasing prison population has been the "privatization" of corrections. Joan Mullen points out: "Confinement service or facility management contracts are another way of expanding corrections capacity—without imposing any burden for facility construction on the government" (1985:4). Private firms have been able to establish and operationalize facilities more quickly than public agencies, which are constrained by a variety of political and bureaucratic requirements. There are several dozen of these facilities; most, but not all, are equipped to handle only minimum security inmates and are, thus, more closely related to halfway houses than traditional prisons. The largest customer of the private facility has been the United States Immigration and Naturalization Service (INS), which has contracted out the detention of illegal aliens to the Corrections Corporation of America, Inc. (CCA) based in Nashville. In 1985 the CCA proposed a takeover of the entire correctional system in Tennessee, but that bid was rejected by the state legislature.

Entry of the private sector into what has traditionally been thought of as a public responsibility is controversial; for example, it has been opposed by the National Sheriffs' Association, although state correction commissioners have tended to be more supportive. Supporters of the idea contend that private operators can maintain or exceed the level of services provided by public agencies at less cost. They are not bound by the bureaucracy or mandated salaries and retirement benefits of government agencies. Opponents question the propriety of handing over so basic a public responsibility as punishment to private entrepreneurs.

While minimum security facilities have generated less concern, the question of turning over medium and maximum security prisoners to a private concern has troubled observers who point out that in such institutions there is the constant threat of the use of force, including deadly physical force. The privately employed security officers are typically trained at the same state academies that train public correction officers, and enjoy the same peace officer powers. Whether private employees should be entrusted by government with such authority is an unanswered legal question. And in at least one case, a guard for a private prison operating under contract with the INS accidentally discharged a shotgun, killing one inmate and wounding another (*Medina* v. *O'Neil,* 589 F. Supp. 1028 (S.D. Tex. 1984). At the other end of the spectrum of possibilities, in 1990 the leader of a multimillion dollar drug ring used a .25 automatic to overpower his guards and escape with two other inmates from a jail being run by the Wackenhut Corporation under contract with Bexar County, Texas. Some opponents contend that private corrections corporations would seek to make Americans even more fearful of crime, through advertising and political campaigns, in order to keep jail and prison space at a maximum level. There are other issues; What will happen in the event of a strike by the private employees of a private prison? What if the firm decides to go out of business or enters into bankruptcy?

There are also any number of legal issues, the most basic being the authority of government to delegate its authority to private entrepreneurs to provide so basic a service as imprisonment. "A private entity," notes Ira Robbins, exercises governmental power when it deprives a person of life, liberty, or property at the behest of government" (1988: 36–37). Since a private prison might have an economic interest in imposing a punishment that denies privileges (thereby decreasing prison costs) or denying good time credits (which keeps the inmate incarcerated from which the firm may benefit financially), they would not typically be permitted control over such actions.

Private Prisons: Pros and Cons

Supporters of contracting out of prison responsibilities argue that:

1. Public prisons have done a poor job of maintaining inmates in a secure and safe environment.
2. The private sector can more quickly and cheaply build prisons and ease overcrowding by avoiding bureaucratic red tape and the need for voter approval for financing prison construction.
3. The private sector can more quickly implement new ideas and programs to better perform correctional functions.
4. The private sector can perform correctional functions more efficiently and less expensively than the public sector. Private institutions usually pay their staff less and employ fewer security personnel. This is accomplished by designing the prisons in such a way as to better control inmates with fewer staff members.

Opponents argue:

1. The power to deprive people of their liberty should not be delegated to private firms.
2. The power to use coercive force, including deadly force, should not be delegated to private firms.
3. Private employees are free to go on strike—who would staff the prison?
4. Private prisons could refuse to accept certain inmates, for example, those with AIDS.
5. The firm could go bankrupt.
6. The profit motive could delay the release of inmates economically beneficial to the private prison.
7. Security and services could be lowered to increase profits.

Source: Zawitz (1988).

Now that we have completed our review of the history of prisons and parole, in the next chapter we will look at the services provided by a parole agency.

REVIEW QUESTIONS

1. What led to the reemergence of positivism in penology after World War II?
2. What are the characteristics of the penological revolution that occurred in California toward the end of World War II?
3. What is meant by the *medical model approach* to criminal behavior?
4. What are the questionable assumptions upon which the medical model approach to corrections is based? Why are they questionable?
5. What is the difference between an *indeterminate* and a *determinate* or definite sentence?
6. What is the basis of criticism of the indeterminate sentence?
7. How do the four types of determinate or definite sentences differ?
8. What is meant by *good time* and how does it affect inmates?
9. What is the relationship between determinate sentencing and plea bargaining?
10. What is meant by *community-based corrections?*
11. What led to the popularity of community-based corrections?
12. What are the programs traditionally included in community-based corrections?
13. What led to the demise of community-based corrections?
14. Why was the corrections approach difficult, if not impossible, to implement in prisons?
15. What were the factors that led to the prison disturbances of the 1960s and early 1970s?
16. What has made the problem of prison discipline more difficult today than in the period of the Big House?
17. What are the pros and cons of using private prisons?

EIGHT
Parole Services

Three basic services can be provided by a parole agency: parole release, parole supervision, and executive clemency. In a number of states that have abolished parole release—California and Illinois, for example—parole officers/agents continue to supervise offenders released (not by a parole board but) on "good time." The administration of parole is less complex than that of probation because parole services are administered centrally on a statewide basis.

ADMINISTRATION OF PAROLE SERVICES

There are two basic models for administering parole services:

1. *Independent Model.* A parole board is responsible for making release (parole) determinations and for the supervision of persons released on parole (and "good time"). It is independent of any other state agency. This is the model used in Alabama, Nevada, and New York.

2. *Consolidated Model.* The parole board is an independent or a semi-autonomous agency within a larger department that also administers correctional institutions. Supervision of persons released on parole (and "good time") is under the direction of the commissioner of corrections. This is the model used in Arkansas, Colorado, and Rhode Island.

In both models, probation services are sometimes combined with parole services in a single statewide agency. For example, Alabama uses an independent model which includes probation services. Vermont uses a consolidated model in which probation services are part of the Department of Corrections. In Pennsylvania the courts have the statutory alternative of referring presentence investigations and the supervision of probationers and (county) parolees to the Board of Probation and Parole, rather than the county probation department.

The Task Force on Corrections (1966) summarized the arguments for the independent model:

1. The parole board is in the best position to promote the idea of parole and to generate public support and acceptance. Since the board is often held accountable (by the public, news media, public officials) for parole failures, it should be responsible for supervising parolees.
2. The parole board in direct control of administering parole services can more effectively evaluate and adjust the system.
3. Supervision by the parole board and its officers properly divorces parole release and parolees from the correctional institution.
4. An independent parole board in charge of its own services is in the best position to present its own budget request to the legislature.

The Task Force (1966) also summarized the arguments for including both parole services and institutions in a single department of corrections:

1. The correctional process is a continuum; all staff, institutional and parole, should be under a single administration rather than be divided, with resultant competition for public funds and friction in policies.
2. A consolidated correctional department has the advantage of consistent administration, including staff selection and supervision.
3. Parole boards are ineffective in performing administrative functions. Their major focus should be on case decisions, not on day-to-day field operations.
4. Community-based programs that fall between institutions and parole, such as work release, can best be handled by a single centralized administration.

Critics contend that the independent model tends to be indifferent or insensitive to institutional programs; that the parole board, in this model, places undue stress on variables outside of the institution. On the other hand, critics of the consolidated model argue that the parole board will be under pressure to stress institutional factors in making parole decisions, although these are of dubious value in making a parole prognosis.

CONDITIONAL RELEASE

Conditional release is the term used to describe inmates released on good time. As noted in previous chapters, inmates in most states are eligible for good time; that is, they can accumulate days-months-years off their maximum sentence by avoiding institutional infractions and/or participating in prison programs. In addition, some states have meritorious good time for exemplary behavior and *emergency good time* provisions to reduce the prison population in cases of severe overcrowding. In states utilizing the indeterminate sentence and parole board, good time can usually be accumulated at the rate of ten days per month—one-third off the maximum sentence. In some of these states good time may also be subtracted from the minimum sentence making the inmate eligible for parole before the minimum sentence has actually been served. In states utilizing determinate sentencing, good time usually amounts to one day off for every day served. In Maryland, which uses indeterminate sentencing, good time is granted at the rate of five days for good behavior, five days for performing industrial, agricultural, and administrative tasks, and an additional five days for making satisfactory progress in vocational and educational training.

In states where parole release has been abolished, most have retained supervision requirements for offenders released on good time—conditional releasees. In California, for example, all persons serving nonlife terms are released to parole supervision that cannot exceed three years. In some of these states decisions regarding good time and/or revocation of conditional release are the responsibility of a variety of boards: in California it is called the Board of Prison Terms; in Illinois, the Prisoner Review Board. In Missouri the Board of Probation and Parole was placed in the Department of Corrections and Human Services where it deals with questions of good time and supervision revocation. In Minnesota, where the parole board has been abolished, supervision of conditional releasees is the responsibility of the commissioner of corrections, who delegates this authority to the executive director of adult release.

These "boards" are also responsible for making parole decisions for persons imprisoned under indeterminate sentencing statutes that have since been repealed, and for persons serving "life sentences." Some also serve as a "pardons board," considering requests for the granting of executive clemency. In California the board has the additional responsibility of reviewing "all determinate sentences to state prison and to notify the sentencing court in any case in which the board determines the sentence to be disparate"—lawful and justified, but, nevertheless, disparate. "The court then has the opportunity to recall the sentence and resentence the defendant in a more uniform manner." (This is accomplished by a computerized system that flags cases falling outside of a normal distribution pattern of Z-scores by plus or minus 1.8.)

In California, as in most states, the Department of Corrections is responsible "for deducting good time credit from the sentence and for establishing procedures to deny good time credit." If good time is denied to an inmate, the person can appeal through department appeals procedures. A final department appeal, however, can be submitted for review to the Board of Prison

Terms, which conducts a hearing on the matter. In Illinois the Prisoner Review Board has broader responsibilities:

> Through panels of at least 3 members [the board has ten members] hear and decide cases brought by the Department of Corrections against prisoners in custody of the Department for alleged violation of Department rules with respect to good conduct credits . . . in which the Department seeks to revoke good conduct credits, if the amount of time at issue exceeds 30 days or when, during any 12-month period, the cumulative amount of credit revoked exceeds 30 days. However, the Board is not empowered to review the Department's decision with respect to the loss of 30 days of good conduct credit for any prisoner or to increase any penalty beyond the length requested by the Department; . . . Upon recommendation of the Department the Board restores good conduct credit previously revoked.

THE PAROLE BOARD

In most states parole board members are appointed by the governor (in Utah they are appointed by the Board of Corrections), although board membership and terms of office vary.

Parole Boards

- The *Alabama* Board of Pardons and Paroles has three members who serve six-year terms.
- The *Arizona* Board of Pardons and Paroles consists of seven members appointed for terms of five years.
- The *Georgia* Board of Pardons and Paroles is composed of five members appointed for seven-year terms.
- The *Hawaii* Paroling Authority consists of a full-time chairman and two part-time members appointed for four-year terms.
- In *Maryland* the Parole Commission consists of seven members who serve terms of six years.
- The *Massachusetts* Parole Board has seven members appointed for terms of five years.
- The *New Jersey* State Parole Board consists of seven members who serve staggered terms of six years.
- The *New York* State Board of Parole has fifteen members who serve six-year terms.
- The *Ohio* Parole Board consists of seven members who are picked for employment from civil services lists and serve indefinite terms.
- The *Pennsylvania* Board of Probation and Parole consists of five members who serve terms of six years.

(Continued)

- In *South Carolina* the Board of Probation, Parole, and Pardons Services consists of seven members who serve six-year terms.
- The *Utah* Board of Pardons has three members who serve six-year terms.
- The *Vermont* Parole Board has five members who serve five-year terms.

Parole boards have been criticized because members may lack any relevant background or education. In only a few states are there any specific professional qualifications for board members. William Parker states that "the only real qualification may be the political responsiveness and reliability of the board members to the appointing power" (1975: 30). New York requires that:

> Each member of the board shall have graduated from an accredited four-year college or university with a degree in the field of criminology, administration of criminal justice, law enforcement, sociology, law, social work, psychology, psychiatry, or medicine and shall have had at least five years of experience in one or more of such fields.

Maryland requires

> at least a B.A. or B.S. degree in one of the social or behavioral sciences or related fields . . . at least three (3) years experience in a responsible criminal justice or juvenile justice position, or equivalent experience in a relevant profession such as law or clinical practice.

In Vermont the governor

> shall appoint as members persons who have knowledge of and experience in correctional treatment, crime prevention or related fields, and shall give consideration, as far as practicable, to geographic representation to reduce necessary travel to the various parole interview centers of the state.

The role of patronage politics in the selection of parole board members is similar to that of many other responsible government positions, although the relatively low salary and extensive travel requirements tend to make it less attractive to those with other opportunities for political appointments.

Parole Board Procedures

Parole board members usually hold release hearings in the state's prisons. The members of the board panel will have available a case folder prepared by an institutional parole officer (or correctional staff person) which contains information about each inmate: the presentence investigation report, institutional reports relative to education, training, treatment, physical and psychological exams, misconduct, and a release plan in the event parole is granted. Typically, from one to three members briefly interview an inmate who is eligible for parole.

Examination by Nelson Harris, Member of the Board of Parole

Re: Smith, Louis, No. 092340136

Q: Louis Smith?

A: Yes.

Q: Smith, I am wondering if you got a chance on parole, what do you think would happen? Do you think the time is right?

A: I would go and pick up my life where I left it before.

Q: Do you think there was anything about the way you were living when you came in that needs changing?

A: A little could be altered so I am quite sure I would change them around now.

Q: Can you pinpoint, tell us some of the areas where you think you will change?

A: There is quite a few areas I can see where I am making mistakes. I am making a mistake coming here, that is one right there.

Q: Anything that you could do to stay out of places like this would definitely be something that would be of good intentions.

A: Yes.

Q: Do you have any plans? How are you going to try and go about making it when you get out of here?

A: First of all, I am starting back to work, which I am doing now and take it on from there.

Q: Staying in the big city area?

A: Yes.

Q: Can you cope with it?

A: I don't understand.

Q: Can you cope with the city, the bigness and all that?

A: Yes, I can.

Q: What is this job that you have?

A: It's the closest thing that they can give me to the job I have in the joint, that was all I have.

Q: Anybody that can get a foothold in that field really has something going for him and can make good money.

A: Yes.

(Continued)

Q: What can you do? How are your skills? What is the most you ever earned from it?

A: Well, the most I earned, brought in in one week was close to $500.

Q: You made that kind of money?

A: Yes.

Q: You noticed I have not referred to the crime?

A: Yes.

Q: You probably talked about it time and again.

A: Not very much, but some.

Q: This is thoroughly reported here. You did not have anything in your past like it and from what I read, it was certainly something you did not intend.

A: You are right, it wasn't intended. It was done through an accident. Mostly I was drinking and that is one problem I think I can handle now.

Q: Do you think you need anything outside yourself with reference to any drinking you did before?

A: I wasn't a regular drinker, I just drank sometimes. Now one thing I learned that if I get a problem, stay away from a bottle, that's what I learned.

Q: As a result of this, you also know that even though you don't drink all the time, it can still be a problem?

A: I found that out.

Q: Okay, your recommendations here are reasonably good and folks that have worked with you say they believe that there is no reason why you can't make it.

A: I hope I can.

Q: In the event you get the opportunity—

A: I hope I can make it.

Q: You feel that way?

A: Yes.

Q: Maybe there is something that you want to call to our attention?

A: No.

Q: Thanks for coming in. We will make a decision and let you know what it is.

In some states this aspect of parole release is handled by hearing examiners who interview the inmate and report back to the board with a recommendation; and some states do not conduct hearings or interviews—decisions are made on the basis of written reports. In New Jersey, for example, a hearing officer considers each inmate for release at an interview session held between four and six months before parole eligibility. If parole is recommended by the hearing officer, the case is reviewed by a panel of parole board members. If they accept the recommendation, a parole release date is set. If the hearing officer recommends against parole, or if the parole panel denies parole, a panel hearing at which the inmate appears is arranged. David Stanley states that the parole hearing is of dubious value. "It is a traumatic experience for the inmate, and parole board members are subjected to the rigors of holding hearings far away from home, with hours spent in travel and in prisons" (1976: 42). Furthermore, Stanley reports that hearings "are of little use in finding out whether the inmate is likely to succeed on parole" and argues that a strong case can be made for abolishing parole hearings:

> In cases where the information in the file and the board's own precedents plainly show that parole must surely be granted or denied, the hearing is a charade. In cases where the outcome is so obvious it is a proceeding in which the inmate is at a great disadvantage and in which he has reason to say anything that will help his chances for parole. The atmosphere at such a hearing is full of tension and latent hostility. Under these circumstances the hearing is an ineffective way to elicit information, evaluate character traits, and give advice, all of which parole boards try to do. (1976: 43).

One way to deal with some of these issues is to permit the inmate to have representation at the hearing. The National Advisory Commission believes that representation helps promote a feeling of fairness, and can enable an inmate to communicate better and thus participate more fully in the hearing. The commission states that "representation can also contribute to opening the correctional system, particularly the parole process, to public scrutiny" (1973: 403). The commission makes note of the fact that representation at parole hearings may be considered "annoying" to parole officials—there is fear that the hearing may take the form of an adversary proceeding—but adds that "these inconveniences seem a small price for the prospective gains."

Nevertheless, most jurisdictions do not permit representation at parole hearings. For example:

> *Pennsylvania:* "As the interview is not an adversarial process, the Board does not permit counsel representation at these interviews."
>
> *Maryland:* "Relatives or other interested and responsible individuals may request a conference with the Commission, submit letters, or other pertinent data relative to an inmate's parole consideration at any time prior to the hearing. They may not appear at parole hearings."
>
> *Wisconsin:* "Representation by legal counsel during the interview is not allowed." [However,] "A spokesperson for the inmate will be allowed . . . in cases of severe speech impediment or where the inmate suffers a severe physical disability which impedes verbal communication, or in cases where the inmate's primary language is not English and the individual lacks adequate fluency to represent himself or herself."
>
> *South Carolina:* While representation by an attorney at a parole hearing is not necessary, "an inmate may retain an attorney, if he so desires."

Vermont: " . . . the Board in its discretion may hear oral statements or arguments by attorneys or other persons with a valid interest in the case before the Board." Furthermore, it is the Board's policy to grant the inmate's legal representative access to the inmate's parole packet at a reasonable time in advance of the parole hearing."

In 1979, the United States Supreme Court (*Greenholtz* v. *Inmates* 442 U.S. 1) ruled that the Constitution does not require that an inmate be given the opportunity to participate in parole board hearings (or to be informed of the reasons for denial of parole). However, Stanley concludes:

Given the present parole system, hearings are necessary as an expression of our national tradition and culture. A man has his day in court before he is convicted and sentenced. In all sorts of situations we feel outraged if a person is not even confronted with the evidence before something adverse is done to him. In the hearing the prisoner is at least given a chance to state his case, correct erroneous statements, and impress the board with his determination (real or alleged) to reform. (1976: 43).

More than thirty states permit victims or their next of kin to appear before the parole board, and about a dozen others permit written statements to be considered at the parole hearing. In Nevada, for example, state law "provides that victims of crimes may attend meetings of the Nevada Board of Parole Commissioners. The Parole Board will provide notice of pending parole hearings if the victim of crime provides the board with a current address and requests such notice." In Alabama, "Victims of violent crimes and families of children who have been abused are notified prior to an inmate's being considered for parole by the Board. The Victim's right to be present at the Parole Hearing and to express their concerns in person and in writing to the Board is provided by law." In New Jersey, at the time of sentencing, the prosecutor notifies any victim injured as a result of a crime in the first or second degree, or the nearest relative of a murder victim, of the opportunity to present a statement to be considered during a parole hearing, or to give in-person testimony before the board concerning the victim's harm. The board notifies victims or relatives who have contacted the board requesting an opportunity to submit a statement or to provide testimony. In South Carolina, in addition to notification, the parole board appoints "an individual on staff to assist victims or witnesses in opposition on any parole or pardon matter." Many states include a victim impact statement as part of the documentation considered by the parole board.

In New York, for example, state law provides that victims or their representatives may submit a written victim impact statement to the parole board which must then consider it in reaching a parole decision. "The contents of the statement may set forth information concerning the offense, the extent of the injury or economic loss, the victim's attitude toward the offender's potential parole release, and other information that the victim may consider appropriate." The information is maintained in confidence.

Parole Board Criteria

In states utilizing the indeterminate sentence, the "parole boards exercise some functions that are exactly the same as judicial sentencing – for example, fixing minimum and maximum terms" (Rubin, 1974: 131). What criteria does a parole board use when it sets the minimum and maximum terms of imprisonment (in those states in which this is left to the parole board), or when it is considering the parole release of an inmate? New York statutes provide:

> Discretionary release on parole shall not be granted merely as a reward for good conduct or efficient performance of duties while confined but after considering if there is a reasonable probability that, if such inmate is released, he will live and remain at liberty without violating the law, and that his release is not incompatible with the welfare of society and will not so depreciate the seriousness of his crime as to undermine respect for law. In making the parole release decision . . . the following [must] be considered: (i) the institutional record including program goals and accomplishments, academic achievements, vocational education, training or work assignments, therapy and interpersonal relationships with staff and inmates; (ii) performance, if any, as a participant in a temporary release program; (iii) release plans including community resources, employment, education and training and support services available to the inmate; and (iv) any deportation order issued by the federal government. . . .

Parole boards usually consider the crime, the length of time served, the inmate's age, prior criminal history, use of alcohol or drugs, and institutional record. Some parole boards may request a recommendation from the prosecutor. All will certainly consider opposition to an inmate's parole from the police and the news media. The widespread use of parole guidelines has reduced the importance of general criteria.

Parole Board Guidelines

As criticism of parole and parole boards began to mount in the 1970s, the United States Board of Parole engaged a group of researchers to develop a model for improved decision making. In particular, the board was interested in a means of reducing disparity and making the decision-making process intelligible to both inmates and the public. The researchers, headed by Donald Gottfredson and Leslie Wilkins, derived a set of variables that they saw as fairly representative of those used by board members in making decisions – the most salient being the seriousness of the offense and parole prognosis. The researchers also conducted a two-year study of 2,500 federal parolees and uncovered a variety of "success factors" which they reduced to seven variables. The combined variables for *severity of offense* and *parole prognosis* were arranged in the form of a grid (see Table 8.1) to determine the actual length of

TABLE 8.1 Guidelines for Decision Making, Customary Total Time to Be Served before Release (Including Jail Time)

Offense Characteristics: Offense Severity (Some Crimes Eliminated or Summarized)	OFFENDER CHARACTERISTICS: PAROLE PROGNOSIS			
	Very Good	Good	Fair	Poor
Category One Low: possession of a small amount of marijuana; simple theft under $1,000.		*Adult Range*		
	≤6 months	6–9 months	9–12 months	12–16 months
		(Youth Range)		
	(≤6) months	(6–9) months	(9–12) months	(12–16) months
Category Two Low/Moderate: income tax evasion less than $10,000; immigration law violations; embezzlement, fraud, forgery under $1,000		*Adult Range*		
	≤8 months	8–12 months	12–16 months	16–22 months
		(Youth Range)		
	(≤8) months	(8–12) months	(12–16) months	(16–20) months
Category Three Moderate: bribery; possession of 50 lb. or less of marijuana, with intent to sell; illegal firearms; income tax evasion $10,000 to $50,000; nonviolent property offenses $1,000 to $19,999; auto theft, not for resale		*Adult Range*		
	10–14 months	14–18 months	18–24 months	24–32 months
		(Youth Range)		
	(8–12) months	(12–16) months	(16–20) months	(20–26) months
Category Four High: counterfeiting; marijuana possession with intent to sell, 50 to 1,999 lb.; auto theft, for resale; nonviolent property offenses, $20,000 to $100,000		*Adult Range*		
	14–20 months	20–26 months	26–34 months	34–44 months
		(Youth Range)		
	(12–16) months	(16–20) months	(20–26) months	(26–32) months
Category Five Very High: robbery; breaking and entering bank or post office; extortion; marijuana possession with intent to sell, over 2,000 lb.; hard drugs possession with intent to sell, not more than $100,000; nonviolent property offenses over $100,00 but not exceeding $500,000		*Adult Range*		
	24–36 months	36–48 months	48–60 months	60–72 months
		(Youth Range)		
	(20–26) months	(26–32) months	(32–40) months	(40–48) months

TABLE 8.1 *Continued*

Offense Characteristics: Offense Severity (Some Crimes Eliminated or Summarized)	OFFENDER CHARACTERISTICS: PAROLE PROGNOSIS			
	Very Good	Good	Fair	Poor
Category Six Greatest I: explosive detonation; multiple robbery; aggravated felony (weapon fired—no serious injury); hard drugs, over $100,000; forcible rape	*Adult Range* 40–52 months (30–40) months	52–64 months *(Youth Range)* (40–50) months	64–78 months (50–60) months	78–100 months (60–76) months
Category Seven Greatest II: aircraft hijacking; espionage; kidnapping; homicide	*Adult Range* 52–80 months (40–64) months	64–92 months *(Youth Range)* (50–74) months	78–110 months (70–86) months	100–148 months (76–110) months
Category Eight[a]	*Adult Range* 100+ months (80+) months	120+ months *(Youth Range)* (100+) months	150+ months (120+) months	180+ months (150+) months

[a]*Note:* For Category Eight, no upper limits are specified because of the extreme variability of the cases within this category. For decisions exceeding the lower limit of the applicable guideline category *by more than forty-eight months,* the pertinent aggravation case factors considered are to be specified in the reasons given (for example, that a homicide was premeditated or commited during the course of another felony; or that extreme cruelty or brutality was demonstrated).

211

Georgia State Board of Pardons and Paroles
Parole Decision Guidelines - Notice of Tentative Action

NAME: _____   DATE: _____

NOTICE:
THE BOARD SPECIFICALLY RESERVES THE RIGHT TO EXERCISE ITS DISCRETION UNDER GEORGIA LAW TO DENY PAROLE EVEN THOUGH GUIDELINES CRITERIA ARE MET BY AN INMATE. IT IS NOT THE INTENTION OF THE BOARD TO CREATE A "LIBERTY INTEREST" OF THE TYPE DESCRIBED IN GREENHOLTZ VS. NEBRASKA PENAL INMATES 442 US 1 (1979).

Parole Decision Guidelines help the Board make a more consistent, soundly based, prompt, and explainable parole decision. Guidelines help the Board decide on a Tentative Parole Month for the inmate or decide that the inmate will complete his sentence without parole. When making decisions, the Board may depart from the Guidelines Recommendation and make an independent decision using the full discretion given it under Georgia Law. The length of the prison sentence imposed by the court will be considered in establishing a Tentative Parole Month.

CRIME SEVERITY LEVEL: Your Crime Severity Level is selected from the table of offenses on the back of this sheet.

PAROLE SUCCESS FACTORS: Your Parole Success Likelihood Score is found by adding the points which apply to you.

A. AGE AT FIRST COMMITMENT
    (26 or over = 5)
    (22–25   = 3)
    (18–21   = 2)   ____
    (17 or less = 0)

B. PRIOR CONVICTIONS (JUVENILE AND ADULT)
    (none   = 3)
    (1   = 2)   ____
    (2–3   = 1)
    (4 or more = 0)

C. PRIOR INCARCERATIONS SINCE AGE 17
    (none   = 2)
    (1   = 1)   ____
    (2 or more = 0)

D. PAROLE OR PROBATION FAILURE
    (No failure   = 4)
    (Probation only = 2)
    (Parole only   = 1)
    (Both   = 0)   ____

E. NO USE, POSSESSION OR ATTEMPT TO OBTAIN HEROIN OR OPIATE
    DRUGS   = 1   ____
    OTHERWISE = 0

FIGURE 8.1   Parole Decision Guidelines, Georgia

F. COMMITMENT OFFENSE(S) DID NOT
   INVOLVE BURGLARY OR FORGERY = 2
   OTHERWISE   = 0   ____

G. FULLY EMPLOYED DURING 6 MONTHS PRECEDING ARREST ON CURRENT
   OFFENSE   = 1
   OTHERWISE   = 0   ____

H. HAD WRAT SCORE OF 8 OR HIGHER
   AT TIME OF INITIAL TESTING = 2
   OTHERWISE   = 0   ____

PAROLE SUCCESS LIKELIHOOD SCORE ____

GUIDELINES RECOMMENDED MONTHS TO SERVE

Read across from your Crime Severity Level and down from your Parole Success Likelihood Score to find your Guidelines Recommended Months to Serve. For Crime Severity Levels I through V the grid reflects a shift in months to serve based on the court imposed sentence length. If your sentence is less than 25% of the statutory maximum penalty, the lesser figure is used. If your sentence exceeds 75% of the statutory maximum penalty, the greater figure is used. For all other sentence lengths, the median figure is used. For Crime Severity Levels VI or VII, the Guidelines Recommendation will be one-third of the court imposed sentence length or the grid recommendation, whichever is greater. The Board, using its discretion in your case, may depart from the Guidelines Recommendation.

PAROLE SUCCESS LIKELIHOOD SCORE

		EXCELLENT 13–20	GOOD 11–12	AVERAGE 9–10	FAIR 6–8	POOR 0–5
	I	4 4 5	5 6 7	6 8 10	10 12 14	14 18 22
	II	5 6 7	6 8 10	7 9 11	11 14 17	17 21 25
CRIME	III	6 8 10	7 9 11	10 12 14	12 15 18	19 24 29
SEVERITY	IV	8 10 12	10 12 14	12 15 18	14 18 22	22 27 32
LEVEL	V	16 20 24	20 25 30	24 30 36	32 40 48	42 52 62
	VI	36	48	54	60	78
	VII	60	72	78	90	102

Crime Severity Level   _____

Parole Success Likelihood Score   _____

Recommended Months to Serve from the Grid, or   _____
   One-third of Court Imposed Sentence

Guidelines Recommended Tentative Parole Month   _____

TENTATIVE BOARD DECISION

All decisions made by the Board herein are considered tentative and may be changed at the discretion of the Board at any time. Only the paragraph with the "X" applies to you.

( ) The Board has tentatively decided to parole you during the above Tentative Parole Month.

( ) Because your Tentative Parole Month is later than your discharge date, you should expect to be discharged from your sentence without parole.

FIGURE 8.1 *Continued*

(   ) The Board has determined that the Crime Severity Level and/or the Parole Success Factors do not adequately reflect the true nature of your case. Therefore, they have departed from the Guidelines Recommendation and have taken the following action:

_____ The specific reasons for departing are listed below:

If you believe your Crime Severity Level or any Parole Success Factor has been scored incorrectly, you may ask the Board, within 30 days, to recompute your scores. The Board will consider any verifiable information submitted to substantiate your request. Such requests may be submitted in any written form and should be directed to the Parole Guidelines Director, State Board of Pardons and Paroles, Floyd Veterans Building, Fifth Floor East, 2 Martin Luther King, Jr., Drive, S.E., Atlanta, GA 30334.

If the Board's tentative decision is to depart from the Guidelines Recommendation, and the number of months to serve is more than three years beyond the Guidelines Recommendation, your case will be reviewed at the Guidelines Recommendation and each three years thereafter.

Your institutional conduct has not been evaluated at this time. The Board expects you to use your time in confinement in a constructive manner. Exemplary conduct may result in a parole release prior to your scheduled release month. Institutional misconduct will result in a delay in your parole release or a decision to deny parole.

FIGURE 8.1 *Continued*

imprisonment. For example, an adult offender convicted of forgery, "Category Two," whose parole prognosis is "Good," would normally be released on parole after serving between eight and twelve months; an offender convicted of multiple robberies, "Category Six," with a parole prognosis of "Poor," would normally serve between seventy-eight and one hundred months before being paroled.

Guidelines typically go well beyond the *rehabilitative/medical model* on which the indeterminate sentence is often presumed to be based. Indeed, satisfactory progress in those institutional programs that are "rehabilitative" may not even affect the parole decision. Kevin Krajick (1978) points out that good institutional behavior is *expected,* not rewarded, although poor behavior can be punished with additional time. In fact, the institutional adjustment of an offender has never been an accurate guide for predicting postinstitutional behavior (for example, see Dolan, Lunden, and Barberet, 1987); there is some evidence that certain offenders (for example, substance abusers, professional criminals) most often perform well in prison and, nevertheless, tend to recidivate.

In effect, the use of guidelines whose primary focus is *just deserts* is a form of deferred sentencing. Some critics claim there is no justification for deferring sentence (the term of imprisonment) and that it creates problems by adding to the offender's uncertainty. Others argue that the parole board is relatively free of the "heat" that certain crimes and criminals can generate. The board does not typically operate with the same high visibility of a court; unlike a sentencing judge, the parole board is not normally under the gaze of the community and news media. These observers stress that the parole board, using guidelines, is better equipped to make a rational decision commensurate with just deserts than is a sentencing judge.

Guidelines used by state parole boards consider the seriousness of the present offense and prior criminal history; most, as in the federal guidelines, also consider rehabilitative items and/or parole prognosis. For example, the Georgia Board of Pardons and Paroles, in a mix of the classical and positive schools, states: "Justice demands that punishment should be tailored to fit both the offense and the offender."

> A Board hearing examiner identifies an inmate's Crime Severity Level from a table of offenses ranked in seven levels from lowest to highest in severity. The higher the severity, the longer the inmate will be recommended to serve. Then the hearing examiner calculates the inmate's Parole Success Likelihood by adding weighted factors with proven predictive value from the inmate's criminal and social history. A history of things such as prior imprisonment, parole or probation failure, heroin use or possession, and joblessness would increase the risk of paroling the inmate and cause him to be recommended for longer confinement.

INSTITUTIONAL SERVICES

Parole services can be divided into those provided by institutional personnel, field personnel, and the separate category of clemency.

The basic responsibility of institutional parole staff is to prepare reports on inmates for the parole board. They also help inmates secure furloughs, work release, or halfway house placement, and they may assist with personal problems ranging from matters relating to spouse and children to questions of a technical or legal nature.

Under ideal conditions, when an offender is first received at the institution he or she is interviewed by a member of the parole staff. The results of the interview, psychiatric and psychological tests, and the information in the presentence report are then used to help plan an institutional program for the inmate. The parole staff periodically updates the material with additional information. They discuss release plans with inmates, and request the field staff to visit and interview family members and prospective employers. When an inmate is ready to meet the parole board, they provide a report on the inmate that includes an evaluation of changes made since the offender was first interviewed at the prison. The report may also contain a completed "parole guidelines" form and a recommendation if this is requested by the board.

Florida Parole and Probation Commission

Pre-Parole Investigation

Date: January 11, 1989
To: Wanda Bryan, Work Processing
From: Karel E. Yedlicka, Jr., Parole Examiner I
Re: Robert L. Smith, FSP #172362

I OFFENSE

The subject was involved in a burglary of a home in which merchandise valued at over $1,800.00 was stolen, and there was damage to the house itself. The presentence report indicates that the victim was in the house at the time of the burglary, but thought it was her son and therefore did not investigate the subject coming into the home by the back door. The subject also received an enhanced penalty on numerous prior felony convictions with a current parole release date of September 1, 1989.

II PERSONAL BACKGROUND

Florida is where he will be temporarily staying with his sister, who has legal custody of the subject's daughter, Judith Smith, age 14. Judith is currently enrolled in Joseph Mittner Junior High School and has been cared for by the subject's sister, Margaret Smith, since the subject's incarceration in 1976. Currently, she is receiving $178.00 per month in Florida Aid to Dependent Children toward the care of Judith. This sum will be reduced when the subject is able to provide support for his daughter. Ms. Smith indicated that the subject has every intention of living with his daughter, securing his own residence, and raising her. He has not had the benefit of being with her very much during the past 12 years. This examiner recommends that as a special condition of parole, the subject be required to provide adequate support for his daughter, whose mother's whereabouts are unknown at this time.

III RESIDENCE

The subject will be residing with his sister Margaret Smith, who, along with her brother Raymond Smith, owns a brick and wood frame home with four bedrooms and one bath located at 1526 Cincinatti Street, Jacksonville. In 1987, the subject's father moved to Charleston, South Carolina, and turned the house over to Margaret and Raymond. Margaret stated that the subject will probably stay with her without a need to pay for room and board until he can get on his feet.

IV EMPLOYMENT

The subject is employed on work release at Briarcliff Manor, a 24-hour nursing home at 1001 Briarcliff Boulevard, Jacksonville. His employment was verified by Mona Mitchell, the bookkeeper. The day supervisor, Melanie Harris, states that the subject is an excellent worker and has experienced no problems. He is employed as a dietician's assistant who helps with meals and other minor duties in the nursing home earning $4.10 per hour, 30–40 hours per week. The subject receives Workmen's Compensation but no other benefits at this time. The nursing home also employs more than 30 other individuals on a 24-hour basis.

The subject has been employed at this job, obtained through the work-release center, since 10-13-88. No driver's license is required in that the subject works exclusively in the facility. However, the subject's sister stated that their father left an old car that the subject can use when paroled for transportation back and forth from northside to southside.

V SPECIAL PROGRAMS OR TREATMENT FEATURES

As previously verified, restitution is owed and the subject should make restitution accordingly, a recommended rate is $25.00 per month for a period of four years. In addition to supporting his daughter, there should be a drug-testing clause reflecting his problem with heroin as indicated in the PSI. In view of the seriousness of his criminal history, the subject will need close supervision.

VI RECOMMENDATIONS

This examiner recommends that the subject be paroled on 3-7-89 for a minimum supervision period of four years due to the severity of the instant offense and the need to pay restitution. The proposed residence appears to be valid and the subject's employment appears to be an excellent opportunity at this time for him to reintegrate back into society. The subject has been out only briefly in the latter part of 1979 before being re-arrested in 1980 with the rest of the time spent incarcerated back to 1976. The subject is now 35 years of age, and if he cannot make parole at this time, it is unlikely that he will make one in the future.

Parole Examiner I

Institutional parole staff may also hold group meetings with new inmates to orient them about parole. These group sessions are then followed up with individual interviews. There are also preparole group sessions at which parole staff attempts to lower anxiety about meeting the board or hearing examiners. When an inmate has been granted parole, or becomes eligible for conditional release, he or she will meet with a parole staff member for a final discussion of the release program and rules of supervision, prior to leaving the prison.

In some jurisdictions institutional parole staff are responsible for notifying victims and/or local law enforcement agencies of the impending release of certain offenders. (Some states require that when an offender is released, the police in the area where the parolee is to reside, or where the crime occurred, be notified. In some instances the parolee must register in person with the local law enforcement agency). The institutional parole staff must determine the probable disposition of any warrants that have been lodged against an inmate. When appropriate, they arrange for an out-of-state program under the Interstate Compact (discussed in Chapter 11). In some states nonparole institutional staff perform the same, or similar, functions as institutional parole officers; these persons sometimes have the title of *correctional counselor.*

Institutional Parole Services in New Jersey

Institutional parole staff service all penal and correctional institutions and training schools. Staff members conduct personal interviews with inmates, counseling on specific matters to resolve problems, and to develop suitable preparole plans. Staff members afford every inmate prerelease classes. They also assist inmates in obtaining necessary clothing and transportation from institutions to residences. The increase in the use of home visits and furloughs and the number of state prisoners in county correctional facilities have added considerably to the workloads of institutional parole office staff.

Institutional Parole Services in New York

Institutional parole officers assigned to correctional facilities guide and direct inmates during their incarceration. They help the inmate develop positive attitudes and behaviors, encourage participation in prison programs, and prepare inmates for their Parole Board appearances. The institutional Parole Officer prepares the inmates' parole records and makes evaluations and recommendations to the Board of Parole to help it reach the best possible decisions concerning granting and denying of parole release.

Street Readiness Program in Nevada

The Street Readiness Program (SRP) of the Department of Probation and Parole was established for inmates about to be released back into the community on parole and those committed for 120-day evaluations who are returning to court for sentencing. These inmates become students three hours a day for a period of three weeks, normally just prior to their release. The curriculum consists of classroom lecture, discussions, activities, and homework. Subjects include: parole orientation, goals, decision-making skills, substance abuse, domestic relations, financial responsibility, citizenship, employment skills, sex education, law, insurance, human relations, and driver training. The program is almost totally dependent on community volunteers, and since it was established in 1981, has graduated more than four thousand offenders.

FIELD SERVICES

Field service staff usually operate out of district offices located throughout the state. The New York State Division of Parole, for example, has field staff assigned to the supervision of parolees and conditional releasees in twenty field area offices throughout New York. They conduct field investigations requested by institutional staff relative to parole release programs, and they supervise parolees and/or conditional releasees. Parole field staff may also be involved in a variety of special programs such as work release and furloughs. In New York: "Some Field Officers are assigned to correctional facilities to supervise Temporary Release participants—inmates permitted by the Department of Correctional Services to work, attend school, provide community service, and re-establish family ties (furloughs)."

Field Services in California

The California Legislature has found and declared "that the period immediately following incarceration is critical to successful reintegration of the offender into society and to positive citizenship. It is in the interest of public safety for the State to provide for the supervision and surveillance of parolees and to provide educational, vocational, family and personal counseling necessary to assist parolees in the transition between imprisonment and discharge."

The overall objective of the Parole and Community Services Division is to reduce the frequency and severity of criminal behavior and to facilitate the community adjustment of adult offenders, fully recognizing their individual and changing circumstances and actions, through a program structure of appropriate prerelease, supervision, and support management functions.

Supervision, surveillance, and services delivery are the responsibilities of parole field staff throughout the State. The primary means by which a parole agent fulfills these responsibilities is through contacts with parolees and persons involved with the parolee. Parole staff will cooperate and collaborate with criminal justice and human service agencies that may be involved with the parolee. It is the duty and obligation of the parole agent to:

1. Obtain information about parolee activities and needs.
2. Intervene in parolee behavior which violates the conditions of parole or which may jeopardize the safety of the public or the parolee.
3. Provide supportive services to assist the parolee in the transition between imprisonment and discharge.
4. Share information about the parolee with law enforcement personnel and the personnel of other agencies who have a demonstrated and/or compelling need to know.

Field Services in Pennsylvania

Once the Board has made a decision to release an inmate on parole, the Board's Bureau of Supervision staff plays a significant role assisting the parolee in adjusting to life in the community. The parole period is a time of transition from the structured, confined environment of the institution to life as a free citizen. Parole is also a time to test the readiness of the parolee to handle the responsibilities of community life.

The immediate goal of parole supervision is the protection of society, which can best be accomplished by reintegrating the offender into the community as a responsible and productive citizen. Specifically, this means helping the parolee obtain and hold a meaningful job; resolving any adjustment problems within the family and the community; meeting education, mental health, or other normative needs, when relevant; and becoming part of the community through participation in activities and organizations which reflect the individual's interests and capability. This involves not only working with the individual under supervision, but also with the various community agencies and resources which have the capability of assisting in solution of problems of parolees.

One of the tools of the supervision staff is "Conditions Governing Parole/ Reparole" established by the Board to be used as a structuring force in the life of the parolee. These conditions define what course of behavior is acceptable if the client wishes to complete the period of parole supervision successfully. While there are a number of common conditions which are to be adhered to, the Board recognizes the needs of the individual offender and has provided for one or more special conditions to be imposed as needed.

Conditions of Parole

Every conditionally released or paroled prisoner is required to sign an agreement to abide by certain regulations. This aspect of parole has its origins in the Ticket of Leave and, as noted in Chapter 6, modern parole conditions resemble Ticket of Leave regulations. Parole conditions are markedly similar throughout most jurisdictions and they are also very similar or identical to probation regulations. Lawrence Travis and Edward Latessa report that since 1969 states have tended to reduce the number of conditions imposed on parolees:

> Exceptions to this trend are found when parole . . . conditions relate directly to the control of illegal behavior and the ability of the parole authority to maintain supervision over released offenders. This is seen particularly in conditions relating to the reporting of arrests, compliance with the law, possession of narcotics, and possession of weapons. (1984: 598)

Conditions of parole can generally be grouped into *standard conditions* applicable to all parolees/conditional releasees, which typically involve restric-

STATE OF OHIO
Department of Rehabilitation and Correction
ADULT PAROLE AUTHORITY

CONDITIONS OF SUPERVISION

In consideration of having been granted supervision on _____ , I agree to report to my probation/ parole officer within _____ , hours or according to the written instructions I have received and to the following conditions:

1. I will obey federal, state, and local laws and ordinances, and all rules and regulations of_____ Common Pleas Court or the Department of Rehabilitation and Correction.

2. I will always keep my probation/parole officer informed of my residence and place of employment. I will obtain permission from my probation/parole officer before changing my residence or my employment.

3. I will not leave the State without written permission of the Adult Parole Authority;

4. I will not enter upon the grounds of any correctional facility nor attempt to visit any prisoner without the written permission of my probation/parole officer nor will I communicate with any prisoner without first informing my probation/parole officer of the reason for such communication.

5. I will comply with all orders given to me by my probation/parole officer or other authorized representative of the Court, the Department of Rehabilitation and Correction or the Adult Parole Authority, including any written instructions issued at any time during the period of supervision.

6. I will not purchase, possess, own, use, or have under my control, any firearms, deadly weapons, ammunition, or dangerous ordnance.

7. I will not possess, use, purchase, or have under my control any narcotic drug or other controlled substance, including any instrument, device or other object used to administer drugs or to prepare them for administration, unless it is lawfully prescribed for me by a licensed physician. I agree to inform my probation/parole officer promptly of any such prescription and I agree to submit to drug testing if required by the Adult Parole Authority.

8. I will report any arrest, citation of a violation of the law, conviction or any other contact with a law enforcement officer to my probation/parole officer no later than the next business day, and I will not enter into any agreement or other arrangement with any law enforcement agency which might place me in the position of violating any law or condition of my supervision unless I have obtained permission in writing from the Adult Parole Authority, or from the Court if I am a probationer.

9. I agree to a search without warrant of my person, my motor vehicle, or my place of residence by a probation/parole officer at any time.

10. I agree to sign a release of confidential information from any public or private agency if requested to do so by a probation/parole officer.

11. I agree and understand that if I am arrested in any other state or territory of the United States or in any foreign country, my signature as witnessed at the end of the page will be deemed to be a waiver of extradition and that no other formalities will be required for authorized agents of the State of Ohio to bring about my return to this state for revocation proceedings.

12. I also agree to the following Special Conditions, as imposed by the Court or the Adult Parole Authority:

I have read or had read to me, the foregoing conditions of my _____ . I fully understand these conditions, I agree to comply with them, and I understand that violation of any of these conditions may result in the revocation of my _____ .

In addition, I understand that I will be subject to the foregoing conditions until I have received a certificate from the Adult Parole Authority, or a Journal Entry from Court if I am a probationer, stating that I have been discharged from supervision.

_____   _____   _____
Witness   Signature   Date

FIGURE 8.2 Ohio Parole Rules

tions on travel, associating with other offenders, drug and alcohol use, employment, and residence; and *special conditions* which are tailored to the individual requirements of a particular offender. For example, persons with a history of sex offenses against children will be prohibited from areas where children typically congregate, such as playgrounds; persons with a history of alcohol abuse may be prohibited from using alcohol or being in facilities, such as bars, where alcohol is consumed.

Length of Supervision

The length of time an offender must spend on parole/conditional release supervision is governed by the length of the sentence and the laws of the state where convicted. In Oregon, a conditional releasee "is subject to a period of supervision similar to parole, not to exceed six months or the maximum date, whichever comes first." In Illinois the length of supervision for conditional releasees varies from one to three years depending on the class of crime for which the offender was convicted. In California, for persons sentenced under a life sentence, the maximum period, including time under parole supervision and time under revocation status, cannot exceed seven years. For persons sentenced under a nonlife sentence the maximum period, including time under supervision and time under revocation status, cannot exceed four years.

In most states a parolee/releasee can be discharged prior to the expiration of sentence or mandated period of supervision. In California, based on satisfactory performance, a nonlife releasee can be discharged from supervision after one year, and a "lifer" after three years. In New York: "If the board of parole is satisfied that an absolute discharge from parole or from conditional release is in the best interests of society, the board may grant such discharge prior to the expiration of the full maximum term to any person who has been on unrevoked parole or conditional release for at least three consecutive years." In Hawaii, any parolee may be discharged from supervision whenever there is "evidence as is deemed reliable and trustworthy that he or she will remain at liberty without violation of the law and that final release is not incompatible with the welfare of society." In any event, parolees under supervision for at least five years, "shall be brought before the Paroling Authority for purposes of consideration for final discharge." In Alabama, however, "Early termination in parole cases may be accomplished only by means of a Pardon, which will be considered after a subject has served five years under supervision." The same board that is responsible for parole in Alabama, Board of Pardons and Paroles, has the power to grant pardons. In Vermont, "although the Board may terminate parole supervision at any time, it will normally consider termination only after successful completion of one half of the maximum parole term."

VIOLATION OF PAROLE/CONDITIONAL RELEASE

While probation violation is linked to the judicial system, parole violation is an administrative function that is typically devoid of any court involvement. While there is some variation with respect to the procedures used, Figure 8.3

PAROLE/VIOLATION FLOWCHART

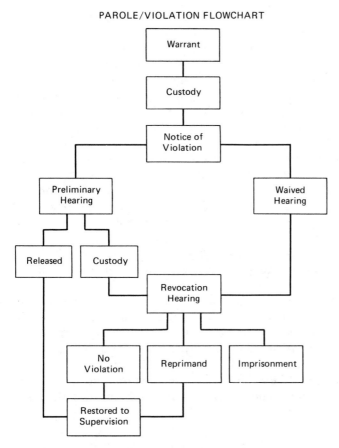

FIGURE 8.3   Parole/Conditional Release Violation Flowchart

presents a general overview of the system and indicates the possibilities available at each stage of the process.

There are two types of parole violation:

1.   *Technical Violation.* This occurs when any of the conditions of parole have been violated.
2.   *New Offense Violation.* This involves an arrest and prosecution for the commission of a new crime. In practice, new offense violations often involve technical violations. A new offense violation, for example, an arrest for robbery that involves a gun, also constitutes a technical violation of the conditions prohibiting possession of firearms.

In either event, the violation process begins when a parole officer (the title varies, for example, probation and parole officer, parole agent, correctional program officer, probation/parole supervisor) becomes aware of a violation. After discussing the situation with a supervisor, a decision is made relative to the issuance of a warrant. This stage has the greatest amount of variance between agencies. In Pennsylvania parole agents can use an "Order to Detain for 48 Hours" in lieu of a warrant when circumstances require it. A similar situation obtains in New York where field parole officers carry a twenty-four-hour detainer-warrant. Thus, in Pennsylvania and New York, a parole agent/officer who becomes aware of a serious violation of parole while in the field, can summarily take the violator into custody and receive telephone authorization for the use of the "Order to Detain" or twenty-four-hour de-tainer-warrant. (These temporary detainers must be replaced by a warrant, in Pennsylvania within forty-eight hours; in New York within twenty-four hours.)

When I was a parole officer in New York, it was not unusual to encounter parolees, unexpectedly, who were in serious violation of the conditions of their release. For example: heavily involved in abusing heroin (and obviously engaging in criminal acts to support the habit); prohibited from the use of alcohol (because of the dangerous nature of their behavior while under the influence) and intoxicated; child molesters found in the company of children. I could take such persons into custody immediately and use the telephone for detainer-warrant authorization.

In jurisdictions which are rather conservative about issuing violation warrants, the process may be quite time consuming and can involve a written request to the board of parole. In Oregon, in lieu of a summary arrest, the parole officer may issue a *citation* requiring the parolee/releasee to appear for a violation hearing. This is authorized when the individual has violated a condition of supervision, but the nature of the violation does not jeopardize the safety of the general public, and the individual, if left undetained, is not likely to flee. In Iowa:

> A parole officer having probable cause to believe that any person released on parole has violated the conditions of parole may arrest such person, or the parole officer may make a complaint before a magistrate, charging such violation, and if it appears from such complaint . . . that there is probable cause to believe that such person has violated the terms of parole, the magistrate shall issue a warrant for the arrest of such person.

In either event, the violator must be taken before a magistrate for consideration of release on bail—"bail is discretionary with the magistrate and is not a matter of right" in Iowa. Many, if not most, jurisdictions do not permit a parole violator to be released on bail.

In Wisconsin, in lieu of an arrest or warrant issuance, a parole agent's immediate supervisor can order the alleged violator to appear for a *case review*.

> The focus of case review is threefold: to determine whether there is probable cause to believe there was a violation of the rules or conditions of probation or parole, to determine whether, if there is probable cause, it makes correctional

sense to revoke, and to determine whether the client should remain in custody during revocation proceedings.

While this case review has many of the characteristics of a preliminary hearing, to be discussed shortly, it is both more broadly focused — can consider issues relating to supervision adjustment — and is less formal:

> It is hoped by making the proceedings less formal and adversary, the client, the client's attorney, the agent and the agent's supervisor can frankly discuss the issues in an atmosphere that focuses attention on the most important issues.

Arizona Department of Corrections
Division of Parole

Request for Parole Violation Warrant

NAME OF SUBJECT: Wilson, Joseph

ID NO.: ADC 8654

DATE: August 26, 1988

Subject was committed to the Department of Corrections on January 30, 1986, for the offense of Burglary, 2nd Degree, a Class 3 felony; he received a sentence of 5 years. On April 30, 1988, the Board of Pardons and Paroles granted the subject parole with the following special conditions:

a. no use of alcohol or illegal drugs;
b. chemical testing for alcohol and illegal drugs;
c. mental health counseling with emphasis on substance abuse;
d. maintain full-time employment during term of parole;
e. restitution to be paid as per court order; and
f. $30 per month supervision fee.

On May 15, 1988 the subject was released from the Arizona State Prison on a Temporary Release, which reverted to parole on May 27, 1988. As per the subject's Departure and Arrival Report, dated May 15, 1988, he will reach his maximum expiration of sentence on October 24, 1989.

On May 15, 1988, subject read, indicated that he understood, and signed the standard conditions form with all of the above special conditions stipulated.

Upon release subject lived with his mother and father, Judith and Harold Wilson at 97 W. Barry Street, Phoenix. Frequent personal and telephonic contacts with his parents indicated that subject reentered the family unit with minimal difficulty. Parents have been cooperative with this PO while the subject has been under supervision; there were no problems reported in the family unit by the parents.

Subject obtained employment soon after his release and has maintained same

(Continued)

---

while under supervision with Biltmore Building Contractors, 1751 Sealy Boulevard, Phoenix. His employer was contacted on several occasions and reported that subject was a "polished" compulsive liar, and frequently failed to come to work on time. Subject was questioned and counseled about his performance at Biltmore.

On May 21, 1988, subject entered the Central Psychological and Substance Abuse Center, 140 Broadway Avenue, Phoenix, as directed, to fulfill his Board-imposed conditions. Subject made all scheduled counseling sessions, but missed two urinalysis screens; subject was questioned and warned. On August 21, and August 24, 1988, subject tested positive for cocaine.

On August 25, 1988, subject was arrested by the Phoenix Police Department and charged with Burglary. The police report (DR #1568) and arresting officer indicate that two witnesses observed the subject in the area of the burglarized apartment located at 1414 N. 34 Avenue, Apt. #95, Phoenix, just prior to hearing the victim's apartment window break. Shortly afterwards they observed the subject near the burglarized apartment carrying something under a jacket. Witnesses obtained the license plate number of the vehicle the subject was driving at the time. He was later positively identified by witnesses in a photo line-up.

On August 25, 1988, this PO placed a Department of Corrections hold on the subject to prevent his release from jail.

Restitution and cost of supervision were current at the time of subject's arrest.

Since there is reasonable cause to believe that Joseph Wilson, ADC 8654, has violated the conditions of his release and has or is probably about to lapse into criminal ways or company, it is recommended that a warrant of arrest be issued for the following violations:

Condition Number Six

> Joseph Wilson was given urinalysis tests at Central Psychological and Substance Abuse Center on or about August 21, 1988, and August 24, 1988, and subsequently tested positive for cocaine.

Condition Number Four

> Joseph Wilson committed the offense of Burglary on or about August 25, 1988.

By _____
Correctional Program Officer

Approved _____
Field Office Supervisor

Preliminary Hearing

If a parolee/conditional releasee has been arrested pursuant to a violation warrant, or if the offender is in custody for a new offense and a violation warrant has been filed as a detainer, the parole officer will provide him or her with a notice of a preliminary hearing and a list of the alleged violations. The purpose of the preliminary hearing is to determine if there is *probable cause* to believe that the offender has committed an act(s) which constitutes a violation of the conditions of release. This hearing is required if the offender is to be detained on a warrant pending a revocation hearing; furthermore, it is required within fifteen days of the time the warrant was executed/filed. If no warrant has been issued—the subject is not being held in custody—but the offender has been summoned to appear for a revocation hearing, a preliminary hearing is not necessary. The offender may also waive the right to a preliminary hearing (see Figure 8.4).

At the preliminary hearing the parolee/conditional releasee will have an

FIGURE 8.4 Waiver of a Preliminary Hearing

DEPARTMENT OF REHABILITATION & CORRECTION

ADULT PAROLE AUTHORITY

WAIVER OF RELEASE VIOLATION PRELIMINARY HEARING

I,_____ Institution Number_____

have been apprised of my right to an On-Site Violation Hearing and the minimum due process which provides

that during this Hearing I have the right to appear and speak in my own behalf; to bring letters, documents, or

other evidence for presentation at the Hearing; and to have any individuals who can give relevant information

to the hearing officer subpoenaed by the Adult Parole Authority to appear in my behalf; furthermore, I

understand I do have the right to request representation by counsel. Persons who have provided evidence

against me will be made available for questioning in my presence unless the hearing officer determines that

the identity of such persons is not known to me and that such persons would be subjected to risk of harm

if their identities were disclosed. If the hearing officer determines that there is probable cause to hold me for

return to the institution I am still entitled to a revocation hearing before the Parole Board upon being

returned to the institution. I also understand that I am entitled to a digest of my On-Site Hearing.

I understand that should I elect to waive said On-Site Hearing, the alleged violations and evidence against me

will be administratively reviewed. Such review may result in a determination to hold a final revocation hearing

by the Parole Board. If I am returned to the institution for a final revocation hearing, I understand that the

hearing will occur within sixty (60) days of the filing of an Adult Parole Authority detainer unless I have been

unavailable to the Adult Parole Authority, in which case my revocation hearing will take place within a

reasonable time of my availability to the Adult Parole Authority.

Being fully advised of these rights and conditions, and having been given notice of my alleged release

violation(s) I do hereby agree to waive my right to such an On-Site Hearing without promise or threat of any

kind having been made.

If releasee is unable to read, the language above was read in his presence and explained to him.

RELEASEE_____ DATE___ WITNESS_____ DATE___

opportunity to challenge the alleged violations and (a limited right) to confront and cross-examine adverse witnesses, including the parole officer, and to present evidence on his or her own behalf. The offender can be represented by legal counsel, although the state is not constitutionally required to provide an attorney. As opposed to the rules of evidence in the criminal process, hearsay is admissible at preliminary hearings (although it is not used alone to determine probable cause). The hearing officer who presides is usually an attorney regularly employed for this purpose by the agency. However, it can be any agency employee who is not directly involved in the case. As a senior parole officer in New York, for example, I frequently served as a hearing officer when personnel normally fulfilling this function were unavailable. Since this hearing is a relatively minimal and informal inquiry, the hearing officer need not hear all of the allegations for a finding of probable cause.

State of Nevada Board of Parole
Summary of Preliminary Inquiry Hearing

RE: Blackstone, John L.
File No. L82-001
Criminal Case No. 28001

The above named subject appeared for a Preliminary Inquiry on Friday, July 19, 1988, at the hour of 2:20 PM at the Carson City Jail.

Rights Verified

Hearing Officer Sally Gomez inquired of defendant Blackstone if he had received copies of the Violation Report dated July 6, 1985 and the "Notice of Preliminary Inquiry Hearing" form listing his rights per the *Morrissey* and *Scarpelli* decisions. Blackstone replied that he had both documents and had read them. He also indicated that he fully understood the charges and his rights during the violation process as explained in the form. It is noted that Blackstone retained as private counsel for this hearing Michael Smith, Esq., of Carson City. Blackstone says he is satisfied with counsel and the time for preparing the defense case. With the indication that Mr. Blackstone fully understands his rights in this matter, we will proceed with the hearing.

Violation Case

Parole and Probation Officer James Richards read in part the Violation Report dated July 6, 1988, which indicates that Mr. Blackstone is charged with violation of Rule 9 of the Parole Agreement, WEAPONS. It was read that Blackstone was found in possession of a snub-nose .38 pistol by Police Sergeant John Brown in the After Hours Bar, 111 N. Carson Street, City of Carson, Nevada at about 11:00 PM on July 4, 1988. Blackstone had shown the weapon to another customer of the bar, a Mr. William Mundy, allegedly stating to Mundy: "Sucker,

I'm going to blow you apart if you keep bugging me tonight." Mundy left the bar and phoned the police to complain of the threat from Blackstone. Sgt. Brown arrived at the bar with several officers and asked Blackstone about the alleged weapon. Blackstone admitted to having an unloaded revolver in his coat pocket, and Sgt. Brown removed same without incident. Blackstone was then placed under arrest for "assault" and an "ex-felon in possession of a firearm." He was transported to the Carson County Jail and booked. Parole Officer Richards placed a Hold for Parole Violation Investigation upon Blackstone the following day, July 5, 1988 at about 10:00 AM.

Officer Richards called William Mundy as his first witness. Mundy told how Blackstone had come into the bar and sat next to him at the counter. Mundy tried to engage Blackstone in some friendly conversation, but Blackstone told him to "shut up and to quit bugging him" or he'd "blow his body apart," showing Mundy a small pistol taken from his coat pocket. Mundy says that he immediately left the bar and called the police, complaining of the incident and asking that the police arrest Blackstone. Mundy identified John L. Blackstone as the person who threatened him in the After Hours Bar on July 4, 1988. Mundy was dismissed after the defense had no questions of him.

Officer Richards called his second witness, Sgt. John Brown of the Carson City Police Department to testify in this case. Brown related that he was dispatched to the After Hours Bar at about 10:55 PM on July 4, 1988 to investigate a citizen's complaint of a man with a gun making threats in the bar to shoot him. Upon arrival, Brown said he was met by Mr. Mundy at the entrance of the bar and that Mundy pointed Mr. Blackstone out for him in the crowded bar. The officer approached Blackstone and asked him if he was carrying a weapon in his coat pocket; Brown said that Blackstone informed him that he had an unloaded pistol in his right hand coat pocket. Sgt. Brown then removed the weapon from Blackstone's right coat pocket and found that it was empty of shells. Sgt. Brown directed Blackstone to step outside the bar with him. Sgt. Brown advised Blackstone that he was being placed under arrest for "simple assault" upon the complaint of Mr. William Mundy and that he would have to come to the jail for booking, but could post bail that evening. Blackstone went along to the jail without incident.

Upon arrival at the Jail, the Head Jailer told Sgt. Brown that Mr. Blackstone was a parolee and should also be booked for the felony charge of "ex-felon with a firearm." Thus, he was so booked. Sgt. Brown was dismissed after the defense offered no cross examination.

Officer Richards rested his Prosecution case, noting that Blackstone has one felony charge of "Felon in Possession of Firearm" pending in Carson Justice Court. A preliminary hearing has been set for July 30, 1988 on the case. The weapon was not present at this hearing, but listed as in the evidence locker of the Carson City Police.

Defense Case

Attorney for the accused Blackstone stated that they would decline to present any evidence or statements at this time regarding the possession of the weapon as the case was a felony charge awaiting disposition in Justice Court. However, attor-

(Continued)

ney Smith did offer a defense witness, Gary Jones, to tell of the alleged threats in the bar. Jones was called into the hearing room and related he was sitting near the counter at a small table next to John Blackstone and Mundy at about 10:30 on July 4, 1988. Mundy, Jones explained, was "pretty drunk" and kept slapping Blackstone on the back, calling him "pal" and "buddy," etc. Blackstone told Mundy to leave him alone and Mundy got mad and left the bar in a "huff," Jones testified. A short time later, Jones testified, police officers took Blackstone out of the bar and that is the last time he saw Blackstone until today. Attorney Smith suggested that Blackstone did not threaten Mundy in the manner alleged by Mundy. Hearing Officer Gomez asked Jones if he saw Blackstone take anything out of his coat pocket and show it to Mundy. Jones replied "No." Richards asked Jones if he could have missed seeing Blackstone show Mundy the gun and say he was going to "blow him apart." Jones was hesitant, but said he was pretty sure; because of the back slapping he was watching the incident pretty close, wondering what Mundy was going to do next.

Then Attorney Smith closed the defense, advising Blackstone not to make any statements to the Hearing Officer until the Justice Court case was held.

Findings

Having considered the evidence presented in this case by both the charging officer and the defendant, this hearing officer finds that there is probable cause to continue detention on the charge of violation of parole rule #9, WEAPONS. The hearing officer has determined that probable cause exists to continue detention pending your formal revocation hearing before the Board of Parole. You are duly notified that at the formal revocation hearing the Board of Parole has the discretion to review and act upon *all* charges which were presented at this preliminary inquiry. With no further evidence to be heard, this hearing will be closed at 3:40 PM, July 19, 1988.

Respectfully submitted,
Sally Gomez
Hearing Officer

If the hearing officer determines that evidence sufficient to make a finding of probable cause has not been presented, the parolee/conditional releasee will be restored to supervision. If probable cause is found, the offender will be held in custody pending a revocation hearing. Prior to the revocation hearing the parole officer will prepare a violation of parole report for use at the hearing.

Revocation Hearing

A revocation hearing is similar to a preliminary hearing except it is more comprehensive. The purpose of the revocation hearing is to determine if the violation of parole/conditional release is serious enough to revoke supervision

STATE BOARD OF PARDONS AND PAROLES
Montgomery, Alabama

REPORT OF PAROLE VIOLATION

Date: ___1/5/89___

Field Office: ___Montgomery___

Name of Parolee ___John Doe___ No. ___123,456___

Race, Sex, & Age ___BM – 30___ County of Conviction ___Montgomery___

Offense ___Theft of Property 1st Degree___ Sentence ___2 years penitentiary___

Date Convicted ___4/10/87___ Date of Parole ___2/17/88___

Date Sentence Expires ___4/10/89___

RESTITUTION

Amount Paid $ ___249.00___

Balance $ ___101.00___

If declared Delinquent, subject can be located at the following place: ___Dan Jones, State Probation Office,___
Room 334, County Courthouse, Montgomery, Alabama 36104

CHARGE NO.1

VIOLATION OF CONDITION NO.7
NEW OFFENSE –BURGLARY III

LEGAL FACTS:

Subject was arrested on 12/24/88, by the Montgomery Police Department for the offense of Burglary 3rd degree, bond was set at $2,000.00. A preliminary hearing was held 1/5/89, and the case was bound to the Grand Jury. Indictment was returned, arraignment held and case set for trial 2/17/89. A Parole Officer's Authorization of Arrest was issued 12/25/88.

DETAILS:

Police reports reflect that at 2 a.m., on 12/24/88, Officer M. D. Jones with the Montgomery Police Department while on routine patrol, observed a black male subject exit Ace Hardware, 4240 Ames Road, Montgomery, Alabama, by way of a back window, in possession of a box. The subject fled on foot but was caught by Officer Jones about three hundred feet from the building. The person was identified as John Doe. He had in his possession property identified as having come from Ace Hardware by the manager, A. L. Pope. It was determined that the hardware store had been entered by forcing open an air conditioning vent at the rear of the store.

Continued:

FIGURE 8.5 Report of Parole Violation

CHARGE NO. 2

VIOLATION OF CONDITION NO. 3
FAILURE TO REPORT

LEGAL FACTS:

A Parole Violator's warrant was issued and given to the Sheriff's Office on
12/25, to prevent the subject's release pending Board action.

DETAILS:

According to the records of the supervising officer, on 12/17/88, subject was
instructed by Officer Dan Jones regarding parole conditions and specifically
that he must report to the Parole Office each month by the 3rd. He stated he
understood all parole conditions.

Subject failed to report or have any contact with the parole officer for the
months of October, November, and December 1988.

On 9/19/88, he reported for the month of September. He stated he forgot to
report by the 3rd. He was reprimanded and encouraged to report in accordance
with instructions.

On 10/10/88, I visited his residence. He was not present. His mother, Mae Doe
said she had not seen him in three days. I asked that she have him report.
On 10/15/88, I wrote subject a letter to report and received no response.
On 10/25/88, I visited his home, his mother said he received my letter.
He was not present. I requested she attempt to have him report and advised
of consequences if he failed.

On 11/5/88, a letter was written to subject reminding and instructing that he
make contact with his parole officer. On 11/19/88, I called his residence
and spoke with his 17 year old sister, Sue Doe, and requested she tell him
to report. On 11/30/88, I visited his father, Joe Doe, at their residence and
requested he have subject report.

On 12/6/88, I visited subject's residence and talked with his parents. They
stated he had been told to report but he refused. On 12/10/88, I wrote him
a letter instructing that he report wihin 7 days or I would file a Report
of Parole Violation, which would likely cause him to be arrested as a parole
violator. He failed to contact the Probation Officer thereafter.

RECOMMENDATION:

I recommend revocation.

Signed and dated at Montgomery, Alabama, this 5th day of January, 1989.

Dan Jones

Dan Jones
Alabama Probation and Parole Officer

DJ/lm

FIGURE 8.5 *Continued*

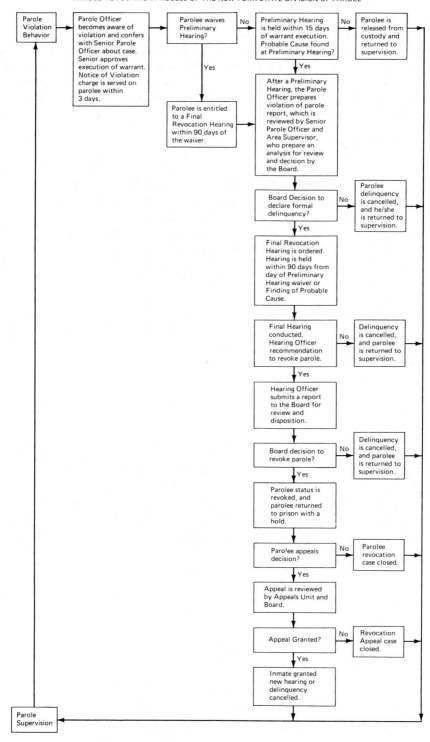

FIGURE 8.6   Parole Revocation Process, New York

and return the offender to prison. In some jurisdictions the revocation is presided over by one or more members of the parole board; in other states it is the responsibility of hearing officers who make recommendations to the parole board for or against revocation. If the board votes against revocation, the offender is restored to supervision.

Street Time

If parole is revoked, the question arises as to just how much time the parolee must serve in prison. This can vary from jurisdiction to jurisdiction. In California, parolees returned to prison for a technical violation can only be confined for one year. In New York a parolee receives credit for the time spent under supervision ("street time") prior to the violation. Thus, in New York, an inmate who is paroled after serving two years of a four-year sentence is required to be on parole for two years, the remainder of the sentence. If, after one year, the parolee violates parole and is returned to prison, he or she will have to serve only the one year remaining on the sentence. However, in a state that does not give credit for street time, this same parolee would be required to serve two years in prison; the one year of satisfactory time on parole would not be credited against the four-year sentence in the event of a parole violation that results in being returned to prison.

CLEMENCY

All states and the federal government (Article II of the Constitution) have provisions for clemency. In thirty-one states and the federal government the chief executive holds the final clemency power, and in most of these states the parole board or a clemency board appointed by the governor investigates clemency applications at the request of the governor (Krajick, 1979). In some states clemency authority is vested entirely in a special board, usually a board of pardons and paroles. Some states conduct formal hearings, and there is generally a requirement that the governor report annually to the legislature on all clemencies granted (National Governor's Association, 1988; this publication provides a state-by-state breakdown of clemency practices). Clemency consists of the reprieve, the commutation, and the pardon.

Reprieve

A reprieve is a *temporary* suspension of the execution of sentence. As was noted in Chapter 2, probation developed, in part, out of the judicial reprieve. Its use today is quite limited and usually concerns cases in which capital punishment has been ordered. In such cases a governor, or the president of the United States, can grant a reprieve—a stay of execution—to provide more time for legal action or other deliberations.

In Georgia, the Board of Pardons and Paroles may grant a reprieve lasting a few hours or a few days to an inmate so that he or she may visit a critically ill member of the family, or attend the funeral of an immediate member of the family. A reprieve may also be granted in Georgia when it is shown that an inmate is suffering from a definable illness for which necessary treatment is available only outside of the state prison system. An inmate granted a reprieve will have the reprieve period credited to the sentence if he or she does not violate any of the conditions of the reprieve.

Commutation

A commutation is a modification of sentence to the benefit of an offender. Commutation has been used when an inmate provided some assistance to the prison staff, sometimes during prison riots. It may also be granted to inmates with a severe illness, such as cancer. The laws governing commutation differ from state to state. In New York an inmate sentenced to more than one year who has served at least one-half of the minimum period of imprisonment, and who is not otherwise eligible for release or parole, may have his or her sentence commuted by the governor. In Georgia the Board of Pardons and Paroles will consider commuting a sentence when it receives substantial evidence that the sentence is either excessive, illegal, unconstitutional, or void; evidence that justice would be served by a commutation; and evidence that commutation would be in the best interests of society and the inmate. The board may also consider commutation of sentences of death after all other legal remedies have been exhausted. A person whose death sentence has been commuted by the board cannot be pardoned or paroled before serving twenty-five years. In Maryland, correctional personnel identify candidates who meet criteria established by the governor's office for commutation, and their names are submitted to the parole board for a recommendation to the governor. Commutations are traditionally granted at Christmas time, and in 1988 the governor granted twenty-eight inmate commutations.

Pardon*

Historical development Following the American Revolution, it was necessary to find a new basis for the pardoning power to replace the English theory that it resided in the king as the fountainhead of justice and mercy. This new basis was found in the theory that the power to pardon was a sovereign power, inherent in the state, but not necessarily inherent in the executive or in any other given branch of the government. Rather, since the people were the

*Information not explicitly cited is from U.S. Attorney General, *Attorney General's Survey of Release Procedures: Pardon* (Washington, D.C.: U.S. Government Printing Office, 1939), pp. 88–90, references deleted.

ultimate sovereign, the power resided in them, and they could provide for its exercise through any agency of government they deemed proper.

And although historically the executive would seem the most natural agency in which to entrust this power, the attitude of the American people after the Revolution was not such as to lead to this conclusion. The struggle with the mother country had left them suspicious of the executive. This was natural enough, for the royal governor was not usually sympathetic to the colonists. The champion of the people was usually the lower house of the legislature. It is, therefore, not surprising that the early constitutions that replaced the colonial charters tended to place restrictions on the governor's power in many respects, including the power to pardon. Only five states left this power in the governor alone. Six, including the newly admitted state of Vermont, provided that the governor could pardon only with consent of the executive council. Georgia deprived the governor of the pardoning power entirely, giving him only power to reprieve until the meeting of the assembly, which then could make such disposition of the matter as it saw fit. Connecticut and Rhode Island continued to function under their colonial charters, by which the pardoning power was exercised by the general assembly.

By the time the federal Constitution was written, however, opinion had begun to swing back toward placing greater power in the hands of the governor. The framers of the Constitution gave the pardoning power to the president without any limitations as to its exercise or any supervision by any other official or agency. The executive councils that several states had set up as a means of preventing too much power from being vested in one person began to lose favor about the same time, and a number of states began abolishing them, giving the sole power to the governor.

Toward the end of the nineteenth century there was an overwhelming movement to give the governor some assistance in this task by providing an advisory pardon officer or pardon board. Some states set up pardon boards not merely to advise the governor, but actually to exercise pardoning power, although the governor was everywhere a member, if not the controlling member, of the board.

The pardon has been used historically in the United States as a form of "parole." In the middle of the nineteenth century pardons accounted for over 40 percent of the releases from U.S. prisons (Hibbert, 1968: 453). In Ohio, for example, whenever the state prison exceeded a certain number of inmates, the governor granted pardons in order to make room for new prisoners. As late as 1938, "parole" was simply a conditional pardon in many states (U.S. Attorney General, 1939: 296, 298). As the intermediate sentence came into use, the pardon boards, developed to advise the governor with respect to release, began to act independently, developing into parole boards. Despite the widespread use of parole, however, the power to pardon has continued.

The basis for a pardon may vary in different states, but it is not used extensively anywhere. In New York the only basis for a pardon is new evidence indicating that the person did not commit the offense for which he or she was accused and convicted. In Florida a pardon is a declaration of record that a person is relieved from the legal consequences of a particular conviction. As in New York, a pardon will be granted only to a person who proves his or her innocence of the crime for which convicted. Florida also has a *first offender pardon,* which carries no implication of innocence and may be granted to an actual first offender. It restores civil and political rights and removes legal disabilities resulting from the conviction. The *ten-year pardon* operates the same way, and may be granted to offenders who have had no convictions for ten years after completing his or her sentence. In Georgia a pardon is a declaration of record by the board that a person is relieved from the legal consequences of a particular conviction. It restores civil and political rights and removes all legal disabilities resulting from the conviction.

A pardon may be granted in two instances. First, a pardon may be granted to a person who proves his or her innocence of the crime for which he or she was convicted under Georgia law. Newly available evidence proving the person's complete justification or nonguilt may be the basis for granting a pardon. Application may be submitted in any written form any time after conviction. Second, a pardon that does not imply innocence may be granted to an applicant convicted under Georgia law who has completed his or her full sentence obligation, including serving any probated sentence and paying any fine, and who has thereafter completed five years without any criminal involvement. The five-year waiting period after sentence completion may be waived if the waiting period is shown to be detrimental to the applicant's livelihood by delaying his qualifying for employment in his chosen profession.

In California, a governor's pardon restores citizenship rights to the individual who has demonstrated a high standard of constructive behavior following conviction for an offense. Individuals who have made a sincere and successful effort to complete a prescribed period of rehabilitation have proved to themselves and others that they have earned the restoration of rights to citizenship.

In accordance with this above philosophy, pardon applications will not be considered unless an applicant has been discharged from probation or parole for at least ten years and has not engaged in further criminal conduct during that period. The ten-year rule may be waived in truly exceptional circumstances if the applicant can demonstrate an earlier need for the pardon.

Effect of a pardon. When a pardon is granted, the Department of Justice and Federal Bureau of Investigation are notified. These agencies' records are then updated to show that a Certificate of Rehabilitation or a pardon has been granted with respect to the conviction.

A person who has been pardoned cannot state that he or she has never been convicted of a felony. The person can state that he or she has been convicted and has been pardoned.

A pardon does not seal or expunge the record of the conviction. The conviction may be used as a prior conviction or prior prison term if the person is subsequently convicted of a new offense.

A California pardon does not pardon convictions suffered in another jurisdiction. A person convicted in another state or in a federal court must apply for a pardon to the other state or the federal government.

Finally, the granting of a pardon does not affect the right or the ability of a licensing agency to consider the conviction that has been pardoned in its determination of whether a license to practice a profession should be granted or restored.

Upon receipt of the application, the governor may request the Board of Prison Terms to conduct a further investigation. Following review, the governor may then grant the pardon. If the petitioner has been convicted of more than one felony in separate proceedings, the California Supreme Court must also approve the grant of a pardon.

In Utah, the Board of Pardons, an independent state agency, has extraordinary powers. This three-member body serves as a board of parole, deciding when and under what conditions persons convicted and serving sentences should be released from imprisonment. In addition, the board can commute sentences of death, reduce terms of imprisonment, and completely terminate an offender's sentence regardless of whether he or she is an inmate or on parole. The board also has absolute pardoning authority for the state; it can forgive the sentence and restore civil rights, although this power is rarely exercised. The Alabama Board of Pardons and Parole has similar powers. Executive clemency is usually limited to deciding on the granting of relief from disabilities, a limited pardon that restores certain civil and political rights, such as the right to apply to vote (local board of registrars make final decision) and hold certain licenses. In order to be considered for such a pardon, a person discharged from prison without parole must wait two years; parolees after five years under supervision or two years after discharge; and probationers two years after discharge from supervision. The pardon report, which is prepared by state probation and parole officers is exhaustive, and allows the board to determine if the applicant has become a law-abiding person and a useful citizen in the community.

In California, the Board of Prison Terms investigates all pardon petitions from persons who have been free of criminal conduct for nine-and-one-half years since discharge from probation, parole, or custody. In Maryland, a pardon requires at least five years of exemplary crime-free behavior following release from incarceration and after expiration of any parole supervision. Pardon requests are received by the parole board which investigates and makes a recommendation to the governor; in 1988 the governor granted twenty-one pardons.

The President of the United States typically grants hundreds of pardons:

Form C-4

State Board of Pardons and Paroles
Montgomery, Alabama

CERTIFICATE OF PARDON WITH RESTORATION
OF CIVIL AND POLITICAL RIGHTS

KNOW ALL MEN BY THESE PRESENTS:

It having been made to appear to the Alabama State Board of Pardons and Paroles that

_____

was convicted in _____ County on _____ , 19____

of _____ , was sentenced to a term of _____ years;

And it further appearing to the Board from the official report of the Parole Officer which is a part of the record in this case, and with no further information to the contrary, that the above named has so conducted himself as to demonstrate his reformation and to merit pardon with restoration of civil rights;

NOW, In compliance with the authority vested in the State Board of Pardons and Paroles by the Constitution and the Laws of the State of Alabama to grant pardons and to restore civil and political rights, it is

ORDERED that a pardon be granted to the above named as a result of the above stated conviction, and all prior disqualifying convictions, and it is further ordered that all civil and political rights which were forfeited as a result of the conviction be and they are hereby restored.

GIVEN UNDER THE HAND AND SEAL of the State Board of Pardons and Paroles,

this the _____ day of _____ , 19 ____ .

STATE BOARD OF PARDONS AND PAROLES

By _____
Executive Director

FIGURE 8.7   Certificate of Pardon

President Gerald R. Ford pardoned former President Richard Nixon in 1974; Jimmy Carter issued 534 pardons during his four years as president, and Ronald Reagan granted 273 during his eight years as president (Moore, 1989).

LEGAL DECISIONS AFFECTING PAROLE

As noted in Part I, legal decisions that affect probation also affect parole. Thus, the decision rendered in *Gagnon* v. *Scarpelli* (discussed in Chapter 5), relating to probation violation, used precedents established in the *Morrissey* v. *Brewer* decision (discussed below), which relates to parole violation. The three theories are also similar, if not identical, to the three theories of probation.

Three Theories of Parole

Traditionally, an individual on parole has not been considered a free person, despite the fact that he or she has been released from imprisonment. The basis for imposing restrictions on a parolee's freedom is contained in three theories:

1. *Grace theory.* Parole is a conditional privilege, a gift from the board of parole. If any of the conditions of this privilege are violated, parole can be revoked.
2. *Contract theory.* Every parolee and (most) conditional releasees are required to agree to certain terms and conditions in return for conditional freedom. A violation of the conditions is a breach of contract, which can result in penalties — a return to prison.
3. *Custody theory.* The parolee is in the legal custody of the prison or parole authorities and, as a result of this quasi-prisoner status, his or her constitutional rights are automatically limited and abridged.

The legal decisions discussed in this chapter often challenge one or more of the foregoing theories.

Parole Release and Hearing

Menechino v. *Oswald* (U.S. Court of Appeals, Second Circuit, 1970) Joseph Menechino was serving a twenty-year to life sentence in New York for murder in the second degree. He was paroled in 1963 and returned to prison as a parole violator sixteen months later. He subsequently appeared before the board of parole and admitted consorting with individuals having criminal records and giving misleading information to his parole officer.

Two years later, Menechino appeared before the board for a release hearing and parole was denied. He brought a court action claiming that his rights were violated by the absence of legal counsel at both his revocation and parole release hearings. The case reached the U.S. Court of Appeals, which rendered a decision in 1970. The court held that:

1. A parole proceeding is nonadversarial in nature since both parties, the board and the inmate, have the same concern, rehabilitation.

2. Parole release hearings are not fact-finding determinations since the board makes a determination based upon numerous tangible and intangible factors.
3. The inmate has "no present private interest" to be protected since he is already imprisoned — has nothing to lose — and this "interest" is required before due process is applicable.

The court further stated that "it is questionable whether a board of parole is even required to hold a hearing on the question of whether a prisoner should be released on parole." Relative to the question of parole revocation, however, the court advised that a minimum of procedural due process should be provided, since at this stage a parolee has a present private interest in the possible loss of conditional freedom.

Although Menechino's case before the federal court was initiated with regard to parole release, it set forth important legal arguments relative to parole revocation. The opinions of the three judges who heard the case clearly indicates that if Menechino had initiated an action concerning his parole revocation, he would have won the case on a 2–1 basis. This fact was duly noted by the New York State Court of Appeals in the second *Menechino* case discussed later.

Greenholtz v. *Inmates of Nebraska Penal and Correctional Complex* (442 U.S. 1, 1979)   In 1979 the Supreme Court reversed a court of appeals decision in a class action brought by inmates of the Nebraska Penal and Correctional Complex. The inmates claimed that they had been unconstitutionally denied parole release by the board of parole.

According to state law, at least once a year initial parole hearings must be held in Nebraska for every inmate, regardless of parole eligibility. At the initial hearing, the board examines the inmate's total record and provides an informal hearing during which the inmate can present statements and documents in support of a claim for release.

If the board determines from the record and hearing that the inmate is a likely candidate for release, a final hearing is scheduled. However, the Nebraska law provides that the board "shall order an inmate's release unless in the final hearing, the board concludes that inmate's release should be deferred for at least one of four specified reasons." This is a somewhat unusual procedure, peculiar, perhaps, to the state of Nebraska. Rolando del Carmen points out that this amounts to a "state-law created liberty interest," an expectation of being granted parole release (1985: 50). As noted above, whenever this "interest" exists some minimum due process is required.

The board then notifies the inmate of the month in which the final hearing will be held. At the final hearing, the inmate may present evidence, call witnesses, and be represented by private counsel of his or her choice. It is not a traditional adversarial hearing since the inmate is not permitted to hear adverse testimony or to cross-examine witnesses who present such evidence. If parole is denied, the board furnishes a written statement of the reasons for the denial within thirty days.

In upholding the procedure used by the Nebraska parole board, Chief Justice Warren Burger, speaking for the Court, stated:

> When the Board defers parole after the initial review hearing, it does so because examination of the inmate's file and personal interview satisfied it that the inmate is not ready for conditional release. The parole determination, therefore, must include consideration of what the entire record shows up to the time of the sentence, including the gravity of the offense in the particular case. The behavior record of an inmate during confinement is critical in the sense that it reflects the degree to which the inmate is prepared to adjust to parole release. At the Board's initial interview hearing, the inmate is permitted to appear before the Board and present letters and statements on his own behalf. He is thereby provided with an effective opportunity to insure, first, that the records before the Board are in fact the records relating to his case; and second, to present any special considerations demonstrating why he is an appropriate candidate for parole. Since the decision is one that must be made largely on the basis of an inmate's files, this procedure adequately safeguards against serious risks of error and thus satisfies due process.
>
> Next, we find nothing in the due process concepts as they have thus far evolved that requires the Parole Board to specify the particular "evidence" in the inmate's file or at his interview on which it rests the discretionary determination that an inmate is not ready for conditional release. The Board communicates the reason for its denial as a guide to the inmate for his future behavior. To require the parole authority to provide a summary of the evidence would tend to convert the process into an adversary proceeding and to equate the Board's parole release determination with a guilt determination. . . . [T]he parole decision is . . . essentially an experienced prediction based on a host of variables. The Board's decision is much like a sentencing judge's choice — provided by many states — to grant or deny probation following a judgment of guilt, a choice never thought to require more than what Nebraska now provides for parole release determination.

Del Carmen and Paul Louis conclude:

> an inmate does not have a constitutional right to be released on parole, nor does he or she enjoy any constitutional right in the parole release process. In more succinct language, the parole board can do just about anything it pleases [with respect to release], and whatever it says and does prevails because it enjoys immense discretion. (1988: 20)

While parole boards are not constitutionally required to provide reasons for denying release, the use of parole guidelines often provides inmates with such documentation.

Parole Revocation

Menechino v. *Warden* (New York State Court of Appeals, 1971) Until the 1970s parole agencies operated without any interference from the judiciary. However, this all changed when the New York Court of Appeals handed down the *Menechino* decision, which granted parolees, for the first time, the right to counsel and the right to call their own witnesses at parole revocation hearings. Although the decision applied only to New York, it indicated the direction in which the courts would rule in future decisions.

This four to three decision, once again involving Joseph Menechino (a "jail house lawyer"), required that an attorney be present at a parole revocation hearing. It also permitted a parolee to call on witnesses who would speak in his or her behalf. The New York court recognized that it was entering into an uncharted area of law. The issue the court was called upon to resolve was stated succinctly at the very beginning of the majority opinion: "whether parolees are constitutionally entitled, under the Federal and State Constitutions, to the assistance of counsel in parole revocation hearings." *Menechino* cited other legal decisions, such as *Mempa* v. *Rhay* (see Chapter 5) and *In re Gault* (see Chapter 3). Although probationers, juveniles, and welfare recipients had already obtained limited due process protections at hearings that might cause the loss of freedom or financial distress, these protections had not yet been extended to parolees.

Morrissey v. Brewer (408 U.S. 471, 92 S.Ct., 1972)   The *Morrissey* decision marked the beginning of the U.S. Supreme Court's involvement with parole revocation procedures. Up until June 1972 the Court had not ruled in this area. The issue in this case was whether the due process clause of the Fourteenth Amendment required that a state afford an individual opportunity to be heard prior to revoking parole.

Morrissey was convicted of the false drawing of checks in 1967 in Iowa. After pleading guilty, he was sentenced to seven years in prison. Paroled from the Iowa State Penitentiary in June 1968, seven months later Morrissey, at the direction of his parole officer, was arrested in his hometown as a parole violator and held in a local jail. One week after review of the parole officer's written report, the Iowa Board of Parole revoked Morrissey's parole, and he was returned to prison. He had received no hearing prior to the revocation decision.

Morrissey violated the conditions of his parole by buying a car under an assumed name and operating it without the permission of his parole officer. He also gave false information to the police and insurance company concerning his address after a minor traffic accident. Besides these violations, Morrissey also obtained credit under an assumed name and failed to report his residence to his parole officer. According to the parole report, Morrissey could not explain any of these technical violations of parole regulations adequately.

Also considered in the *Morrissey* case was the petition of Booher, a convicted forger who had been returned to prison in Iowa by the Board of Parole without any hearing. Booher had admitted the technical violations of parole charges to his parole officer when taken into custody.

The Supreme Court considered all arguments that sought to keep the judiciary out of parole matters, and it rejected the "privilege" concept of parole as no longer viable. The Court pointed out that parole is an established variation of imprisonment of convicted criminals—it occurs with too much regularity to be simply a "privilege."

> It is hardly useful any longer to try to deal with this problem in terms of whether the parolee's liberty is a "right" or a "privilege." By whatever name the liberty is valuable and must be seen within the protection of the Fourteenth Amendment. Its termination calls for some orderly process however informal.

The Court pointed out that parole revocation does not occur in just a few isolated cases—it has been estimated that 35 to 40 percent of all parolees are subjected to revocation and return to prison. The Court went on to state that with the numbers involved, protection of parolees' rights was necessary. The Court did note, however, limitations on a parolee's rights:

> We begin with the proposition that the revocation of parole is not part of the criminal prosecution and thus the full panoply of rights due to the defendant in such a proceeding does not apply to parole revocation. Supervision is not directly by the court but by an administrative agency which sometimes is an arm of the court and sometimes of the executive. Revocation deprives an individual not of absolute liberty to which every citizen is entitled but only the conditional liberty properly dependent on observance of special parole restrictions.

Also found in the decision is the New York State Court of Appeals response to the problem raised by the *Menechino* case. The Supreme Court held:

> Society thus has an interest in not having parole revoked because of erroneous information or because of an erroneous evaluation of the need to revoke parole, given the breach of parole regulations. See Parole ex rel *Menechino* v. *Warden.*

In *Morrissey* the Supreme Court viewed parole revocation as a two-stage process: (1) arrest of the parolee and preliminary hearing, and (2) the revocation hearing. Because there was usually a significant time lapse between the arrest and revocation hearing, the Court established an interim process for all parole violators, a hearing prior to the final or revocation hearing:

> Such an inquiry should be seen in the nature of a preliminary hearing to determine whether there is probable cause or reasonable grounds to believe that the arrested parolee had committed acts which would constitute a violation of parole conditions.

The Court specified that the hearing officer conducting this preliminary hearing need not be a member of the parole board, only someone who is not involved in the case; that the parolee be given notice of the hearing, and that its purpose be to determine whether there is probable cause to believe that the parolee has violated a condition of parole. On the request of the parolee, persons who have given adverse information on which parole violation is based are to be made available for questioning in the parolee's presence. Based upon this information presented before the hearing officer, there should be a determination if there is reason to warrant the parolee's continued detention (pending a revocation hearing). The Court stated that "no interest would be served by formalism in this process; informality will not lessen the utility of this inquiry in redressing the risk of error." This writer served as an auxiliary hearing officer, conducting preliminary hearings in New York. These were held at local correctional facilities. All persons were placed under oath, and a legal reporter recorded all testimony verbatim. The parole officer alleging the violation "prosecuted" the case, although in significant cases a legal advocate was provided by the Division of Parole for that purpose. Following all of the testimony, the writer would write down his decision in summary form: the violation of parole charges considered and sustained were listed and a copy given to the parolee. If none of the charges were sustained, the parole officer would be directed to arrange for the parolee's release from custody.

In reference to the revocation hearing, the Court stated:

> The parolee must have an opportunity to be heard and to show if he can that he did not violate the conditions or if he did, that circumstances in mitigation suggest the violation does not warrant revocation. The revocation hearing must be tendered within a reasonable time after the parolee is taken into custody. A lapse of two months as the state suggests occurs in some cases would not appear to be unreasonable.

The Court also suggested minimum requirements of due process for the revocation hearing:

> Our task is limited to deciding the minimum requirements of due process. They include (a) written notice of the claimed violation of parole; (b) disclosures to the parolee of evidence against him; (c) opportunity to be heard in person and to present witnesses and documentary evidence; (d) the right to confront and cross-examine adverse witnesses (unless the hearing officer specifically finds good cause for not allowing confrontation); (e) "neutral and detached" hearing body such as a traditional parole board, members of which need not be judicial officers or lawyers; and (f) a written statement by the fact finders as to the evidence relied on and reasons for revoking parole.

The Supreme Court left open the question of counsel when it stated: "We do not reach or decide the question whether the parolee is entitled to the assistance of retained or to appointed counsel if he is indigent." In practice, parole boards have permitted parolees to be represented by counsel, although they usually do not provide such assistance.

Parole Board Liability

Martinez v. California (444 U.S. 277, 1980)   In a unanimous decision, the Supreme Court affirmed the constitutionality of statutory provisions that provide parole officials with immunity from tort claims. In this instance,

Thomas, a parolee convicted of attempted rape, tortured and murdered fifteen-year-old Mary Martinez five months after his parole release from prison. Thomas had been labeled as not amenable to treatment and it was recommended by the sentencing court that he not be paroled. Nevertheless, after serving five years of a one-to-two-hundred-year sentence, Thomas was paroled. The deceased girl's parents argued that in releasing Thomas parole authorities subjected their daughter to deprivation of her life without due process of law.

Justice Stevens delivered the opinion for the Court:

> Like the California courts, we cannot accept the contention that this statute deprives Thomas' (a paroled offender) victim of her life without due process of law because it condoned a parole decision that led indirectly to her death. The statute neither authorized nor immunized the deliberate killing of any human being. This statute merely provides a defense to potential state tort law liability. At most, the availability of such a defense may have encouraged members of the parole board to take somewhat greater risks of recidivism in exercising their authority to release prisoners than they otherwise might. But the basic risk that repeat offenses may occur is always present in any parole system.

While parole boards act in a quasi-judicial capacity, they do not enjoy the total immunity conferred on judges. Justice Stevens pointed out that in this decision "We need not and do not decide that a parole official could never be deemed to 'deprive' someone of life by action taken in connection with a prisoner on parole."

Parole Officer Liability

While there is no definitive Supreme Court decision concerning the liability of parole officers in the supervision process, state and federal cases have established liability for crimes committed by parolees under their supervision within a narrow set of circumstances. The common element in these circumstances, note del Carmen and Louis, is the rather unclear concept of a "special duty" on the part of the parole officer. In order for this "special duty" to attach there must be a *reasonably foreseeable risk* which

> exists when the circumstances of the relationship between the parolee and a third party suggest that the parolee may engage in criminal or antisocial conduct related to his or her past conduct. This, in turn, results from a combination of three factors: (a) the parolee's job; (b) his or her prior criminal background and conduct; and (c) the type of crime for which he or she was convicted. For example, it is reasonably foreseeable that a parolee convicted of child sexual assault would commit a similar act if employed in a child care center, but not if employed as a janitor on a college campus. (1988: 37)

Now that we have completed our examination of the historical, administrative, and legal aspects of probation and parole, in the next section we will turn to treatment of supervision in probation and parole.

REVIEW QUESTIONS

1. Why is the administration of parole less complex than that of probation?
2. What are the three basic services provided by a parole agency?
3. What are the two basic models for administering parole services? What are the arguments in favor of each?
4. What is conditional release and how does it differ from parole?
5. Why have parole release hearings been criticized?
6. Why do most parole boards deny inmates the right to legal representation at parole release hearings?
7. What are the two most important factors considered when making a parole release decision?
8. What led to the development of parole release guidelines?
9. What is the relationship between institutional rehabilitation and parole release guidelines?
10. Why can the parole board be in a better position than the sentencing judge to render a decision based on just deserts?
11. What is the primary responsibility of institutional parole staff? What other services might they provide?
12. What is the purpose of a preliminary parole violation hearing?
13. What is the difference between a preliminary parole violation hearing and a parole revocation hearing?
14. What are the different forms of clemency?
15. What are the three theories that have traditionally formed the basis for imposing restrictions on parolees?
16. What are the due process requirements mandated by the *Morrissey* decision?

PART THREE

Treatment and Supervision in Probation and Parole

NINE
Treatment Theory

Some modes of treatment are more easily applied to probation and parole (hereafter p/p) practice than others. Some require more training than most p/p officers have received, and their use may require an expenditure of time that is not realistic in most p/p agencies. In practice, p/p officers use a variety of treatment techniques, tailoring them to different clients. They often use techniques without understanding the theoretical base or even recognizing it as part of a particular mode of treatment — "flying by the seat of your pants" is characteristic of p/p. Treatment, however, no matter the discipline, requires a theoretical base — abstract knowledge and principles applied to specific cases.

There are three basic theoretical models for treatment in p/p:

1. social casework
2. reality therapy
3. behavior/learning theory

To better understand these models, it is necessary to review the theory behind a method of treatment that is not used extensively, if at all, in p/p. The methods of treatment discussed in this chapter can be delineated according to the degree to which they accept, use, or reject psychoanalytic theory and methods.

PSYCHOANALYSIS AND PSYCHOANALYTIC THEORY

Psychoanalysis is a method of treatment based on a body of theory fathered by Sigmund Freud (1856-1939). Over the years both theory and method have undergone change, although Freud's basic contribution, his exposition of the importance of unconscious phenomena in human behavior, remains. (For a discussion of the different models of psychoanalytic theory, see Greenberg and Mitchell, 1983.)

Stages of Psychological Development

Freud postulated unconscious processes which, although not directly observable, were inferred from case studies with patients. He divided unconscious mental phenomena into two groups:

1. *preconscious:* thoughts and memories that can easily be called into conscious awareness, and
2. *unconscious:* repressed feelings and experiences that can be made conscious only with a great deal of difficulty.

"The unconscious is essentially dynamic and capable of profoundly affecting conscious ideational or emotional life without the individual's being aware of this influence" (Healy, Bronner, and Bowers, 1930: 24).

Unconscious feelings and experiences are related to normal stages of psychosexual development through which each person passes on the way to adulthood (psychosexual maturity). These stages of psychosexual development are repressed and, therefore, unconscious—not part of an individual's conscious or preconscious memory—and, yet, serve as a source of anxiety and guilt, the basis for psychoneurosis and psychosis. In brief, they appear as follows:

1. *Oral* (birth to eighteen months): the mouth, lips, and tongue are the predominant organs of pleasure for the infant. In the normal infant, the source of pleasure becomes associated with the touch and warmth of the parent who gratifies oral needs. When this is lacking, deviant behavior, particularly drug and alcohol abuse, is to be expected in the adult. Depressant drugs such as heroin and alcohol serve as a substitute for maternal attachment, and drug abuse is seen as a narcissistic regression back to an unfulfilled oral stage. The infant actually enters the world a "criminal," that is, unsocialized and devoid of self-control.

2. *Anal* (eighteen months to three years): the anus becomes the most important site of sexual interest and gratification. Pleasure is closely connected to the retention and expulsion of feces, as well as the bodily processes involved and the feces themselves. During this stage, the only partially socialized child acts out rather destructive urges, breaking toys or even injuring living organisms, such as insects or small animals. A great deal of psychopathology in the adult, including violent behavior and sociopathological personality disorders, is traced to disruptions during this stage. Depressant drugs such as heroin and barbiturates can provide a way of managing sadistic and masochistic impulses — self-medication — that were not dealt with adequately during the anal stage. On the other hand, use of stimulants, cocaine and amphetamines, for example, in the adult, can be then traced to separation anxiety and accompanying depression for the child who was unable to relinquish the dependent attachment to the maternal object necessary to move on to the next stage of development.

3. *Genital* (three to five years): the main sexual interest begins to be assumed by the genitals, and in normal persons is maintained by them thereafter. During this period of life the child experiences *Oedipus* (in boys) and *Electra* (in girls) *wishes* in the form of fantasies of incest with the parent of the opposite sex.[1] In the healthy child, he or she must relinquish the dependent paternal/maternal attachment, and deal with the feelings of sadness that result. Sexual problems and drug and alcohol abuse are traced to failures during this stage of development. The use of heroin by the adult can be attributed to a need to suppress the sexual urge that is fixated in unresolved (unconscious) incestuous feelings. Drugs that stimulate sexual desire, such as cocaine and amphetamines, may be necessary for the adult whose unresolved incestuous feelings would otherwise make adult sexual performance difficult or impossible.

4. *Latent* (five years to adolescence): there is a lessening of interest in sexual organs during this period and an expanded relationship with playmates of the same sex and age.

5. *Adolescence-adulthood* (thirteen years to death): there is a reawakening of genital interest and awareness; the incestuous wish is repressed and emerges in terms of mature (adult) sexuality. Adolescence is typically the stage at which most drug abusers begin experimenting with psychoactive substances. In the psychosexually disturbed adolescent, drugs become a way of dealing with the strong psychological and biological sexual awakening experienced during this stage of development.

---

[1]Based on his treatment of middle-class women in Vienna, Freud reported that they fantasized sexual activity with their fathers and other male relatives: "almost all my female patients told me that they had been seduced by their fathers. Eventually I was forced to the conclusion that these stories were false, and thus I came to understand that hysterical symptoms spring from phantasies and not from real events: (Freud, 1933: 164). This "seduction theory" is the most controversial aspect of Freud's psychoanalytic theory. It has recently been revealed that, in fact, many of Freud's female patients had been sexually abused as children by their fathers and/or male relatives.

The stages overlap, and transition from one to the other is gradual, the time spans being approximate. Furthermore, each stage is left behind, but never completely abandoned. Some amount of psychic energy (*cathexis*) remains attached to earlier objects of psychosexual development. When the strength of the cathexis is particularly strong, it is expressed as a *fixation*. For example, instead of a boy transferring his affection to another woman in the adolescent-adult stage, he may remain fixated on his mother (or a girl on her father). When a person reverts to a previous mode of gratification, it is referred to as regression. This type of behavior can be seen in young children who revert to thumb-sucking or experience elimination "accidents" when a sibling is born.

When a person is passing through the first three stages of psychosexual development, concomitantly, the mind undergoes the development of three psychic phenomena:

1. *Id.* This mass of powerful drives seeks discharge or gratification—it is asocial, devoid of values and logical processes. Comprising wishes, urges, and psychic tensions, according to Freud, the id is "a cauldron of seething excitement" seeking pleasure and avoiding pain (1933: 104). The id is the driving force of the personality, and from birth until about seven months of age, it is the total psychic apparatus.

2. *Ego.* Through contact with the reality around them and the influence of training, infants modify their expressions of id drives. This ego development permits them to obtain maximum gratification with a minimum of difficulty in the form of restrictions that their environment places upon them. For example, an id drive (desire) to harm a sibling rival is controlled by the ego (an awareness of the consequences of one's action—the punishment that may result). Without the ego to act as a restraining influence, the id would destroy the person through its blind striving to gratify instincts in complete disregard for reality. As a result of disturbances in psychosexual development, a person may remain at the ego level of development: "The child remains asocial or behaves as if he had become social without having made actual adjustment to the demands of society" (Aichhorn, 1963: 4). Feelings of rage and aggression associated with the anal stage lurk in the background awaiting an opportunity to break through to satisfaction—unless they are controlled by the superego, or the person self-medicates with the use of depressant drugs. The adult may use stimulants because of a self-directed and intensely competitive personality, and/or to ward off feelings of boredom and depression by artificially stimulating the ego.

3. *Superego.* The superego is often viewed as a conscience-type mechanism, a counterforce to the id. It exercises a criticizing power, a sense of morality over the ego: "it represents the whole demands of morality, and we see all at once that our moral sense of guilt is the expression of tension between the ego [which strives to discharge id drives] and the super-ego" (Freud, 1933: 88).[2] The superego is tied to incestuous feelings of the genital stage, at which time the development of controls becomes an internal matter and no longer exclusively dependent upon external forces (parents, for example). The healthy superego is the result of an identification with a parent(s) that is accomplished during the genital stage of psychosexual development. In other words, "The role which the super-ego undertakes later in life, is at first played by external power, by parental authority" (Freud, 1933: 89). The use of drugs can reduce the anxiety caused by unresolved inner conflicts, while the harmful aspects of drug use provides external punishment demanded by an overactive superego (discussed below).

Id drives impel a person (via the ego) to activity leading to a cessation of the tension or excitement caused by the drives—the person seeks discharge or gratification. For example, the hunger drive will cause activity through which the person hopes to satisfy (gratify) the hunger experience. These drives are divided into two categories, but elements of each appear whenever either drive is activated:

1. *Primary process:* that which tends toward immediate and direct gratification of the id impulse.

2. *Secondary process:* the tendency to shift from the original object or method of discharge when something blocks it—for example, the superego—or when it is simply inaccessible, to another object or method. For example, a desire to play with feces arising out of an anal cathexis, will be transferred to playing with mud or clay as a result of toilet training. This transfer is called *displacement,* and it is one of the many defense mechanisms that the human mind employs to adapt to its environment. Other defense mechanisms include:

> *Repression:* activity of the ego that prevents unwanted id impulses, memories, emotions, desires, or wish-fulfilling fantasies from entering conscious thought. Repression of charged material (such as incestuous fantasies) requires the expenditure of psychic energy and sets up a permanent opposition between the id and the ego. The delicate balance (equilibrium) between the charged material and its opposing expenditure of energy can shift at any time, usually as a result of some stress. When repression is inadequate for dealing with charged material, psychoneurotic symptoms develop.

[2]Eli Sagan (1988) points out that there is a substantial difference between the superego and the conscience. While the latter implies an objective sense of morality, the superego in a Nazi society commands one to live up to genocidal ideals.

Reaction formation: a mechanism whereby an individual gives up some form of socially unacceptable behavior in favor of behavior that is socially acceptable. This more acceptable behavior usually takes the form of being opposite to the real desire (drive). For example, a child who desires to kill a sibling will become very loving and devoted. In adult behavior, a sadistic impulse toward animals can result in a person becoming involved in the care and treatment of persons or animals.

Projection: a person's attribution of his or her own wish or impulse to some other person(s). This is pathological in cases of paranoia.

Sublimation: when a drive that cannot be experienced in its primary form, such as a desire to play with feces, is accommodated by modeling clay or, perhaps, becoming a proctologist.

There is a delicate balance maintained by unconscious forces as a person experiences various sociocultural and biological aspects of existence. When the balance is upset, the psyche passes from the normal to the psychoneurotic and/or the psychotic (mental illness). It is basic to psychoanalytic theory that there is a very thin line between the normal and the neurotic, and between the neurotic and the psychotic. In fact, there is only a difference of degree between the "normal" and the "abnormal." The degree to which there is a malfunctioning in psychic apparatus is the degree to which a person is "abnormal" or "sick," that is, socially dysfunctional.

Crime and the Superego

The "psychoanalytic theory of crime causation," notes Gerhard Falk, "does not make the usual distinction between behavior as such and criminal action"; the distinction is a legal one—that is, crime is behavior defined by a society as illegal, an issue discussed in Chapter 1. Antisocial behavior is seen as a neurotic manifestation whose origin can be traced back to early stages of development: "There is no fundamental difference between the neurotic criminal and all those socially harmless representatives of the group of neurotic characters; the difference lies merely in the external fact that the neurotic lawbreaker chooses a form of acting out his impulses which is socially harmful or simply illegal" (Alexander and Staub, 1956: 106).

According to August Aichhorn:

. . . the superego takes its form and content from identifications which result from the child's effort to emulate the parent. It is evolved not only because the parent loves the child, but also because the child fears the parent's demands. (1963: 221)

However, Freud states that "the superego does not attain to full strength and development if the overcoming of the Oedipus complex [in males] has not been completely successful" (1933: 92).

It is the superego that keeps primitive (oral and anal) id impulses from being acted upon. Persons with a poorly developed superego are restrained only by the ego — sociopaths — which alone cannot exercise adequate control over id impulses. Such persons suffer little or no guilt as a result of engaging in socially harmful behavior.

At the other extreme are persons whose superego (internal parental voice) is destructive. Their superego is overwhelming and cannot easily distinguish between *thinking bad* and *doing bad*. Unresolved conflicts of earlier development and id impulses that are normally repressed or dealt with through other secondary processes (such as reaction formation or sublimation, see above) create a severe sense of (unconscious) guilt. This guilt is experienced (at the unconscious level) as a compulsive need to be punished. To alleviate this (unconscious) guilt, the actor is impelled toward committing acts for which punishment is virtually certain. Delinquents of this type are the victims of their own morality (Aichhorn, 1963). Persons employed in the criminal justice system often see cases in which the crime committed was so poorly planned and executed that it would appear that the perpetrator *wished* to be caught.

In sum, criminal behavior is related to the superego function, which is a result of an actor's relationship to parents (or parental figures) during early developmental years. Parental deprivation through absence, lack of affection, and/or inconsistent discipline, stifles the proper development of the superego. Parental influence is thus weakened by deprivation during childhood development, and in adulthood the actor is unable to adequately control aggressive, hostile, or antisocial urges. Overly rigid and/or punitive parents, on the other hand, can lead to the creation of a superego that is likewise rigid and punitive, for which the actor seeks punishment as a way of alleviating unconscious "guilt."

It is obviously important for a p/p officer to be able to distinguish between those offenders with an inadequate superego from those with a punitive one. With the latter, attempts to deter criminal behavior through the application of threats may actually have an the opposite effect. With the former, the p/p officer may need to act in a parental role in place of a poorly developed superego. (For a discussion of psychoanalytic theory and drug abuse, see Abadinsky, 1989.)

Psychoanalytic Treatment

Psychic disorders are treated by psychoanalysis or one of its variants such as psychotherapy. According to Freud psychoanalysis "aims at inducing the patient to give up the repressions belonging to his early life and to replace them by reactions of a sort that would correspond better to a psychically mature condition." To do this, a psychoanalyst attempts to get the patient "to recollect certain experiences and the emotions called up by them which he has at the moment forgotten" (Reiff, 1963: 274). To the psychoanalyst, present symptoms are tied to repressed material of early life—the primary stages of psychosexual development. The symptoms will disappear when the repressed material is exposed under psychoanalytic treatment.

To enable the patient to relive the early past, the analyst uses *dream interpretation* and *free association,* whereby a patient verbally relates ideas as they come to mind. In addition, psychoanalysis takes advantage of the phenomenon of *transference.* This is the development of an emotional attitude, positive or negative, by the patient toward the therapist. It is a reflection or imitation of emotional attitudes that were experienced in relationships that had an impact on psychosexual development. Thus, the therapist may (unconsciously) be viewed as a parental figure by the patient. Through the use of transference the therapist recreates the emotions tied to early psychic development, unlocking repressed material and freeing the patient from his or her burden. As Freud noted, transference "is particularly calculated to favor the reproduction of these (early) emotional conditions" (Reiff, 1963: 274).

Psychoanalysis is not used in p/p treatment because it requires highly trained (and thus expensive) practitioners; treatment takes many years; and it needs a level of verbal ability in patients beyond that of most persons on p/p. In fact, psychoanalytically oriented therapists may underestimate how hard it is to verbalize experience, even for otherwise verbal patients (Omer and London, 1988). Instead of psychoanalysis, in probation and parole psychoanalytic theory is applied through the use of social casework.

SOCIAL CASEWORK

Social work has its roots in charity work and the supplying of concrete services to persons in need; solving problems rather than changing personalities. Mary Richmond, whose colleagues included many physicians, presented the practice of social work as including (nonpsychoanalytic) psychological and sociological aspects of a person's behavior. She also set the groundwork for what is sometimes referred to as the *medical model* of treatment, dealing with nonphysiological problems through the method of *study, diagnosis,* and *treatment.*

Social casework is one of the three basic specialties of social work, the others being group work (discussed below) and community organization. Swithun Bowers offers the following:

> Social casework is an art in which knowledge of the science of human relations and skills in relationship are used to mobilize capacities in the individual and

resources in the community appropriate for better adjustment between the client and all or any part of his total environment. (1950: 127)

According to Thomas Brennan and his colleagues, casework "can be defined essentially as the development of a relationship between worker and client, within a problem-solving context, and coordinated with the appropriate use of community resources: (1986: 342). The purpose of social casework is "the solution of problems that block or minimize the effectiveness of the individual in various roles" (Skidmore, Thackeray, and Farley, 1988: 64).

Following World War I, Freudian thought impacted on social work — caseworkers began examining the client's feelings and attitudes in order to understand and "cope with some of the unreasonable forces that held him in their grip" (Perlman, 1971: 76). The client's behavior was conceived of as purposeful and determined, but some of the determinants are unconscious. Casework was thus expanded to include work with psychological as well as social or environmental stress. Although social casework borrowed much of its theory from psychoanalysis, it avoided the psychoanalytical goal of trying to effect personality changes. Instead the caseworker helps clients to maintain constructive reality-based relationships, solve problems, and achieve adequate and satisfying independent social functioning within the client's existing personality structure (Torgerson, 1962). To accomplish this task, social workers use encouragement and moral support, persuasion and suggestion, training and advice, comfort and reassurance, together with reeducation and some sort of guidance (Kasius, 1950).

Modern social casework, Margaret Yelloly points out, has been influenced by neo-Freudians who stress the impact of social and cultural factors and have deemphasized the instinctual and biological aspects of psychoanalytical theory, and by ego psychologists "who have focussed attention on the psychology of the ego and its development through object-relationships" (1980: 5). In contrast to psychoanalytic approaches, she states, the ego psychology favored in social casework pays primary attention to those aspects of the ego which derive from its reality orientation, on the causal significance of consciousness and affective states.

The importance of social casework in p/p practice goes beyond theory and into the skills and training that schools of social work provide. These include "an extension and refinement of information on how to interview, how to obtain facts about the client's background, how to identify and distinguish surface from underlying problems, what community resources exist, and how to refer" (Wilensky and Lebeaux, 1958: 288–89). Harold Wilensky and Charles Lebeaux note that such practice is pragmatic, based on rule-of-thumb experience rather than on theory. (This writer, as a parole officer, was sent to graduate school for a degree in social work and found both the theory and skills that resulted quite relevant and useful for p/p practice.)

There are three basic operations practiced in social casework methodology (Perlman, 1957: 61):

1. *Study:* fact-finding activities;
2. *Diagnosis:* thinking about and organizing facts into a meaningful goal-oriented explanation; and
3. *Treatment:* implementation of conclusions as to the "what" and the "how" of action upon the problem(s).

Although we shall review these three operations separately, it should be noted that "study-diagnosis-treatment" have a "close mutual relationship and form one theme." Roland Ostrower also notes that although for teaching purposes these steps are referred to separately, they "are not actually performed in sequence, but are interwoven and in reality comprise a unity" (1962: 86).

Study

During the initial phase the worker must establish a relationship with his or her client. To be able to do this, the worker must be what Gordon Hamilton calls "a person of genuine warmth" (1967: 28). Using face-to-face interviews, the worker conveys acceptance and understanding. Walter Friedlander notes that "caseworkers communicate their respect for and acceptance of the client as a person whose decisions about his own living situation are almost always his own to make" (1958: 22). Of course, the p/p officer-as-caseworker may be bound by statute or agency regulation to make decisions about the client's living situation. Workers know that the way they communicate will have an effect on clients' perception of them and the worker-client relationship. Therefore, workers must be cognizant of the way they greet clients; their tone of voice, facial expressions, and posture; and the way they express themselves verbally. In p/p practice, workers who exude authority, who are curt, and who emphasize the enforcement aspect of their position will encounter difficulties in establishing a sound casework relationship.

Workers engage clients in the helping process and they make certain judgments about a client's motivation, how much he or she wants to change, and how willing the client is to contribute to bringing about change. Workers recognize that a client brings attitudes and preconceptions about being on probation or parole. The p/p client is fearful, or at least realistically on guard, since he or she recognizes the power of the p/p worker.

An anxious client will be resistant to a worker's efforts, and in the mandated setting that is probation and parole practice, a worker can easily raise a client's anxiety level, thus increasing *resistance:* "evasive, angry, and uncooperative behaviors" (Hutchinson, 1987: 591). Psychoanalytic theory also posits resistance that is unconscious. P/p clients frequently have negative impressions of all authority figures. This is usually based on experiences with parents, school officials, police officers, court officials, training schools, or prisons. In addition, a client may have a low self-image, a severe superego, or a chronically high anxiety level. The result will be resistance. It is important for the worker not to become defensive about client resistance; not take it personally.

There are ways of lessening resistance. Workers can discuss the client's feelings about being on p/p, allowing him or her to ventilate some of their feelings and anxiety. This will also enable workers to clear up any misconceptions that clients have about p/p supervision. Elizabeth Hutchinson suggests "letting it all hang out":

> It is essential for the social worker to make early acknowledgement of client reluctance toward the mandated transactions and to validate such reluctance as understandable. This makes the issue explicit rather than latent and assures the client of the acceptability of his or her feelings as well as the genuineness of the social worker. (1987: 592)

The client's motivation can also be influenced by *transference.* The client may view the worker as a friendly parent, or an authoritarian and demanding mother or father. The worker can be influenced by *countertransference,* since he or she may view the client as a childlike figure, or, when there is a significant age difference between the worker and client, the former may view the latter as a parent or older sibling.

The caseworker prepares a psychosocial study of the client. In nonprobation/parole agencies workers often stress the importance of early childhood development and experiences with a view toward applying psychoanalytic explanation to the client's behavior. This is not the usual practice in p/p settings, where it is more relevant and appropriate to analyze "the unique constellation of social, psychological, and biological determinants of the client's current stressful situation" (Friedlander, 1958: 47). In p/p practice, the primary focus is on the present or the recent past.

The probation/parole worker seeks information that will provide an indication of the client's view of his or her present situation. The p/p officer is concerned with the client's plans for improving the situation and weighs the sincerity and intensity of the latter's commitment to change. The caseworker reviews the client's relationship with his or her family and evaluates the impact of the client's current situation. While engaged in study, the worker must also be aware of the cultural, racial, and ethnic factors that influence the client.

In p/p, material from the unconscious is not sought. However, with clients who are mentally ill, material that in the better-functioning person is normally repressed may be brought to the fore. In such situations, the worker must direct efforts toward keeping the client in touch with reality, and should usually avoid exploring the normally repressed material.

Diagnosis

A diagnosis is a "summation of the symptoms of some underlying causation" (Friedlander, 1958: 146). It determines the nature of the client's difficulty and provides a realistic assessment for individualized treatment. Some of the questions that a diagnosis seeks to answer include (1958: 84–85):

1. What are the client's social-role problems?
2. What are his or her dominant and alternate modes of adaptation?
3. What are the etiological factors that can be traced to the client's present situation?
4. What are his or her ego strengths and weaknesses?

The diagnosis focuses particular attention on ego functioning. The client's capacity to deal consciously with difficult inner forces is dependent on ego functioning, a facet of personality that develops its strengths through interaction with other persons (Friedlander, 1958). Ego adequacy will have a direct impact on the client's efforts to deal with his or her difficulties.

Helen Perlman suggests that the diagnosis in casework consists of:

1. The nature of the problem and the goals sought by the client, in their relationship to
2. The nature of the person who bears the problem, his or her social and psychological situation and functioning, and who needs help with his or her problem, in relation to
3. The nature and purpose of the agency and the kind of help it can offer and/or make available. (1957: 169)

For a diagnosis to be complete, psychological testing and/or a psychiatric evaluation is necessary. The results of a clinical examination will indicate if the client is in need of any special treatment—for example, if he or she is psychotic. In many, if not most instances in p/p, however, a psychological or psychiatric report will not be available.

In discussing the etiology of the client's malfunctioning, Perlman refers to the "history of his development as a problem-encountering, problem-solving human being"; she notes that "this can provide the worker with an understanding of the client's present difficulties and the likely extent of his or her ability to cope with them" (1957: 176).

Walter Friedlander notes that "in an on-going relationship, diagnoses are continually reformulated, as the caseworker and the client engage in appropriate corrective action or treatment" (1958: 22).

Treatment

It is a basic concept in social work that the worker has no right to impose his or her goals on the client. The client has a right to *self-determination*. Obviously, the authority inherent in the p/p officer's role necessarily limits self-determination. How is this reconciled when social casework is the mode of treatment?

A review of some of the literature on this issue, notes Dale Hardman (1960), is confusing, since it reveals that authority is considered:

1. Impossible
2. Possible only in mild cases of delinquency
3. Both detrimental and beneficial; or
4. Essential but not necessarily harmful.

Hardman (1960: 250) states that "authority conflict is a major causative factor in delinquency," a proposition that is widely accepted in correctional treatment. Therefore, helping the offender come to grips with the reality of authority is a basic goal of p/p treatment. The client's relationship with a p/p worker is often the only positive experience he or she has ever had in dealing with an authority figure. Brennan and his colleagues report that "many clients' involvement with the law expresses a need for control they cannot themselves provide. If used with respect and care, the authority of the court can be invoked by the forensic social worker to strengthen the client's weak motive to get treatment and to improve impulse control" (1986: 345).

However, social caseworkers in other than correctional settings must also deal with the reality of their authority. They require clients to keep appointments, provide personal information, and pay fees — usually under the threat, implied or expressed, of denying the client the help or service for which the client is asking. Workers in child welfare agencies may even be required to remove children from their parents or guardians in neglect or child abuse cases. In addition, because of the impact of any agency setting, or the phenomenon of transference, the caseworker is always an authority figure. The concept and the use of authority and the limits placed on self-determination by reality are not alien to the practice of social casework. (See Hutchinson (1987) and Hasenfeld (1987) for a discussion of this issue.)

However, we should consider the admonition of Alexander Smith and Louis Berlin, who state that "no matter how evident the need for counseling . . . appears to the probation and/or parole officer, it cannot be forced upon the offender unless it is directly related to his crime" (1974: 3). For example, according to Smith and Berlin, a client who has a history of drug usage that has resulted in the need to steal could be required to accept counseling because it is "directly related to his crime." However, I question the usefulness of "counseling" that has to be "forced upon the offender." I would recommend instead that no form of treatment be forced upon any offender. This will preserve the client's right not to be treated, while allowing the worker to better use treatment time and skills with clients who both need and want help.

The illusion "that all, or most all, offenders need and will respond to rehabilitative efforts, if such efforts are sufficiently massive and persistent," note Bernard Ross and Charles Shireman, has led to assigning "most offenders to programs of active intervention in their lives. The result is the choking of programs with large numbers of individuals who do not need, do not want, and cannot use the sort of relationship-and-communication-based treatment that is the basis for most probation or parole services" (1972: 24).

In any event, the plan for treatment in social casework will use procedures that, it is hoped, will move the client toward the goal of enhancing the ability to function within the realities placed on him or her by society in general, and the client's present probation/parole status in particular. There are three basic techniques involved.

Changing the environment This may involve obtaining needed resources if these are available from the agency, or locating other agencies that can provide them. In using this technique the worker may assume a *mediator* or *advocate* role when the client is unable to secure a service that he or she needs and to which the client is entitled. In p/p practice this is a common role for the worker. The technique is used by the juvenile p/p officer when seeking placement for a youngster in a foster home, group home, or residential treatment center. The aftercare worker who is trying to place a juvenile back in public school after a stay at a juvenile institution is often a *mediator/advocate*. The worker may have to intervene on behalf of clients who require financial assistance from the welfare department. P/p workers may help a client to secure a civil service position or a necessary license/certificate to enter a particular trade or profession.

The p/p worker may help the client by talking to an employer or school official, at the same time helping the probationer or parolee to modify behavior relative to problems encountered at work or school. Many p/p clients have had few positive work or school experiences, and their difficulty with authority extends to employers and teachers. By using role playing, reflection, and suggestion the worker tries to modify the client's behavior, at least to the degree required for continued schooling or employment.

The p/p worker, while being of direct assistance when necessary, should promote independence on the part of the client. The worker realizes that he or she is not continually available, and treatment is rarely indefinite. *The worker should not do anything for the client that the client is capable of doing for him- or herself.*

Ego support   The use of this technique entails attempts by the worker to sustain the client through expressions of interest, sympathy, and confidence. The worker, through the use of a relationship with the client, promotes or discourages behavior according to whether the behavior is consistent with the goals of treatment. The worker encourages the client to ventilate and deals with any anxiety that may inhibit functioning.

Central to the treatment process is the relationship between the client and the worker. The worker imparts a feeling of confidence in the client's ability to deal with problems. He or she makes suggestions about the client's contemplated actions and indicates approval or suggests alternatives relative to steps that the client has already taken. The worker may, at the very least, provide a willing and sympathetic ear to a troubled and lonely client. It is not unusual for the p/p worker to be the only person available to an offender to whom he or she can relate and talk. When the relationship is a good one, the client cannot help but view the worker as a friend.

The worker is also supportive of the client's family, parents, or spouse. In p/p practice, home visits are a usual part of the worker's responsibilities. During the home visit, the worker has an opportunity to observe the client's environment directly. This adds another dimension to the worker's knowledge of the client.

The knowledge that a client lives in substandard housing and/or in a high-delinquency area is easy for the worker to incorporate into his or her working methodology. But the concept is an intellectual one. A home visit provides the smell of urine in the hall, the roaches, the broken fixtures and bathroom facilities; housing that is hot in the summer and cold in the winter; it enables the worker to experience the presence of drug addicts huddling in a hallway, waiting for their connection. The worker is able to see, hear, and smell the environment in which a client is forced to live and to understand the hostility and frustration that fills the life of many p/p clients almost from the time they are born.

By working directly with parents or a spouse, in addition to working with the client, the p/p officer broadens his or her delivery of help to the client. The worker can make referrals for the client's children when special aid is necessary—indeed he or she can intervene on behalf of the client in the role of *mediator/advocate* to get services for any family member. The p/p officer can assist with marital problems. Marital discord is an acute problem in many parole cases where a client has been incarcerated for several years. The worker may try to deal with the problem directly or may provide a referral to a specialized agency for the client and spouse. It is not unusual for a distraught wife to call the p/p officer to complain about her husband. Sometimes she is merely seeking some way of ventilating her feelings; at other times the situation may be more serious—for example, she may have been subjected to physical abuse.

When a client is living with parents, the worker strives to involve them in the rehabilitation effort. This is often difficult. The client may be the perennial black sheep in a large family. He or she may come from a family that also has other members on probation, in prison, on parole. This may dissipate the family's energy and resources, and directly affect their ability to help the client.

Clarification Clarification, states Florence Hollis, is sometimes called counseling because it usually accompanies other forms of treatment in casework practice. Clarification includes providing information that will help a client to see what steps he or she should take in various situations. The worker, for example, may help the client weigh the issues and alternatives to provide a better picture on which to base a decision. Hollis notes that the client "may also be helped to become more aware of his own feelings, desires and attitudes" (1950: 418–19).

The client is encouraged to explain what is bothering him or her. If the problem is external, this may be relatively easy. If the difficulty is internally caused, however, it may go deep and provoke anxiety. This will cause resistance, and the p/p officer will need great skill to secure enough information about the problem to be able to be of assistance. In response to the information, the worker may provide a direct interpretation to the client; more often, the p/p officer will ask questions and make suggestions designed to help the client to think out the problem more clearly and to deal with it in a realistic manner.

SOCIAL GROUP WORK

Groupwork provides a helping milieu wherein individuals agree to help one another; in contrast with the worker in social casework, it is the group that is the agency of help. The basic operating premise of social group work is that "Groups of people with similar needs can be a source of mutual support, mutual aid and problem solving" (Brown, 1986: 10). In the group, notes Allan Brown (1986: 11), "every member is a potential helper." Helen Northern states that "one of the advantages of the use of groups in social work is that stimulation toward improvement arises from a network of interpersonal influences in which all members participate" (1969: 52). The theory underlying the use of the group is that the impact provided by peer interaction is more powerful than worker-client reactions within the one-to-one situation of social casework.

In probation/parole, groups consist of members who share a common status, in this case legally determined. Groups in p/p may also be organized on the basis of age, or around a common problem such as substance abuse. The group is a mutual aid society in which members are given an opportunity to share experiences and assist each other with problems in a safe, controlled environment. The group helps to confirm for each member the fact that others share similar problems—"are in the same boat"—thus reducing the sense of isolation. With the help of the worker, members are able to share a sense of purpose and develop a commitment to helping each other through patterns of group interaction. "As members offer solutions to common problems, make supportive comments, and share in the skill development of fellow members by participating in group exercises, they become committed to helping each other" (Shaffer and Galinsky, 1989: 26).

The group can reduce the anxiety of having to report alone to a p/p officer; it tends to offset the more direct authority of the one-to-one situation; and it tends to lower the impact of sociocultural differences between client and worker. As Gisela Konopka points out, "In a group members support each other; they are not alone in the face of authority" (1983: 93). In a group, she notes, the offender is surrounded by equals; he or she is not a client, but a *member.* This permits "feelings of identification that are impossible to achieve on an individual basis with even the most accepting social caseworker" (1983: 97). Group work also requires a level of skill and training that is not widely available in social work in general, and p/p practice in particular.

There are a variety of approaches to group work that can be applied in correctional settings, often depending on the theoretical stance of the agency or worker, including: gestalt therapy, transactional analysis, and psychoanalytic group therapy, all of which are rooted in psychoanalytic theory; guided group interaction, which is based on sociological, small group theory, and behavior modification. Within the profession of social work there are a number of different approaches to group work, for example, those espoused by William Schwartz (1976), Robert Vinter (1985), Helen Northern (1969), and Sheldon Rose (1977).

LEARNING THEORY/BEHAVIOR MODIFICATION

If we view the various modes of treatment used in probation and parole practice as if they were on a continuum represented by a straight horizontal line, with total acceptance of psychoanalytic theory/treatment on the extreme left, and total rejection on the extreme right, social casework would tend to be left of center, while reality therapy, discussed later, would tend toward the right of center; learning theory/behavior modification would be firmly on the extreme right of our imaginary line.

Psychoanalytic Theory . . . . Reality Therapy . . . . Learning Theory
(Social casework)   (Behaviorism)

Behavior modification, the application of learning theory, which emanated from the science laboratory and experimental psychology, rejects psychoanalytic theory as an unscientific basis for an even more unscientific mode of treatment. Ian Stevenson, a psychiatrist, is extremely critical of the paucity of evidence indicating that the therapeutic procedures that are based on psychoanalytic theory are effective (Wolpe, Salter, and Reyna, 1964: 7). B. F. Skinner, America's foremost behaviorist, argues that analytically oriented therapists "rely too much on inferences they make about what is supposedly going on inside their patients, and too little on direct observation of what they do" (Goleman, 1987: 18). For Skinner, the mind is irrelevant as a basis for understanding human behavior ("B. F. Skinner Insists It's Just Matter Over Mind," 1987).

Behaviorists, on the other hand, take pride in displaying and subjecting to rigorous scientific analysis their methods and results. Indeed, the use of behavior modification requires the maintenance of extensive objective treatment data, including outcomes in quantifiable terms (American Psychiatric Association, 1974). Psychological dictionaries define *behaviorism* as an approach to psychology that emphasizes the importance of an objective study of actual responses.

Behavior modification proceeds on the theory that all forms of behavior are the result of learning responses to certain stimuli. "Disturbed" behavior, for example, is a matter of learning responses that are inappropriate (London, 1964). The behaviorist contends, and has been able to prove, that animal behavior, human and otherwise, can be modified through the proper application of behaviorist principles. Indeed, such techniques as *conditioned reflex therapy* are "based completely on the work of Pavlov and Bechterev" (Salter, 1964: 21), who demonstrated that such observable and measurable activity as the flow of a dog's saliva could be controlled by the use of laboratory conditioning. (Nobel prize winner Ivan Pavlov's dogs were conditioned to salivate at the sound of a bell.) When behavior modification moved out of the laboratory, its use was "confined to specific problems such as children's fears and bedwetting and alcoholism" (Reyna, 1964: 170).

The basic principle in behaviorism is *operant conditioning*. As noted by Skinner, when some aspect of (animal or human) behavior is followed by a certain type of consequence—reward—it is more likely to occur again. The reward is called a *positive reinforcer*. When a negative consequence is used to decrease the likelihood that some aspect of behavior will be repeated, it is called a *negative reinforcer*. These terms form the basis for operant conditioning, whereby patterns of behavior are *shaped* incrementally by reinforcement (Skinner, 1972). Antisocial behavior is merely the result of learning directly from others, for example peers, or the failure to learn how to discriminate between competing norms, lawful and unlawful, because of inappropriate reinforcement. When conforming behavior is not adequately reinforced, or perhaps negatively reinforced, an actor can more easily be influenced by competing, albeit antisocial, sources of positive reinforcement. "Behavior modification, then, involves altering the nature of the controlling conditions, rather than imposing control where none existed before" (Stolz, 1975: 1037). To be effective for learning, however, reinforcement must follow rather closely the behavior that is to be influenced. When these principles are applied in treatment, therefore, timing is crucial.

The behavioral therapist begins with a functional analysis in order to develop a treatment program designed to deal with specific target behaviors. The analysis deals with the day-to-day functioning of the subject in order to discern the independent variables causing maladaptive behavior/dependent variables. The therapist attempts to elicit specific descriptions of actual events that constitute a problem so that he or she can evaluate which components of the situation are amenable to change by behavioral techniques (Kanfer and Goldstein, 1975). The specific description, whenever possible, is based on direct observation or interviews with the client and/or significant others (for example, parents or spouse), and a review of any relevant records. Maladaptive behavior is analyzed in terms of intensity and/or frequency, and is often presented in the form of graphs. Offenders have problematic reinforcement contingencies. They often engage in behavior that provides an immediate pay-off, but which has negative long-term consequences. The therapist recommends, among other techniques, teaching the client to conduct his or her own functional analysis for subsequent self-produced modification of the environmental contingencies that are reinforcing the maladaptive behavior.

The functional analysis can be combined with self-monitoring techniques. Highly motivated clients maintain a daily log of the specific problem; for example, lack of temper control. The client records the number of times he or she exhibits the specific manifestations of a lack of temper control. While this technique can be combined with other forms of therapy, alone it seems to have the power to modify behavior since it

> increases awareness and makes the response sequence less automatic. This may provide the opportunity for the person to suppress the response or engage in some incompatible behavior. Additionally, self-monitoring may encourage the person to reward or punish himself depending upon whether appropriate gains have been made. Investigators have shown that self-reinforcing statements such as "I am doing well" are important in maintaining one's own behavior. A recording system which facilitates this process undoubtedly will be effective in helping people to change their own behavior as well. (Bootzin, 1975: 11)

The need for timely reinforcement makes operant conditioning difficult to apply in probation and parole practice. For example, stimulants such as cocaine and depressants such as heroin, are powerful reinforcers—they provide instant gratification to those who find their use pleasant; competing with this reality in many cases is difficult, often impossible. Albert Bandura points out, however, that in humans, "Outcomes resulting from actions need not necessarily occur instantly" (1974: 862). This is because humans, as opposed to lower animals, "can cognitively bridge delays between behavior and subsequent reinforcers without impairing the efficacy of incentive operations" (1974: 862). The cognitive position maintains that it is necessary to look to thoughts, memory, language, and beliefs. The emphasis is on inner rather than environmental determinants of behavior (Hollin, 1990). Bandura argues that to "ignore the influential role of covert reinforcement in the regulation of behavior is to disavow a uniquely human capacity of man." Of course, self-reinforcement can also operate in a manner that enhances antisocial behavior. Reinforcement, however, particularly in humans, can take on many tangible or symbolic dimensions. In reality therapy, to be discussed later, praise and encouragement are dispensed by the therapist; in correctional settings the positive reinforcements are often privileges dispensed through secondary reinforcers or *tokens*.

Token Economy

Operant conditioning has been used extensively in prisons (and other "total institutions") where reinforcing variables can be controlled to a degree not possible elsewhere. In the controlled setting of the total institution, the application of behavior modification is often referred to as the *token economy*. In some correctional programs inmates are issued punch cards with numbers every morning. As they move through the various prison activities during the day, points are earned and punched out on the cards by correction officers trained in behavior modification techniques. Points can be earned for a variety of "good" behavior — bed making, vocational and educational performance, and so on. The points accumulated on the punch cards are convertible into access to certain privileges, such as the television room, cigarettes, movies, and snacks. Such programs can often reduce the need for standard forms of coercion typically used in correctional institutions.

A widely heralded token economy was used by Harold Cohen at the National Training School for Boys (NTS) in Washington, D.C. (Cohen and Filipczak, 1971). The project involved forty-one adjudicated juvenile delinquents whose crimes ranged from auto theft to homicide. A point system was tied to educational work and academic achievement. The points that were earned allowed a boy to purchase refreshments, clothing, and even items selected from a mail-order catalog. Cohen reports that by establishing this incentive plan, the program enabled youngsters to increase their academic growth from two to four times the average for American public school students.

Cohen notes that the conventional method used in the public school system and correctional institutions is to assign students on the basis of their IQ score and reading level. Those who score low are assumed to be basically incompetent to perform in such areas as algebra and physics. They are assigned to tasks considered appropriate to their level of ability, and these usually do not require reading and other academic skills. Before Cohen arrived at the NTS, this was the method used there.

Cohen began his program by considering every inmate as a potential student capable of upgrading. His goal was to prepare them to return to public school or to pass the high school equivalency test. He set up a planned environment that included choices and perquisites that, while normally available to the average employed person, were not typically available to youths in prison. At the NTS residents could earn points for academic performance with which they paid for their rooms, clothing, amusements, and gifts. Even showers had to be rented with points. And points could not be gained except through "work"—they could not be given away, loaned, traded, or stolen. Family members were permitted to visit, but were not permitted to purchase any items for residents—they were completely dependent on the NTS program. In addition, residents were able to earn nonmonetary reinforcements: respect and approval from staff and peers.

The principal objective of the program was the development of appropriate academic behavior. No assumptions were made by the program originators relative to the resident's behavior when he returned to the community. However, a follow-up on recidivism indicated that during the first year after release from the NTS, the rate of recidivism was two-thirds less than the norm, although by the third year the rate was near the norm. Cohen reports that the program evidently delayed a return to delinquent behavior, but did not necessarily prevent it.

Thomas Stampfl points out:

> One obvious disadvantage related to TE [token economy] is that rather close control over environmental contingencies is required. The status of the S [subject] whose behavior is to be modified is that of a "captive." In the absence of environmental control, it is not possible to introduce critical contingencies. If control is present initially, but is then lost for whatever reason, the removal of the contingencies allows the altered behavior to revert in the direction of its original baseline rate. In an effort to maintain behavior when the subject has lost his status as a captive, operant conditioners have attempted to gradually alter the manipulated contingencies in respect to the behavior being modified so that the changed behavior itself would tend to result in natural intrinsic reinforcement. (1970: 105)

The difficulty inherent in the latter approach, Stampfl notes, is that delinquents/criminals "tend to be highly resistant to the usual types of natural or intrinsic reinforcement that appear to function so effectively for other 'normal' populations" (1970: 105).

Other Behavior Modification Systems

Operant conditioning can also use punishment: *aversive* therapy. This involves the avoidance of punishment in a controlled situation in which the therapist specifies in advance an unpleasant event that will occur if the subject performs an undesirable behavior. According to a report by the American Psychiatric Association, "the most effective way to eliminate inappropriate behavior appears to be to punish it while at the same time reinforcing the desired behavior" (1974: 25). This method of treatment is obviously controversial, and many behaviorists disapprove of the use of punishment on both ethical and treatment grounds — its effects do not seem to last as long as results conditioned by positive reinforcement. According to Skinner, "What's wrong with punishments is that they work immediately, but give no long term results. The responses to punishment are either the urge to escape, to counterattack, or a stubborn apathy. These are the bad effects you get in prisons or schools, or wherever punishments are used" (Goleman, 1987: 18).

There have been some "horror stories" about the use of aversive therapy, which was portrayed in the Stanley Kubrick movie *A Clockwork Orange*. In real life, California prisoners were injected with Anectine (succinylcholine), a muscle relaxant that causes brief paralysis but leaves the subject conscious. The prisoners were unable to move or breathe voluntarily, a sensation that simulates the onset of death. At the same time the therapist would tell the subject that he must change his behavior. Some observers state that this program was not an example of aversive conditioning, but rather merely punishment. Indeed, conventional aversive therapy usually involves having the patient *imagine* negative consequences when certain behaviors are suggested; for example, thinking about vomiting when alcohol or drugs are suggested.

Criticism of Behavior Modification

There is considerable opposition to behaviorism in theory and practice. To many cognitive therapists learning theory lessens the dignity of a human being, reducing people to the level of animals, with techniques used reminiscent of animal training. Ogden Lindsley, a noted behaviorist, for example, humorously reminisces about his early days with behaviorism, stating "that if the bottom fell out of the whole thing, I would drop out of graduate school and try to get a job with Ringling Brothers' circus training gorillas to dance and play the piano" (Hilts, 1974: 7).

Much of what is done in the name of behavior modification is dependent on one's definition of the situation. As a learning tool behaviorism is amoral and politically neutral and thus easily lends itself to misuse. Some critics maintain that behavior modification is simply a tool for keeping persons with legitimate grievances from expressing or acting on them — behavior modification, as noted, has been successful in helping to maintain prison discipline and order. Where legitimate dissent ends and disorder begins is often a matter of obvious subjectivity. "Behavior modification," note Beth Sulzer and G. Roy Mayer, "is an approach that is concerned with how to change behavior, not which behaviors should be changed" (1972: 7). Unlike other forms of treatment, behavior modification does not require the acquiescence of its subjects in order to be successful. In fact, it may at times be more successful when used without the knowledge of those whose behaviors are being subjected to it. Since behavior modification serves to modify *undesirable* behavior or attitudes, who is to determine what is undesirable? What one observer considers *learning,* another views as *brainwashing*. This was made quite vivid during the Korean War (1950–53), when a number of U.S. servicemen, prisoners of war, were subjected (unknowingly) to behavior modification. The success of this practice with some captive G.I.s was not viewed as "learning" by officials in the United States, who coined the term *brainwashing* to describe the behavior modification methods used by the Chinese and North Koreans. (For a discussion of the social, moral, and political implications of behavior modification, see Wheeler (1973).)

"Frequently, the goal of effective behavior modification in a penal institution," note Stephanie Stolz, Louis Wienckowski, and Bertram Brown, "is the preservation of the institution's authoritarian control." That is, "making the prisoners less troublesome and easier to handle, thus adjusting the inmates to the needs of the institution" (1975: 1049). A major problem with behavior modification programs in prisons, they argue, "is that positive programs begun with the best intentions may become subverted to punitive ones by the oppressive prison atmosphere" (1975: 1040).

As in psychoanalytic theory, learning theory does not distinguish between behavior as such and criminal behavior; both are seen as based on the same principles of learning. In expounding the behaviorist position on crime, C. Ray Jeffrey states that "There are no criminals, only environmental circumstances which result in criminal behavior. Given the proper environmental structure, anyone will be a criminal or a noncriminal" (1971: 177). In both theories—psychoanalytical and learning—the person defined as a criminal is not in control of his or her behavior—a denial of *free will*—which raises serious legal issues with respect to holding persons accountable for their actions; in law known as *mens rea*.

Psychoanalytically oriented therapists have been critical of behavior modification over the issue of *symptom substitution*. These therapists do not question the ability of behaviorists to remove or diminish certain undesirable behavior. However, according to traditional psychoanalytic theory, this symptom reduction will merely lead to new symptoms that will replace the old ones with each new emotional difficulty experienced by the subject. Thus, Aichhorn argues that the disappearance of a symptom does not indicate a cure. When a psychic process is denied expression and the psychic energies determining it remain undischarged, a new path of discharge will be found along the line of least resistance, and a new form of delinquency will result. (1963: 39)

Psychic disturbances are thus conceived of as producing a lightning-like force which if manipulated in a way that prevents discharge (that is, by behavior modification), will merely strike harmfully in another direction. The American Psychiatric Association (APA) Task Force states, however, that this is not necessarily so. Furthermore, they argue, reduction of unwanted behavior provides an opportunity to teach a person more desirable behavior (APA, 1974: 53).

Behaviorists analyze symptoms in terms of observable behavior components. The therapist keeps a record of "frequency counts" on a particular behavioral component. For example, a parent will be asked to record the number of outbursts exhibited by a youngster within a given period of time. The therapist then makes a functional analysis designed to determine the circumstances under which the undesirable behavior seems to occur, and the elements within the environment that may be supporting (and thus encouraging) the behavior. In this case, the parent may be told to ignore the outbursts, no matter what the intensity, while providing positive reinforcers for positive behavior. The results of this approach will be measured against the original baseline of frequency counts. The empirical nature of the behaviorist approach has significant appeal; however, human behavior is driven by subjective meanings that may be known only to the actor.

Positive reinforcement, the timely application of rewards, is more easily accomplished in an institutional setting where the environment can be controlled and manipulated to reinforce certain behaviors, than in the community where most probation/parole treatment occurs. This accounts for the paucity of articles on the use of behavior modification in p/p in professional journals. In one published report (Thorne, Tharp, and Wetzel, 1967), probation officers were trained in behavior techniques and they in turn gained the cooperation of parents whose youngsters were on probation. The officers explained the behavior techniques to be used and taught the parents how to apply them. Behavior was monitored by the parents, and charts were used to record frequency counts. Positive reinforcers were given for desired behavior, such as attendance at school, scholastic work, and satisfactory behavior, and were withheld when the child misbehaved. The rewards were specific and related directly to the positive behavior. For example, a girl on probation was given telephone privileges and permitted weekend dates, contingent on her attendance at school all day. In this case the attendance teacher would give a note to the child at the end of the school day attesting to her attendance. When the child gave her mother the note, she earned the privilege of receiving and making calls that day. If she received four notes, she earned a weekend date; five notes earned two weekend dates.

In another case, rewards included both tangible and intangible items. For example, for studying thirty minutes a day, the youngster was both praised and given permission to ride his bicycle. Money, access to TV, and other rewards were used as reinforcers for specific behavior on a specified schedule basis. This form of treatment is often referred to as *behavioral contracting:* "an agreement in which the performance of predetermined responsibilities or duties results in receipt of privileges or rewards" (O'Leary and Wilson, 1975: 480). It has been used predominantly with children since (in noninstitutional settings) they can be subjected to greater environmental controls than adults. In another published study on contingency management with adult drug offenders on probation, probation officers used reduction in probation time as a reinforcer (Polakow and Docktor, 1974).

Robert Polakow and Ronald Docktor note that "experimental literature on behavioral approaches to probation work with adults is almost nonexistent" (1974: 63). And the quality of behavioral research in p/p, note Michael Nietzel and Melissa Himelein, "is quite disappointing" (1987: 127). Bob and Marina Remington state that while they have "little doubt as to the promise of behavior modification in probation service contexts," their review of the literature indicates that "the promise has yet to be adequately fulfilled" (1987: 170).

REALITY THERAPY

Reality therapy (RT) was developed as a mode of treatment by William Glasser, a psychiatrist. It is probably the easiest of the three modes of treatment to describe, and simplicity has been a major reason for its popularity in probation and parole practice. Glasser's book, *Reality Therapy* (originally published in 1965), contains only 166 pages. Glasser describes RT as a method "that leads all patients toward reality, toward grappling successfully with the tangible aspects of the real world" (1975: 6).

Although Glasser accepts the developmental theories of psychoanalytic theory, he rejects them as a useful basis for treatment. "It is wishful thinking to believe that a man will give up a phobia once he understands either its origins or the current representation of its origin in the transference relationship" (1975: 53). Glasser believes that conventional treatment "depends far too much on the ability of the patient to change his attitude and ultimately his behavior through gaining insight into his unconscious conflicts and inadequacies" (1975: 51). The reality therapist denies the claims of psychoanalytic theorists that cure depends on the recovery of traumatic early memories that have been repressed. The ability of psychoanalysis to cure persons, states

Melitta Schmideberg (1975), a psychiatrist whose mother was eminent in the field of psychoanalysis, has never been clinically substantiated.

In a later work (1976), Glasser reiterates some of his previous positions and elaborates on others. Various mental problems, Glasser argues, are merely symptomatic illnesses that have no presently known medical cause. They act as companions for the lonely people who *choose* them. Glasser states that in cases of so-called mental illness, the behaviors or symptoms are actually chosen by the person from a lifetime of experiences residing in the subconscious. In place of conventional treatment, the reality therapist proposes first substituting the term *irresponsible* for mental health labels (neurotic, personality disorder, psychotic). A "healthy" person is called *responsible,* and the task of the therapist is to help an irresponsible person to become responsible. Furthermore, notes Schmideberg, the psychoanalytic approach of "dwelling on the past encourages the patient to forget his present problems, which is a relief at times, but often — undesirably — the patient feels that after having produced so many interesting memories he is now entitled to rest on his laurels and make no effort to change his attitude or plans for the future" (1975: 29).

This diverts attention from the client's current problem(s), which is a reality that should be dealt with directly. Glasser argues that conventional treatment does not deal with whether a client's behavior is right or wrong, in terms of morality or law, but "Rather, it contends that once the patient is able to resolve his conflicts and get over his mental illness, he will be able to behave correctly" (1975: 56). Societal realities, however, particularly in probation and parole practice, require direct interventions with a client, with the therapist not accepting "wrong" behavior.

"Reality therapy is based upon the theory that all of us are born with at least two built-in psychological needs: (1) the need to belong and be loved and (2) the need for gaining self-worth and recognition" (Glasser, 1980: 48). According to Glasser, people with serious behavior problems lack the proper involvement with someone, and lacking this involvement, they are unable to satisfy their needs. Therefore, to be a helping person, the therapist must enable the client to gain involvement, first with the worker and then with others. Whereas the traditional therapist maintains a professional objectivity or distance, the reality therapist strives for strong feelings between worker and client. This type of relationship is necessary if the worker is to have an impact on the client's behavior. The worker, while always accepting of the client, firmly rejects irresponsible behavior. He or she can then teach the client better ways of behaving.

To accomplish this reeducation, the worker must know about the client's reality — the way he or she lives, his or her environment, aspirations, *total reality*. Reality is always influenced by culture, ethnic and racial group, economic class, and intelligence. The worker must be willing to listen open-mindedly and learn about the client (Schmideberg, 1975). While doing this the worker develops a relationship with the client, a relationship that can effect an influence leading to responsible behavior. Alluding to the fact that RT does not always work, Glasser states that the fault is with the therapist who is unable to become involved in a meaningful way with the client. However, George Harris and David Watkins point out that the mandated correctional client may avoid counseling because of their difficulties with intimacy:

> For many people it feels safer to reject someone trying to help them than to risk accepting that help only to be disappointed. Such clients try to create physical and emotional distance in relationships. Paradoxically, a warm and empathic counselor often is met with barriers to bonding in the therapeutic relationship, and too much pursuit of the client to bring about intimacy only intensifies the client's anxiety. (1987: 18).

Glasser expresses a great deal of support for the work of probation and parole officers, although he cautions persons in corrections, as well as other fields, against the use of punishment. "For many delinquents," he notes, "punishment serves as a source of involvement. They receive attention through delinquent behavior, if only that of the police, court, probation counselor, and prison [workers]. . . . A failing person rationalizes the punishment as a reason for the anger that caused him to be hostile" (1976: 95).

Like behavior modification, RT is symptom-oriented. The p/p client is in treatment because he or she has caused society to take action as a result of their behavior. If the worker can remove the symptoms and make the client responsible, that will satisfy society and relieve the client of anxiety caused by fear of being incarcerated. Schmideberg (1975: 24) states that for a delinquent symptom to disappear, it is usually necessary for the person to accomplish three interrelated tasks:

1. Face it full with all of its implications and consequences.
2. Decide to stop it and consider the factors that precipitate it.
3. Make a definite effort to stop it.

She maintains that a general and nondirective method is not likely to change symptoms that a client may find quite satisfying (drugs to the addict, excitement and money to the robber, forced sex to the rapist).

Richard Rachin outlines fourteen steps that the reality therapist follows to attain responsible behavior in his or her client (1974: 51–53):

1. *Personalizes.* The reality therapist becomes emotionally involved. He is a warm, tough, interested, and sensitive human being who genuinely gives a damn — and demonstrates it.
2. *Reveals self.* He has frailties as well as strengths and does not need to project an image of omniscience or omnipotence. If he is asked personal questions, he sees nothing wrong with responding.

3. *Concentrates on the "here and now."* He is concerned only with behavior that can be tried and tested on a reality basis. He is interested only with the problems of the present, and he does not allow a client to waste time and avoid confronting reality by dwelling on the past. He does not permit a person the luxury of blaming irresponsible behavior on past difficulties.

4. *Emphasizes behavior.* The reality therapist is not interested in uncovering underlying motivations or drives; rather, he concentrates on helping the person act in a manner that will help him meet his needs responsibly.

5. *Rarely asks why.* He is concerned with helping a client understand what he is doing, what he has accomplished, what he is learning from his behavior, and whether he could do better than he is doing now. Asking a person the reasons for his actions implies that they make a difference. To the reality therapist irresponsible behavior is just that — he is not interested in explanations for self-defeating behavior. He conveys to the client that more responsible behavior will be expected.

6. *Helps the person evaluate his behavior.* He is persistent in guiding the client to explore his actions for signs of irresponsible, unrealistic behavior. He does not permit the client to deny the importance of difficult things he would like to do. He repeatedly asks the person what his current behavior is accomplishing and whether it is meeting his needs.

7. *Helps him develop a better plan for future behavior.* By questioning *what* the person is doing now and *what* he can do differently, he conveys his belief in the client's ability to behave responsibly. If the client cannot develop his own plan for future action, the reality therapist will help him develop one. Once the plan is worked out, a contract is drawn up and signed by the person and the reality therapist. It is a minimum plan for behaving differently in matters where the person admits he has acted irresponsibly. If the contract is broken, a new one is designed and agreed upon. If a contract is honored, a new one with tasks more closely attuned to the person's ability is designed.

8. *Rejects excuses.* He does not encourage searching for reasons to justify irresponsible behavior, thus avoiding the implication that the client has acceptable reasons for violating his agreement. Excuses are not accepted — only an honest scrutinizing examination of his behavior.

9. *Offers no tears of sympathy.* Sympathy can indicate that the worker lacks confidence in the client's ability to act responsibly. Sad tales, past and present, are avoided. Sympathizing with a person's misery and self-pity will not lead to more responsible behavior. The worker must convey to his client that he cares enough about him that, if need be, he will try to force him to act more responsibly.

10. *Praises and approves responsible behavior.* The worker makes appropriate indications of recognition for positive accomplishments. However, he does not become unduly excited about the client's success in handling problems that he previously avoided or handled poorly.

11. *Believes people are capable of changing their behavior.* The worker's positive expectations enhance the client's chances of adopting a more productive lifestyle, regardless of what has occurred in the past. The worker is encouraging and optimistic.

12. *Tries to work in groups.* The use of a peer group allows for more influence or pressure on the members. It enables the members to express themselves before

people with similar problems. It enables the member to test out "reality" in a controlled environment.

13. *Does not give up.* The worker rejects the idea that anyone is unable to learn how to live a more productive and responsible life. Historical information contained in long case records is not allowed to interfere with the worker's involvement with his client, and his belief that all persons can begin again.

14. *Does not label people.* Avoids the diagnostic rituals, and does not classify people as sick, disturbed, or emotionally disabled — they are either responsible or irresponsible.

Glasser developed reality therapy while he was a psychiatrist at the Ventura School, an institution for the treatment of older adolescent girls who had been unsuccessful on probation. Because this technique evolved within the field of corrections and the realities of dealing with delinquent behavior, it has been widely accepted and applied to p/p treatment. RT flows easily from the p/p officer's need to hold offenders accountable for their behavior. Some maintain that the value emphasis in RT coincides with the paternalistic and perhaps authoritarian attitudes of some p/p officers. Carl Bersani states that, "Glasser's writings do not provide a systematic methodology for clearly separating the moral standards of the counselor from that of the client" (1989: 188). Although Glasser does not deal with theory and RT is practice-oriented, the theoretical underpinnings are quite close to those in behavior modification. Instead of manipulating the environment or using tangible reinforcers, the therapist develops a close relationship with the client and uses praise or concern as positive and negative reinforcers. In order for this method to be carried out effectively, the worker needs to be a genuinely warm and sympathetic person who can easily relate to persons who have often committed very unpleasant acts, and whose personalities may leave a great deal to be desired — no easy task. Thus, while it may be relatively easy to train someone in the use of RT, success requires qualities of personality that are not part of the basic qualifications for becoming a probation or parole officer.

Now that we have examined psychological theories and methods of treatment, let us look at some sociological theories that have application to probation and parole practice.

SOCIOLOGICAL THEORY

Psychological theory attempts to identify causes of criminal behavior within the individual actor, and to treat the causes accordingly. While it does not necessarily offer specific approaches to treatment, sociological theory approaches crime in a social context and can add dimension to understanding individual offenders. We will briefly review those sociological theories most relevant to p/p practice.

Anomie

The concept of anomie, derived from the Greek meaning "lack of law," was developed by the French sociologist Emile Durkheim (1858-1917) to explain variations in suicide rates. Durkheim (1951) pointed to periods when abnormal social conditions (for example, an economic depression) weaken cohesion, causing each individual to pursue his or her own solitary interests. Rapid industrialization and urbanization, for example, can lead to a breakdown of social controls as large numbers of people are suddenly thrown out of adjustment with their typical ways of life (Clinard, 1964). The individual is left with a sense of "normlessness" — anomie — leaving him or her adrift without customary guideposts — social constraints on behavior. There is an accompanying growth of individualism as weakened social controls encourage a breakdown in discipline and allow unbridled human appetite to reign free — a high level of deviance such as crime and suicide can be expected. In 1938, Robert Merton "Americanized" the concept of anomie.

Merton argued that no other society comes so close to considering economic success as an absolute value. Furthermore, he states, in the United States

> the pressure of prestige-bearing success tends to eliminate the effective social constraint over the means employed to this end. The 'end-justifies-the-means' doctrine becomes a guiding tenet for action when the cultural structure unduly exalts the end and the social organization unduly limits possible recourse to approved means. (1938: 681)

Ian Taylor and his colleagues argue: "The desire to make money without regard to the means in which one sets about doing it, is symptomatic of the malintegration at the heart of American society" (1973: 93).

According to Merton, anomie results when people are confronted by the contradiction between goals and means and "become estranged from a society that promises them in principle what they are denied in reality [economic opportunity]." Despite numerous success stories — the poor boy from humble origins who becomes rich and famous — "we know that in this same society that proclaims the right, and even the duty, of lofty aspirations for all, men do not have equal access to the opportunity structure" (1964: 218). This is particularly true of the most disadvantaged segments of our population who become the clients of our probation, prison, and parole systems.

How do persons respond to the anomic condition? Most simply scale down their aspirations and conform to conventional social norms. Some rebel, rejecting the conventional social structure and seek, instead, to establish a "new social order" through political action or by establishing alternative lifestyles. Two responses, retreatism and innovation, are of particular interest for probation and parole practice.

Retreatism means that all attempts to reach conventional social goals are abandoned in favor of a deviant adaptation—a "retreat" to alcohol and drug abuse. Time and energy are now expended to reach an attainable goal: getting "high." *Innovation* is a term used by Merton to describe the adoption of illegitimate means to gain success. Societal goals of success have been incorporated and accepted, but the person finds access to legitimate means for becoming successful quite limited—anomie results. Crime is viewed as a basically utilitarian adaptation to the anomic situation. Thus, with the innovation response "the ends justify the means," while with retreatism the ends ("getting high") are sufficiently reduced as to make the means readily accessible.

What does the theory of anomie offer the probation/parole officer and the very real problems of p/p practice? One consideration has to do with aspirations. Offenders often have quite unrealistic goals; their aspirations surpass their ability. In such cases, if anomie is to be avoided, the p/p officer must help the client to make a realistic assessment of the situation, and then to assist him or her with achieving goals that are both constructive and reality based. Each client should be encouraged to achieve to the limits of his or her ability. The officer also has a responsibility to see to it that the client's goals are not blocked by such barriers as discrimination. In such instances the PO must make use of the various agencies that are responsible for enforcing equal opportunity laws.

Differential Association

As proposed by Edwin Sutherland (1883–1950), differential association explains how criminal behavior is transmitted (not how it originates). According to Sutherland (1973) criminal behavior is learned, and the principal part of learning criminal behavior occurs within intimate personal groups based on the degree of intensity, frequency, and duration of the association. The individual learns, in addition to the techniques of committing crime, the drives, attitudes, and rationalizations that add up to a favorable precondition to criminal behavior. Much criminal and noncriminal behavior have the same goal: securing economic and personal status. Differential association accounts for the difference in selecting criminal or noncriminal methods for achieving the goals.

The basis for this theory is a set of beliefs that:

1. Criminal behavior is learned (it is not the result of biological or psychological variables).
2. Criminal behavior is learned in interaction with other persons in a process of communication.
3. The learning of criminal behavior occurs primarily within intimate personal groups (in contrast to the influence of teachers, books, etc.).
4. The learning of criminal behavior includes the techniques, motives, and attitudes of a criminal.

5. The specific direction of motives and drives is learned from definitions of the legal code as favorable or unfavorable (mixed attitudes to which the individual is exposed).

6. A person becomes delinquent because of an excess of definitions favorable to violation of law over definitions unfavorable to violation of law (attitudes to which the person is exposed determine behavior).

7. Differential associations may vary in frequency, duration, priority, and intensity (the strength of association determines influence).

8. The process of learning criminal behavior by association with criminal and anticriminal patterns involves all of the mechanisms that are involved in any other learning (Boy Scouts or gangsters, their behavior is learned in the same manner).

9. While criminal behavior is an expression of general needs and values, it is not explained by those general needs and values, since noncriminal behavior is an expression of the same needs and values (both criminals and the law-abiding experience the same drives and motivations).

In sum, criminal behavior results from the strength or intensity of criminal associations and is the result of an accumulative learning process. A pictorial portrayal of differential association can easily be conceived of in terms of a balanced scale that starts out level. On each side is accumulated the varying weights of criminal and noncriminal associations. At some theoretical point criminal activity will result if there is an excess of criminal associations over the noncriminal or prosocial associations.

What import does this theory have for p/p practice? As noted earlier in the discussion of p/p regulations (Chapters 5 and 8), they usually contain prohibitions against certain associations. A person on p/p is usually cautioned against associating with others similarly situated. This can easily be seen as a practical attempt to respond to the theory of differential association. In addition, the p/p officer can provide exposure to prosocial associations; an exposure and influence that conceivably can help to balance out our theoretical scale. The officer can assist the client with securing and/or encouraging association with community, charitable, religious, athletic, fraternal, and other such organizations.

The emphasis on crime as a *learning* process is similar to behaviorist (*learning theory*) views of criminal behavior. This led Robert Burgess and Ronald Akers to reformulate Sutherland's central premise into a "differential association *reinforcement* theory" of criminal behavior:

a person will become delinquent if the official norms or laws do not perform a discriminate function and thereby control "normative" or conforming behavior. We know from the law of differential reinforcement that the operant which produces the most reinforcement will become dominant. Thus, if lawful behavior did not result in reinforcement, the strength of the behavior would be weakened, and a state of deprivation would result. This, in turn, would increase the probability that other behaviors would be emitted which are reinforced and hence would be strengthened and, of course, these behaviors, though common to one or more groups, may be labeled deviant by the larger society. Also such behavior patterns themselves may acquire conditioned reinforcing value and subsequently be reinforced by the members of a group by making various forms of social reinforcement, such as social approval, esteem, and status, contingent upon that behavior. (1969: 315)

Differential/Limited Opportunity

Richard Cloward and Lloyd Ohlin (1960) attempt to integrate anomie with differential association in order to explain how delinquent subcultures arise, develop various law-violating ways of life, and persist or change over time. They distinguish between three types of delinquent subculture that are a result of anomie and differential association:

1. *Criminal Subculture:* gang activities devoted to utilitarian criminal pursuits, for example, racketeering;
2. *Conflict Subculture:* gang activities devoted to violence and destructive acting out as a way of gaining status; and
3. *Retreatist Subculture:* activities in which drug abuse is the primary focus.

Each of these subcultural adaptations arises out of a different set of social circumstances, or *opportunity*. Cloward and Ohlin state that the dilemma of many lower-class people is that they are unable to locate alternative avenues to success or goals: "Delinquent subcultures, we believe, represent specialized modes of adaptation to this problem of adjustment" (1960: 107). The criminal and conflict subcultures provide illegal avenues, while the retreatist "anticipates defeat and now seeks to escape from the burden of the future." Criminal behavior is viewed, not as an individual endeavor, but as part of a collective adaptation.

Cloward and Ohlin note that

> many lower-class adolescents experience desperation born of the certainty that their position in the economic structure is relatively fixed and immutable—a desperation made all the more poignant by their exposure to a cultural ideology in which failure to orient oneself upward is regarded as a moral defect and failure to become mobile as proof of it. (1960: 106–107)

The turn toward alternative means of success is to be understood in terms of this social-psychological phenomena. However, Cloward and Ohlin also point out that illegitimate means of success, like legitimate means, are not equally distributed throughout society: "Having decided that he 'can't make it legitimately,' he cannot simply choose among an array of illegitimate means, all equally available to him" (1960: 145). Thus, for the average lower-class adolescent, a career in professional or organized crime (see Sutherland, 1972;

Abadinsky, 1983) can be as difficult to attain as any lucrative career in the legitimate sphere of society.

This warns the p/p officer of the need to be able to differentiate persons involved in "professional" or "organized" criminality, from the more frequent offender who has only limited skills and contacts. Professional and organized criminals are not usually good candidates for the rehabilitative efforts of probation and parole agencies. Such persons are not likely to give up criminal skills and status, which were achieved only after a considerable expenditure of time and effort, for a more conventional and law-abiding lifestyle. In these cases the investigative and control—not the therapeutic—skills of the p/p officer must be utilized.

The application of the hybrid theory of differential opportunity to p/p practice is similar to the two strains on which it is based: anomie and differential association. In California, the Los Angeles County Probation Department has responded to the activities of a conflict subculture by moving in the direction of law enforcement. The Department's "Specialized Gang Supervision Program" has as its objective improved control and surveillance of gang-oriented probationers and "the prompt handling of all violations and the return of these offenders to Court for appropriate disposition."

Social Control Theory

If, as control theorists generally assume, most persons are sufficiently motivated by the potential rewards to commit criminal acts, why do only a few engage in criminal behavior? According to control theorists "delinquent acts result when an individual's bond to society is weak or broken" (Hirschi, 1969: 16). The strength of this bond is determined by internal and external restraints. In other words, internal and external restraints determine if we move in the direction of crime or law-abiding behavior.

Internal restraints include what psychoanalytic theory refers to as the *superego,* they provide a sense of *guilt.* As noted above, dysfunction during early stages of childhood development, or parental influences that are not normative, can result in an adult who is devoid of prosocial internal constraints; some refer to this as psycho- or sociopathology. (There is also evidence tying psychopathology to a brain defect; see Goleman, 1987.) Criminal behavior, devoid of any genuine remorse, can be explained according to this dimension. Whether they are conceived of in terms of psychology or sociology, internal constraints are linked to the influence of the family (see, for example, Hirschi, 1969), an influence that can be supported or weakened by the presence or absence of significant external restraints—the probation/parole officer.

External restraints include social disapproval linked to public shame and/or social ostracism and fear of punishment. In other words, people are typically deterred from criminal behavior by the possibility of being caught and the punishment that can result, ranging from public shame to imprisonment (and in extreme cases capital punishment). The strength of official deterrence — force of law — however, is measured according to two dimensions: risk versus reward. Risk involves the ability of the criminal justice system to detect, apprehend, and convict the offender. The amount of risk is weighed against the potential rewards. Both risk and reward, however, are relative to one's socioeconomic situation. In other words, the less one has to lose, the greater is the willingness to engage in risk — and vice versa. This theory explains why persons in deprived economic circumstances would be more willing to engage in certain criminal behavior. However, the potential rewards and a perception of relatively low risk, can also explain why persons in more advantaged economic circumstances would engage in remunerative criminal behavior such as corporate crime.

Instead of conforming to conventional norms, through differential association some persons organize their behavior according to the norms of a delinquent or criminal group with which they identify or to which they belong. This is most likely to occur in environments characterized by relative social disorganization, where familial and communal controls are ineffective in exerting a conforming influence. Under such conditions, conforming, prosocial behavior may be dependent on the ability of the p/p officer to monitor the client carefully combined with a realistic threat of punishment.

Delinquent Subcultures

James Short explains that "subcultures are patterns of values, norms, and behavior which have become traditional among certain groups. These groups may be of many types, including occupational and ethnic groups, social classes, occupants of 'closed institutions' [e.g., prisons, mental hospitals] and various age grades." They are "important frames of reference through which individuals and groups see the world and interpret it" (1968: 11).

Albert Cohen (1965) argues that in certain lower-class subcultures there is a negation of middle-class values, and this negation is a severe handicap. Cohen says that there are certain cultural characteristics that are necessary to achieve success in our society, and the middle-class child is more likely to have these characteristics as a result of his upbringing:

- ambition
- a sense of individual responsibility
- skills for achievement
- ability to postpone gratification
- industry and thrift
- rational planning (for example, budgeting time and money)
- cultivation of manners/politeness

- control of physical aggression
- respect for property
- a sense of "wholesome" recreation

Cohen states that class-linked differences "relegate to the bottom of the status pyramid those children belonging to the most disadvantaged classes, not by virtue of their class position as such but by virtue of their lack of requisite personal qualifications resulting from their class-linked handicaps" (1965: 86). These youngsters simply lack the attributes listed above, and react in a manner that Cloward and Ohlin have referred to as the conflict subculture.

According to Cohen the delinquent ("conflict") subculture "takes its norms from the larger culture but turns them upside down." Thus, the subcultural delinquent's conduct is correct "by the standards of his subculture, precisely *because* it is wrong by the norms of the larger culture." His delinquent activities are totally nonutilitarian; they are "malicious, negativistic — 'stealing for the hell of it' — and apart from considerations of gain and profit" (1965: 80). The goal is status, not financial profit. According to Cohen, rules (those of the wider society) are not something merely to be evaded, they are to be *flouted:* there is an element of active spite, malice, contempt, ridicule, challenge, and defiance.

Short disagrees with Cohen. He concludes that the subcultural delinquent gang merely discourages expression of conventional values, and "values which are given active support within the context of gang interaction, for example, toughness and sexual prowess, are not conducive to conventional types of achievement" (1968: 16). Walter Miller (1958) states that law-violating acts committed by members of adolescent street corner groups in lower-class communities are not geared toward flouting conventional middle-class norms. Instead, the delinquent is merely adhering to forms of behavior as they are defined within his community. The delinquent subculture, according to Miller, did not rise in conflict with the larger, middle-class culture, nor is it geared to the deliberate violation of middle-class norms. Instead, lower-class culture is simply *different,* the focal concerns being:

1. Trouble — law-violating behavior;
2. Toughness — physical prowess, daring;
3. Smartness — ability to "con," shrewdness;
4. Excitement — thrills, risk, danger;
5. Fate — being lucky; and
6. Autonomy — independence from external restraint.

Trouble often involves fighting or sexual adventures while drinking; troublesome behavior for women frequently means sexual involvement with disadvantageous consequences. Miller contends that any desire to avoid troublesome behavior is based less on a commitment to legal or larger social order norms, than on a desire to avoid the possible legal and other undesirable consequences of the action. This would justify the threat of a probation/ parole violation as a valuable tool for p/p officers. While trouble-producing behavior is a source of status, nontrouble-producing behavior is required in order to avoid legal and other complications. This is a source of conflict for the lower-class youngster which may be resolved in a legitimate manner by becoming part of an organization with high levels of discipline, such as the military or the police.

The emphasis on *toughness* is traced by Miller to the significant proportion of lower-class males reared in female-dominated households and the resulting concern over homosexuality, which "runs like a persistent thread through lower-class culture" (1958: 9). Gambling, which is also prevalent in lower-class culture, has its roots in the belief that "their lives are subject to a set of forces over which they have relatively little control" (1958: 11). Miller refers to some of the sentiments commonly expressed in lower-class culture: "No one's going to push me around . . ." and "I'm gonna tell him to take the job and shove it!" He states that expressions of autonomy often contrast with actual patterns of behavior; that many lower-class persons actually desire a highly restrictive social environment (ranging from prison to the armed forces) with strong external controls over their behavior. Miller contends that for the lower-class person "being controlled is equated with being cared for" (1958: 13). Thus, the p/p officer will find clients resentful of controls, yet acting in such a manner as to insure recommitment after a short period of relative freedom. The p/p officer must strive to moderate these extremes for the benefit of the client.

Albert Cohen believes that the delinquent subcultural rejection of middle-class standards is more apparent than real. He contends that the standards of the wider society actually linger on, requiring, for example, a reaction-formation in the form of acts that are grossly antisocial. Walter Miller, on the other hand, asserts that the lower-class culture is distinct, significantly different from the larger middle-class culture. *Trouble* results because of culture conflict: the standards of the middle-class emerge as legal codes, thus entangling the lower-class person, who is acting according to his cultural standards, in a web of officialdom. Gresham Sykes and David Matza (1957) disagree with Cohen and Miller; they refer to a social psychological mechanism — *neutralization* — which permits a delinquent to accept the social norms of the wider society and, at the same time, violate these norms.

Neutralization   Gresham Sykes and David Matza maintain that the delinquent actually retains his belief in the legitimacy of official, middle-class norms: "The juvenile delinquent frequently recognizes both the legitimacy of the dominant social order and its moral rightness" (1957: 664). They argue that if there existed in fact a delinquent subculture such that the delinquent viewed his illegal behavior as morally correct, we could reasonably suppose that he would exhibit no feelings of guilt or shame at detection or confinement. Instead, the major reaction would tend in the direction of indignation or a sense of martyrdom.

However, the authors note, many delinquents do indeed experience a sense of guilt, "and its outward expression is not to be dismissed as a purely manipulative gesture to appease those in authority" (1957: 664–65).

Sykes and Matza postulate that:

1. The delinquent does not necessarily regard those who abide by the legal rules as wrong or immoral; and
2. It is doubtful if many delinquents are totally immune from the demands for conformity made by the dominant social order.

Therefore,

the juvenile delinquent would appear to be at least partially committed to the dominant social order in that he frequently exhibits guilt or shame when he violates its proscriptions, accords approval to certain conforming figures, and distinguishes between appropriate and inappropriate targets for his deviance. (1957: 666)

They conclude that "the delinquent represents not a radical opposition to law-abiding society but something like an apologetic failure, often more sinned against than sinning in his own eyes" (1957: 667).

By using various *techniques of neutralization* the delinquent is able to avoid guilt feelings for his actions. He is able to do this by contending that rules are merely qualified guidelines limited to time-place-person conditions. This line of reasoning is in accord with the legal code that requires *mens rea,* criminal intent, to be present in order for penal sanctions to be imposed. The delinquent justifies his actions in a form that, while it is not valid to the larger society, is valid for him. Sykes and Matza present five types of neutralization:

1. *Denial of responsibility*—rationalizing that it was not his fault, for example, he was simply a victim of circumstances.
2. *Denial of injury*—nobody got hurt; it was just a prank, or the insurance company will cover it.
3. *Denial of the victim*—he deserved it, for example, he's a "fag."
4. *Condemnation of the condemners*—dwells on the weakness and motives of those in authority of judgment: police, school officials, judges (they are corrupt, hate kids, etc.).
5. *Appeal to higher loyalties*—had to do it for friends, family, neighborhood, etc.

These sentiments, or variants of them, are often encountered by p/p officers in the course of presentence investigations or p/p supervision. Sykes and Matza caution against dismissing them as merely postact rationalizations since they indicate a genuine commitment to societal norms, a basis for rehabilitation.

Drift   Does the juvenile delinquent move on to become an adult criminal, or does the youngster mature—and *drift*—into becoming a law-abiding member of society? David Matza views the delinquent's lifestyle as not fully committed: "he drifts between criminal and conventional action" (1964: 59). Matza denies the portrayal of a juvenile delinquent as a person committed to an oppositional culture; instead, the delinquent reveals a basic ambivalence toward his behavior. Matza believes that juveniles are less alienated than others in society, and that most of the time the delinquent behaves in a noncriminal manner:

> The image of the delinquent I wish to convey is one of drift; an actor neither compelled nor committed to deeds nor freely choosing them; neither different in any single fundamental sense from the law abiding, nor the same; conforming to certain traditions in American life while partially unreceptive to other more conventional traditions. (1964: 29)

While Matza does not contradict the idea of a delinquent subculture, he finds that the subculture is not a binding force on its members: "Loyalty is a basic issue in the subculture of delinquency partially because its adherents are so regularly disloyal. They regularly abandon the company at the age of remission for more conventional pursuits" (1964: 158). The "age of remission" is a time when adolescent antisocial behavior is abandoned in favor of adult prosocial or conventional behavior. The crime-prone years for males are roughly fifteen to twenty-five, remission occurring after age twenty-five. Matza's theory has important policy implications: justice system intervention can stigmatize a juvenile, thereby blocking entry into a conventional lifestyle as he or she matures into adulthood.

Labeling

A stigma, sometimes referred to in terms of labeling or *societal reaction theory,* is the concern of a sociological perspective known as *symbolic interactionism:*

> Symbolic interactionists suggest that categories which individuals use to render the world meaningful, and even the experience of self, are structured by socially acquired definitions. They argue that individuals, in reaction to group rewards and sanctions, gradually internalize group expectations. These internalized social definitions allow people to evaluate their own behavior from the standpoint of

the group and in doing so provide a lens through which to view oneself as a social object. (Quadagno and Antonio, 1975: 33)

The focus is not the behavior of any social actor (person), but on how that behavior or actor is viewed by others—society.

The societal reaction labels—stigmatizes—the actor which results in a damaged self-image, deviant identity, and a host of negative social expectations. Think about the societal reaction to the terms: *ex-convict* or *parolee.* Furthermore, it is argued, the damaged self-image and its ramifications can result in a "self-fulfilling prophesy." Edwin Schur notes that "once an individual has been branded as a wrongdoer, it becomes extremely difficult for him to shed that new identity" (1973: 124). Furthermore, according to Edwin Lemert, the labeled deviant reorganizes his or her behavior in accordance with the societal reaction and "begins to employ his deviant behavior, or role based upon it, as a means of defense, attack, or adjustment to the overt and covert problems created by the consequent societal reaction to him" (1951: 76). Lemert has termed this process *secondary deviation.* There is a saying among the "sages" of the street: "If you got the *name,* might as well play the *game.*"

The p/p officer is constantly faced with the dynamics of labeling as clients encounter difficulty in returning to school, securing employment, obtaining housing, making friends—because of the stigma (label) inherent in the terms *delinquent/criminal/probationer/parolee.* The label results in a negative self-image whereby the offender's view of him- or herself is that of an inferior and unworthy person. In such a condition, he or she may seek the companionship of others similarly situated; may engage in further antisocial activities in an effort to strike back at the society that is responsible for the labeling.

Conflict Theory

This view considers the conventional criminal as an inevitable product of a stratified capitalist society into which the individual is born poor and powerless. The view encompasses a wide spectrum of ideas including those of Karl Marx and Max Weber. What they share in common is the belief that society is better characterized by conflict than by consensus; that what passes for crime and criminal justice actually represents the interests of powerful class interests. Otherwise, they argue, how could a burglary netting a few dollars be classified as a felony, while corporate officials who pad defense contracts with millions of dollars in overcharge, who flagrantly violate safety and restraint of trade laws, avoid incarceration or even the labeling that accompanies the processing of conventional (read: *poor*) delinquents/criminals. As noted in Chapter 6, it is always a specific class of persons who inhabit our prisons—the poor.

The conflict approach eschews theory that treats criminal behavior as a manifestation of individual pathology. Instead, crime is seen as a phenomenon generated by a capitalist system. Capitalism leads to a class system of severely differentiated wealth and power; inequities in wealth and power—in life chances—cause alienation; an alienated segment of the underclass, those whose interests are not furthered by capitalism, react in ways defined as criminal. The legal apparatus, including a monopoly over sanctions and the use of force, serves to control the alienated population and helps to perpetuate domination by the ruling class. The criminal justice system is simply a mechanism through which the self-interests of the ruling classes are protected by functionaries in their employ. Their rule is given legitimacy by an ideology of democracy, free enterprise, and property rights whose benefits accrue primarily to those who already have wealth and power. As Karl Marx pointed out, the ideas of the ruling class are always the ruling ideas.

Within this approach criminal behavior is sometimes romanticized as "rebellion," and criminals as some type of "primitive rebel," although most conventional crime is committed by the underclass against the underclass. During the 1960s and early 1970s, it was not unusual to hear conflict theory being espoused by offenders on probation or parole, or prison inmates—a reflection of a politically active era. Conflict theory sensitizes the p/p officer to some of the basic inequities in our society, certainly as they are reflected in criminal justice. Although it is beyond the role of the p/p officer, as such, to deal with system inequities, he or she does have an advocate role which will be discussed in the next chapter.

REVIEW QUESTIONS

1. How is psychoanalytic theory applied in probation and parole practice?
2. According to psychoanalytic theory, what is the importance of unconscious feelings and experiences?
3. According to psychoanalytic theory, what are the causes of behavior defined as criminal?
4. How do psychoanalytic and learning theory contradict each other in the concept of free will and *mens rea?*
5. What is the relationship between social casework and the medical model?
6. What is the basis of changing behavior in reality therapy?
7. Why has reality therapy been attractive to probation and parole agencies?
8. According to behavior modification/learning theory, what is the cause of behavior defined as criminal?
9. What are the techniques for changing behavior according to learning theory?
10. Why is it difficult to apply behavior modification techniques to probation and parole practice?
11. What are the advantages of social group work over the more traditional one-to-one approach to counseling in probation and parole?
12. What is the difference between psychological and sociological explanations of criminal behavior?

13. How does Robert Merton use the concept of anomie to explain certain types of criminal behavior in the United States?
14. According to the theory of differential association, what determines if a person becomes a criminal?
15. According to Richard Cloward and Lloyd Ohlin (differential opportunity), what are the three types of delinquent subcultures that are the result of anomie and differential association?
16. According to control theory, what determines if persons engage in criminal behavior?
17. What are the characteristics which Albert Cohen states are necessary to achieve success in our society—characteristics which lower class youth do not possess?
18. What is meant by techniques of neutralization?
19. What are the negative results of labeling?
20. What is the conflict view of criminal behavior?

TEN
Classification and Supervision

Prisons have traditionally classified inmates on the basis of the security needs of the institution and the physical limitations — handicaps — if any, of the prisoner. With the advent of the *corrections model,* the classification process was expanded to include items relevant to treatment programs offered by the correctional department in its various facilities. According to the National Advisory Commission on Criminal Justice Standards and Goals (1973), classification is a process for determining the needs and requirements of offenders and thereby assigning them to programs according to their needs and existing resources. This can be done by officials at the institution where the offender will serve his or her sentence, or at a reception center that receives all inmates for the purpose of classification and assignment to the appropriate institution.

Classification in California

A person sentenced to incarceration is first sent to a reception center for two to four weeks. Here the inmate is examined by physicians, psychologists, and educators. A correctional counselor works with this team to determine which of the sixteen institutions is appropriate for the inmate.

The counselor calculates a sociometric score for each inmate to determine custody classification, based on the following factors:

1. length of sentence
2. age

---

3. marital status
4. employment history
5. social stability
6. education
7. warrants from other jurisdictions
8. escape or attempts
9. prior commitments
10. past behavior in prison

Although the score typically determines prison and program, the counselor can make a special placement based on extenuating factors, such as the inmate's physical and mental health, prison space available, and security concerns.

At the receiving prison, a classification committee meets within fourteen days to assign the inmate to a primary program. The committee offers the inmate a variety of programs; if all programs are declined, the inmate cannot earn time ("good time") off the court-imposed sentence.

Inmates and institutions are classified into four levels reflecting security factors (escape potential, violence potential, and inmate needs) posed by the inmate and the resources of the institution to deal with the risk. The goal of classification in corrections is to place inmates in the lowest custody level consistent with public safety.

Level I consists of open dormitories without a secure perimeter for inmates with less than a thirty-month sentence, minor histories of criminality, and some history of social stability. About 35 percent of all inmates are Level I.

Level II utilizes open dormitories but with secure perimeter fences and armed coverage. It is for inmates with sentences over thirty months, minor histories of criminality, few escapes, low potential for institutional violence, and few indications of social stability. About 15 percent of inmates are Level II.

Level III consists of individual cells surrounded by fenced or walled perimeters and armed coverage. These institutions are for inmates with somewhat longer sentences, significant prior criminal history, prior "walk-away escapes," disciplinary problems during prior incarcerations, and a general lack of social stability. About 25 percent of inmates are Level III.

Level IV institutions have cells surrounded by fenced or walled perimeters, electronic security, more staff and armed officers both inside and outside the institution. These inmates have long histories of extensive criminal behavior and serious disciplinary problems during past incarcerations, a history of escapes, or a term of such length that escape is highly probable, and no social stability. About 25 percent are Level IV.

The deemphasis of the corrections model has, correspondingly, lessened the importance of institutional classification (at least for treatment). However, there has been a noticeable upsurge in the use of classification in probation and parole/conditional release supervision. (Hereafter, p/p will stand for probation, parole, and conditional release.)

CLASSIFICATION IN PROBATION AND PAROLE

During the 1970s it was becoming increasingly clear to p/p administrators that their resources would never be sufficient even to approach the service needs of their clientele. They also realized that the typical p/p officer approximated agency objectives (protection of the community and rehabilitation of the offender) through the use of an unofficial and unarticulated classification system. Christopher Baird and his colleagues note that

> because not all offenders require the same level of supervision or exhibit the same problems, most experienced probation and parole agents utilize an intuitive system of classifying offenders into differential treatment or surveillance modes, usually based on their judgments of client needs and their perception of the client's potential for continued unlawful behavior. It seems reasonable to assume that without this type of case load management, successes would diminish and failures increase. (1982: 36)

However, "this untested, highly individualized approach does not provide information necessary to rationally deploy staff and other resources" (1982: 36). Enter: The Risk/Needs Assessment.

RISK/NEEDS ASSESSMENT

During the late 1970s and early 1980s there was a remarkable expansion in the use of formal classification in probation and parole supervision. This movement was led by the state of Wisconsin, which in 1975 received funding from the Law Enforcement Assistance Administration for a Case Classification/ Staff Deployment Project. After four years the Risk/Needs Assessment was designed, implemented, and evaluated statewide. The basic strength of the Risk/Needs Assessment system is in its completeness, simplicity, and its utility to management.

The risks/needs concept developed in Wisconsin was adopted as a model by the National Institute of Corrections and, subsequently, many other probation and parole jurisdictions. While there are variations between jurisdictions, all risks/needs classification schemes quantify variables along two dimensions:

1. the degree to which the offender presents a *risk* of recidivating (committing new offenses); and,
2. the degree to which the offender requires assistance, *needs,* from the probation/ parole agency.

Taken together, these two dimensions allow for a prognostication that has implications for the level of supervision required and thus for caseload management and deployment of personnel.

The system tested in Wisconsin demonstrated its effectiveness in predicting success or failure in completing probation/parole terms. In a sample of 8,250 clients, the percentage of individuals rated low risk and later revoked was 3 percent; of the cases rated high risk 37 percent were revoked. Other jurisdictions have also tested the system. The Los Angeles Probation Department found that the risk scale, as compared to intuitive judgments by probation officers, did very well in predicting which cases would be successful and which would not; the needs scale, however, was found to have almost no predictive value (Program Services Office, 1983). In Massachusetts, Marjorie Brown (1984) found that with a variation of the Wisconsin instrument half the clients classified as "maximum risk" were subsequently recidivists, as compared to 36 percent of those classified as "moderate" and 17 percent of those classified as "minimum." It was also discovered that the predictive ability of the assessment could be improved by utilizing four levels of supervision/risk: intensive, maximum, moderate, minimum. A test of the Wisconsin Juvenile Probation and Aftercare Risk instrument by Jose Ashford and Craig LeCroy (1988) revealed that it was not a suitable basis for predicting recidivism.

Supervision Levels in Georgia

Administrative Classification

Although there is no standard of supervision required for this classification, probationers who have absconded, who are serving a prison sentence on a new offense and have not been revoked on the present offense, and probationers receiving no direct supervision per court approval, should be classified as Administrative.

Minimum (Nondirect Supervision)

1. (Division minimum requirement). Mail in change of address or employment, monthly payment of fine, restitution, court cost, etc.
2. Monthly mail-in report.
3. Monthly telephone contact with probationer.

Minimum (Direct Supervision)

1. (Division minimum requirement). Monthly telephone contact with probation officer.
2. Quarterly face-to-face contact with probation officer.
3. Monthly telephone contact with probation officer *and* quarterly face-to-face contact with probation officer.

(Continued)

Medium

1. (Division minimum requirement). Monthly telephone contact with probation officer *and* quarterly face-to-face contact with probation officer.
2. Monthly face-to-face contact with probation officer.
3. Monthly face-to-face contact with probation officer and one field contact or collateral contact quarterly.

High

1. (Division minimum requirement). Monthly face-to-face contact with probation officer *and* one field contact or collateral contact quarterly.
2. Monthly face-to-face contact with probation officer *and* monthly field contact or collateral contact (two contacts per month).
3. Two monthly face-to-face contacts with probation officer, monthly field contact, *and* monthly collateral contact. (Four contacts per month).

Maximum

1. (Division minimum requirement). Two monthly face-to-face contacts with probation officer, monthly field contact, *and* monthly collateral contact. (Four contacts per month).
2. Two monthly face-to-face contacts with probation officer *and* two monthly field contacts. (Four contacts per month).
3. Four monthly face-to-face contacts with probation officer, two monthly field contacts, *and* two monthly collateral contacts. (Eight contacts per month).

The p/p officer interviews a new client and with the help of the presentence report, institutional reports (for parolees), and other relevant documents, fills out a risk/needs instrument (see Figure 10.1). From the scoring of information on the instrument a total is derived which is plugged into a particular level of supervision; there is typically a reassessment every six months. Since clients with a higher level of supervision require a greater expenditure of p/p officer time, equity is determined, not simply on the total number of clients supervised (*caseload*), but, on the basis of the anticipated amount of time each case will demand (*workload*). This quantification allows for the easy use of computers which can determine the need for more p/p officers in a particular jurisdiction (or, if additional officers are not economically feasible, a corresponding reduction in the amount of supervisory time devoted to each case). The Probation Division of the Georgia Department of Offender Rehabilitation sets out the purpose for probation classification:

The purpose of case classification is (1) to improve the effectiveness of service delivery to the probationer; (2) to develop a uniform standard for classification on a statewide basis; and (3) to provide a data base for budgeting and staff deployment on a workload rather than on a caseload model.

Let us examine the instrument used in by the Pennsylvania Board of Probation and Parole (Figure 10.1) that is typical of most jurisdictions. The PO places a number in a box that corresponds with the case record and/or the officer's assessment for each of the eleven *risk* assessment variables. Then the officer adds up the score and records that in a box labeled "Total." He or she then proceeds to do the same for the thirteen *needs* assessment variables. Afterwards, the two final scores are compared; whichever is higher (risk or needs), determines the level of supervision—reduced, regular, close, intensive. (In some jurisdictions there are only three levels of supervision: minimum, medium, maximum). There is some flexibility in that the procedures provide for an override: "If, after completing the Initial Client Assessment or Client Reassessment, there is a compelling reason to raise or lower the client's grade of supervision, the agent may recommend such a change to his/her supervisor for review and approval/disapproval."

Differential Supervision in New York

Demonstrating through empirical evidence that 80 percent of the parolees who violate their parole conditions do so during their first fifteen months under supervision, the critical determinant of Differential Supervision is time under supervision. In order to target agency resources to parolees with the greatest risk potential, those within their first fifteen months on the street are designated "intensives." After fifteen months, the offender is placed on a "regular" supervision with less stringent contact standards. While regular caseloads average 97 parolees, parole officers with intensive cases supervise 38 parolees. In areas where density of parolees is sparse and traveling between clients poses an obstacle to efficient supervision, parole officers have mixed—intensive and regular—caseloads on a weighted formula of 2.55.

PROBATION/PAROLE SUPERVISION

The supervision process in both probation and parole is similar, if not identical. In fact, probation and parole are handled by the same agency in some states. However, parolees, by definition, have been imprisoned, and imprisonment generally reflects the severity of the offense and the criminal history of the offender. Therefore, parolees are generally considered a greater danger to the community than are probationers.

COMMONWEALTH OF PENNSYLVANIA
BOARD OF PROBATION AND PAROLE
PBPP.20 (1/85)

INITIAL CLIENT ASSESSMENT

CLIENT NAME (Last, First, Middle Initial)	PAROLE NO.	AGENT NAME	OFFICE	DATE

RISK ASSESSMENT

1. Age at First Conviction: (or juvenile adjudication)
- 24 or older 0
- 20-23 2
- 19 or Younger 4

2. Number of Prior Probation/Parole Revocations: (adult or juvenile)
- None 0
- One or more 4

3. Number of Prior Felony Convictions: (or juvenile adjudications)
- None 0
- One 2
- Two or more 4

4. Convictions or Juvenile Adjudications for:
(Select applicable and add for score. Do not exceed a total of 5. Include current offense.)
- Burglary, theft, auto theft, or robbery 2
- Worthless checks or forgery 3

5. Number of Prior Periods of Probation/Parole Supervision:
(Adult or Juvenile)
- None 0
- One or more 4

6. Conviction or Juvenile Adjudication for Assaultive Offense within Last Five Years: (An offense which involves the use of a weapon, physical force or the threat of force.)
- Yes 15
- No 0

7. Number of Address Changes in Last 12 Months:
(Prior to incarceration for parolees)
- None 0
- One 2
- Two or more 3

8. Percentage of Time Employed in Last 12 Months:
(Prior to incarceration for parolees)
- 60% or more 0
- 40%-50% 1
- Under 40% 2
- Not applicable 0

9. Alcohol Usage Problems: (Prior to incarceration for parolees)
- No interference with functioning 0
- Occasional abuse; some disruption of functioning 2
- Frequent abuse; serious disruption; needs treatment 4

10. Other Drug Usage Problems: (Prior to incarceration for parolees)
- No interference with functioning 0
- Occasional abuse; some disruption of functioning 1
- Frequent abuse; serious disruption; needs treatment 2

11. Attitude:
- Motivated to change; receptive to assistance 0
- Dependent or unwilling to accept responsibility 3
- Rationalizes behavior; negative; not motivated to change. 5

TOTAL

INITIAL ASSESSMENT SCALES

Risk Scale		Needs Scale
0-5	Reduced Supervision	8-10
6-18	Regular Supervision	1-10
19-30	Close Supervision	11-25
31 & above	Intensive Supervision	26 & above

SCORING AND OVERRIDE

Score Based Supervision Level ..... Intensive ▢　　Regular ..... ▢
　　　　　　　　　　　　　　Close .... ▢　　Reduced ..... ▢

Score Override .... No ...... ▢　　Yes .... ▢

FINAL GRADE OF SUPERVISION .... Intensive ▢　　Regular ..... ▢

Override Explanation:　　　　　Close ...... ▢　　Reduced ..... ▢

NEEDS ASSESSMENT

1. Academic/Vocational Skills
- High school or above skill level .... −1
- Adequate skills; able to handle everyday requirements 0
- Low skill level causing minor adjustment problems .... + 2
- Minimal skill level causing serious adjustment problems . + 4

2. Employment
- Satisfactory employment for one year or longer .... −1
- Secure employment; no difficulties reported; or homemaker, student or retired 0
- Unsatisfactory employment; or unemployed but has adequate job skills .... + 3
- Unemployed and virtually unemployable; needs training ... + 6

3. Financial Management
- Long-standing pattern of self-sufficiency; e.g., good credit rating − 1
- No current difficulties 0
- Situational or minor difficulties .... + 3
- Severe difficulties; may include garnishment, bad checks or bankruptcy .... + 5

4. Marital/Family Relationships
- Relationships and support exceptionally strong .... − 1
- Relatively stable relationships 0
- Some disorganization or stress but potential for improvement . + 3
- Major disorganization or stress .... + 5

5. Companions
- Good support and influence .... − 1
- No adverse relationships 0
- Associations with occasionally negative results .... + 2
- Associations almost completely negative .... + 4

6. Emotional Stability
- Exceptionally well adjusted; accepts responsibility for actions .. − 2
- No symptoms of emotional instability; appropriate emotional responses 0
- Symptoms limit but do not prohibit adequate functioning; e.g., excessive anxiety .... + 4
- Symptoms prohibit adequate functioning; e.g. lashes out or retreats into self .... + 7

7. Alcohol Usage
- No interference with functioning 0
- Occasional abuse; some disruption of functioning .... + 3
- Frequent abuse; serious disruption; needs treatment ..... + 6

8. Other Drug Usage
- No interference with functioning 0
- Occasional substance abuse; some disruption of functioning . + 3
- Frequent substance abuse; serious disruption; needs treatment . + 5

9. Mental Ability
- Able to function independently 0
- Some need for assistance; potential for adequate adjustment; mild retardation .... + 3
- Deficiencies severely limit independent functioning; moderate retardation .... + 6

10. Health
- Sound physical health; seldom ill 0
- Handicap or illness interferes with functioning on a recurring basis + 1
- Serious handicap or chronic illness; needs frequent medical care . + 2

11. Sexual Behavior
- No apparent dysfunction 0
- Real or perceived situational or minor problems .... + 3
- Real or perceived chronic or severe problems .... + 5

12. Recreation/Hobby
- Constructive 0
- Some constructive activities .... + 1
- No constructive leisure-time activities or hobbies ...... + 2

13. Agent's Impression of Client's Needs
- Minimum .... − 1
- Low 0
- Medium .... + 3
- Maximum .... + 5

TOTAL

FIGURE 10.1　Initial Client Assessment, Pennsylvania

Parolees differ from probationers as a result of their prison experiences. Elliot Studt (in Law Enforcement Administration, 1973) reports that there are certain highlights of the reintegration process that stand out in most parole cases. She notes that the changeover from prison life to community living requires a major readjustment. In prison the offenders' lives are rigidly controlled: they are told when to sleep, when to eat, when to work, and when to have recreation. When they are released into the community they must adjust to managing their own lives. This may be compounded by police harassment, particularly in smaller communities. Social agencies often do not recognize parolees' needs and somehow believe that they should be receiving assistance from the parole agency. Unfortunately, most parole (and probation) agencies are extremely limited in their ability to deliver tangible services. This fact, coupled with the usual lack of employable skills, often makes parolees a burden on their families, worsening what may have been an already difficult family situation.

Parolees have told this author that even so minor an experience as taking a bus ride can be traumatic to a newly released offender. Several stated they were not aware of the required fare and they had a feeling that everyone on the bus, especially the driver, recognized that they had just been released from prison. Being in prison also isolated them from normal social contacts with members of the opposite sex. They were very self-conscious and often felt that because of the way they looked at women, everyone would realize that they had been in prison.

Studt points out that parolees must "unlearn" prison habits and acquire new patterns of behavior if readjustment is to be accomplished quickly. Parolees are often subjected to social rejection because of their status, and they usually lack the necessary connections and economic resources that are effective in dealing with crisis situations.

Case Assignment

The supervision process begins when the offender is placed on the caseload/workload of a p/p officer. This aspect of supervision, case assignment, can be accomplished in a variety of ways, depending on the practice used by the particular agency and the scope of its jurisdiction. In agencies that have statewide jurisdiction (such as all parole agencies), there are district/area offices located throughout the state and each office covers a specific geographic area. County probation agencies, depending on the size of the county, may also have (sub)offices scattered throughout the jurisdiction. Offenders on probation/parole are directed to report to the office responsible for the area in which they (intend to) reside. At the p/p office they will be assigned to a caseload either on a totally random basis, or according to the specific area in which they plan to reside. Caseloads incorporating geographic considerations are advantageous insofar as they limit the travel time involved in supervising the offender. Each officer also gains greater familiarity with his or her territory, the social and law enforcement agencies therein, (not to mention places to eat and clean washrooms) that can enhance the supervision process. In more rural areas, where travel will be extensive, the caseloads will be smaller than in urban areas, where offenders are usually clustered in certain areas of the city. In the caseload assignment process, the agency typically attempts to achieve parity by keeping the size of caseloads roughly equal.

There may also be *specialized caseloads* wherein offenders are assigned by virtue of a salient characteristic such as history of drug abuse or mental retardation. (The use of specialized caseloads will be discussed in Chapter 11.) A final model utilizes classification schemes; quantitative weights are assigned to each case based on the level of supervision prognosticated by case (for example, risk/needs) classification, and workloads are balanced by maintaining ongoing comparative statistics for p/p officers assigned to field supervision. While this is the most rational approach to achieving parity in supervision, it is also the most difficult to operationalize, particularly for an agency that has statewide responsibilities.

Initial Interview

The first meeting between the client and the p/p officer usually takes place in the probation or parole office—it is a time of apprehension and anxiety. Jose Arcaya states that the officer "represents a power that can, and does, limit his freedom." The offender is in the office *involuntarily* in a situation "where two individuals are joined by legal force in a counseling . . . relationship" (1973: 58–59). The offender encounters the p/p officer for the first time with a mixture of fear, weariness, and defiance. Ann Strong notes: "Particularly difficult is the nonvoluntary nature of the probationer; this individual places a premium on the skills of the probation officer who must counter resistance with patience, persistence, and good will" (1981: 12).

The "sizing up" process at the time of the initial interview works both ways. The p/p officer is meeting a stranger who is usually known only through information in the case record and/or presentence investigation report. While the record may say a great deal about the offender's background, it may not accurately reflect his or her current attitude toward p/p supervision. How will the client deal with current problems? Will the probationer/parolee follow regulations? Will he or she abscond from supervision if pressured or frustrated? Will the officer be responsible for having a warrant issued and having the offender sent to prison? Will this be, instead, an easy case with a minimum of problems?

The client is asking similar questions. Will the p/p officer give me a hard time? Will my PO be rigid about every minor rule? Is he or she quick to seek delinquency action? Does the officer have the knowledge and ability to help me secure employment, training, education, a place to live?

Illinois Probationer Reporting Form

_____   DATE: _____
PROBATION OFFICER'S NAME

_____   PHONE: _____
PROBATIONER'S NAME

_____
PROBATIONER'S CURRENT ADDRESS   CITY   COUNTY   STATE

I. Have there been any changes this month in the following areas?

   1. Residence: Yes ____No ____Explanation _____

   2. Who the probationer is living with: Yes ____No ____Explanation _____
      (Spouse, Parents, Friend, Etc.)

   3. Employment: Yes ____No ____Explanation _____
      (New Job, Place of Employment, Job Title, Salary, Etc.)

   4. School: Yes ____No ____Explanation _____
      (New School, Attendance, Grades, Suspensions, Etc.)

II. Have there been any changes in driving status? Yes ____No ____Explanation ____
   (License Returned, Auto Accidents, Traffic Violations, New Car, Etc.)

III. Have there been any changes in financial debt status? Yes ____No ____Explana-
tion _____
   (Are Bills Delinquent, Being Paid Off, Paid Off, New Debts, Etc.)

IV. Are any of the following still outstanding: Yes ____No ____Explanation _____
   1. Court Fines _____ 2. Court Cost _____ 3. Restitution _____
   (Amount paid and balance due should be shown in explanation section.)

V. If Public Service, Therapeutic or Social Service Programs are in the conditions of
probation or probation plan, respond to the following:
   1. Has program been completed? Yes ____No ____Explanation _____
   (Give brief summary of attendance, attitude, therapeutic progress, and date of
completion.

VI. Have there been subsequent Police or Court Contact? Yes ____No ____Explana-
tion* _____

   I certify the above information to be true and correct and I understand that any
falsification of my answers is a violation of my court-ordered probation/supervision.

_____
SIGNATURE OF PROBATIONER   DATE

_____
SIGNATURE OF PARENT OR GUARDIAN IN THE CASE OF A JUVENILE
PROBATIONER   DATE

PROBATION OFFICE USE ONLY

_____
DATE RECEIVED: RECEIVED BY: BY MAIL   IN PERSON   DEPARTMENT ID
                                                  NUMBER
*FOR EXPLANATION PLEASE USE ADDITIONAL SHEET OF PAPER

FIGURE 10.2 Probationer Reporting Form, Illinois

During an initial interview the officer explains the p/p rules, answering questions while attempting to set realistic standards for a client. Several items are usually emphasized:

1. The need to make in-person, telephone, or mail reports.
2. The need to keep the p/p officer informed of his or her place of residence.
3. The need to seek and maintain lawful employment.
4. The need to avoid unlawful behavior and report contacts with law enforcement officers.

Where there is a special problem, the officer may set special conditions. An offender with a history of sex offenses against children will be required to keep out of areas where children normally congregate, such as playgrounds. An offender with a history of alcoholism may be directed to refrain from using any intoxicating beverages. A young offender may be required to keep a curfew. Offenders with substance abuse (drugs and alcohol) problems may be required to attend treatment programs, such as Alcoholics Anonymous.

The p/p officer explains that he or she will be visiting the offender's residence periodically. Officers offer clients assistance with employment or other problems. Some clients may need financial assistance. One of the immediate problems frequently encountered by a newly released parolee is financial. The amount of money that an inmate receives upon release, *gate money,* is usually inadequate for even immediate housing and food needs.* A parolee may have some funds as a result of prison work, but wages are well below that received by free labor. The p/p officer may refer the client to the department of welfare or to private agencies such as the Salvation Army or a halfway house.

The initial interview in p/p practice is considered a crucial time in the supervision process. The New York State parole officer is provided with the following guidelines relative to the initial interview.

Initial Interview

As the name implies, this is the first major interview between the parole officer responsible for the supervision of the case and the newly released parolee. If the arrival report is taken by the parole officer who will supervise the case, it may be combined with the initial interview. It is at this time that the parole officer initiates a counseling or casework relationship with the parolee.

Since the parole officer is endeavoring to establish this relationship with

---

*Richard Berk and his colleagues (1980: 766–86) found that support payments to just-released prisoners in Georgia and Texas reduced recidivism.

individuals whose knowledge of and acceptance of parole varies to a great degree, the interview must be planned and handled with best casework skills. There are those whose attitudes toward parole are based on prejudices, doubt, and fears brought about by rumors. With this group, only patience and skill will overcome the hostility and resistance to a working relationship.

This is the interview on which the planning for future supervision of the parolee will be based. Therefore, it is important that the parole officer prepare for it by studying all the pertinent information contained in the case folder. It is also important that this interview be well planned, unhurried, and without interference, if possible. It is the key to the future of the case.

The parole officer undertakes the initial interview with four major objectives in mind:

1. Establish a casework relationship with the parolee.
2. Secure the parolee's participation in an analysis of his/her problems.
3. Make constructive suggestions that will give the parolee "something to do" toward beginning the overall parole program.
4. Leave the parolee with some positive assurance of what there is to look forward to as the parole period progresses.

Suggested Content of Initial Interview

The initial interview will vary with the needs and problems, both immediate and long-range, of the individual case. However, the following items are presented as a general guide to areas that the parole officer might wish to cover in conducting his or her initial interview with the parolee. Several of these areas would have been addressed during the parolee's arrival report, if it was conducted at an earlier time. In that case, these items should now be discussed further to ascertain if there are any continuing or additional problems, and to learn whether the parolee's situation has altered.

1. Description of the Parolee

At this time, the parolee's physical appearance should be updated from the time of his arrival report, with any particular changes, such as his mode of dress and attitude, noted. It should be borne in mind that an individual's habit of dress and mannerisms often offer nonverbal communication that can tell us much about how a person regards himself and those about him. (From time to time during the parolee's period of supervision, the parole officer should note whether there are any significant changes in the parolee's mode of dress and mannerisms, as these may signal changes in how the parolee regards himself or in his adjustment pattern.)

2. Analysis of Problems and Initiating the Casework Process

In conducting an initial interview, the parole officer is expected to encourage the parolee's participation in discussion of his problems and goals. This discussion should be based upon information contained in the parolee's folder, other knowledge that the parole officer might have, and the parolee's input.

There should be a discussion of the parole program. Both the residence and

(Continued)

employment aspects of the program should be carefully reviewed to ascertain that it is as approved, and the parole officer should take pains to fill in any information regarding the residence and employment that may otherwise be missing in the reports. Care should be exercised to make sure that any questions or concerns the parolee has regarding his program are addressed.

The parole officer should ensure that the parolee understands his employment program, and, if necessary, arrangements should be made for the parolee to report to his employer. The parolee's prompt reporting to his prospective employer or employment program, is, of course, a necessity. The parolee's actual employment or participation in employment program should be verified as soon as possible by the parole officer.

If the parolee has no specific employment or alternative program, he should report promptly to any party or agency that may have offered him approved assistance in securing employment. If no such program has been previously established, the parole officer must assist the parolee during the initial interview to devise a plan for seeking employment. If possible, the parole officer may provide the parolee with referrals to potential employers or parties who might assist the parolee in securing employment.

Information should be provided to the parolee concerning the provisions for discharge after three years of successful parole supervision as well as possible eligibility for a Certificate of Relief from Disabilities or a Certificate of Good Conduct.

Before concluding the initial interview, the parole officer should make every attempt to determine whether or not the parolee has any questions, reservations or misconceptions concerning his relationship with parole and the conditions of parole to which he is subject. This should be done in such a manner as to ensure him that the parole officer is ready and willing to assist him in any constructive manner with the problems which might arise during his time on parole.

3. Reporting Instructions

Before concluding the initial interview, the parolee should be clearly told why office reports are necessary and helpful. He should also understand when, where, and with what frequency he is to report to his parole officer. If he is to report to his parole officer at a different location, he should be given the address of that location and the time to report. The parole officer should give the parolee one of his official business cards, writing the parolee's name on the front and reporting instructions on the back.

Further, the parolee is to be clearly informed that, should he be unable to make a scheduled report, he must contact his parole officer in advance, for permission to miss a scheduled report and to obtain an alternative appointment.

4. His attitude toward the Parole Officer and the Interview

In noting the parolee's attitude toward the parole officer and the interview, the parole officer should include a description of the parolee's attitudes, interpretation of these attitudes, and his basis for such interpretation.

Recording the Interview

The initial interview is the foundation on which the relationship between the parolee, the parole officer and the parole system is established. The way it is conducted and its content are highly important to that relationship. It is also important, from both a casework and a legal perspective, that what transpired during this initial interview be clearly and promptly recorded in the parole case folder. Since much of the information discussed during the initial interview is already recorded in the case folder, it is not necessary to repeat that information except where it relates directly to the problems that were discussed during the initial interview.

In recording the initial interview, the parole officer should bear in mind any immediate problems the parolee has and any long range problems that the parole officer anticipates. In making this assessment, the parole officer should also indicate what immediate intervention on the parolee's behalf has been undertaken or is contemplated, what immediate and obtainable goals have been established for, or preferably with, the parolee, and what long-range plans for the parolee are being considered.

Montgomery County, Ohio
Adult Probation Department
Probation Orientation Program

Each probationer will be expected to attend one probation orientation program within the first thirty days of his placement under probation supervision. At least two orientation programs will be presented each month—that is, the first and third Mondays.

Purpose

Probationers often have a personal view of what probation is all about as influenced by their own assigned probation officer or fellow probationer. There is often a thought that there is a difference between probation officers—the way officers handle their cases in terms of service to the client, police tactics, use of special conditions of probation, and so on. The orientation programs are meant to give each client a clearer understanding of the official probation processes and, more important, to introduce them to the services that are available to them through the Community Resource Division of the Adult Probation Department. It is further hoped that the orientation program schedule will allow each client to participate in an orientation session before the formulation of case plans. With the background of the orientation program, the probationer should have more of an opportunity to discuss with the probation officer the types of needs and concerns that he or she personally has that can be addressed by programs within

(Continued)

the department, or directly or indirectly supported by it. It is also an opportunity to convey to the new probationers that they can have an active part in the development of programming within the department.

The Work Roles of the Probation/Parole Officer

Ann Strong (1981) provides eleven work roles of the probation/parole officer:

1. *Detection.* Detection can involve identifying when a client is at risk or when the community is at risk (from the client). The first objective for the officer is to identify the individuals who are experiencing difficulty (at crisis) or who are in danger of becoming a risk to the community. A second objective is to identify conditions in the community itself that may be contributing to personal problems of the client and which might raise his/her assigned risk level (such as lack of jobs/training, influx of easily available controlled substances). A third objective is to determine when the community is at risk from the probationer and take steps to protect the community.

2. *Broker.* The primary objective is to steer (refer) clients to existing services that can be of benefit to them. Its focus is on enabling or helping people to use the system and to negotiate its pathways. A further objective is to link elements of the service system with one another. The essential benefit of this objective is the physical hookup of the person with the source of help and the physical connection of elements of the service system with one another.

3. *Advocate.* The primary objective is to fight for the rights and dignity of people in need of help. The key assumption is that there will be instances where practices, regulations, and general conditions will prevent individuals from receiving services, from using resources, or from obtaining help. This includes the notion of advocating changes in laws, rules, and regulations, on behalf of a whole class of persons or segment of society. Advocacy aims at removing the obstacles or barriers that prevent people from exercising their rights or receiving the benefits and using the resources they need. When I was a parole officer in New York, because of Department of Motor Vehicles regulations, parolees with legitimate employment needs had a difficult time obtaining a motor vehicle license. Advocacy on the part of the Parole Officers Association was effective in changing these regulations and removing the unnecessary obstacles.

4. *Evaluator.* This involves gathering information, assessing personal or community problems, weighing alternatives and priorities, and making decisions for action.

5. *Mobilizer.* The foremost objective is to assemble and energize existing groups, resources, organizations, and structures; or to create new groups, organizations, or resources and to bring them to bear on problems that exist; or to prevent problems from developing. Its principal focus is on available or existing institutions, organizations, and resources within the community.

6. *Enabler.* The primary objective is to provide support and to facilitate change in the behavior patterns, habits, and perceptions of individual clients. The key assumption is that problems may be alleviated or crises may be prevented by modifying, adding, or extinguishing discrete bits of behavior, by increasing insights, or by changing values and perceptions.

7. *Information manager.* The primary focus is the collection, classification, and analysis of data generated within the community. Contents would include data about the individual case and the community.

8. *Mediator.* The primary objective is to mediate between people and resource systems and among resource systems. The key assumption is that problems do not exist within people nor within resource systems, but rather in the interactions between people and resource systems and between systems. As opposed to the advocate, the mediator stance is one of neutrality.

9. *Educator.* Instruction is used in the sense of an objective rather than a method. The primary objectives are to convey and impart information and knowledge and to develop various kinds of skills. A great deal of what has been called social casework or therapy is simple instruction.

10. *Community planner.* This involves participating in, and assisting neighborhood planning groups, agencies, community agents, or governments in the development of community programs to assure that client needs are represented and met to the greatest extent feasible.

11. *Enforcer.* The enforcer role requires the officer to use the authority of his or her office to revoke the probationer/parolee's standing due to changes in the status quo which involves heightened community or individual risk outside of the control of the officer.

Probation/Parole Officer Roles and Agency Models

What role will the p/p officer assume toward the client? Harry Allen and his colleagues report that a review of the literature reveals four basic role typologies (1979: 58):

1. *The punitive/law enforcement officer,* whose primary concern is the protection of the community through control of the p/p client.
2. *The welfare/therapeutic officer,* whose primary concern is the improved welfare of the p/p client.
3. *The protective/synthetic officer,* who attempts to effect a blend of treatment and law enforcement.

4. *The passive/time server officer,* who has little concern for the welfare of the community or the client, but sees the work merely as a sinecure, requiring minimum effort.

Role four is meaningless since it is not particular to p/p or even criminal justice settings in general. The first three roles are deficient when discussed outside a particular agency context or model, of which there are three:

Control Model . . . . Combined Model . . . . Social Service Model

1. *Control Model.* Control of the p/p client's activities is the primary focus. Unannounced home and employment visits, checks for drug use, and a close working relationship with law enforcement agencies are the standard practice.
2. *Combined Model.* Requires p/p officers to provide social services, while also attending to control functions.
3. *Social Service Model.* Focuses on the client's needs: employment, housing, and counseling that provides social and psychological support.

Most probation and parole agencies would fall somewhere between the combined and social service models, with parole agencies tending toward the combined model and probation agencies tending toward the social service model. The control model would not be found in its pure form, although there may be specific programs — electronic monitoring, intensive supervision (discussed in Chapter 11) — that are based on a control model. Now if we return to the p/p role typologies, we can see that the punitive/law enforcement officer is more likely to be found in — indeed, would be appropriate for — the control model agency. The welfare/therapeutic officer would be most likely found in the social service model agency. The issue, then, is not what role the p/p officer will assume with respect to clients but, rather, whether the role is compatible with the agency model. In the combined model some use can be made of p/p officer role variation (I prefer the term *style*). Supervisors can assign cases on the basis of matching the officer's style with the salient characteristics of the offender. For example, an officer with a more authoritarian style would be matched with "heavy" (that is, professional or career) criminals. An officer with a gentler style would be appropriate for certain situational offenders or perhaps youthful clients.

In a combined model agency, officers should integrate their control or community protection role with their social service role, while maintaining flexibility to stress one over the other in an individualized response to each case. For example, a young offender under supervision for joyriding in a stolen car will receive a different response than an experienced offender who is associated with organized criminal activity. In p/p treatment officers adapt those methods that are useful to their practice, while sacrificing the rest, sometimes cynically, on the altar of reality. Support for combining the social service with control function comes from Elizabeth Hutchinson (1987), who argues that social workers should avoid sending out other people to carry out coercive actions.

THE PROBATION/PAROLE OFFICER
AS TREATMENT AGENT

In Chapter 9 a variety of treatment approaches were reviewed—the implications being that p/p officers could operationalize these approaches with their clients. However, requirements for p/p officer positions are usually a bachelor's degree, hardly adequate to provide the background, let alone the skill, for carrying out a sophisticated treatment role. Shelle Dietrich points out that "the probation officer usually has not received extensive specialized training for the function of change agent; that is, the function of being competent to facilitate another person's changing his behavior, attitude, affect, or personality style" (1979: 15). Generally the p/p officer is not educated or trained to be a treatment agent: "It is an unrealistic expectation of probation [and parole] officers to expect themselves to be competent in an area for which they have not received adequate training" (1979: 15).

In a review of the literature purporting to advise p/p officers whose background is otherwise deficient how to become effective change agents, Dietrich found it simplistic and at times potentially harmful to the client. Thus, she argues, professional intrusion is often advocated into areas where the p/p officer lacks training. Cynically, she proposes, "Why not go ahead and prescribe medications, prepare legal documents, or write an insurance plan for the probationer?" (1979: 17). Dietrich cautions: "And what about the probationer? Certainly his position in relation to the probation officer is a vulnerable one. Shouldn't the probationer be protected from being the involuntary patient of an unlicensed and untrained person, even if the person's intentions are the most purely humanistic?" (1979: 18).

Dietrich raises two other related issues:

1. Is the therapeutic enterprise possible in a p/p setting? And given a positive response to this question,
2. Is it realistic to expect the delivery of treatment in p/p, where caseloads usually average between 80 and 100? [While 80 to 100 may have been standard when Dietrich was writing, at the turn of the decade the range was closer to 100 to 200.]

She argues that even if the p/p officer "were optimally skillful in such therapeutic endeavors," without the full promise of confidentiality (impossible in a p/p setting), full and open discussion, the basis for a therapeutic relationship, is not possible (1977: 18). Dietrich, however, is using a rather narrow definition of *therapy,* and within that definition she is correct—therapy is not possible in a p/p setting. I believe that therapy is more usefully defined here as the purposeful use of self to improve the social and psychological functioning of a client, and thus therapy is possible within the confidentiality limitations of a p/p agency. Therapy, however, is *not* possible given the lack of adequate education and training and the usual excessive caseloads encountered in p/p practice.

THE PROBATION/PAROLE OFFICER
AS BROKER OR ADVOCATE

The provision of necessary services in p/p practice often requires an advocacy stance on the part of the p/p officer. Private and public agencies may view the p/p client as undesirable or even undeserving. Welfare, mental health, and educational agencies may see the client as threatening. Their responses to a client's needs may lead to frustration and a frustrated client who reacts in a manner that does indeed appear threatening—frustration control is often a problem with p/p clientele—a self-fulfilling prophecy.

Eric Carlson and Evalyn Parks see the *brokerage* approach in p/p as almost diametrically opposed to the treatment approach, since the p/p officer "is not concerned primarily with understanding or changing the behavior of the probationer, but rather with assessing the concrete needs of the individual and arranging for the probationers to receive services that directly address these needs" (1979: 120). They point out that

> there is significantly less emphasis placed on the development of a close, one-to-one relationship between the probation officer and the probationer. The probation officer functions primarily as a manager or broker of resources and social services which are already available from other agencies. It is the task of the probation officer to assess the service needs of the probationer, locate the social service agency which addresses those needs as its primary function, to refer the probationer to the appropriate agency, and to follow up referrals to make sure that the probationer actually received the services. Under the brokerage approach, it can be said that the probation officer's relationship with community service agencies is more important than his relationship with an individual probationer. The brokerage approach does share with the casework approach the importance of the probationer's participation in developing his own probation plan. (1979: 120–21)

They note that "the essential tasks of the brokerage orientation to probation are the management of available community resources and the use of those services to meet the needs of probation clients."

> There is little emphasis on the quality of the relationship which is developed between probation officers and the probationer; rather, more emphasis is placed upon the close working relationship between the probation officer and the staff members of community social service agencies. Counseling and guidance are

considered inappropriate activities for the probation officer; no attempt is made to change the behavior of the probationer. The primary function of the probation officer is to assess the concrete needs of each probationer and make appropriate referrals to existing community services. Should the needed service not be available in the community, it is the responsibility of the probation officer to encourage the development of that service. (1979: 123)

Carlson and Parks point out that the brokerage approach is amenable to the team approach to p/p supervision.

Team Supervision

In contrast to the more typical one-to-one approach, Frank Dell'Apa and his colleagues argue in favor of the team approach to probation and parole supervision, a version they refer to as Community Resources Management Team — CRMT. According to Dell'Apa, Tom Adams, and Herbert Sigurdson (1976: 38):

1. Probation and parole services are in need of improved service delivery system models.
2. Most offenders are not pathologically ill; therefore the medical (casework) model is inappropriate.
3. Most probation and parole officers are not equipped by education and experience to provide professional casework counseling even if it is needed.
4. Existing probation/parole personnel are unlikely to be expanded. Consequently, those people must come to view their roles in different and perhaps radically new terms if they are to deal with the increasing numbers of offenders under supervision.
5. Services needed by the offender to "make it" in society are available in the community social service network rather than in the criminal justice system.
6. Probation and parole staff must assume advocacy roles in negotiating appropriate community-based services for offenders. They must assume a community organization and resource development role for needed services that do not exist.
7. A team approach represents a powerful and visible alternative to the autonomous and isolated individual officer and "case" relationship.

They argue that in the traditional caseworker role the p/p officer attempts to be all things to everyone on the caseload — a jack-of-all-trades — and turns out to be master of none, so that the client suffers. Instead they offer several different team models (1976: 43):

Basic agency team   The team is composed of a manager, no fewer than two line field staff, a clerical staff person, and a staff specialist. The team has the responsibility of meeting all of the needs of a caseload in a specific geographic area. Decisions are made at team meetings led by the team manager.

Agency-community extended team   The team is composed of a manager, no fewer than two line field staff, a trainee, one or more ex-offenders, a clerical staff person, with support from interested community social service agents from legal aid, welfare, employment security, mental health, minority group organizations, health, and education agencies. In addition, community persons such as successful ex-offenders and citizens' group leaders serve as resources to the team. The team's caseload is made up of a fixed number of clients who usually are drawn from a cross section of the agency's clientele, who have distinct needs for supervision and assistance. They may come largely from one geographic area, be designated as drug- and alcohol-related offenders, represent distinct minority groups, or fall within definite age groupings.

The team is analyzed to determine the skills of each member, and the workload is the determinant of who does what. Team staff serve as brokers of the services and coordinators among the attached support specialists. The team members meet regularly to assess community resources and needs, as well as workload needs upon which the division of labor is based. The clients may be served by all members of the team or only one or any combination. This model obviously depends on a high level of cooperation between the team staff and those from support community agencies.

Specialist resource team   The team is composed of two or more line field staff and a manager. Support persons from the community may be used whenever possible. The team's caseload is specialized, persons with a history of drug abuse, for example. The team marshals community resources that provide services to the specialized clientele.

Rob Wilson (1978) notes that evaluations of the CRMT approach have shown a marked increase in p/p revocations. He views this as a positive development, an indication that the approach requires client accountability. An alternative explanation is more troubling: clients having difficulty relating to or dealing with a concept as amorphous as a team. "*Who* is *my* PO?" has no answer. The obverse is that team members are more detached from their clients—hence invoking delinquency action is less personal and perhaps easier. An equally formidable problem is the relationship between persons in the client's life (such as spouse, parents) and their ability to relate to or deal with a team.

Let us look at one type of situation that, despite a myriad of variations, is typical in p/p practice. Charlie Smith's wife calls the p/p officer: "That s.o.b. husband of mine has been out all night drinking, and he slapped me around this morning. Unless the PO comes out here and straightens him out, I'm callin' the cops and having his ass locked up!" The men and women I worked with who had Charlie Smith on their caseload could respond quickly and effectively. Instead of four uniformed officers and a broken nightstick—a lot of "Charlies" are resentful of police authority—the PO goes to the house.

Charlie breaks down and cries, explaining the reason for his behavior. In many cases that I have experienced, both as a parole officer and supervisor of parole officers, the PO was the only variable capable of maintaining Charlie in the community. I am not sure what the team response would be; perhaps it is simply sending out the police or warrant officers and a revocation decision that doesn't help Charlie or his wife.

The team, structured with a rational division of labor and responsibilities, can provide services more efficiently and economically than can the traditional one-to-one casework approach. However, in the real world of probation and parole there is a price to pay for this efficiency.

A variant of the team approach in Georgia provides an example. In 1982, faced with the reality of prison overcrowding, the Department of Offender Rehabilitation inaugurated its "Intensive Probation Supervision Program" (IPS). IPS provides "close community supervision" to selected offenders who normally would have entered prison if it were not for the existence of the program:

> The IPS team, composed of an experienced Probation Officer and a Surveillance Officer, supervise a maximum caseload of twenty-five (25) offenders who present no unacceptable risk to the community in which they are supervised. The caseload consists primarily of non-violent felony offenders who have been convicted of property offenses.

According to the plan, the IPS probation officer is supposed to provide typical professional casework services, while the probation surveillance officer (with less education, training, and salary) provides "24 hour surveillance capability through day, night, and weekend visits and telephone contacts." Surveillance officers, however, developed greater rapport with clients and their families than did probation officers. The surveillance officer had more direct contact with, and was more easily accessible to, the client and his family. Billie Erwin and Lawrence Bennett report:

> One of the most interesting findings of the IPS evaluation is the near impossibility of separating treatment from enforcement. The Georgia design places the Probation Officer in charge of case management, treatment and counseling services, and court-related activities. Surveillance Officers, who usually have law enforcement or correctional backgrounds, have primary responsibility for frequently visiting the home unannounced, checking curfews, performing drug and alcohol tests using portable equipment, and checking arrest records weekly. The Surveillance Officer becomes well acquainted with the family and is often present in critical situations. Both the Probation and Surveillance Officers report a great deal of overlap of functions and even a reversal of their roles. (1987: 6)

In practice, the surveillance officer was doing the work of a professional PO, while the latter's role was either redundant or was often reduced to that of a paper-pushing case analyst.

THE PROBATION/PAROLE OFFICER
AS LAW ENFORCEMENT AGENT

The p/p officer as law enforcement agent is related to the *control model* of supervision in much the same way as the treatment or broker-advocate role is related to the *social service model*. For a discussion of the law enforcement role of p/p officers to be meaningful, it must be considered within the context of agency model. However, many critics of a law enforcement role for p/p officers render unequivocal statements without any discussion of the model. Thus, without any attention to agency model, the American Correctional Association, in its *Standards for Adult Probation and Parole Field Services,* states (1981: 36):

> Probation/parole officers do not routinely carry weapons in the performance of their duties.

A more productive approach is to identify the agency model and then decide if it is compatible with a law enforcement role.

Paul Keve states that agencies "suffer sharp internal problems when agency policy seems to require surveillance and arrest activities while at the same time the agency prohibits use of firearms" (1979: 432). New Jersey, for example, modified its Parole Act to authorize arrest powers for parole officers, but made no provision for the carrying of firearms (although they carry handcuffs). The state of Florida provides the following description of the activities of its correctional probation officers:

> Provides security and protection to the community through investigation, control, and supervision of offenders which require investigative and security skills. This is accomplished through surveillance of offenders in the community and by enforcing the Florida Statutes and special conditions of the Circuit Courts and the Parole Commission. Surveillance of the offender entails continuous investigation of the offender while under jurisdiction of the Department of Corrections. Such surveillance and investigation frequently involves regular visits to high crime areas to contact offenders and others. Searches of offenders under supervision are conducted where indicated and arrests are made upon probable cause of violation in accordance with Florida Statutes. . . .

But correctional probation officers do not routinely carry firearms! A more rational approach was taken by the Texas Adult Probation Commission which voiced its opposition to *both* arrest powers and the carrying of firearms for probation officers.

In 1975 I surveyed fifty-three adult parole agencies in the United States (the fifty states, the District of Columbia, Puerto Rico, and the U.S. Division of Probation which also supervised parolees). The survey (Abadinsky, 1975) indicated that parole agencies differ greatly with respect to officers carrying firearms and arresting violators. Several years later, Keve (1979) conducted a similar survey of top administrators in probation and parole in the United States and found that a little more than half of the jurisdictions prohibited the carrying of a firearm. In 1986 the Oklahoma Department of Corrections surveyed all fifty states with respect to the carrying of firearms by probation and parole officers. "The study indicated that about 48 percent of all probation and parole agencies allowed their officers to carry a gun on the job. Only 24 percent of the jurisdictions polled said their officers routinely carried a weapon" (Jones and Robinson, 1989: 90).

In recent years, as more and more probation and parole agencies move toward a control model of supervision, arrest powers and the carrying of firearms by p/p officers has become increasingly common, for a number of compelling reasons. In many jurisdictions, particularly in high-crime urban areas, the police/sheriff are either unwilling or unable to provide sufficient warrant-enforcement services. If the agency does not enforce its own warrants, they go unattended; the potential danger to the public is obvious as hundreds or, in larger jurisdictions, thousands of probation/parole warrants go unenforced. Or, warrants turned over to outside agencies may be used to force p/p violators into becoming informants (or in some cases the warrants are used for corrupt purposes). Many agencies are confronted by p/p personnel who feel endangered by having to enter high-crime areas, particularly during evening hours, to visit serious offenders at home. These officers are demanding protective training and the right to carry firearms.

Hazards of Parole Supervision

The very nature of parole work subjects parole officers to potentially hazardous events on a routine basis. Fortunately, not every parole officer has had a bad or harrowing experience, but many have. On one occasion, Tom Brancato was strangled almost to the point of unconsciousness in a remote wooded area where he stopped to see his parolee at work. This attack occurred by surprise after Officer Brancato had asked the parolee to have a seat in his car. As soon as they were seated the parolee reached over, grabbed Officer Brancato by the throat and wedged him between the bucket seats of his Volkswagen. His right arm and gun were pinned beneath him. After considerable effort he managed to get his gun with his left hand and stick the barrel in the parolee's ear.

Source: New York State Division of Parole *Annual Report,* 1986.

In practice, probation and parole agency policy with respect to firearms falls into one of three categories:

1. *Officers are not permitted to carry firearms at any time based either on state law or agency policy.* For example:

    • In Arizona, while they maintain their constitutional right to carry a weapon when they are not on duty, "Under no circumstances may an adult parole officer carry a weapon in the performance of their duty."
    • In Maryland parole and probation agents are social workers and have no peace officer responsibilities or powers.
    • In South Dakota parole agents are not by statute considered law enforcement officers and do not carry weapons.
    • In New Jersey the state supreme court has determined that probation work is guidance and assistance, not law enforcement, and has directed that probation officers not be permitted to carry firearms.

2. *Officers are by statute peace/law enforcement officers, but the agency either restricts or discourages the carrying of weapons.* For example:

    • The Montgomery County (OH) Adult Probation Department allows officers to carry firearms *only* on special assignments such as transportation of a probation violator; or in emergency situations, such as the escape of a dangerous offender, or a "highly threatening office disturbance" [sic].
    • The Georgia Department of Offender Rehabilitation allows probation officers to carry firearms only in the course of arresting or transporting a probation violator or conducting business in an area known to be potentially dangerous.
    • The Adult Probation Department of Allen County (IN) states that, while its personnel are allowed by statute to carry firearms and arrest probationers, the court discourages the carrying of a firearm.
    • The Contra Costa County (CA) Probation Department, although its probation officers are by state law peace officers, prohibits them from carrying firearms in the course of their work. They are required, however, to complete that portion of the peace officers training that relates to powers of arrest.
    • The Florida Department of Correction restricts the carrying of firearms by correctional probation officers to time-limited situations when the officer's life has been threatened.

3. *Officers are by statute peace/law enforcement officers and the agency permits or requires all qualified personnel to carry firearms.* For example:

    • Employment as a probation and parole officer in Nevada requires firearms qualification and carrying of weapons, either a .38 or a .357 revolver, while on duty.
    • Firearms training is mandatory for all California (adult and youth) parole agents, New York State parole officers, and Oklahoma probation and parole officers, and they are issued departmental firearms.
    • Illinois, Massachusetts, Ohio, and Pennsylvania parole officers/agents are permitted to carry firearms provided they have met applicable training and proficiency standards.
    • All training certified probation and parole officers in Kentucky are authorized to carry firearms.
    • All state probation and parole officers in Alabama are required to qualify with firearms and all training certified p/p officers are required to carry a firearm on duty.
    • Firearms are authorized for all probation officers in Bibb County, Georgia.

- Dauphin County (PA) probation officers who have qualified in the handling of weapons may carry a firearm.
- Nassau County (NY) probation officers who have completed firearms training are authorized to carry firearms.

Should probation/parole officers make arrests and carry firearms? In 1975, while still a parole officer, I answered with a resounding "Yes." Almost two decades later, I find myself still in agreement with the legendary parole chief in New York, David Dressler, who wrote: "I am convinced a parole system worth its salt *has* to make its own arrests" (1951: 152). I believe that departments which fail to provide the maximum amount of community protection possible within a probation/parole setting are in danger of having their services shifted or contracted out to public or private social service agencies. The privatization of prisons and, in certain instances, presentence investigation reports, should serve as a warning to the self-interests of p/p personnel.

While many (typically nonpractitioner) observers bemoan the existence of a role conflict in probation and parole—incompatibility between control and treatment—this writer never experienced such conflicts in practice—nor did any of his colleagues in New York. Indeed, given the nature of p/p clientele, sound treatment demands the use of appropriate methods of control—offenders under supervision often engage in behavior that is self-destructive and dangerous to the community. As a trained social worker (with a master's degree in social work), I found that the application of casework principles was enhanced by the legal powers inherent in probation/parole settings. Indeed, if there is role conflict inherent in p/p practice, as Todd Clear and Edward Latessa note, such is the nature of many professional positions. However, "Among other professions, role conflict is seldom seen as a justification for eviscerating the profession of a few less salient tasks; rather, it is felt that the 'true' professional finds a way of integrating various role expectations, balancing them and weighing the appropriateness of various expressions of the roles" (1989: 2).

As a private citizen with a working knowledge of probation and parole, I have certain concerns about personal safety—that of my family, friends, and neighbors. It is from this (I believe typical) layperson's perspective that I evaluate a p/p agency. Let me provide some typical examples. It is not unusual during the course of an office or home visit for a p/p officer to discover that a client is using heroin or cocaine. If the offender is unemployed, the drug habit is probably financed by criminal activities—the client is a clear and present danger to him- or herself and to the community. A p/p agency whose officers cannot immediately (and safely) arrest such an individual is not providing an adequate level of client service or community protection. P/p agencies also supervise offenders who have been involved in (1) sex offenses against children, (2) vehicular homicide as a result of intoxication, (3) burglary, and (4) armed robbery. A p/p agency whose officers have no responsibility to enforce prohibitions, through investigation and arrest, against (1) frequenting play areas, (2) drinking and driving, and (3) carrying tools for forced entry, or who cannot (4) investigate money or a lifestyle that cannot be supported by the offender's employment status, is not providing the minimum acceptable level of community safety.

Furthermore, the adult (and frequently the juvenile) p/p client is a serious law violator who has proved to be a potential danger to the community. Many have been involved in crimes of violence, and the public and elected officials expect that probationers and parolees, if they are to remain in the community, will be under the scrutiny of p/p authorities. This is why the law of most jurisdictions empowers p/p agencies with law enforcement responsibilities. However, the question is often raised whether the p/p officer should be the law enforcer or merely the treatment agent. Probation and parole agencies may employ warrant officers or use outside law enforcement officers to do their enforcement work—the "dirty work." Do arrest powers and the carrying of a firearm interfere with the p/p officer's ability to form a casework relationship with which to provide treatment? I am of the opinion that they do not. Indeed, because of the p/p officer's relationship with their clients, in delinquency situations, they are able to effect an arrest without the tension and hostility that often accompanies arrests made by other law enforcement officers (who have no relationship with the client). In fact, whether the p/p officer actually makes the arrest, the client knows that the p/p officer initiated the warrant action. As noted, p/p clients are potentially dangerous, and usually reside in high-crime neighborhoods, reason enough to be armed.[1] A study by William Parsonage and Conway Bushey in Pennsylvania highlights the danger of probation/parole work: They found that the "victimization of Pennsylvania probation and parole workers is extensive and pervasive" (1989: 24).

Absconder Apprehension Task Force

In most states, probation and parole agencies expend few, if any, resources on the problem of absconders, and overburdened police departments and sheriffs are generally not interested in enforcing probation and parole warrants. Although absconders represent a serious risk to the public, probation and parole warrants usually remain unenforced until the violator is arrested for a new crime.

---

[1]This facet of parole work was dramatically revealed while I was a parole officer in New York. My colleague, thirty-two-year-old Donald Sutherland, attempted to arrest a parole violator and was shot to death. The parolee was subdued at the scene by other parole officers. After being convicted of murder, the parolee escaped from prison and eluded law officers for several weeks, on one occasion after an exchange of gunfire. He was finally killed after refusing to surrender to a combined force of city and state police and parole officers.

In New York, the Division of Parole has always made the apprehension of absconders a priority, and in 1986, created a special unit to intensify its efforts. The Absconder Apprehension Task Force consists of twelve investigative teams and four supervisors. Each team is comprised of one parole officer and one New York City Police Department investigator. The task force targets career criminals and/or persons wanted on outstanding police warrants, and has significantly increased the apprehension of dangerous parole violators.

ONGOING SUPERVISION

Offenders are usually relieved to be out of the office after the first visit. They generally leave with mixed feelings. If the officer has been warm, concerned, and helpful, positive feelings will predominate. If the officer was not sensitive to the attitude conveyed and did not evince a feeling of acceptance, negative feelings will predominate. Claude Mangrum notes that "there is nothing necessarily incompatible between warmth and acceptance and firm enforcement of the laws of the land. We must take whatever corrective measures are necessary, but these must not permit us to demean the dignity of the individual" (1972: 48).

During the periodic visits to the client's residence, the p/p officer should try to spend enough time to be able to relate to the client and/or the client's family. The home visit provides an opportunity to meet family members and interpret the role of the p/p agency to them. The worker should leave a business card and invite inquiries for information or help. The home visit also provides an opportunity to ensure that spouse or child abuse is not a problem. When visiting the home, it is incumbent upon the officer to try to protect the confidentiality inherent in each case. Officers do not advertise their business or draw unnecessary attention to the visit to a client's home. In many cases, the client's p/p status is known to neighbors, and the officer may be a familiar figure in the neighborhood. It is not too unusual for a client or client's family to escort the officer back to his or her automobile or public transportation, as a gesture of concern in high-delinquency areas.

The following excerpt from a case record shows how increased understanding of an offender caused a change in the direction of treatment. It also reveals the value of home visits as a means of gaining new insights into an offender's situation.

Quarterly Summary, March

3/9   Office report.
3/23   Failed to report.
3/30   Home visit. Mother and aunt seen.

(Continued)

4/6   Failed to report. Notice sent, giving 48 hours to report.
4/8   Reported.
4/13   Failed to report.
4/20   Home visit. Offender and aunt seen.
4/27   Reported.
5/1   Contact made with Community Settlement.
5/11   Reported.
5/25   Reported.

During March and April attempts were made to get the offender to look for work. Early in March, he reported that he had a temporary job as a truck driver, and thought that because of this he did not have to report. I corrected this idea and emphasized the importance of keeping his appointments. He had little to say but seemed amenable to conforming. The failure to report in April was excused because of illness.

During home visits, the mother reported that the offender is keeping reasonable hours. She informed me that he spends most of his spare time at the Community Settlement and recently won a trophy for basketball. The aunt, a single woman who lives in the home, takes an active interest in him. She said that the offender is really very shy and needs special attention, which she tries to give him because the mother has little time to spare from the younger children. She has accompanied him to the State Employment Office, where he has been trying to obtain work, but as he is unskilled, he has few opportunities. Such protectiveness seems inappropriate for a nineteen-year-old youth.

I called at the Community Settlement and talked with the director, Mr. Apt. He is very much interested in the offender, but told me confidentially that he is afraid the subject might be getting into a neighborhood gang that is beginning to form. He has noticed that when the offender leaves the settlement, he often joins other young men, some of whom have been in trouble. The settlement has an employment service for members and will try to help the offender obtain employment. When the offender reported, I suggested that he apply at the settlement employment service. The next day, Mr. Apt telephoned. The offender had been referred to a job in a downtown warehouse. He returned to the settlement in tears. He was so frightened that he had been unable to apply. He doesn't think he could do such work, although it is simple unskilled labor. Mr. Apt thinks that the offender needs psychiatric attention, but this may be the first time the offender has tried to seek work by himself.

At the time of the last report, the offender discussed some of his fears about work. He speaks warmly of the personnel at the settlement, but somewhat resentfully of his mother and aunt, who "keep nagging" him about work.

It is planned to try to encourage this offender by building up his self-esteem, giving recognition to his success in settlement activities and, by planning visits when he is at home, dealing with him directly rather than with relatives. The possibility of psychiatric referral will be explored.

The following description of an interview with an offender in jail indicates how the probation officer approached a hostile and uncooperative offender. It is important to note that the officer guides the interview to avoid futile and repetitive rationalizations, but explores to find some area in which he and the offender can work constructively together.

Peter, aged eighteen, has been on probation for two months. He was accorded youthful offender treatment following indictment for an assault during which he threatened to, but did not, use a knife. During the course of our contact, he has been on a weekly reporting schedule. I have concentrated on trying to help him get work. He has conformed in rather surly fashion, and never has volunteered to discuss any of his problems. He lives at home with his mother, a divorcee, and an older brother, who is a conforming person who did well in school, has regular employment, and generally does everything he should, thereby winning the mother's approval.

Recently, Peter was arrested for drunk and disorderly conduct. He pleaded guilty and received a thirty-day jail sentence, which he is just beginning to serve. The arresting officer's report indicated that he was assaultive and that it required three policemen to get him to the station. I visited him at the jail to obtain information for a violation report to be submitted to the court for action regarding his probation status. When I explained this, Peter went into what threatened to be a long harangue against the police and everyone connected with the current offense. He was in jail, he said, only because his girlfriend's father objected to him and was trying to keep him from dating her. I stated briefly and flatly what I knew about his present situation and noted that his own conduct was the reason for his being here. I asked him to tell me something about his girl, but he cut this off by saying that she and her family had moved to get the girl away from him, and he would not be seeing her any more. I asked what he had been assigned to do in jail. He was just washing dishes and it was a bore and everyone here was a jerk. Had his family visited him? His mother had, but not his brother. I wondered how he got along with his brother. As if I had turned on a faucet, the story of his resentment toward his brother gushed out. He recalled things that had happened when he was only about six years old, and revealed that he is conscious of his jealousy over the mother's favoritism.

OFFENDER EMPLOYMENT

The securing and maintaining of employment or training for employment are crucial aspects of p/p supervision: "Perhaps the greatest single factor influencing the quality of life of parolees in their communities is the ability to secure and maintain employment" (Davidoff-Kroop, 1983: 1). It is generally believed that there is a relationship between successful employment and avoidance of further legal difficulties. A study in California revealed that unemployment and underemployment are closely associated with recidivism (Grogger, 1989). Joy Davidoff-Kroop (1983: 1) states: "Two recent parolee follow-up studies [in

New York] showed a high rate of unemployment amongst parolees returned to prison." Mary Toborg and her colleagues state (1978: 2; references deleted):

> The observed relationship between criminality and unemployment has been explained in different ways. Some researchers have proposed that there is a *causal relationship* between unemployment and crime, while analysts have agreed that unemployment and recidivism are highly correlated only because each is associated with another factor (e.g., the influence of family members or a decision to "go straight") which induced widespread behavioral change. Whatever the explanation, unemployment and recidivism are often closely related.

Thus, the variable *employment* may not be the cause of the variable *go-straight*, but both variables may actually be dependent on the (independent) variable *motivation*. In other words, whatever it is that motivates an offender to seek and maintain gainful employment also tends to motivate that offender to avoid criminal behavior.

                        ——Employment
          Motivation
                        ——Go straight

In addition to providing economic rewards, employment also enhances the self-worth and image of the client. When the economic conditions are poor, when unemployment is high, this has a direct effect of p/p supervision. Davidoff-Kroop notes: "Given the present day realities of high unemployment, parolees [and probationers] who are often under-educated and with few skills learn that finding work is problematical and frustrating" (1983: 1). The employment problem for parolees is often a great deal more difficult than for probationers. The parolee has been separated from employment and community contacts, usually for at least eighteen months, often longer. The prison environment offers little help. The Comptroller General of the United States (1979) has reported that federal and state prison systems have been deficient in their approach to training and educating inmates for employment. In view of the shift toward "just deserts" there is no reason to believe the situation has gotten better since that report was published.

In assisting clients with employment p/p officers make direct referrals to particular employers if they have the necessary contacts, or they may refer clients to other agencies, such as state employment services, for help. Officers may have to provide guidance and counseling concerning some of the basic aspects of securing employment, items that for middle-class persons are taken for granted. For example, officers will emphasize the need to be on time for interviews—in fact, the need to arrive a few minutes early. They will help to fill out applications or help the client to prepare for this aspect of the job search. Some officers may use role playing to accustom clients to job-interview situations. It is often important to discuss various aspects of good grooming and what type of clothing to wear on an interview. The following checklist is an example of interview instructions that might be given to a client:

Checklist for Offender Employment*

Greet Receptionist

1. Give your name and reason for visit. Example—"Good morning, my name is John Smith and I have a 10:00 A.M. employment interview with Mr. Jones."
2. Be punctual. Example—For a 10:00 A.M. interview, try being there by 9:30 or 9:45 A.M..
3. Be prepared to fill out an application. Example—(refer to No. 2)—By arriving at 9:30 A.M. or 9:45 A.M., you can fill out an application and go in at 10:00 A.M. to see Mr. Jones.
4. Have a copy of your social security number, names of past jobs with addresses and dates, names of references with addresses, etc., written on a card to aid you in filling out the application.
5. Be prepared to take a test for the job you are applying for if required. Example—Electronic, clerical or industrial machines, etc.
6. Have a list of questions you wish to ask prepared. Example:
   a. How old is the company?
   b. How many employees are with the company?
   c. What is the potential for promotion and growth?
   d. What are the duties that the job entails?
   e. What is the starting salary?
   f. What is the top salary potential?
   g. What are the working hours?
   h. Is there paid overtime?
   i. What benefits are offered by the company?
   j. Does the company offer tuition for night school?
   k. Does the company promote from within?

Procedure for the Interview

1. Walk slowly and quietly, stand right, hold your head up.
2. Greet the interviewer.
   a. Shake hands firmly if interviewer offers his hand.
   b. Look interviewer in the eye and say, "How do you do, Mr. Jones."
   c. Stand until the interviewer asks you to be seated.
   d. Wait for the interviewer to start the interview and lead it.
   e. You may smoke if the interviewer states so.
   f. Be prepared to answer questions. Examples:
      Why do you want to work for this company?
      Where do you see yourself in five years?

(Continued)

Are you planning to further your education?

What do you know about this company?

Do you have any particular skills or interests that you feel qualify you for a position with this company?

What makes you feel you are qualified for this particular job?

Do you have any plans for marriage in the immediate future?

Now is when you present your questions.

Attitudes and Behavior During the Interview

1. Sit up straight, feet on floor, hands in lap.
2. Sit quietly (do not keep moving around or fidget).
3. Use your best manners.
    a. Be attentive and polite.
    b. Speak slowly and clearly.
    c. Look interviewer in the eye (do not wear sunglasses).
    d. Use correct English, avoid slang.
    e. Emphasize your good points.
4. Speak of yourself in a positive manner.
5. Talk about what you can do.
6. Do not apologize for your shortcomings.
7. Do not talk to excess about your personal problems.

What an Interviewer Sees Immediately During an Interview

1. Hygiene.
    a. Bathe just before an interview.
    b. Clean and clip nails if necessary.
    c. Brush teeth.
    d. Use a good deodorant.
    e. Wear an outfit that is clean and conservative regardless of the fashion trend or style.

Interviewer Closes the Interview

1. Do not linger when he indicates it is time to stop.
2. Be sure to thank the interviewer as you leave.

Staying on the Job

1. With the great shortage of available jobs, employers can afford to be highly selective in choosing an employee.
2. Accept positions in related fields so when positions are re-opened, you will have first choice at these positions.

In Conclusion

Remember the four A's.

1. Attendance
2. Attitude
3. Appearance
4. Ability

*From Phyllis Groom McCreary and John M. McCreary, *Job Training and Placement for Offenders and Ex-Offenders* (Washington, D.C.: Government Printing Office, 1975), pp. 79–80.

One critical aspect of employment for ex-offenders is the question of revealing their record. I allowed my clients to decide for themselves. However, I did provide guidance by discussing the experiences of other clients relative to this issue. Many clients reported that their candor resulted in not securing employment. Others reported that some employers were interested in providing them with an opportunity. Unfortunately, many, if not most, employers will not hire an ex-offender if there is any alternative.

Some offenders are required by law or p/p agency policy to reveal their records when applying for certain jobs. For example, most positions with the government require individuals having a criminal conviction to reveal this fact; and they are frequently fingerprinted for this purpose. Banks, hospitals, and other sensitive areas of employment may also require disclosure. Certainly, allowing an offender with a history of drug abuse to work in a hospital or similar situation, would not be advisable, especially if the employer did not know of the person's record.

An expert in the field of ex-offender employment, Sol Tropp, recommends that "the employer should be made aware of an offender's status only when the pattern of the offender's behavior may result in anti-social behavior," such as a former drug addict working in a medical setting (*Vocational Counseling,* 1965: 8). The vocational director of the Osborne Association, a prison reform group, states: "We do not lie about the individual's record but, because of the prejudice that employers may have, we try to postpone complete revelation until the employer has had a chance to try out the offender on the job" (*Vocational Counseling,* 1965: 8).

THE STIGMA OF CONVICTION

John Reed and Dale Nance have stated what is all too often obvious in p/p practice: "A record of conviction produces a loss of status which has lasting consequences." They note that although probation and parole, in terms of rehabilitation, are thought of as more desirable than prison, "both visibly display the offender in the community under a disability—his conditions of probation or parole. In some jurisdictions, he must register as a criminal, supposedly for the protection of the community. The unintended effects of registration are to broadcast his conviction and preserve his criminal stigma" (1972: 27). Reed and Nance refer to this as a form of value conflict, whereby the protective concerns of society run counter to the rehabilitative philosophy that is espoused.

One of the few studies on the impact of a criminal conviction was conducted by Richard Schwartz and Jerome Skolnick (1962). They studied the effects of a criminal record on the employment opportunities of unskilled workers. Four employment folders were prepared, which were the same in all respects except for the criminal record of the applicant, as follows:

1. The first folder indicated that the applicant had been convicted and sentenced for assault.
2. The second, that he had been tried for assault and acquitted.
3. The third, also tried for assault and acquitted, but with a letter from the judge certifying the finding of not guilty.
4. The fourth made no mention of any criminal record.

The study involved one-hundred employers who were divided into units of twenty-five, with each group being shown one of the four folders on the mistaken belief that they were actually considering a real job applicant. The results:

1. Of the employers shown the "no record" folder, 36 percent gave positive responses.
2. Of the employers shown the "acquitted" folder with the judge's letter, 24 percent expressed an interest in the application.
3. Of the employers shown the "acquitted" folder, 12 percent expressed an interest in the applicant.
4. Of the employers shown the "convict" folder, only 4 percent expressed interest in the applicant.

Since a majority of persons on probation and parole are unskilled, the ramifications of these findings are obvious.

In an effort to minimize the legal harm caused by a criminal record, some states have removed various statutory restrictions on gaining licenses necessary for employment, and a few have even enacted "fair employment" laws for ex-offenders. New York, for example, prohibits the denial of employment or license because of a conviction unless there is a *direct relationship* between the conviction and the specific employment or license, or unless it involves an "unreasonable risk" to persons or property. A direct relationship requires a showing that the nature of the criminal conduct for which the person was convicted has a direct bearing on the fitness or ability to carry out duties or responsibilities related to the employment or license. The statute requires that a public or private employer provide, upon request, a written statement setting forth the reasons for a denial of license or employment, and provides for enforcement by the New York State Commission on Human Rights. And the U.S. Department of Labor has a long-standing program which provides bonding (up to $10,000) for probationers and parolees without any cost to either employee or employer.

States vary in the method and extent to which they provide relief from disabilities incurred by probationers and parolees. Some states have adopted automatic restoration procedures upon satisfactory completion of p/p supervision, and a large number of states have statutes designed to restore forfeited rights, although they may be subjected to restrictive interpretation in licensing and occupational areas. Pardon is another method, although its use is generally limited; some states, however—for example, Alabama, Florida, and Georgia—have limited forms of pardon that restore certain rights (discussed in Chapter 8). In New York, the judiciary and parole board have the power to restore certain rights through the granting of a "Relief from Disabilities."

New York State Relief from Civil Disabilities

I. Certificates of Relief from Disabilities

A. Effect of a Certificate of Relief

A Certificate of Relief removes any legal bar or disability imposed as a result of conviction of the crime or crimes specified in the certificate, although specific disabilities (such as those relating to weapon possession) may be excepted by the Board of Parole. In addition, by law, the Certificate of Relief may not enable an individual to retain or be eligible for public office. While removing legal bars does restore to the certificate holder the right to apply, it does compel the granting of employment or license or prevent the potential employer or licensing agency from taking the criminal record into consideration. *Possession of a certificate does not authorize an individual to deny that he/she has ever been convicted of a crime.*

B. Eligibility

A Certificate of Relief may be issued by the Board of Parole to any eligible offender who has been committed to an institution under the jurisdiction of the New York State Department of Correctional Services. The Board of Parole may also issue a Certificate of Relief to an eligible offender who has been convicted in any other jurisdiction and who now resides in New York State. By law an eligible offender is defined as one who has *not been convicted more than once of a felony.* (Two or more felony convictions stemming from the same indictment count as one conviction. Two or more convictions stemming from two or more

(Continued)

separate indictments filed in the same court prior to conviction under any of them count as one conviction.) A plea or a verdict of guilty upon which sentence or the execution of sentence has been suspended or upon which a sentence of probation, conditional discharge, or unconditional discharge has been imposed *shall be deemed to be a conviction.* (It should be noted that Juvenile Offenders are eligible for Certificates of Relief. Those Juvenile Offenders, however, who have been granted Youthful Offender status have incurred no state disabilities and do not require Certificates of Relief.)

A certificate may be issued upon an eligible individual's release from a correctional facility or at any time thereafter.

II. Certificates of Good Conduct

A. Effect of a Certificate of Good Conduct

A Certificate of Good Conduct has the same effect as the Certificate of Relief. In addition, the Certificate of Good Conduct may restore the right of an individual to apply for public office. The certificate may be issued to remove all legal bars or disabilities or to remove only specific bars or disabilities. The Board may subsequently issue a supplementary certificate removing those disabilities or bars not previously removed.

B. Eligibility

The Certificate of Good Conduct is available to those individuals convicted of more than one felony. Such individuals, however, do not become eligible for a Certificate of Good Conduct until a minimum period of time has elapsed from the date of conviction, or, if incarcerated, from the date of unrevoked release from custody by parole or termination of sentence. In those cases where the most serious conviction is a misdemeanor, the minimum period of good conduct required is one year. In those cases where the most serious conviction is a C, D, or E Felony, the minimum period of good conduct is three years. In those cases where the most serious conviction is an A or B Felony, the minimum period is five years.

THE PROBLEM OF AIDS

As in many other areas of society, the problem of AIDS has impacted on probation and parole. Since persons with AIDS and AIDS-related illnesses present a significant management problem for institutional officials, there is a great deal of pressure for their early release. Under community supervision AIDS clients confront probation and parole agencies with many serious problems. Probation and parole staff require education and training on handling these special clients who will need a great deal of medical attention, and often assistance with housing and support. And there are important legal issues.

Should high-risk clients — for example, intravenous drug users — be required to take an AIDS test? Who should be notified of a client's condition —

spouse, girlfriend, boyfriend? Should there be special conditions of supervision imposed, and how are they to be enforced? Probation and parole agencies are still grappling with these issues (see Takas and Hammett, 1989; Hunt, 1989).

PROBATION AND PAROLE OFFICERS

The selection of probation and parole officers is typically by a process similar to that used to select most public employees. One of three systems is generally employed: the merit system, the appointment system, or a combined system.

Merit system   Under the merit system applicants who meet the minimum qualifications for the position are required to pass a competitive written examination. Persons who score at or above the minimum passing grade are placed on a ranked list. It is from this list that candidates are selected, generally in the order of their rank. In some systems applicants are graded on the basis of their education and employment background. The merit system was developed to remove public employment from political patronage. Critics argue, however, that a written examination cannot determine who will be a good probation/parole officer.

Appointment system   Under the appointment system, applicants who meet minimum requirements are hired on the basis of an evaluation by the agency. Applicants do not take a written examination, although they are usually interviewed by an agency representative(s). This system provides agency officials with the greatest amount of flexibility; it also has a history of being used for political purposes.

Combined system   Some jurisdictions use elements of both the merit and appointment systems. Applicants are first screened through a qualifying examination. Those who receive a passing grade are placed on a list from which candidates are selected, usually after an interview with an agency representative(s).

Personal Qualities

The characteristics generally considered desirable for probation and parole officers can be classified into four categories:

1. *Basic knowledge.* A p/p officer should have a working understanding of psychology, sociology, the criminal statutes, police operations, and the court and correctional systems.
2. *Individual characteristics.* A p/p officer needs the ability to relate to all offenders and to deal with their sometimes subtle or overt hostility, to exercise authority in

an appropriate manner, to work well with other staff members, and to be able to organize work properly and prepare written reports in a coherent and timely manner.

3. *The agency.* The p/p officer must be willing to accept the responsibilities engendered by working for a public agency that handles offenders, and to enforce rules and adhere to regulations.

4. *Other agencies.* The p/p officer has to be able to deal effectively with many kinds of agencies and persons, usually divided into criminal justice (police, prosecutors, judges, correctional officials), and social service (treatment, welfare, employment, educational). These agencies often have varying attitudes toward offenders that must be handled appropriately.

Qualifications for Probation/Parole Officers

The American Correctional Association sets the following standard (*#2-2041*) for entry level probation and parole field positions:

> An entry-level probation or parole officer possesses a minimum of a bachelor's degree or has completed a career development program that includes work-related experience, training, or college credits providing a level of achievement equivalent to a bachelor's degree.

These are standards set by various jurisdictions throughout the United States:

Alabama (Probation and Parole Officer I). Any combination of training and experience equivalent to graduation from a four-year college with major course work in sociology, social casework, criminology, penology, education, or psychology.

California (Santa Clara County Deputy Probation Officer I). Bachelor's degree with specialization in sociology, criminology, penology, or a related major, preferably with an emphasis in the correctional field. (Youth Authority Parole Agent I). Education equivalent to graduation from college and one year of social casework, group guidance work, or community organization experience, or one year of graduate education in social work, guidance, psychology, sociology, or criminology.

Georgia (Probation Supervisor). Bachelor's degree or completion of two years of college and one year of professional or paraprofessional experience in law enforcement, social work, counseling, or related human service delivery areas.

Illinois (Probation Officer). Bachelor's degree. (Corrections Parole Agent I). Knowledge, skill, and mental development equivalent to the completion of four years of college with a bachelor's degree in the behavioral or social sciences or law enforcement.

Indiana (Probation Officer). Bachelor's degree.

Kentucky (Probation and Parole Officer). Bachelor's degree; professional experience in probation/parole work can be substituted for the required education on a year-for-year basis.

Maine (Probation/Parole Officer, Juvenile Caseworker). Bachelor's degree and six months experience in probation/parole work, youth/adult counseling, law enforcement, or directly related experience/training.

Maryland (Parole and Probation Field Supervisor). Bachelor's degree with thirty hours in social, behavioral, or correctional sciences and one year of counseling or other relevant experience.

Massachusetts (Probation Officer). Bachelor's degree and one year experience in human or allied services or a graduate degree in the behavioral sciences, education, administration, management, law, or criminal justice. (Junior Parole Officer). Two years of experience in probation or parole work, social work, vocational counseling, employment counseling, rehabilitation counseling. College education may be substituted for the required experience on the basis of one year of such education for six months of the required experience.

Missouri (Probation and Parole Officer). Bachelor's degree in the field of criminal justice, social work, psychology, or sociology. (Jackson County Deputy Juvenile Officer). Bachelor's degree in behavioral science or related field. Prefer graduate counseling education and/or social work experience.

Nevada (Adult Probation and Parole Officer I). Graduation from high school and four years experience in parole and/or probation supervision or duties above the journey level in the correctional system (sergeant or above); or four years in the area of social work or similar activities; or a bachelor's degree in the behavioral sciences or law enforcement.

New Jersey (Probation Officer). Bachelor's or master's degree in psychology, sociology, corrections, criminology, criminal justice, penology, or social work.

New York (Parole Officer). Bachelor's degree and two years of relevant experience in social work or counseling or thirty graduate credits in social work, psychology, sociology, guidance, or a law degree. (Nassau County Probation Officer I). Bachelor's degree and two years of counseling or casework experience or a master's degree in social work, education, public administration, sociology, psychology, criminology, law, or a related field.

Ohio (Adult Probation Officer Trainee). Any combination of training and work experience which indicates possession of the skills, knowledge, and abilities required for a probation officer. A bachelor's degree in psychology, sociology, social work, corrections, or a related field qualifies for this position. (Parole Officer I). Completion of an undergraduate major program with core coursework in behavioral or social science, or criminal justice; or two years training and/or experience in probation and parole field services.

Oklahoma (Probation and Parole Officer). A bachelor's degree with twenty-four credits in the behavioral/social sciences, education, or police science.

Pennsylvania (Juvenile Probation Officer). A bachelor's degree with at least eighteen credits in a social science. (Parole Agent I). Bachelor's degree or any equivalent experience or training. (Philadelphia Probation Officer Trainee). Bachelor's degree in social work, psychology, criminal justice, sociology, law enforcement, corrections, criminology, counseling, guidance.

Texas (Adult Probation Officer). Bachelor's degree and one year of graduate study in sociology, social work, counseling, criminology, psychology, or law; or one year of full-time casework or counseling experience with offenders or disadvantaged persons. Candidates must pass a certifying examination promulgated by the Texas Adult Probation Commission.

PARAPROFESSIONALS

Many jurisdictions also employ workers (sometimes referred to as *paraprofessionals*) who assist in the probation/parole supervision process, but who do not have the full responsibilities or qualifications of a probation/parole officer. For example, Georgia employs Probation/Parole Aides, Nevada employs Probation Aides, and Santa Clara County (CA) employs Probation Community Workers. Typically, experience in such a position can qualify the person for employment as a probation/parole officer.

Paraprofessionals are frequently recruited from among persons sharing the same social, economic, racial, or ethnic background as a large number of probation/parole clients. In some states this has opened probation and parole employment to ex-offenders. The basic motives for employing paraprofessionals emerged during the years of President Lyndon Johnson's "War on Poverty" (*Overview Study,* 1974: 44):

1. To compensate for the shortage of skilled personnel, particularly workers trained at the graduate level.
2. To increase employment opportunities among disadvantaged workers and the unemployed poor.
3. To develop an efficient division of labor so that personnel with different levels of skill could be assigned appropriate duties.
4. To modify organizations so that the resulting service delivery system could be more directly related to the problem of clients and more efficient in meeting their needs.
5. To provide work experience in which workers, by helping clients with problems similar to their own, improve social functioning and become better prepared for work.

Paraprofessionals are likely to come from the same environment as the largest segment of the p/p population. Indeed, this is a (or perhaps *the*) basic reason for employing ("indigenous") paraprofessionals in p/p; they are seen as better able to relate to persons alienated from middle-class society. In his essay "Changing Criminals," Donald Cressey (1955) argues that the reduction of alienation is a first step in rehabilitating criminals. This is effected by "positive association" with prosocial persons who are "just like me." According to Carlson and Parks:

> It is very difficult for the professional to serve as an effective role model. The indigenous worker, conversely, has often experienced situations and problems similar to those that confront certain clients. The indigenous worker has the advantage of proximity in time and space, while typically the professional is limited to a nine to five, Monday to Friday schedule, living some distance from those served. The indigenous worker, living closer to his clients, has much greater familiarity with their environments, and has greater freedom to move about at times other than business hours. Inter-racial tensions in certain areas point out

the need for non-professionals recruited from groups having an ethnic or racial affinity with certain offender populations. A communications gap resulting from social and cultural differences between middle-class professionals of any race and lower class minority group members is a growing problem in rehabilitation services. (1979: 192)

In p/p the use of paraprofessionals has included hiring ex-offenders— this is sometimes the basis of a paraprofessional program. The use of ex-offenders can be seen as a logical extension of Cressey's stress on correctional workers who are "just like me." Toborg and her colleagues review some of the advantages of using ex-offenders as counselors:

Ex-offenders are often considered to make good counselors, because they can more easily identify with the client. This may result both in greater understanding of the client's needs and in a lesser likelihood of being manipulated (or "conned") by the client. Additionally, some staff members think that certain clients may be more at ease with ex-offender counselors and that this will lead to greater honesty and openness, resulting in early identification of problems and high levels of client success. (1978: 13)

There are also disadvantages, as Toborg and her colleagues point out:

Ex-offender counselors may pose problems, however. One problem which may occur from selecting an insufficiently mature ex-offender of the same background as the client is that the two may become stuck on the point of their fight against the "establishment" [which] becomes the scapegoat; no behavior change is demanded, and no responsibility is accepted, though the staff member may teach the participant how to beat the system.

Another problem arises when ex-offender staff think that their status as ex-offenders automatically makes them good counselors. Such staff members may resist efforts to train them in counseling techniques. In addition, ex-offenders may experience a number of role conflicts, caused by having "establishment" jobs where they deal with clients experiencing a community readjustment which the ex-offender counselors may themselves have undergone quite recently. Also, in some cases ex-offender staff may be so assertive about rejecting their criminal past that they antagonize clients, rather than creating the rapport with them which is often considered an advantage of ex-offender counselors. (1978: 13)

Paraprofessionals receive a lower salary than professionals employed by the same agency. Some professionals in p/p agencies may believe that the presence of lower-paid personnel doing essentially the same work may undermine their efforts at securing greater salary and employment benefits. Some contend that the willingness of paraprofessionals to accept lower rates of pay than professionals is often the *real* reason that they are employed.

Some probation and parole officers maintain that paraprofessionals overidentify with clients, sometimes in opposition to the agency and its policies. However, others maintain the opposite: that paraprofessionals tend to overidentify with the agency (and middle-class values) and are less flexible than their professional colleagues. Still other observers have found neither criticism valid.

VOLUNTEERS

Probation in the United States originated as a volunteer service, and it is in probation that the tradition was reactivated in 1959 by Keith J. Leenhouts, Judge of the Royal Oak, Michigan, Municipal Court. In that city, the municipal (misdemeanor) court probation department was staffed entirely by volunteers. Through the efforts of Judge Leenhouts a national organization, *Volunteers in Prevention, Probation, and Prisons, Inc., or simply VIP,* was formed. (VIP merged with the National Council on Crime and Delinquency in 1972; in 1983 it reverted to independent status. For more information write to VIP, 527 N. Main Street, Royal Oak, MI 48067.) In 1961 the juvenile court in Boulder, Colorado began to utilize volunteers as a major part of the court rehabilitation service to supplement the services already offered by probation officers, and with the help of VIP the use of volunteers spread throughout criminal justice. A VIP study in 1979 revealed an estimated 500,000 volunteers in about 5,000 courts, jails, prisons, juvenile institutions, prevention, diversion, probation, and parole programs.

Carlson and Parks report four volunteer service models (1979: 237):

1. *One-to-one model.* On a one-to-one basis, volunteers seek to obtain the trust and confidence of p/p clients and help them to maintain their existence, clarify their role in society, and plan for the future.
2. *Supervision model.* Working as a case aide to a p/p officer, the volunteer provides services to a number of clients at the direction of the PO.
3. *Professional model.* The volunteer is a professional or semi-professional in his or her field — a teacher or mechanic, for example — who provides specialized services to a number of clients, for example, help with literacy or skills training. In Florida, the Department of Corrections has volunteer financial planning specialists available to assist probationers with help in maintaining a realistic family budget.
4. *Administrative model.* The volunteer assists with project administrative functions and interacts only indirectly with clients.

Victim Witness Services
Juvenile Court of Jackson County

In Kansas City, Missouri, the Juvenile Court of Jackson County has a victim assistance program staffed by volunteers. The program assists victims by empowering them with knowledge of the juvenile court process and being with them at the court hearing. Among the services provided by the volunteers:

1. Volunteers visit victims in cases of delinquency and prepare an impact statement that informs the court of the victim's losses and attitude toward the offense and the offender.
2. They provide referrals for those requiring crisis counseling, repair of property, emergency funding, and other vital services.
3. They inform the victim of the ability to file a civil action to recover losses.
4. They assist in the filling out of victim compensation claims.
5. They assist victims in recovering their property from police departments where it is being held as evidence.
6. When necessary, volunteers provide transportation to court.
7. They prepare letters for victims/witnesses for employers relative to any loss of work time.
8. They meet with victims/witnesses prior to their court appearance and stay with them until the hearing is complete.
9. They provide for mediation of restitution payments, if the court decides that the victim should meet with the offender, and the victim agrees.
10. They provide information to the public on the juvenile court process.

Volunteers are used by the Missouri Board of Probation and Parole and the Delaware Department of Correction on a one-to-one basis. Both agencies utilize volunteers to increase the services available to probation/parole clients. In Missouri they are provided with training in reality therapy (discussed in Chapter 9) and are expected to influence behavior by setting an example while being patient listeners. The volunteer helps the client to develop and carry out realistic plans, provides advice and encouragement, and may offer concrete assistance by helping the client secure employment.

Some p/p agencies and staff members are critical of the use of volunteers. They may view the efforts of volunteers as interference with their prerogatives, and they may be concerned about sharing information with volunteers because of the confidential aspect of p/p practice.

Chris Eskridge and Eric Carlson (1979) report that in some agencies the regular probation/parole workers see volunteers as a threat to their jobs. Some probation/parole officers resent the fact that volunteers are able to play the "good guy" while they have control and enforcement functions. Some complain of volunteers acting as advocates for the offender in opposition to the regular worker.

Since volunteers are not paid, they need to derive some satisfaction from their efforts. Satisfaction results when there is a level of success, and to be successful volunteers require adequate training and supervision. In other words, the successful use of volunteers is not "cost free"; staff is required for the training, coordination, and supervision of volunteers. If additional staff is not to be employed for these tasks, it has to take away from the working time of regular probation/parole agency personnel. Eskridge and Carlson (1979) report that lack of success in volunteer programs is a function of management operations rather than the volunteer concept. Faulty management includes the inability to assign volunteers expeditiously, inadequate volunteer training, poor supervision and/or support for volunteers, and a lack of communication between volunteers and officers.

Now that we have examined the details of probation and parole supervision, in the next chapter we will look at special programming in probation and parole.

REVIEW QUESTIONS

1. What are the reasons for the classification of prison inmates?
2. How did the advent of the corrections model alter the prison classification process?
3. What led to the widespread use of classification in probation/parole?
4. What are the two dimensions weighed by a Risk/Needs Assessment instrument?
5. What are the purposes of classifying offenders in probation/parole?
6. What is the difference between a *caseload* and a *workload* in probation/parole?
7. Why do parolees often encounter difficulties not experienced by probationers?
8. What are the various methods for assigning cases to probation/parole officers?
9. Why can the first meeting between probation/parole officer and client be characterized as a time of apprehension and anxiety?
10. What are the various work roles of the probation/parole officer?
11. What are the three basic probation/parole agency models?
12. What are the four basic role typologies that may be assumed by probation/parole officers?
13. What are the three basic categories with respect to agency policy regarding probation/parole officers making arrests and carrying firearms?
14. What are the arguments for and against probation/parole officers making arrests and carrying firearms?
15. What are the advantages and disadvantages of the team approach in probation/parole?
16. What are the factors that hamper treatment in probation/parole settings?
17. What are the various problems in probation and parole supervision generated by clients with AIDS?
18. How can there be a relationship between employment and "going straight" that is not causal?
19. What are the systems used to select probation/parole officers?
20. What are paraprofessionals, and what are the reasons they are used in probation and parole?
21. What are the advantages and disadvantages of using volunteers in probation and parole?

ELEVEN
Special Programs

Probation and parole agencies utilize numerous special programs. In this chapter we will review both popular and unique programs and services with which probation and parole officers and agencies are involved.

INTERSTATE ADULT AND JUVENILE COMPACTS

In the Crime Control Consent Act of 1934, Congress authorized two or more states to enter into agreements or compacts for cooperative efforts and mutual assistance in the prevention of crime. Pursuant to this legislation, in 1937 a group of states signed the *Interstate Compact for the Supervision of Probationers and Parolees,* which enabled them to serve as each other's agents in the supervision of persons on probation and parole. By 1951 all forty-eight states (and now all fifty states and the District of Columbia), Puerto Rico, and the Virgin Islands, were signatories of the compact. The compact provides a system whereby a person under supervision can leave the state of conviction and proceed to another state for employment, family, or health reasons, and at the same time guarantees that the receiving state will provide supervision of the offender. The state of original jurisdiction (where the offender was convicted) retains authority over the probationer/parolee and is kept advised of his or her whereabouts and activities by the receiving state. The compact also provides for p/p violators to be returned without the need to resort to time-consuming extradition procedures. Because it is based on a federal statute and governed by the substantive law of contracts, the Interstate Compact supersedes state law. (The Supreme Court has never ruled on the constitutionality of the compact, having denied certiorari whenever the issue has been raised.)

Prior to the establishment of the compact, thousands of convicted felons were permitted to leave the state of conviction with no verified or approved plan of residence and employment in the receiving state. On occasion, dangerous criminals were released by states and permitted (sometimes forced: "internal exile" or "sundown probation/parole") to enter other states without any provision for supervision or even the knowledge of any official body in the receiving state. The compact provides a systematic method for supervision purposes for the receiving state to verify and approve a plan of residence and employment or education before a probationer or parolee is permitted to enter the state. The compact also regulates interstate travel by probationers and parolees; each state issues a travel pass, a copy of which is sent to the interstate administrator, who notifies the receiving state of the impending visit (see Figure 11.1). After a probationer or parolee is accepted for supervision by the receiving state, the latter sends quarterly "progress and conduct" reports to the sending state (see Figure 11.2).

The Association of Administrators of the Interstate Compact, (now called the Parole and Probation Compact Administrators' Association), formed in 1946 and to which each state has designated an administrator, meets at least once per year, prepares uniform reports and procedures, and attempts to reconcile any difficulties that have arisen with respect to the compact. The Council on State Governments serves as a secretariat for the association and publishes the *Interstate Movement of Probationers and Parolees Under the Probation and Parole Compact*.

Some problems remain. One problem exists because of the differences in probation and parole administration. In all states parole is an executive function with statewide procedures; interstate activities are centralized through a compact administrator in each state. Probation, however, is often administered on a county basis, and it may lack statewide coordination. The local autonomy that often exists in the judicial branch can cause difficulties in utilizing and administering the pact in probation cases. In such cases, the probation officer of the sending state may need to make direct contact and arrangements with the court of the receiving jurisdiction.

Another problem results from different approaches to supervision in various states. One state may exercise close control and require strict enforcement of the conditions of probation or parole. Another state may be more flexible, or it may simply be incapable of close supervision and control because of the size of caseloads. When a "strict" state notifies a "permissive" sending state that one of its probationers or parolees is in violation, the sending state may not consider it serious, and may leave the offender in the receiving state with a request that they continue supervision. In some cases the sending state may not wish to incur the expense of transporting the violator back to one of its state prisons, which are probably overcrowded anyway. The receiving state

```
                          STATE OF ARIZONA
                      DEPARTMENT OF CORRECTIONS


                           TRAVEL PERMIT
                            (Out-of-State)
                                              Date Issued_____
     TO WHOM IT MAY CONCERN:

     _____     _____   _____
                  (Parolee's Name)                     (Number)              (Age)

     Address in Arizona _____

     By order of the Director or his authorized representative, and under the provisions of the appropriate Interstate Compact, per-
     mission is hereby granted for the abovenamed parolee to go to the following destination:_____
                                                                              (Street Number)


     _____     _____
            (City)                (State)                   (Name of person to be visited & relationship)

     Reason for trip: _____

     Parolee will leave_____ and will travel by_____
                               (Date)
                                                   _____
                                                                  Companions on this trip will
         (If by auto, give license number and name of owner)

     be:_____
                        (Name and relationship, if any, to parolee)

     If permission is for emergency visit only (fill in the following): Parolee is to return to Arizona address shown above by_____

     _____


     SPECIAL INSTRUCTIONS TO PAROLEE:

     I have been given this permission with the understanding I am to continue to follow the rules and regulations of my
     parole, that I am to cooperate with my supervising officer, or any authorized officer of the Arizona Department of
     of Corrections while on this trip. If I should be arrested in any other state, I will waive extradition and will not resist
     being returned to the State of Arizona. I fully understand that I am to return to Arizona under the terms of this permit
     within 30 days of the date hereof or be in violation of my parole.



     ISSUING OFFICER:

     _____     _____
                                                Parolee's signature

     By:_____     Date: _____

     Prepared in quadruplicate
     Distribution as follows:

                 Original - Parolee
                 Copy 2  - Parolee's file in appropriate Parole Field Office
                 Copy 3  - For mailing to Receiving State
                 Copy 4  - Parolee's Master File - Central Office
```

FIGURE 11.1   Out-of-state Travel Permit

has two options: continue to supervise an offender it considers in violation, or discontinue supervision and leave the offender without any controls at all. And there are also problems associated with the collection of restitution and supervision fees. These types of situations may make a receiving state reluctant to accept future cases from a particular sending state, a situation that needs to be reconciled at the compact administrator's meeting.

O.S. PROBATION & PAROLE FORM IV
PROGRESS AND CONDUCT REPORT
INTERSTATE COMPACT UNIT
ALABAMA BOARD OF PARDONS AND PAROLES
750 Washington Avenue
Suite 312
Montgomery, Alabama 36130
(205) 261-5533

To _____ State of Georgia _____ Date of Report ___ 1-14-89 ___

_____ Date Forwarded _____

Re: _____ John C. Doe _____ No. __ OS 24,115 ____ State ____ Georgia ____

Address of Parolee or Probationer:
  Route 1, Box 14
  Montgomery, Alabama 36114

Name and Relationship of Others in Home:
  Jane Doe - wife
  3 children

Contact Dates:
  8/5/88, 9/3/88, 10/4/88 and 12/6/88

Marital Status:
  Married

Employer — Address:
  Dana Corporation
  Route 2
  Montgomery, Alabama 36104

Is Subject's Record Known to Employer:
  No

Type of Work — Hours — Wages:
  Laborer
  40 hr/wk $5.85 hr.

Conduct, Progress and Attitude:
  Subject's conduct has been good. He received two traffic
  citations in November, 1985, but has had no other contact
  with Law Enforcement Officials. Attitude remains good.

Jack C. Smith	*Michael Jones*
Alabama Probation & Parole Officer	Interstate Compact Administrator
Montgomery	
Field Office	

FIGURE 11.2 Progress and Conduct Report

    States sometimes allow probationers or parolees to go to a receiving state
under the guise of a visit, when the offender's intentions are to stay permanently. The receiving state is then contacted by the sending state to investigate

"with a view toward accepting supervision." The receiving state is faced with a *fait accompli.*

Interstate Compact for the Supervision
of Parolees and Probationers

Consented to by the Congress of the United States of America, 1934
The Uniform Enabling Act

(Contains the exact wording of the Interstate Compact for the
Supervision of Parolees and Probationers)

AN ACT PROVIDING THAT THE STATE OF . . . MAY ENTER INTO A
COMPACT WITH ANY OF THE UNITED STATES FOR MUTUAL HELP-
FULNESS IN RELATION TO PERSONS CONVICTED OF CRIME OR OF-
FENSES WHO MAY BE ON PROBATION OR PAROLE

Be it enacted, etc.:
　Section 1. The governor of this state is hereby authorized and directed to
execute a compact on behalf of the state of ＿＿＿＿＿＿＿＿＿＿＿＿＿＿＿＿＿＿＿＿
with any of the United States legally joining therein in the form substantially as
follows:

A Compact
　Entered into by and among the contracting states, signatories hereto, with the
consent of the Congress of the United States of America, granted by an act
entitled "An act granting the consent of Congress to any two or more states to
enter into agreements or compacts for cooperative effort and mutual assistance
in the prevention of crime and for other purposes."
　The contracting states solemnly agree:
　(1) That it shall be competent for the duly constituted judicial and administrative authorities of a state party to this compact (herein called "sending state"), to
permit any person convicted of an offense within such state and placed on
probation or released on parole to reside in any other state party to this compact
(herein called "receiving state"), while on probation or parole, if
　　(a) Such person is in fact a resident of or has his family residing within the
receiving state and can obtain employment there;
　　(b) Though not a resident of the receiving state and not having his family
residing there, the receiving state consents to such person being sent there.
　Before granting such permission, opportunity shall be granted to the receiving
state to investigate the home and prospective employment of such person.
　A resident of the receiving state, within the meaning of this section, is one who
has been an actual inhabitant of such state continuously for more than one year
prior to his coming to the sending state and has not resided within the sending
state more than six continuous months immediately preceding the commission of
the offense for which he has been convicted.

(Continued)

(2) That each receiving state will assume the duties of visitation of and supervision over probationers or parolees of any sending state and in the exercise of those duties will be governed by the same standards that prevail for its own probationers and parolees.

(3) That duly accredited officers of a sending state may at all times enter a receiving state and there apprehend and retake any person on probation or parole. For that purpose no formalities will be required other than establishing the authority of the officer and the identity of the person to be retaken. All legal requirements to obtain extradition of fugitives from justice are hereby expressly waived on the part of states party hereto, as to such persons. The decision of the sending state to retake a person on probation or parole shall be conclusive upon and not reviewable within the receiving state, *Provided, however,* That if at the time when a state seeks to retake a probationer or parolee there should be pending against him within the receiving state any criminal charge, or he should be suspected of having committed within such state a criminal offense, he shall not be retaken without the consent of the receiving state until discharged from prosecution or from imprisonment for such offense.

(4) That the duly accredited officers of the sending state will be permitted to transport prisoners being retaken through any and all state parties to this compact, without interference.

(5) That the governor of each state may designate an officer who, acting jointly with like officers of other contracting states, if and when appointed, shall promulgate such rules and regulations as may be deemed necessary to more effectively carry out the terms of this compact.

(6) That this compact shall become operative immediately upon its execution by any state as between it and any other state or states so executing. When executed it shall have the full force and effect of law within such state, the form of execution to be in accordance with the laws of the executing state.

(7) That this compact shall continue in force and remain binding upon each executing state until renounced by it. The duties and obligations hereunder of a renouncing state shall continue as to parolees or probationers residing therein at the time of withdrawal until retaken or finally discharged by the sending state. Renunciation of this compact shall be by the same authority which executed it, by sending six months' notice in writing of its intention to withdraw from the compact to the other state party hereto.

Section 2. If any section, sentence, subdivision or clause of this act is for any reason held invalid or to be unconstitutional, such decision shall not affect the validity of the remaining portions of this act.

Section 3. Whereas an emergency exists for the immediate taking effect of this act, the same shall become effective immediately upon its passage.

There is also an *Interstate Compact on Juveniles* that governs the movement of juvenile cases interstate. In the early 1950s, legal and financial problems involving the supervision, transportation, and control of juvenile cases among states reached the point where most of those involved acknowledged the need for some form of interstate compact patterned on the one used for adult cases. In 1954, the National Council on Juvenile Court Judges drafted a preliminary compact on juveniles. Later that year a number of groups, under the coordination of the Council on State Governments, drafted the Interstate Compact on Juveniles. In 1955, ten states adopted the compact and currently all states and the District of Columbia are signatories. In addition to providing for cooperative supervision, the compact provides for the return of juvenile probation and parole absconders and escapees and the return of nondelinquent runaways (see Figure 11.3).

FIGURE 11.3   Requisition for Runaway Juvenile

STATE OF MISSOURI

INTERSTATE COMPACT ON JUVENILES

REQUISITION FOR RUNAWAY JUVENILE

TO   : _____   DATE:_____

FROM : _____

RE   : _____

  This court requisitions the return of_____in accordance to the Interstate Compact on Juveniles, Article IV, Return of Runaway. Said juvenile is believed to be in your jurisdiction. (Additional information attached, if available).

  On the basis of the evidence before it, this court finds said juvenile was born on_____. Juvenile's physical description: Height _____, Weight _____, Eyes_____, Hair_____. Identifying marks or scars:_____ _____.

  This court further finds that said juvenile should rightfully be in the custody of_____, who is the _____and who is
              (Relationship to Juvenile)
located at_____, within the territorial jurisdiction
   (address)
of this court; that said juvenile has run away without permission; and that said juvenile's continued absence from rightful custody and control is detrimental to the best interest of said juvenile and the public.

  If requisition is honored, please notify_____
          (Name, title, address and telephone)
_____by collect telephone call or wire when minor will be available for release to our agent.

  Attached are: Petition for Requisition to Return a Runaway Juvenile verified by Affidavit, and certified documents verifying petitioner's entitlement to the juvenile's custody.

        Signed:_____
             Judge

FIGURE 11.4   Application for Compact Services

MISSOURI INTERSTATE COMPACT ON JUVENILES

Application for Compact Services

To: _____

    I, _____, hereby apply for supervision as a parolee or probationer pursuant to the Interstate Compact on Juveniles. I understand that the very fact that supervision will be in another state makes it likely that there will be certain differences between the supervision I would receive in this state and supervision which I will receive in any state to which I am asking to go. However, I urge the authorities to whom this application is made, and all other judicial and administrative authorities, to recognize that supervision in another state, if granted as requested in this application, will be a benefit to me and will improve my opportunities to make a good adjustment. In order to get the advantages of supervision under the Interstate Compact on Juveniles, I do hereby accept such differences in the course and character of supervision as may be provided, and I do state that I consider the benefits of supervision under the Compact to be worth any adjustments in my situation which may be occasioned.

    In view of the above, I do hereby apply for permission to be supervised on (parole/probation) in _____, for the following reasons:
                                   (state)

    I have read the above or have had the above read and explained to me, and I understand its meaning and agree thereto.

Signed _____
                              (Juvenile)

Witnessed by _____
Date _____

Signed _____
                            (Guardian Ad Litem or person or agency having legal custody)

In contrast to the compact for adults, the juvenile compact has mandatory and discretionary cases. Thus, the receiving state must accept supervision whenever a juvenile will be returning to or has already been placed in the home of his or her legal parents or guardians, and each state must accept its own residents. Other cases are discretionary. When supervision has been arranged, the sending state retains jurisdiction and the receiving state becomes the agent of the sending state. Because of variations in state laws regarding juveniles, a person who is a juvenile in one state may be considered an adult in another. The compact overcomes this problem by applying the law of the state from which the juvenile has run away or from which he or she was sent for supervision: If a person is a juvenile under law in his or her home state, he or she is a juvenile to all member states. While the compact does not deal with child custody cases, it can provide for the return of a child to wherever a court has determined legal custody is maintained.

INTERMEDIATE PUNISHMENTS

The trend in favor of the classical school, just deserts, and determinate sentencing, has been intertwined with jail and prison overcrowding. Widespread support for punishment and deterrence through greater use of incarceration has encountered serious financial limitations. Judges have been unwilling to permit conditions of incarceration that violate the Eighth Amendment's prohibition against cruel and unusual punishment, thereby increasing the cost of a punishment-by-way-of-incarceration policy. In response, there has been a scramble to create alternative systems that satisfy a public appetite for punishment, while limiting the financial costs involved. This has led to the development of intermediate punishments that are community-based, although Belinda McCarthy argues that cost-effectiveness is not the only reason:

> The vast majority of "correcting" has always been done in the community, because this is the best place to deal with offenders. While it *can* be the most economical site for dispositions, the community *is* invariably the most humane setting and the richest environment in which to meet offender needs. If community corrections today is suffering from a lack of credibility, it is because we have used many community programs, especially our richest option—probation—unwisely. Too many offenders have been poorly supervised by overworked and undertrained staff with a confused sense of purpose. (1987: 3)

Under the category of *intermediate punishments* are two increasingly popular special programs that are community based—criminal justice in general, and corrections in particular, has always suffered from a "bandwagon" mentality—intensive probation/parole supervision and home confinement/electronic monitoring.

INTENSIVE PROBATION/PAROLE SUPERVISION (IPS)

If one can judge by the amount of agency literature and research efforts, intensive supervision has become the most popular program in probation and parole. Early versions of intensive supervision were based on the premise that increased client contact would enhance rehabilitation while affording greater client control. Current programs are simply a means of easing the burden of prison overcrowding.

In probation, intensive supervision is usually viewed as an alternative to incarceration. In other words, persons who are placed on intensive probation supervision are supposed to be those offenders who, in the absence of intensive supervision, would have been sentenced to imprisonment. In parole, intensive supervision is viewed as risk management — allowing for a high-risk inmate to be paroled but under the most restrictive of circumstances. In either case, intensive supervision is a response to prison overcrowding. Thus, while intensive supervision is invariably more costly than regular supervision, the costs "are compared not with the costs of normal supervision but rather with the costs of incarceration" (Bennett, 1988: 298).

Intensive supervision takes many shapes. In Texas, for example, intensive probation supervision is simply an experienced probation officer whose maximum caseload does not exceed forty. We will review representative IPS programs in several jurisdictions.

Texas Intensive Supervision Program (ISP)

Created in 1981 to deal with prison crisis, the Texas ISP attempts to divert selected felony offenders by offering an alternative to incarceration. For these offenders intensive supervision is a condition of probation. In most Texas probation departments ISP caseloads do not exceed forty, and the probation officers are specially selected and trained for the assignment. In some Texas jurisdictions, however, probation officers supervise a mixed ISP and regular caseload. Whenever this occurs, the mixed caseloads can compromise no more than 125 regular probationers prior to receiving the first ISP case, and then they must be reduced by five regular cases each time a new ISP case is assigned to the caseload. Cases are received either directly from the court after sentencing, or they involve persons facing probation revocation, and shock probationers (discussed below). In order to qualify, offenders must meet one or more of the program's criteria:

- one or more prior jail or prison commitments
- one or more convictions
- documentable
    chronic unemployment
    alcohol dependency

drug dependency
mental retardation or psychological problem
* seriousness of current offense

Using a risk/needs assessment classification, the ISP officer develops a supervision plan that outlines behavioral objectives to be met by the offender within specific time frames. By contracting with various community resources, the ISP officer negotiates for the exact type of services needed for each client. There is a formal reassessment every ninety days. Typically, an ISP client remains under intensive supervision for one year or less, and is then transferred to regular supervision. However, the court may amend the terms of probation to continue the offender under intensive supervision for an additional year. In rare and exceptional cases, the period may last beyond two years.

Texas also has a *superintensive supervision* program they call "surveillance probation." It is reserved for cases whose regular probation has been revoked, those sentenced to shock probation, or as a special judicially imposed condition pursuant to a grant of probation. Each offender remains in the program for ninety days, although an extension can be granted, during which time two probation officers (who supervise no more than twenty cases) maintain a minimum of five contacts a week, three of which are in person. There is a mandatory curfew and frequent drug and alcohol testing.

Georgia Intensive Probation Supervision

Intensive probation supervision began in Georgia in 1982 as a pilot program, but has now become a routine method of keeping down prison commitments. In addition to seeking to divert offenders from prison, the program attempts to accomplish the goal of punishment. Program standards include:

* five face-to-face contacts per week
* 132 hours of mandatory community service
* mandatory curfew
* mandatory employment
* weekly check of local arrest records
* automatic notification of arrest elsewhere via the state crime information system
* routine and unannounced alcohol and drug testing

Supervision is provided by a team consisting of a probation officer and one (twenty-five cases) or two (forty cases) surveillance officers. Georgia IPS skims off low-risk offenders for the program—persons who are nonviolent property offenders and drug- and alcohol-related offenders—although most have been sentenced to imprisonment. An analysis of the program revealed that as a result of IPS, the percentage of offenders sentenced to prison has decreased and the number of probationers has increased. Furthermore, the "kinds of offenders diverted were more similar to prison inmates than to regular probationers, suggesting that the program selected the most suitable offenders" (Erwin and Bennett, 1987: 2). However, Michael Sullivan (1987) points out that about 85 percent of the prisoners released by the Georgia parole board have been confined for nonviolent offenses, including driving with a suspended drivers license, punishable in Georgia by up to five years in prison. In other words, the program is indeed diverting offenders from prison, but there is a serious question of why such persons are being subjected to imprisonment in the first place. As noted in Chapter 6, Georgia is in the "top ten" when it comes to rates of incarceration.

Florida Community Control

According to the Florida Department of Corrections, their program of community control "is not intensive probation. It is a distinctively different type of program that is punishment oriented and allows selected offenders to serve their sentences confined to their homes under 'house arrest' instead of prison." That is, they must remain home when not at, or travelling to and from, their place of employment or mandated public service job. They are supervised by special (community control) correctional probation officers (persons with surveillance, arrest, search, and self-defense training, but who are unarmed) who have a maximum caseload of twenty. The officers are equipped with portable radios for quick access to law-enforcement assistance.

Persons may be placed on community control by the sentencing judge if found guilty of a noncapital felony but are considered unsuitable for regular probation; or they may be probation or parole violators. The target population, however, is offenders who have committed nonviolent crimes and would not otherwise be placed on regular probation due to the seriousness of their criminal history (Baird and Wagner, 1990). Officers are required to make a minimum of seven contacts per week with the offender and others in the community—for example, employers and law enforcement agencies. Two of these visits must be in person including at least one in the field. The offender is required to make weekly office visits during which he or she can be subjected to urinalysis. The officer also makes at least sixteen personal telephone contacts to insure that the offender is at home as required by curfew restrictions.

Dauphin County (PA) Intensive Juvenile Probation

The Dauphin County (PA) Probation Department has a juvenile intensive probation supervision program geared to reduce the level of institutional commitments. Each youngster is placed on a suspended commitment to an appropriate juvenile institution with the understanding that he or she would have been committed to this institution if intensive supervision did not exist. Each case is screened to insure that the youngster is not a distinct serious threat to either him- or herself or the community. In addition, there must be sufficient family stability so that the probation officer can work with the family as a unit. And the family has to be willing to cooperate with the program. If the screening PO determines that the case is appropriate for intensive supervision, the youngster is scheduled for a juvenile court hearing and the PO recommends that the respondent be sentenced to a suspended commitment to an appropriate institution and placed in the intensive supervision program.

Each caseload with a maximum of eighteen cases is supervised by one probation officer and one part-time PO; the term of IPS supervision is six to nine months. Each juvenile must follow regulations that include a curfew and mandatory school or work attendance. There is a treatment plan based on the needs and interests of each client. Each youngster is seen three to five times weekly, which includes counseling sessions in the office and at home, in both individual and family sessions. The IPS officer maintains a high level of visibility with both the client and the community.

Home Confinement with Electronic Monitoring

Home confinement with electronic monitoring (EM) is used instead of jail for defendants awaiting trial (see, for example, Cooprider and Kerby, 1990), or as a more restrictive setting for persons on probation and parole, and for probation/parole violators. New York has initiated a pilot EM program that provides an alternative to incarceration for parole violators, who must remain confined to their homes for not less than sixty days nor more than one hundred and twenty days. Home confinement can be used without electronic monitoring, and electronic monitoring can be used for purposes other than home confinement. In this section it is home confinement with electronic monitoring as an alternative to incarceration that is of primary interest.

Home confinement with electronic monitoring has proven appealing because it has the potential to satisfy the goals of imprisonment without the social and financial costs normally associated with imprisonment:

- satisfy the demand for punishment
- provide a deterrent effect
- provide for community protection

In 1988, electronic monitoring was being used in thirty-three states for 2,277 offenders; "most of those monitored were sentenced offenders on probation or parole, participating in a program of intensive supervision in the community" (Schmidt, 1989: 2). EM can serve to enforce curfews, usually restricting the offender from leaving home at night; for detention—a more strict curfew— requiring the offender to remain at home at all times except for employment, education, or other specified activities such as medical treatment (Bureau of Justice Assistance, 1989).

The first system of electronic monitoring was apparently inspired by Ralph Schwitzgebel (1968, 1969a, 1969b) who proposed "electronic parole" as an alternative to imprisonment. The Schwitzgebel-inspired research program monitored the location of parolees, mental patients, and volunteers in Massachusetts from 1964 through 1970. Roger Przybylski suggests that while there was always interest in electronic monitoring of offenders, until the crisis in prison overcrowding "market conditions were never attractive enough to make the technology commercially available" (1988: 1). Reputedly inspired by a "Spiderman" comic strip, Albuquerque District Court Judge Jack Love asked Michael Goss to develop a device suitable to monitor probation curfews. The "Gosslink" was first attached to the ankle of a thirty-year-old probation violator for a one month period starting in 1983. Judge Love subsequently sentenced four other offenders to monitored home confinement.

Meanwhile, a Monroe County, Florida, judge tried a new (Moody) EM system with twelve offenders over a six-month period; they served house-confinement sentences ranging from two days to four months. As a result, the state of Florida incorporated electronic home confinement in the Correctional Reform Act of 1983, and the following year a pilot program was initiated in Palm Beach County for misdemeanants, mostly drunken drivers. By the beginning of 1986, there were more than five thousand offenders on electronically monitored home confinement in Florida. By the beginning of 1987, there were more than fifty programs in twenty-one states using some form of monitored home confinement; and according to the National Institute of Justice there are more than a dozen firms marketing systems designed to verify that an offender is in a specified location at a given time (Przybylski, 1988; Petersilia, 1988b; Ford and Schmidt; 1985).

There are several different types of systems used for electronic monitoring, but they can be divided into two basic categories (Przybylski, 1988): (1) active/continuously signalling; and (2) passive/programmed contact.

Continuously signalling systems   There are two primary types of continuously signalling systems, those that use telephone lines and those that use a radio-like transmitter and receiver.

One system that uses the telephone lines involves the offender wearing a battery-powered moisture- , water- , and shockproof transmitter that is about the size of a pack of cigarettes and weighs about six ounces. The device is securely fastened by riveted plastic straps just above the ankle or on the wrist. Once strapped on it can only be removed by stretching or cutting the straps in an easily detected manner. A circuit board contained in the transmitter has an individually calibrated and unique identification code. The transmitter emits a signal at regular intervals with a range of about 100 to 150 feet. The signal is monitored by a receiver connected to a 110 volt A/C outlet and a standard

FIGURE 11.5 A, B, AND C   Electronic monitoring devices.

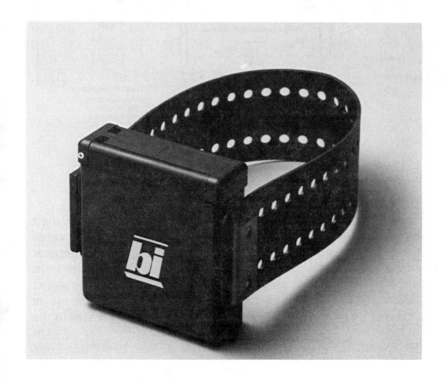

FIGURE 11.5C   *Continued*

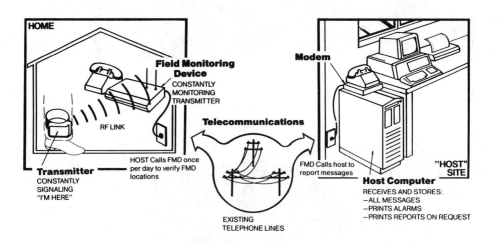

FIGURE 11.6   Continuously signalling system. *Source:* BI Home Escort,
Boulder, CO 80301.

telephone jack installed in the residence. The receiver automatically dials
a central computer describing the time the person goes beyond the range
of the signal, or returns within range, and automatically dials the computer
when it has been subjected to tampering. If the dialer is disconnected or loses
its source of power (by a power outage, for example), the message is stored
until such time as the unit is reconnected to the A/C power and telephone; at
that time a delayed message describing the times of each activity is sent to the
computer.

   Simpler continuously signalling systems that do not use a telephone consist of only two basic components: a transmitter and a portable receiver. The transmitter, which is strapped to the offender's ankle or wrist, or worn around the neck, emits a radio signal which travels about one city block. The portable receiver is placed in a supervising officer's car. By driving past the offender's residence, place of employment, or treatment center, the officer can verify his or her presence.

Programmed contact systems   One of these systems relies on the telephone and computerized voice identification. The computer records the offender's voice and is then programmed to call him or her at random times and request that a series of words or phrases be repeated. They are then matched with the earlier recording to verify presence. In the event of a failure to answer the phone or a voice verification failure, the computer reports a monitoring infraction. Another programmed contact system uses visual verification through telephone units that transmit black-and-white still pictures of the callers on a three-inch screen, while another program uses an encoder device attached to a wrist band; the band cannot be removed without breaking it. The encoder must be inserted into a verifier box attached to the telephone whenever a computer-generated call is received.

Intensive supervision and electronic monitoring are both used as mid-level responses to probation and parole violations, an alternative to incarceration.

Home Detention Project

In an effort to address the problem of the repeat drunk driving offender, Kent County and the Maryland Division of Parole and Probation began a home detention project alternative to incarceration for second and third time offenders. These persons who would have normally been sent to jail, are allowed to remain in the community under probation supervision, but are restricted to their homes during the evening hours. This latter aspect of supervision is accomplished via a computer that dials the client's home phone number on random days and times during evening hours. The client answers and by placing an electronic bracelet attached to his or her wrist to the phone, sends a code to the computer. The computer then asks several questions of the client. After the call has been processed, a report is sent to the office that confirms that the client's phone number was dialed, verified, and the date and time. The report is reviewed by the parole and probation agent on the following morning.

In addition to community-based intermediate punishments are those utilizing short-term incarceration that "shock" the miscreant while saving prison space.

SHOCK PROBATION/PAROLE/INCARCERATION

Shock probation/parole was pioneered by the state of Ohio, which enacted legislation in 1965 permitting the early release from prison of convicted felons either on probation (within 30 to 120 days of imprisonment) or parole (within 6 months of imprisonment). Since that time a number of other states (such as Idaho, Indiana, Kentucky, North Carolina, Maine, and Texas) have adopted similar statutes. To be eligible for shock probation in Ohio, the offender must be otherwise eligible for a sentence of probation and must file a petition with the court. Those not eligible for probation may file a request with the parole board for shock parole (which excludes those convicted of such crimes as rape, armed robbery, kidnaping, major drug violations, and some burglaries).

Shock probation was authorized by the Texas legislature in 1977 as a rehabilitation technique in which an offender is given a sample of prison or jail, and is then placed on probation for the remainder of the sentence. Data from Texas indicates that the typical shock probationer is a white, single male in his early twenties, a laborer with a tenth- or eleventh-grade education. He was convicted of burglary as a first offense, and the crime is usually drug or alcohol related.

The state of New Jersey utilizes a form of shock probation that includes intensive supervision as an intermediate form of punishment; that is, punishment which is less costly than prison, but much more onerous than traditional probation, to achieve the criminal justice objective of deterrence—general and specific—as well as rehabilitation. The program is highly restrictive: only persons serving a sentence for a nonviolent felony are eligible, and no more than five hundred persons can be in the program at any one time.

Offenders typically serve four months before entry into the New Jersey program (Pearson, 1988), and to be eligible the inmate must develop a personal plan which will govern activities upon release. The plan must include provisions for such diverse activities as finding living accommodations and meeting financial obligations. If appropriate, the inmate must develop a plan for drug or alcohol treatment, education, vocational training, or restitution. The plan must include a series of realistic and relevant goals against which the viability of the applicant's admission is assessed by a three judge resentencing panel.

Each applicant must obtain a community sponsor who will be responsible for the applicant's actions while in the community. The sponsor serves as an adjunct to and a resource for the probation officer. Specific activities can include:

- providing transportation to work
- checking on compliance with curfew or other restrictions
- assisting with emergent problems with respect to housing, employment
- maintaining contact with the probation officer

The offender is required to perform community service, usually physical labor, "which contributes to the goal of intermediate punishment in the program" (Pearson, 1988: 440). Probation supervision is "intensive": the PO is responsible for a minimum of five contacts per week per participant.

In the first six months of supervision the frequency of contact per case averages thirty-one per month, including twelve face-to-face, seven curfew (10 P.M. to 6 A.M.) checks, and four urinalysis. And,

> A program requirement is that participants who fail to abide by the program rules will be immediately returned to prison. IPS officers go out in the field actively looking for violations. They conduct curfew checks; they test for drug use; they do not tolerate nonperformance of community service [sixteen hours per month] or nonpayment of fines, restitution, and so on, and in various ways run a tight program. (Pearson, 1988: 439)

New Jersey Conditions for Placement of Adults on Intensive Supervision

I have applied for, and been granted, an opportunity to be placed on intensive supervision by the Resentencing Panel for a period of _____.
Based on the plan I submitted, the Resentencing Panel believes that I am capable of living a useful and law-abiding life in the community and has suspended my sentence with the condition that I comply with the provisions of the intensive supervision program. My being granted the opportunity of intensive supervision is subject to my compliance with the plan I submitted as part of my application along with the conditions listed below. If there is probable cause to believe that I have committed another offense or if I have been held to answer thereto, the Resentencing Panel will commit me to the institution to which I have been sentenced, without bail, to await trial on the new charges. I am required to notify promptly my ISP officer if I am arrested at any time during my sentence to the intensive supervision program.

1. I will obey the laws of the United States, and the laws and ordinances of any jurisdiction in which I may be.
2. I will report as directed to the court or my ISP officer.
3. I will permit the ISP officer to visit my home.
4. I will answer promptly, truthfully, and completely all inquiries made by my ISP officer and report any address or residence change to that officer. If the change of address or residence is outside the region in which I am under supervision, I will request approval of my ISP officer at least thirty days in advance of such change.
5. I will cooperate in any medical and/or psychological examinations, tests and/or counselling my ISP officer recommends.
6. I will support my dependents, meet my family responsibilities, continue gainful employment, and/or pursue such alternatives as may be part of the

(Continued)

program and promptly notify my ISP officer prior to any change in my place of employment or if I find myself out of work.

7. I will participate in a counseling program as scheduled by my ISP officer.
8. I will not leave the state of New Jersey without permission of my ISP officer.
9. I will not have in my possession any firearm or other dangerous weapon.
10. I will perform community service in accordance with the ISP program.
11. I will participate in group activities scheduled by my ISP officer.
12. I will maintain a diary of my activities while under supervision.
13. I will maintain weekly contact with my community sponsor and network team.

I will comply with the following conditions of intensive supervision imposed in accordance with N.J.S.A. 2C:45-1 *et. seq.,* as communicated to me by my ISP officer:

_____ I will pay a fine of $_____ in strict accord with the terms described.

_____ I will make restitution of $_____ in strict accord with the terms described.

_____ I will pursue the course of study or vocational training described.

_____ I will attend/reside in the facility described for the required period of time.

_____ I will refrain from frequenting the unlawful or disreputable places or consorting with the disreputable persons described.

_____ I am required to satisfy the following additional conditions as outlined in my plan:

_____

_____

_____

Boot Camp Shock Probation/Parole

In 1983, the states of Georgia and Oklahoma, in an effort to deal with their problems of prison overcrowding, devised *boot camp shock incarceration* (SI). By the end of 1988, eleven states had initiated similar programs; except for New York and Michigan they are all in the South. The boot camp resembles its military counterpart—a Spartan regimen of rigorous discipline and exercise. The SI program requires short stays of imprisonment—three to six months—combined with shaved heads, marching, close order drills, exercise, and harassment by correction officer/drill instructors during twelve-hour days. There are no television, radio, or telephone privileges.

One program operates in the medium security prison near Baton Rouge, Louisiana: At dawn there is reveille, and inmates quickly dress in fatigue uniforms, make tight beds, and a half hour later have formed into four platoons marching to breakfast in step and cadence (Spencer, 1987):

> *Warden, warden can't you see*
> *What this program's done for me.*
> *Sat me down in a barber chair*
> *Turned around and had no hair.*
> *Took away my faded jeans*
> *Now I'm wearing army greens.*

At a prison facility in Beaver Dams, (in Schuyler County) New York: A bugle blares at precisely 5:30 A.M. and thirty-two inmates leap from their bunks:

> "Good morning, Sir!" they scream to the scowling corrections officer/drill instructor.
> "Are you motivated?" he barks.
> "Motivated! Motivated! Motivated! Sir," the young inmates shout.

In a fury they are dressed, beds made tight, and roaring in unison they are out the door single file. The last man out, a drug dealer from the Bronx, grabs the platoon flag as he runs by (Martin, 1988: 15). This regimen lasts six months, and upon successful completion the inmates are released to parole supervision. The program is limited to persons under twenty-six who have been convicted of nonviolent crimes and are serving their first prison sentence (Bohlen, 1989).

The idea behind shock incarceration "is to break the prisoners down, strip them of their street identity, and then systematically build them up by providing discipline and self-control" (Spencer, 1987: Sec. 3: 1). Offenders must be young, usually seventeen to twenty-five, in good health, and they must volunteer for the program — drop-outs return to complete their sentence of imprisonment, and many drop out (Parent, 1988).

SPECIALIZED PROBATION/PAROLE UNITS

It has long been recognized that offenders with certain salient characteristics could benefit from the services of a specialist — a p/p officer who, as a result of education, training, and/or experience, is in a better position to provide social services and control functions. As a result, many p/p agencies have specialized units for particular offenders. Traditionally, these have included:

- drug-abusing offenders
- alcohol-abusing offenders
- dangerous felony offenders
- gifted offenders
- mentally ill offenders

- retarded offenders
- young offenders

New York, for example, has specialized units for all of these categories. More recently, some probation agencies have expressed concern for the problem of DWI (driving while intoxicated) by establishing special units to deal with such offenders.

Nassau County DWI Unit

Increasing public concern, if not outrage, over the fatalities resulting from driving while intoxicated, has led to increased penalties for those convicted of DWI. However, this response has impacted on correctional officials attempting to deal with jail and prison overcrowding; hence the logic for community-based responses that protect the public while not contributing to the jail/prison crisis. In New York, the state has funded DWI supervision units which now operate in more than thirty-five counties.

In Nassau County (Long Island), New York, the DWI unit is provided with a list of DWI defendants for whom presentence investigation (PSI) reports have been requested by the court. Each case is computer-checked for prior criminal record, outstanding warrants, and motor vehicle record. Cases with multiple DWI arrests are flagged, and their names entered into a pre-screening log. This log is used by the unit supervisor to monitor DWI court activity in anticipation of future screening and assignment to probation supervision. This information is then sent to the PO assigned to conduct the PSI.

When the case is flagged by the DWI unit, the PSI officer sends it to the mental health unit, where a consultant determines if the defendant is a candidate for the county's drug and alcohol abuse agency. The consultant also makes a recommendation regarding therapy that will accompany the final PSI report sent to the sentencing judge. The judge revokes the defendant's motor vehicle license at this time (six months for misdemeanors and one year for felonies), and the case is submitted for DWI unit screening. Eligible defendants are those:

- with a blood/alcohol level of .15 or above at the time of arrest or who refused to submit to a chemical test;
- with two or more DWI arrests (including the instant offense);
- who are county residents;
- not on parole or a defendant in another case;
- for whom alcohol is the primary drug of abuse;
- without an extensive psychiatric history;
- whose evaluation indicates they are suitable for therapy;
- available for evening therapy sessions; and they require
- participation by a concerned member of the family.

Each unit PO maintains a caseload of no more than thirty DWI probationers in a designated area of the county (which is periodically updated in
order to better conform to the distribution of DWI clientele). The PO is
responsible for the program objectives:

1. To hold DWI offenders accountable for their behavior through individual and
   group treatment.
2. To hold the probationer accountable for observing all the laws of the state of
   New York including those involving vehicular traffic.
3. To interrupt the cycle of the disease of alcoholism within the family unit.
4. To provide vocational services as needed.
5. To provide alcohol support services to other family members.

DWI supervision requires the offender to report weekly to a designated
agency where he or she completes a ten-week alcohol education program and a
twenty-four-week closed group therapy session program. The group sessions
are co-led by a probation officer and alcohol counselor. Individual counseling is made available on an as-needed basis. Clients are subjected to random alcohol testing, and a positive reading can result in a variety of sanctions.
On completion of the agency program the client is encouraged to participate
in an Alcoholics Anonymous program. The client is required to report in
person to the PO, and the officer makes periodic home visits. On successful
completion of the program a letter is sent to the department of motor vehicles
indicating that the subject is no longer prohibited from securing a driver's
license.

Philadelphia Drug Unit

The Pennsylvania Board of Probation and Parole operates a drug unit in
Philadelphia which utilizes extensive urinalysis. Caseloads are limited to fifty
and all offenders referred for supervision must have been actively involved in
drug use for at least three years. Parole agents assigned to the unit have
undergone specialized training and are rotated every two to three years to
regular units "to avoid burnout." All clients are tested for drug use upon being
assigned to the unit and they are tested every ninety days thereafter, unless
circumstances demand more frequent testing. Offenders who remain drug free
for nine months are reviewed for transfer to general supervision units. Immediately prior to such a transfer, however, there is a final urinalysis.

Clients whose test results are positive are tested weekly; two positive
opiate urinalyses within a four-month period requires placement in a withdrawal treatment program. If the parole agent believes that a client's pattern of
drug abuse is disruptive to the reintegration and treatment process, or if the
client's behavior constitutes a threat to the community or the client, the agent
may place the offender in "protective custody" for forty-eight hours. If the

agent believes that the client should be subjected to violation of parole procedures, the detention continues until the preliminary hearing.

Pretrial Probation and Diversion

The President's Commission on Law Enforcement and Administration of Justice (1972) pointed out that prosecutors often deal with offenders who need treatment or supervision, but for whom criminal sanctions would be excessive. Programs implementing this theory are referred to by many names, including *pretrial diversion* and *deferred prosecution*. These programs use the fact that an arrest has occurred as a means of identifying defendants in need of treatment or, at least, not in need of criminal prosecution. They generally incorporate specific eligibility criteria, a service program, and the opportunity to monitor and control the decision not to prosecute. In eligible cases, the prosecutor agrees not to prosecute for periods ranging from three to twelve months, contingent on satisfactory performance during the pretrial period, often under the supervision of a probation officer or similar worker. At the end of a successful pretrial supervision period, the charges are dismissed. This type of diversion helps to remove minimal-risk cases from crowded court calendars while providing services to those who are in need of such help (Mullen, 1974).

The Des Moines Pre-Trial Release Project, patterned after a bail project of the Vera Foundation in New York City, permits defendants who are not able to make bail to be released on their own recognizance (ROR) or under supervision. Each defendant is interviewed after arrest by a counselor. If he or she is unable to provide bail, the interviewer completes a pretrial instrument that provides information about the defendant's roots in the community: length of time residing in the Des Moines area; family ties (married, children, parents); employment history; prior criminal record. Each category is linked to a quantitative score, and if the defendant scores at a specific level, he or she becomes eligible for the pretrial release program.

The program proceeds on the premise that a defendant who is incarcerated while awaiting trial has the probability of obtaining probation reduced "because of his inability to obtain or maintain those positive personal and environmental circumstances that courts look to in evaluating an individual's potential for community rehabilitation" (Mullen, 1974: 17). This use of pretrial supervision is geared toward helping defendants "cope with problems, aiding the development of a more stable behavior pattern for the defendant and thereby obtaining a more favorable disposition of his case" (Mullen, 1974: 19). The program does not concern itself with the guilt or innocence of the defendant.

Onondaga County (Syracuse), New York, has had a diversion program in place for more than twenty-five years whose goal is to ensure that no individual arrested for a crime remains in jail solely because of an inability to post bail. The unit is staffed by five probation assistants who screen all detained defendants and, when appropriate, recommend individuals for pretrial release (PTR) and community supervision:

> Each weekday, a probation assistant screens those defendants who have been arrested in the past twenty-four hours. The defendant's prior record is reviewed and those individuals who are selected as possible candidates for pre-trial release are then individually interviewed. Referral and acceptance of appropriate services is often a condition of these individuals' release. Alcohol and drug abuse are the most frequent problems of defendants being considered for pre-trial release. . . . If it is determined that there is an appropriate community treatment program where the defendant will not present a threat to the community and will likely reappear in court, the defendant is recommended to the court for pre-trial release.

As with probation cases, PTR clients are required to abide by individual conditions that may include weekly contact with a probation assistant, referrals to community agencies, and continuance in school or employment. The PTR unit also provides a liaison function for the probation department and the courts. PTR staff appear at calendar calls to make PTR recommendations, dispense information on individuals placed on probation, and gather requests for presentence investigations.

The Florida Department of Corrections operates a Pretrial Intervention Program that diverts first-time defendants who are accused of third-degree felonies or misdemeanors from prosecution; they must volunteer for the program and agree to abide by deferred prosecution conditions of supervision that include restitution and payment of supervision costs. Consent must also be given by the victim, prosecutor, and judge. The subject is placed under the supervision of a correctional probation officer for a period that generally lasts from ninety days to six months. Those who successfully complete the program have their charges dismissed; those who fail are subject to prosecution for their original offense.

WORK RELEASE

Many states have prison work-release programs, and in some instances these programs involve p/p staff. Work release allows individuals serving sentences to work in the community, returning each evening to the institution. They are still subject to institutional controls (and absconding is considered an escape from confinement), and there are additional regulations relative to their extra-institutional status. Under this system inmates are able to earn a salary and pay taxes, contribute to their families' income, repay debts, make restitution, and even contribute to their keep at the institution. In addition, work release enhances an inmate's self-image.

Legislation authorizing work-release programs was enacted in Wisconsin in 1913, but it took more than forty years before it spread to other states: California and North Carolina enacted work release legislation in 1957. By 1965 twenty-four states had such legislation, and by 1975 all fifty states and the federal government had legislation authorizing some form of community work and education release (Rosenblum and Whitcomb, 1978).

States vary with respect to the criteria used in selecting inmates for work-release programs; some automatically excuse those serving life sentences or inmates who have detainers filed against them. In some states the court must authorize work release; in others the parole board has this responsibility. The final responsibility for selecting candidates, however, is usually under the aegis of the correctional authorities who administer the program. Most states do not have specific restrictions governing who may participate in work release, but often use such general expressions as "not a high security risk" or "not likely to commit a crime of violence" (Root, 1972). States vary in the number of inmates involved in work release, and in some the program is combined with furloughs enabling eligible inmates to leave the institution for specific periods of time to seek employment or educational opportunities.

Unfortunately, many, if not most, correctional institutions are isolated from urban areas where employment opportunities are more readily available. Responding to this deficiency, some states operate a variety of facilities for housing work-release participants in proximity to areas of employment. These facilities include minimum security prisons or work-release centers, halfway houses, or rented quarters in hotels or YMCAs.

There are typically basic restrictions on the employment situation available to inmates (Root, 1972):

1. Inmates cannot work in a skilled area where there is already a surplus labor force.
2. Conditions of employment must be commensurate with nonoffenders.
3. If a union is involved, it must be consulted, and no work releasee can work while a labor dispute is in progress.

Montgomery County (MD) Prerelease Program

In 1968, the state legislature passed a law authorizing the establishment of a work-release program through the county's detention center. That same year Montgomery County enacted a law defining the nature of and general regulations to be utilized in implementing the work-release program. In 1969 the "Work Release Dorm" handling up to sixteen carefully selected inmates was opened. Only minor offenders (such as nonsupport cases) participated. The inmates worked in the community during the day and returned to detention for the remainder of the day. Since that time the program has been modified and expanded. It was subsequently determined that the detention center was not a suitable atmosphere to operate the program and, just as important, it was concluded that offenders had many other problems they needed to deal with besides employment.

In 1972 a separate facility was established that employs counselors, community release coordinators, and other service personnel, so a more conducive atmosphere can be maintained while utilizing available resources of the community. In 1973 the program became coeducational, the very limiting restrictions on eligibility were removed, and the courts began utilizing this program as an alternative to security incarceration for selected offenders. Although the majority of center residents are male, female participation has increased dramatically since the first years of operation and they now make up about 12 percent of the residents.

Pre-Release Center

The Pre-Release Center is actually a complex made up of three separate correctional units (one thirty-six-bed women's unit and two forty-four-bed male units). Each unit is operated by a separate staff treatment team. Each unit contains bedrooms, a game/television room, visiting area, laundry room, telephone and vending machine area, control desk, staff offices, supply room, and records room. The central services area includes a lobby, dining room, kitchen, library, classrooms, audio-visual room, medical and administrative office space. Outside areas include patios, a basketball court, an outside visiting area, and a parking lot. The center is located in the heart of the county in a commercial area and is close to public transportation.

Program Criteria

County law dictates the standards and process for selecting participants for the program. The individual must be within six months of release back into the community, without serious court charges or detainers outstanding from other jurisdictions, no escapes within two years, no revocation from a work-release program in last two years, and physically and psychologically capable of performing in the program. The program has been modified to handle short-term cases (sixty day sentences) and provide specialized alcohol monitoring and treatment for chronic DUI offenders.

Key Features of Program

About four hundred residents a year participate in *behavioral contracting* at the Detention Center. Prior to transfer to the PRC each individual identifies personal issues and states specifically what he or she will do and accomplish in the program. The contracting process insures accurate expectations are set and increases residents' understanding, acceptance, and use of program opportunities.

Thorough individual assessment, treatment planning, and program imple-

(Continued)

mentation are carried out by a *staff treatment team,* which provides the service delivery. There is a staff treatment team for each separate unit (twenty-four hours a day, seven days a week).

In the area of *employment,* vocational aptitude testing, job interview skill training (utilizing videotape), intensive employment counseling, and job placement services are provided by the PRC work release coordinators. Residents are usually employed within three weeks, most in jobs at semiskilled levels with upward mobility potential. Vocational training, typically, is in the form of O.J.T. (on-the-job training). Experience indicates this is the most effective means of attaining skill development for this population.

Educational opportunities occur at all levels. Reading-impaired residents participate in individual tutoring provided by community volunteers. GED opportunity is provided. College-level education is available through the Montgomery College and local universities.

In the area of developing more adequate personal adjustment, a variety of strategies are used. Each resident is assigned a staff primary counselor who provides intensive *individual counseling.* The residents meet with their staff counselor one to three times a week to discuss, on a personal level, needs and frustrations the resident is having in coping with community life. Using the *reality therapy* process, staff assist residents in defining more clearly their needs, values, and goals, and in developing effective strategies for reaching their goals. Throughout the process, staff teach residents and reinforce the concept that it is up to them to choose responsible problem-solving behaviors that lead to goal attainment and freedom in the community. Counseling staff also work closely with residents' families and assist in resolving problems they confront as a family unit.

The Life Skills program includes twenty seminars designed to improve residents' skills in preparing for successful independent living upon final release to the community. The one-and-a-half-hour seminars are held two evenings each week. They include experimental activities such as role plays, group go-rounds, small task-oriented problem-solving groups, and so on; group participation plays a major role in the facilitation of the individual's learning. Community resource persons also assist in presentations to share their expertise. The seminars include topics such as work adjustment, value clarification, decision making, communication skills, leisure time, stress management, drugs and alcohol, family involvement, problem solving, and money management. Although each seminar has its own specific goals and strategies, the seminars also serve to improve the resident's self-image and self-confidence through group support and participation. Through this process residents develop an increased sense of responsibility, as well as improved problem-solving and coping skills.

The center provides additional *training in stress management* (six sessions) through a contract clinician. This special training is designed for those residents who are continuously frustrated and agitated and are least capable of managing the daily stresses of life. The center also contracts with a biocriminologist who individually *assesses* highly stressed residents for *food allergies, hypoglycemia,* and other *biochemical factors* that affect behavior. Female offenders participate in a *special women's group* led by a contract clinician who focuses on such issues as self-image, sex roles, and parenting.

Residents also become involved in and pay for *community special focus treatment services* (such as drug, alcohol, and family counseling) as their needs may dictate. Residents identify the critical issues on which they want to focus. Based on these issues, the community release coordinators refer residents to appropriate community treatment services and then follow up on both service delivery and resident use of the resource.

During their free time, residents participate in the center's *structured leisure activity program.* By having the opportunity to develop new leisure interests and activities, residents can begin to change their leisure-time life-style and can develop appropriate ways of relaxing, reducing stress, and building greater personal strength. Prior to their PRC experience, most of their leisure time was consumed in an intoxicated state of one kind or another. Since more crime occurs during the free time, the development of ways to use leisure time constructively is critical.

Responsible behavior is reinforced, while irresponsible behavior results in the loss of freedom. The staff uses a behavioral rating scale, and each resident is accountable for his or her actions. Those demonstrating responsibility receive increased freedom, furloughs, and eventual release. Those who demonstrate irresponsible behavior experience decreased freedom and eventual reincarceration.

Financial guidance is also provided to residents, as well as assistance in locating *housing* prior to release.

The center assesses residents' preparedness for release and presents this information to the Parole Commission or the court. In Montgomery County parole release is earned on the basis of program performance. Services do not necessarily stop upon release.

Postrelease follow-up is provided through intensive parole and probation supervision by an agent assigned to the Pre-Release Center. As necessary, the center assists the releasees.

HALFWAY HOUSES

"The concept of halfway houses was introduced in 1817 by the Massachusetts Prison Commission. This group recommended the establishment of temporary homes for destitute released offenders as a measure to reduce recidivism" (Rosenblum and Whitcomb, 1978: 9):

> It is intended to afford a temporary shelter in this building, if they choose to accept it, to such discharged convicts as may have conducted themselves well in prison at a cheap rate, and have a chance to occupy themselves in their trade, until some opportunity offers a placing of themselves where they can gain an honest livelihood in society. A refuge of this kind, to this destitute class, would be found perhaps humane and politic. (Commonwealth of Massachusetts Legislative Document, Senate No. 2, 1830)

According to Donald Thalheimer (1975: 1):

> The very name halfway house suggests its position in the corrections world: halfway-in, a more structured environment than probation and parole; halfway-out, a less structured environment than institutions. As halfway-in houses they represent a last step before incarceration for probationers and parolees facing or having faced revocation; as halfway-out houses, they provide services to pre-releasees and parolees leaving institutions. Halfway houses also provide a residential alternative to jail or outright release for accused offenders awaiting trial or convicted offenders awaiting sentencing.

Victor Goetting notes that "it is accepted that these facilities are based upon sound correctional theory; in order to ultimately place a person in society successfully that person should not be any further removed from that society than is necessary" (1974: 27). When used in conjunction with prison or training school release programs, the halfway house provides: (1) assistance with obtaining employment, (2) an increased ability to utilize community resources, and (3) needed support during the difficult initial release period (Griggs and McCune, 1972).

The various types of halfway houses operated by public and private agencies and groups can be divided basically into those that provide bed, board, and some help with employment, and those that provide a full range of services, including treatment. The latter includes a variety of methods, from guided group interaction, to psychotherapy, reality therapy, or behavior modification. A halfway house may be primarily for released inmates, for parolees, or for probationers as an alternative to imprisonment. Halfway houses may also be used for probationers or parolees who violate their conditions of supervision but not seriously enough to cause them to be imprisoned.

The Texas Adult Probation Commission has funded a series of halfway houses (called residential treatment facilities) throughout the state. These facilities house felony offenders in need of a brief residency in a structured environment which offers treatment services, rather than placing them in prison or on regular probation. These offenders often need treatment for drug or alcohol abuse, job skills training, and basic education. The facilities offer a home like atmosphere with a minimum of security measures. Residents are classified according to their individual needs and assigned to a treatment regimen which usually includes counseling, educational classes, and vocational training; they also share in the housekeeping responsibilities. As residents advance in the program, they are allowed to check in and out of the facility to go to work or training in the community. If unemployed they may be assigned to do community service work. When residents have advanced to an acceptable level in their treatment plan, they are released from the center and placed under regular probation supervision.

The Georgia Department of Offender Rehabilitation has established more than a dozen halfway houses (called residential diversion centers) to provide judges with an option for sentencing "marginal cases" — an alternative between imprisonment and regular probation. There are two centers for female offenders. The program requires residents to work, pay for their room and board, and provide restitution to their victims. In order to qualify for the program a defendant must:

1. be one who would otherwise be incarcerated;
2. be a nonviolent property offender;
3. not be regarded as a habitual criminal; and
4. be capable of maintaining employment.

Each center has the capacity for between forty and fifty residents who serve an average of four to five months before being released to regular probation supervision. The centers provide counseling, basic education, high school equivalency exam preparation, and recreation. Release is based on a satisfactory completion of a treatment contract which the offender needs to qualify for the program. The centers serve three daily meals, and pack-out lunches are furnished to residents who are out to work. Residents are responsible for maintaining the facility and are allowed visitors on the weekends during specified hours. After the fourth week residents may earn weekend passes. Failure to comply with rules and regulations, or absconding from the facility, means imprisonment.

Massachusetts Halfway Houses, Inc. (MHHI)

MHHI is a private nonprofit corporation that began its operations in 1965 serving thirty-one parolees in a fifteen-bed facility. The corporation now operates halfway house programs in eight locations providing residential services to more than 1,300 juvenile and adult offenders each year. In addition to its extensive residential program, MHHI also offers nonresidential vocational and employment placement services. Most clients are from the greater Boston area, although MHHI now has contracts with the sheriffs of Suffolk and Norfolk Counties to provide services to prerelease residents as a result of overcrowding at county jails. There is also a preparole residential program for state prison inmates who have been granted parole, and a residential program for parole violators "whose parole adjustment might be enhanced by a structured community environment as an alternative to reimprisonment in an overcrowded and costly state or county institution."

The basic residential program lasts from sixty to ninety days and each resident is assigned a counselor to work with. The program utilizes a mutual agreement contract to set specific goals to be achieved within that time frame. These include full-time vocational activity, money management, steps to overcome any specialized problem such as substance abuse, family difficulties, and the develop-

(Continued)

ment of a network of community resources – for example, new peer associates and new recreational activities. Once developed, reintegration plans are formalized into a written mutual agreement program contract. This document spells out the mutual responsibilities of residents and staff in each of the primary areas as well as time-frames for achievement of specific objectives. The counseling process follows the tenets of reality therapy, a behavior-focused approach which recognizes that people are responsible for their own actions, concentrates on the here and now, and maintains that the option to succeed is open to those willing to apply themselves to that end. The counselor initially acts as the resident's advocate in dealing with community agencies.

St. Leonard's House

St. Leonard's House, on Chicago's West Side, was established in 1956 by, and continues to be operated under the auspices of, the Episcopal Church. The facility provides residential and rehabilitative services for twenty-three men recently released from prison who are under parole supervision; there is a close working relationship between parole agents and house staff. Each resident stays between thirty and ninety days, and there are many more requests for services than the facility can handle. St. Leonard's enforces a curfew and residents are permitted to have visitors as well as weekend passes. Drugs, alcohol, sex, threats, violence, stealing, gambling, or lending money results in immediate expulsion.

Staff members include job counselors, addiction counselors, mental health counselors, former residents, as well as numerous volunteers. The program is staffed twenty-four hours a day; from 6:30 A.M. to 9 P.M. the counseling staff staggers hours in order to be available to clients, especially in the early hours before school and job training and before the search for employment begins. They are on duty again late in the day when the men return for supper and evening meetings at the house. Education leading to a GED is available at the house.

No fees are charged, although residents are expected to complete various housekeeping chores. A personal program for each resident begins at intake, during which he spends several hours a day, over a period of three to five days, being interviewed. While his needs are assessed he begins to feel his way into the program and with the help of counselors sets personal goals. There follows a program of personal and group counseling, peer meetings, opportunities to meet with the chaplain and the employment counselor – all designed to assure that each resident gets as much help as possible in reestablishing and reordering his life.

The major difficulty with opening and maintaining a halfway house is community reaction. A Lou Harris poll, for example, found that whereas 77 percent of the representative U.S. sample favored the halfway-house concept, 50 percent would not want one in *their* neighborhood, and only 22 percent believed that people in *their* neighborhood would favor a halfway house being located there. Experts stress the importance of getting community support for the project before opening a halfway house. Among some of the strategies used in gaining support is the formation of an advisory board made up of influential community people. Community residents may be placed on the board of directors and hired as staff for the facility. Victor Goetting (Bakal, 1974) notes that local citizenry often fear that unwanted criminal elements will come into the area, and he suggests two ways of dealing with such fears; first, the facility can be restricted to serve individuals who would ordinarily reside in the community; or, if outside persons are to be brought in, a screening panel can be formed to alleviate some of the fear. The committee can be made up of community persons who work for the police, sheriff, courts or probation/parole agencies.

Now that we have completed our examination of special programs, in the final chapter we will review research into the effectiveness of probation and parole.

REVIEW QUESTIONS

1. What is the purpose of the Interstate Compact in probation and parole?
2. What is the purpose of an intensive supervision program in probation and parole?
3. Why are specialized units in probation/parole advantageous?
4. What led to the use of electronic monitoring in probation/parole?
5. How is electronic monitoring accomplished?
6. What are the advantages of shock probation/parole?
7. What are the advantages of shock incarceration?
8. What are the purposes of a pretrial probation program?
9. What are the two types of halfway house; what are their purposes?
10. Why is a work-release program difficult to implement?

TWELVE
Research in Probation and Parole

In this chapter we will look at a variety of research efforts designed to test the degree to which probation or parole, or a variety of component programs, are "successful," and the results are often contradictory. The methodology of some efforts is simply unsound; however, even methodologically sound research has not allowed us to answer the question: *Probation and parole: success or failure?* For example, Mark Jay Learner (1977) found that parole supervision in New York markedly reduced the postrelease criminal activity of a group of (conditional) releasees compared to a group of dischargees released from the same institution without supervision. A similar study by Howard Sachs and Charles Logan (1979) found that in Connecticut parole supervision resulted in only a modest reduction in recidivism. In California, however, Deborah Star found (1979) no significant difference in the recidivism rates of persons released with or without parole supervision.

Of course, a major part of the problem is the word "success." For example, Mark Wiederanders (1983: 4), a researcher for the California Youth Authority, very candidly portrays his own findings:

> Depending on which statistics one decides to use, parole behavior in the sample of wards can be made to look quite good, especially considering the high levels of pre-Youth Authority crime, or quite bad. For example, only 13% were sent to state prison for parole-period offenses during the 24 months of followup, resulting in an 87% "success rate" by this criterion. Some correctional jurisdictions who report spectacularly high success rates, in fact use such a restricted measure. Alternatively, regarding the same sample we could accurately report that 77% of

the sample had been arrested or temporarily detained during the 24 months leaving a "success rate" by this criterion of only 23%.

We will return to the problem of "success" after reviewing the research.

INTENSIVE PROBATION/PAROLE SUPERVISION (IPS)

Before we begin our examination of the effectiveness of intensive supervision, we should note that the establishment of IPS programming was not based on careful research and evaluation, but is simply a response — perhaps ill-conceived — to jail and prison overcrowding (Clear, Flynn, and Shapiro, 1987). And policy implications of evaluative research into IPS may be irrelevant: "If the results are negative . . . then these findings will be viewed as support for both the continued use of incapacitation and the development of even more intrusive, surveillance-oriented community control programs" (Byrne, 1990: 8). In fact, while evidence of the effectiveness of IPS is wanting, the program has been a public relations success (Clear and Hardyman, 1990).

As noted in Chapter 11, intensive supervision, usually accomplished by severely reducing caseload size per p/p officer, is based on the assumption that it will lead to increased contact between the officer and the client or their significant others (such as spouse or parents), and that this increased contact will improve service delivery and control and, thus, reduce recidivism. Some programs, however, have had difficulty achieving *intensity:* "While it may be inconceivable for intensive supervision to occur in caseloads that exceed some finite number, such as fifty persons, it is certainly conceivable that much smaller caseloads might not result in significant levels of intensity" (Clear and Hardyman, 1990: 44). Eric Carlson and Evalyn Parks claim that intensive supervision does indeed increase case contacts, often by 50 percent or more, while the amount of time spent in contact also increases significantly. "The difference between spending one-half hour per month with a client and spending an hour per month," however, "is, relatively speaking, an extremely small difference considering the magnitude of the treatment and service provision task which the probation officer is trying to accomplish" (1979: 72). Research into this question dates back to 1953, when California conducted "probably the most extensively controlled experiment in American correctional history" (Glaser, 1969: 311).

California   The Special Intensive Parole Unit (SIPU) experiment ran from 1953 until 1964 during which time caseload sizes were varied from fifteen to thirty-five. In addition, research was conducted into the impact of increased supervision on particular risk classes of offender. There was a positive outcome only with those parolees classified as "lower-middle-risk" — they had significantly fewer violations. In a review of this research, however, Robert Martinson (1974: 47) found that the successful cases were concentrated in northern California, where agents were more apt to cite both the experimentals and the controls for violating parole at a higher rate than in southern California. The limited success, Martinson argues, was not due to the intensive nature of supervision, but was the result of a realistic threat of reimprisonment. There is also a problem with using parole violation as a criteria for success because of what researchers refer to as the "halo effect," a tendency on the part of p/p officers to tolerate greater levels of misbehavior than is usual, in order to prove the experiment successful.

More recent research into California IPS was conducted in three counties. Cases were randomly assigned from a pool of high risk offenders on probation to IPS caseloads of forty (Contra Costa), nineteen (Ventura), and thirty-three (Los Angeles), or control caseloads that averaged one-hundred and fifty to three hundred offenders. After six months it was clear that IPS clients received more intensive supervision: two to three times the usual number of contacts. About 30 percent of the IPS cases had a technical violation, a much higher rate than the control caseloads; however, there was no statistically significant difference between new arrest rates for IPS or control cases. The research revealed that intensive supervision in these counties did not impact on the rate of new arrests: IPS failed to enhance the rehabilitative or control function of supervision (Petersilia and Turner, 1990).

Georgia   Research in Georgia has produced mixed results for the concept of intensive supervision. Probationers in the intensive supervision program (which was discussed briefly in Chapters 10 and 11) are under the joint supervision of a probation officer and a surveillance officer in caseloads that do not exceed twenty-five. One comparison of outcomes (Erwin, 1984) for IPS probationers (N = 542) and a matched sample (n = 752) of regular probationers, revealed that while 13.7 percent of the IPS group had their probation revoked for new crimes (none for violent crimes), the figure for the control sample was 10.2 percent. The IPS group had a higher rate of technical violations (11.8 percent) than the control sample (6.5 percent) — which the researchers argue is to be expected considering the intensive supervision — and there was little difference in the absconder rate: 2.2 for the IPS, 2.4 for the control sample. A second study of the program (Erwin and Bennett, 1987) revealed that 18.5 percent of the IPS probationers and 24.0 percent of the regular probationers were convicted of new crimes. However, 42.3 percent of prison releases during the same period were convicted of new offenses, and "59.4 percent of the IPS cases were more similar to those incarcerated than to those placed on probation" (1987: 4).

According to Joan Petersilia (1988), any number of states have adopted IPS programming based on the apparent success of the Georgia program. However, she cautions, judges in Georgia, like those in many southern states, tend toward the punitive, imposing more sentences of imprisonment and for longer terms than elsewhere. Thus, there is a greater pool of IPS prospects — nonviolent offenders — than would be expected outside of the south in general, and Georgia in particular. In fact, when it comes to the risk of new criminal behavior, IPS clients are not markedly different from the regular probation population in Georgia. The basic claims of IPS in Georgia with respect to cost-effectiveness, diversion of offenders, and improved public safety "are not supported by the available research evidence" (Clear, Flynn, and Shapiro, 1987: 35). In fact, "a convincing argument can be presented that the Georgia evaluation actually demonstrates the opposite" (Byrne, Lurigio, and Baird, 1989: 27).

New Jersey   IPS in New Jersey (discussed under shock probation in Chapter 11) is limited to five-hundred highly select offenders who are diverted from prison after several months of incarceration. IPS cases were compared with a sample of offenders who were eligible for the program but were, instead, incarcerated and released on parole. Frank Pearson (1988) reports that the IPS participants' new conviction rate averaged roughly 10 percentage points lower than that of the comparison group. He concludes that New Jersey IPS

> works fairly well with felons who are neither dangerous nor habitual criminals. The program does save a modest amount of prison space without increasing recidivism; it has been cost-effective compared to ordinary terms of imprisonment and parole; it has been monetarily beneficial (in terms of earnings, taxes, payments to a fund for victims, and so on); and it does provide a level of punishment between probation on the one hand and ordinary imprisonment on the other. (1988: 447)

But the "New Jersey program evaluation — by design — should make the IPS program look quite good since it compares IPS cases with a group of class 3 and class 4 felons who represent the poorest risks and who receive the harshest treatment by the New Jersey corrections system" (Byrne, Lurigio, and Baird, 1989: 30). And other researchers find it ironic that the relatively low-risk offenders in the New Jersey program are receiving intensive supervision, while the far higher risk parolee joins a caseload in excess of one hundred cases (Clear, Flynn, and Shapiro, 1987).

New York   Research conducted by the New York State Division of Parole (Collier, 1980) indicates that intensive supervision can have a modest effect on violent felony offenders. In 1978 the legislature provided funding for the supervision of violent felony offenders. In 1979, all released inmates who had been convicted of a violent felony (crimes ranging from robbery to arson — most were imprisoned for robbery) were placed in intensive units whose parole officers supervised no more than thirty-five cases: 97 percent were male; the median age was 27.3; blacks constituted 57.5 percent, whites 23 percent, and Hispanics 19.5 percent; 62 percent completed less than the twelfth grade and 80 percent were unskilled laborers. Interestingly, two-thirds of this group had little or no prior criminal history.

After one year the violent felony offenders released in 1979 and placed under intensive supervision (N = 1,905), were compared with the same population released in 1978 to regular supervision (N = 1,732), with the following results:

1. 12.6 percent of the (1978) controls and 1.8 percent of the (1979) intensives were returned to prison for a new offense;
2. 3.3 percent of the controls and 4.0 percent of the intensives were returned to prison for technical violations of parole;
3. 5.0 percent of the controls and 3.4 percent of the intensives absconded from supervision; and
4. as of the end of the one-year research period (3/31/80), 6.5 percent of the controls and 3.9 percent of the intensives had parole violation or court hearings pending.

It should be noted, however, that even regular parole supervision in New York, as contrasted with that typically operating in other states, is relatively "intensive." During this writer's almost fifteen years as a parole officer and senior parole officer (supervisor), the average caseload size rarely exceeded sixty, and was usually closer to fifty, and there was a high number of in person client contacts between officers and offenders, particularly unannounced visits to the client's residence.

Ohio   Edward Latessa and Gennaro Vito (1988) conducted research into the intensive probation supervision of shock probationers in Lucas County (Toledo), Ohio. Funded by a state probation subsidy program, the Incarceration Diversion Unit (IDU) consists of four probation officers, each with a caseload maximum of twenty-five, with the exception of the supervisor, who is assigned fifteen. The IDU probationers were compared to a group of shock probationers under regular supervision. (The study did not indicate the size of regular shock probation caseloads.) The researchers found that the IDU officers recorded almost four times as many client contacts, and more social services were provided to their clients. However, there were no statistically significant differences with respect to recidivism; the IDU group did have significantly less technical violations which the researchers conclude was the result of a realistic fear of being sent to prison because of the nature of IDU supervision and strict violation practices. (An alternative hypothesis would raise questions about the quality of the supervision.) Latessa and Vito (1988: 327) conclude that their study "should provide a word of caution to officials seeking ways to limit incarceration rates" by using intensive supervision.

A study conducted by Susan Noonan and Edward Latessa (1987) in

Montgomery County (Dayton), Ohio, compared matched samples from IPS units, with twenty-five cases per officer, and regular units. The research revealed that 11.7 percent of the intensive supervision cases ended with a felony conviction, against 3.8 percent for regular supervision; 1.2 percent of the intensive cases were incarcerated for misdemeanors as opposed to 6.2 percent of the regular cases. Interestingly, the IPS officers, on average, made fewer than one face-to-face contact per month with their clients in the client's home—hardly an *intensive* level of supervision.

State of Washington The objective of the Adult Corrections Division was to save tax dollars by removing *low-risk offenders* from the state's prisons. Persons released into the program had on average served less than three months in prison. They (N = 289) were placed under the intensive supervision of a parole officer whose caseload did not exceed twenty. At the end of one year, it was determined whether the individual's behavior warranted a conditional discharge from supervision or whether further supervision by a regular parole officer was indicated.

In order to evaluate the program a matched historical sample (n = 102) was selected as the control group. Random assignment was ruled out because of "equal treatment under the law considerations." The control group was made up of inmates who were paroled at the same time as those selected for early release and intensive supervision. However, the control group subjects were released after having served normal sentences to a parole officer who supervised an average caseload of seventy-three. A person in the control group was selected on the same criteria as those in the test group. David Fallen (1981) and his colleagues report the following outcomes:

1. After one year of supervision, 19 percent of the test (IPS) group had been arrested or convicted for new (nontraffic) offenses, while the figure for control cases was 40 percent;
2. however, the IPS parole officers showed a strong tendency to invoke delinquency action: after one year 42 percent of the test group had been cited for technical parole violations as opposed to 24 percent for the control group; and
3. the one-year revocation rate for the IPS group was 17 percent; for the control group it was 6.1 percent (the average for general supervision in Washington is 15 percent).

The researchers speculate on explanations for their findings:

1. Intensive parolees were less likely to commit new offenses because of a fear of detection produced by increased supervision.
2. By brief incarceration, intensive parolees received the initial "shock value" of prison but were not in long enough to learn the "skills" or adopt the values of the incarcerated criminal population.

3. Because many intensive parolees received formal technical violations, these served as effective warnings that undesirable behavior would not be tolerated.
4. Because many intensive parolees were revoked for technical violations only, this may have screened out those disposed to commit new offenses.

Wisconsin   In 1984 the Wisconsin Division of Corrections established an experimental IPS program for high risk offenders. Thirty offenders (later increased to forty) were supervised by two-agent teams in two locations. The research did not indicate the caseload for non-IPS parole agents. The experienced agents screened all new cases in their areas and selected only high risk offenders (HRO) as clients. To qualify as an HRO, the client must have a history of assaultive behavior; other distinguishing characteristics include a lengthy criminal record, poor prison adjustment record, poor attitude toward community supervision, as well as an unwillingness to participate in drug or alcohol abuse, or mental health programs.

As part of intensive supervision, specialized rules were tailored for each offender; these restricted certain associations, use of motor vehicles, and evening hours. "The general tactic is to establish rules which restrict behavior(s) associated with a past criminal pattern" (Wagner, 1989: 23). Offenders were required to provide a weekly schedule revealing where they will be at any given time. Each client registered with the local police, submitting a photograph, fingerprints, handwriting sample, past offense history, and current address. The police were expected to assist in the offender-monitoring process. Parole agents made at least four in person contacts each month, including two visits, scheduled and unscheduled, to the offender's residence. There were frequent collateral visits with police, employers, landlords, and associates. In at least one case, school officials and parent association members were informed of the release of a child sex offender so they could aid in the surveillance process.

The HRO group under IPS was compared to a matched sample that received regular supervision. The results were dramatic; after one year, only 3 percent of the IPS parolees had been convicted of a felony; it was 27 percent for the control group. The statistics for parole violation provide at least a partial explanation for these differences: while only 12 percent of the control group were returned to prison for parole violations, the number was 40 percent for the IPS group. Dennis Wagner, a researcher for the state of Wisconsin, concludes that the IPS program "suppresses criminal behavior by pre-empting it" (1989: 26). The research does not indicate how many of the remaining IPS clients successfully completed their entire supervision period.

Intensive Supervision: Discussion

In order to evaluate IPS, we need to examine the two premises on which it is based.

Premise One: Intensive probation supervision will divert offenders who would otherwise be incarcerated. In any number of jurisdictions this is not being accomplished. Judges continue to send probation-eligible offenders to prison, while using IPS for those who would be sentenced to probation in any event. Needless to say, this will affect the results of any research on an IPS program. In order for the diversion goal to be accomplished, cases need to be assigned to IPS *after* a sentence of imprisonment. Only after conviction, sentence, and remand to jail pending transportation to prison, should the IPS screening officer review the case and, if appropriate, submit a recommendation for resentencing. Cases not intercepted should proceed to state prison. With respect to parole, parole boards often assign cases to intensive supervision that would have been granted parole even in the absence of an IPS program. If intensive supervision is to serve the goal of reducing the prison population, it should be reserved for cases that have been denied parole. An IPS screening officer (institutional parole officer) should review the case *after* parole has been denied and, if appropriate, submit a recommendation for reconsideration of parole with IPS.

In sum many, if not most, intensive supervision programs are not actually diverting offenders—they are simply providing judges and parole boards with an additional supervision option that is not being used in lieu of prison. While this may not have the effect of lowering prison commitments, it certainly has merits of its own. For example, the Florida IPS (Community Control) Program received offenders who were often more serious than those on probation or in jail, but less serious that those sentenced to prison. And an undetermined number of these borderline cases, perhaps more than half, would have been sent to prison in the absence of IPS (Baird and Wagner, 1990). Many IPS programs, however, appear to be accepting those offenders who are not at high risk, who probably should have been on regular probation in the first instance. In some counties, the probation department routinely recommends inappropriate cases for IPS. This serves two intertwined purposes: first, it ensures that the IPS program will deliver "good stats;" and second, it helps to keep down regular caseloads by shifting some cases to probation officers funded by special allocations (and the continuation of these allocations is dependent on "good stats").

However, intensive supervision for inappropriate cases unnecessarily increases the cost of probation and it may be harmful to the client: "Behavioral scientists have long speculated that the addition of strains and controls to a human system can, at some time, result in a reaction that is contrary to the direction of the controls" (Clear and Hardyman, 1990: 55). According to the labelling perspective (discussed in Chapter 9), an offender inappropriately identified as "high risk" by virtue of IPS status, may indeed assume that role and organize his or her behavior accordingly.

And there is an additional problem: offenders who feel that intensive supervision is as punitive as imprisonment. "In many states, given the option of serving prison terms or participating in IPS, many offenders have chosen prison" (Petersilia 1990: 23; emphasis deleted). Joan Petersilia points out that for many/most serious offenders, imprisonment and the stigma that can result are not the frightening phenomenon that they are for the community at large. "For many offenders, it may seem preferable to get that short stay in prison over rather than spend five times as long in an IPS" (1990: 25). Under these conditions, in order for intensive supervision to work, it may be necessary to offer it as an option for much more serious offenders than are now being subjected to IPS.

In sum, large amounts of scarce resources are being allocated to the less serious offenders, while more dangerous offenders are released to the community under parole supervision that is often inadequate due to lack of funding (Clear, Flynn, and Shapiro, 1987), or is simply non-existent in those states that have discontinued post-prison community supervision. It is the worst "Alice-in-Wonderland" situation when armed robbers and other dangerous offenders are released from prison with inadequate or no supervision, while property offenders are placed on intensive probation supervision.

This irrational approach to crime and justice is exemplified by a Texas study (Texas Adult Probation Commission, 1988). IPS cases were compared to cases eligible for probation but sentenced to imprisonment, and cases not eligible for probation and sentenced to imprisonment, using the "risk" part of the Texas Risk/Needs Assessment form. The mean scores were:

1. intensive probation supervision = 20.10
2. eligible for probation but incarcerated = 18.93
3. ineligible for a sentence of probation = 26.26

In other words, while the IPS program was apparently diverting offenders from prison (a risk mean of 20.10), there were less serious risks (risk mean of 18.93) who were, nevertheless, imprisoned; and the high risk offenders (risk mean 26.26) who were imprisoned will be released to parole supervision that is not intensive. A similar situation existed in Illinois where the state funded extensive IPS programs, while in 1987 60 percent of the state's parole agents were laid off causing caseloads to approach the four hundred mark. (The positions were restored in 1989, and caseloads went to one hundred and ten.)

Alan Schuman (1989: 29) argues that

> The new IPS concept actually depicts local communities' original image of how probation services should operate. IPS provides the type of comprehensive surveillance services, restitution payments, drug testing and treatment, employment verification, and networking with other community services that should be expected of all probation agencies that are adequately funded.

Gerald Buck (1989: 66) argues that intensive supervision "*is* probation practiced as it was originally intended to be. Other probation programs are a sham that ought not to be called probation supervision."

Premise Two. More of whatever it is that the probation/parole agency does with routine cases will have a salutary effect on cases at greater risk. Although a number of research studies have challenged this premise, there is a strong, if unproven, belief in probation and parole that *more is better.* I want to dwell on the question of *more* of *what?* The implication of intensive supervision—the bait that hooks funding from elected officials—is that offenders will be closely monitored, under surveillance, made to fear detection for any violations they might be inclined to commit. Probation and parole officers are portrayed as making unannounced contacts with offenders, whom they are monitoring around the clock, ready to take immediate action to prevent any danger to the community. For agencies whose officers are armed and trained in law enforcement, this approach is a natural extension of the services they are already providing.

Agencies in which officers do not have adequate law enforcement training or authority, however, cannot live up to the image of *intensive.* Indeed, agencies that adopt a meaningful form of intensive supervision—one that does indeed increase unannounced face-to-face in field contacts—but fail to equip and train their officers accordingly, place these officers in danger. In Vermont, for example, officers expressed a great deal of concern for their safety since intensive supervision meant frequent unannounced visits by unarmed officers. When I worked as a parole officer in New York, unannounced visits found parolees with firearms left on the dresser, large amounts of heroin and drug paraphernalia on the kitchen table, and other potentially dangerous situations. For protection in Florida, community control officers—specially chosen correctional probation officers—are provided with radios and advised to wear clothing and shoes "suitable for running" [sic].

IPS programs are typically set up outside of the traditional supervision structure: clients and officers are hand picked; the latter receive special training, sometimes salary increases, and report to their own supervisory chain of command. This can impact on general agency morale since the IPS unit receives a disproportionate share of resources and attention. And there is strong pressure on these "special" units to demonstrate results:

> This is one reason why these programs often seem to be encased in an atmosphere of caution—they are very vulnerable to errors. Based on a rationale of effective offender control, and in contrast to seemingly more lenient traditional probation methods, the idea of intensive probation can be seriously damaged by even one publicized incident of serious client failure, such as a violent crime. Therefore, despite the control rhetoric, program officials seem to bend over backwards to avoid the riskiest clients and to resist giving accepted clients many chances to violate probation. (Clear, Flynn, and Shapiro, 1987: 42)

This accounts for the relatively high rate of probation violations in most IPS programs.

In New York, when I was a parole officer, each caseload had some (usually two or three out of about forty-five) cases that were designated "intensive" by the parole board. These cases required at least one face-to-face home visit and at least four in person office visits each month. Cases were subjected to more supervisory review, and there was less latitude—in the event of a technical violation of the rules, such offenders were more likely to be taken into custody and returned to prison. This system avoided the "elitism" that has apparently reared its head in other probation/parole agencies with IPS programs.

ELECTRONICALLY MONITORED HOME CONFINEMENT

The appeal of this method of responding to offenders is easy to understand when we consider that the cost of imprisonment is $10–20,000 per year, and the cost of building a new prison is $50–100,000 per bed. (Unfortunately, as noted by Douglas McDonald, 1989, accurate estimates of the cost of imprisonment and the cost of community supervision, intensive or otherwise, do not exist.) However, startup costs for electronic monitoring are costly—Albuquerque paid $100,000 for its first twenty-five devices. To offset these costs offenders can be required to pay supervision fees or pay for the cost of installing the monitoring telephone, a practice that raises important ethical and legal issues. Should an offender who is otherwise qualified for home confinement be denied access to the program—and thereby face imprisonment—because he or she lacks the ability to pay fees, or does not have a residence? And if the answer is "no," how far should the county or state go in providing a residence and, in some systems, a telephone? The answers will impact on the cost-effectiveness of any electronic home-confinement program. Some firms rent and monitor the equipment, but this can be costly, about seven to ten dollars a day per offender, and this does not include personnel costs involved in responding to signal disruptions or checking to see that the equipment has not been tampered with.

Candidates for electronic home confinement are typically low-risk offenders who, in most jurisdictions, would be candidates for probation. Thus, the program may actually be adding to the cost of supervision without affecting the problem of jail/prison overcrowding. On the other hand, the system is typically used for drunk drivers, and there is criticism that home confinement does not serve as a significant deterrent for a crime that is potentially life-threatening, while leaving the offender in a position to repeat his or her criminal act. And, of course, home confinement is devoid of any rehabilitative dimension: it provides no services to persons who often have extensive social service needs.

Richard Ball, Ronald Huff, and Robert Lilly (1988) found that the electronic surveillance programs they examined have not impacted on jail or prison commitments in any noticeable manner. And they found that the persons selected for EM are typically from social and economic circumstances that, in any event, would predict a positive outcome. The researchers also expressed concern over the impact of such programming on probation/parole officers: "Are these professionals going to see their relationships to offenders change from helping agents to surveillance agents?" (1988: 97). EM has the potential to downgrade the role of p/p officers. Furthermore, there has been no research on the impact of home confinement on the offender's family.

EM has been associated primarily with probation, and there is very little literature on its use in a parole setting. Utah has used continuously signalling EM on a very limited scale to supplement curfew restrictions:

> A parole officer assisted by a correctional technician operates the program according to policies and procedures established for IPS. Staff of a community correctional center in Salt Lake currently monitor the host unit for alarms and play a role in the primary response to an alarm. If the center is unable to verify that an offender is at his/her residence, a parole agent is paged. Parole officers have vehicles and other necessary equipment with which to respond to alarms. Backup is provided by other parole officers in the field or law enforcement. (Bureau of Justice Assistance, 1989: 17)

SHOCK INCARCERATION/BOOT CAMP

Critics of the "shock" approach argue that it has not proven to have any salutary effect on the offender, and (even) short-term imprisonment exposes the offender to the destructive effects of institutionalization, disrupts his or her life in the community, and further stigmatizes the offender for having been imprisoned (National Advisory Commission, 1975). Furthermore, the shock incarceration (SI) inmate is released without having received any additional education or having developed any additional employment skills. There is no doubt that these programs do release strong, healthy, unemployed young men into the community after only a brief term of incarceration. However, in one Oklahoma study, SI graduates returned to prison at a higher rate than other inmates, while a Georgia study found no difference in return rates between SI and regular inmates (Parent, 1989).

Research in Louisiana revealed that there were no differences in post-release new crime arrests for SI inmates and parolees with similar characteristics who served regular sentences (MacKenzie, 1989). In New York, 23 percent of shock parolees were returned to prison within one year of their release, compared to 28 percent of a comparison group (Office of Policy Analysis and Information, 1989).

The boot-camp programs are in place to save prison resources; an offender sent to a shock program avoids long-term incarceration. Of course, this assumes that in the absence of such programming, the offender would have been sent to prison and not placed on probation. In Florida, for example, candidates for SI are selected from among those sentenced to traditional imprisonment, although one study found that they tended to be those who were less serious offenders (Sechrest, 1989). In Georgia, however, SI is used by judges as part of probation sentences. While SI might not meet the needs of rehabilitation and community safety, it appears to meet the short-term needs of political officials who can boast of "doing something" about crime and criminals. Dale Parent found that SI was given to "the very offenders who would likely have been given non-confinement sentences if SI were not available—thus using more, not less, prison space" (1989, 12). This is not the case in New York, where Department of Corrections (DOC) personnel, not judges, have charge of the program:

> New York law defines SI eligibility criteria. NYSDOC screens prison admissions to identify cases that meet these criteria. If inmates pass their physical examinations, they may volunteer to participate. Judges have no veto power. When inmates complete the program, they are released by the Parole Board, not by judges. By consulting New York's parole guidelines, NYSDOC estimates that the average inmate who completes SI will shorten his or her prison term by 12-18 months. (Parent, 1989: 15)

And there is an element of absurdity in the prison-as-boot camp approach, particularly in light of the fact that the military has drastically changed the way it trains recruits, away from abusive or degrading methods. "The very idea of using physically and verbally aggressive tactics in an effort to 'train' people to act in a prosocial manner is fraught with contradiction" (Morash and Rucker, 1990: 214). Such programs run the risk of turning out young men who are more aggressive and hostile than they would have been under routine imprisonment. "The irony in emphasizing an aggressive model of masculinity in a correctional setting is that these very characteristics may explain criminality" (1990: 216).

FELONY PROBATION

Joan Petersilia and her colleagues (1985: v), researchers for the Rand Corporation, note that "over one-third of California's probation population consists of felons convicted in Superior Court—persons who are often quite different from the less serious offenders probation was originally conceived and structured to handle." They found that 51 percent of a sample of California felony probationers who were sentenced in 1980 and tracked for forty months were reconvicted, 18 percent for violent crime. They conclude (1985: vi) that "felons granted probation present a serious threat to public safety" and this threat is not being adequately managed by probation agencies in California (and probably elsewhere).

But research into felony probation in Missouri and Kentucky, revealed a very different outcome. Both studies were designed to replicate that of Petersilia and her colleagues in California to determine whether felony offenders placed on probation in Missouri and Kentucky presented risks similar to those in California. And there significant differences were found (McGaha, Fichter, and Hirschburg, 1987):

	CALIFORNIA	MISSOURI	KENTUCKY
Rearrests	65.0%	22.3%	22.1
Reconvictions	51.0%	12.0%	17.7
Violent Felony	18.0%	7.1	4.1

The results of research into felony probation in New Jersey fell about midway between the findings in California and those in Kentucky and Missouri: four years after they were sentenced to probation, 40 percent had been rearrested, and 35 percent were reconvicted (Whitehead, 1989).

Petersilia, et al. (1985: 64), argue that "routine probation, by definition, is *inappropriate for most felons.*" What, other than imprisonment, is *appropriate* for most felons?

> We believe that the criminal justice system needs an alternative, indeterminate form of punishment for those offenders who are too antisocial for the relative freedom that probation now offers, but not so seriously criminal as to require imprisonment. A sanction is needed that would impose intensive surveillance, coupled with substantial community service and restitution. It should be structured to satisfy public demands that the punishment fit the crime, to show criminals that crime really does not pay, and to control potential recidivists (1985: ix).

The Rand Corporation researchers (1985: xiii) recommend a form of probation which this writer has been advocating since the first edition of this book was published in 1977:

> In response to changes in the probation population, the system should redefine the role and powers of probation officers. Probation officers cannot deal with felony probationers in the same ways they have dealt with misdemeanants. We certainly do not recommend that they abandon their counseling or rehabilitative roles; however, because the probation population includes a large number of active criminals, we support the growing legal and policy trend toward quasi-policing roles for probation officers, whenever the situation warrants it. Attention should be paid to the recruitment and training of probation officers. Different skills may be required of officers whose primary responsibility is surveillance rather than rehabilitation.

PROBATION/PAROLE: SUCCESS OR FAILURE?

The effectiveness of a probation or parole system is usually conceived of in terms of recidivism (Maltz, 1984: 54):

When recidivism is discussed in a correction context, its meaning seems fairly clear. The word is derived from the Latin *recidere,* to fall back. A recidivist is one who, after release from custody for having committed a crime, is not rehabilitated. Instead, he or she falls back, relapses, into former behavior patterns and commits more crimes. This conceptual definition of recidivism may seem quite straightforward; however, an operational definition, one that permits measurement, is not so simple.

The 1976 edition of the *Dictionary of Criminal Justice Data Terminology* defines recidivism as "the repetition of criminal behavior; habitual criminality." However, the 1981 edition avoids providing a definition and, instead, notes:

> Efforts to arrive at a single standard statistical definition of recidivism have been hampered by the fact that the correct referent of the term is the actual repeated criminal or delinquent behavior of a given person or group, yet the only available statistical indicators of that behavior are records of such system events as rearrests, reconvictions, and probation or parole violations or revocations. It is recognized that these data reflect agency decisions about events and do not closely correspond with actual criminal behavior.

Jay Albanese and his colleagues (et al., 1981: 51) point out:

1. There is a wide disparity in the definition of revocation and recidivism.
2. Revocation/recidivism rates without a standardized definition have little comparative value.
3. A criterion (or criteria) of "effectiveness" is not well defined.

Gordon Waldo and David Griswold (1979: 230) point out that being arrested and convicted for any crime is not sufficient as an operational definition of recidivism. They quote Charles Tittle: "Being arrested for gambling cannot be accepted as evidence of recidivism for a burglar." In addition, the extensive use of plea bargaining means that merely looking at the crime for which a person is convicted does not allow for a determination of whether the individual has committed the same crime again, or a less serious or more serious crime. Then there is the problem of technical violations — do we rate them as "recidivism?" There is no consistent definition of recidivism and "one cannot state with any degree of assurance whether a given recidivism rate is high or low; there is no 'normal' recidivism rate as there is a normal body temperature" (Maltz, 1984: 23).

The Goal of Probation and Parole

What is the goal of probation and parole? Success can only be measured against anticipated outcome. If a p/p agency is based on a *service model,* success is measured by the delivery of, or by referral to, services such as education, training, employment, and counseling, and client-consumer satisfaction with the level of service. This type of agency will often be affected by variables beyond its control. For example, a probation agency in Los Angeles, which has a relatively low unemployment rate, will presumably do better at job placement than the same agency in Detroit, which has a relatively high rate of unemployment. Similarly, an agency located in a community with a variety of available social services will be more likely to show a greater level of success than one in a community with a paucity of such agencies.

If a p/p agency is based on a *control model,* success is measured according to the agency's ability to limit recidivism. However, recidivism may also be related to unemployment — and to the extent that it is, the success of this type of agency will be dependent in part on the state of the economy. Recidivism is also related to other practical issues. First, we obviously cannot account for undetected criminality; and second, arrest and prosecution are often a measure of the law enforcement activity in a given community. Thus different levels of law enforcement will produce different levels of official (statistical) recidivism, regardless of p/p agency effectiveness. Indeed, a more effective *control model* agency may enhance the law enforcement function (for example, through close cooperation with the police) and will thus help to *produce* more recidivism — arrests and convictions of agency clientele. David Stanley points out that if we use recidivism as a measure, "An offender can be unemployed, ignorant, promiscuous, and drunk but still a success as far as the criminal justice system is concerned if he commits no crime" (1976: 173). Indeed, a cynic (realist?) might suggest encouraging drug abusers to become alcoholics instead.

Two related issues need to be considered. How are technical violations of p/p rules to be treated (statistically) with respect to agency goals? More vigorous (that is, intensive) supervision may *produce* more technical violations (although the research is still not clear on this issue), whereas an agency that provides little or no supervision will have few (detected) technical violations, hence fewer revocations of p/p. The level of individual and agency tolerance for technical violations will also affect the revocation rate, and a higher revocation rate of technical violations may result in a lower number of convictions — higher-risk offenders screened out of supervision before they can be arrested for new crimes. A second issue concerns the screening of agency clients by judges and parole boards. A conservative judge/parole board, or perhaps one just fearful of an adverse public reaction, will release fewer offenders to probation or parole. Those who are placed on probation or parole will tend to be the "boy scouts" — lower-risk offenders who will probably *produce* impressive (statistical) measurements of success for the agency. The reverse of this situation is also true.

For example, research has identified a number of variables that correlate well with success or failure on probation: age (younger offenders have greater difficulty adhering to probation conditions); employment (those who are employed and financially stable do better); marital status (those who are married are less likely to violate probation); offense (those on probation for theft-related crimes have higher recidivism rates) (Liberton, Silverman, and Blount, 1990).

Since neither the *social service* nor the *control model* agency need make any claim about rehabilitation, the question of postsupervision arrests and convictions need not be raised. In agencies that include rehabilitation as a (or perhaps *the*) goal, this issue will need to be considered. How long does the agency retain (statistical) responsibility for success or failure of a client who has completed supervision — six months, a year, life? The implication is that such an agency will succeed in producing a lasting change in client behavior. An added question is how to weigh recidivism where the instant offense is a great deal less serious than the original crime, for example, an armed robber convicted of shoplifting — success or failure?

Perhaps the most difficult agency to evaluate in terms "success or failure" is one based on a *combined model.* Most p/p agencies in the United States fall into this category. In this type of agency there is usually an explicit or implicit claim relating to service, rehabilitation, *and* control. An agency with such broad purposes — a plethora of complicated goals — cannot *fail,* nor can it *succeed* — it presents no clear-cut basis for measuring anticipated outcome. The claims are too broad, too many, and too dependent on variables beyond agency control (such as the economy, level of law enforcement in the community, screening of offenders by judges/parole boards, availability of resources in the community, and so on) for a research effort to analyze in any relevant manner. As a result, this type of agency has been subjected to criticism on the basis of research that "microscopes" one goal and finds it wanting. The goals are literally picked apart, leaving the agency vulnerable to those who would discredit probation or parole.

Perhaps we should turn to the very reason that probation and parole exist. As penological history in the United States indicates, probation and parole (devoid of the humanistic dynamic) exist for *economic reasons.* If p/p were as costly (in terms of budgetary considerations) as, or even equal in cost to, imprisonment, it would be so severely restricted as no longer to constitute an important issue in criminal justice.

A Direction For Probation and Parole

A viable alternative to imprisonment must provide the maximum level of protection possible within a community setting. This writer envisions a state-wide agency — *Department of Offender Supervision* (DOS) — based on a *control model.* DOS would receive for supervision all persons placed on probation or released from sentences of incarceration via a parole board or conditional release, the total cost of supervision would be borne by the state. Offenders would be supervised by DOS agents whose primary responsibility would be protection of the community. Under this model no pretense is made about rehabilitation. Counseling and other services generally classified as "rehabilita-tive" would be offered to—but not forced upon—the offender. This approach is supported by David Fogel (1984) who argues that a "justice model" for probation should offer help to probationers and, furthermore, those refusing, or not amenable to, rehabilitative efforts should be placed under close surveil-lance.

Risk classification would determine the level of supervision and the rules to which an offender would be required to conform. Very high-risk offenders would be placed under house arrest with electronic surveillance, or encum-bered with severe curfew and travel restrictions. Changes in classification based upon behavior would result in reduced supervision and a modification of the restrictions. Low-risk offenders would be placed on a form of "paper supervision" with only spot checks—unannounced home visits or surveillance. This approach is consistent with the "justice model of probation" which views the surveillance aspects of supervision as punishment—"just deserts" (McAnany, Thompson and Fogel, 1984). DOS agents would be trained and equipped to investigate rule-violative behavior or reversion to criminal activ-ity—in addition to possessing counseling and referral skills. They would be empowered to take offenders into custody if there was evidence of an immedi-ate threat to public safety. Custody might be for only a few days, or in more serious cases, until a preliminary hearing was held as per the *Morrissey* and *Gagnon* decisions.

The effectiveness of the proposed model would be predicated on proba-tion/parole supervision as an economic necessity. Claims of effectiveness, "success," would be restricted to an evaluation of recidivism—return to serious criminal behavior—during the period of supervision. Part of the evaluation would include the role of the DOS agent in providing information that caused an offender to be subjected to prosecution for new criminal activity; technical violations would not be considered—they would constitute a "neutral" case outcome.

The Violent Felony Offender Project, the Bureau of Special Services, and the Absconder Search Unit of the New York Division of Parole provide methodologies and data for implementing the DOS proposal. The California Department of Corrections "High Control Project" (1977–1980) provides ad-ditional methodology and data. (*Investigation and Surveillance in Parole Supervision,* 1981).

The High Control Project was the last of several new programs imple-mented as part of a three-year evaluation effort undertaken by the Department of Corrections to determine more effective ways of running the parole system in the future. The project tested control-oriented models of parole supervision, where specially trained parole agents conducted intensified investigative and surveillance activities on selected high-risk parolees. The objectives of the project were to:

1. Identify those parolees who presented the most serious threat to public safety.
2. Deter those parolees who had not returned to criminal activity but had a high potential for doing so.
3. Increase the frequency and severity of sanctions applied to those parolees verified as having returned to criminal activity.

The high-control model of parole supervision differed from traditional approaches to parole supervision on several dimensions. First, it represented an exclusively control-oriented, as opposed to a service-oriented or mixed approach to supervision. Second, it placed primary emphasis on monitoring parolee activity indirectly through a variety of means (as opposed to direct agent-parolee contact). Third, it targeted a group of parolees selected by agents as being higher-risk cases. Fourth, by using specialist (as opposed to generalist) agents working within a small team of agents (rather than independently), it utilized a different organizational and management structure.

This direction brings with it the danger that probation and parole will become simply offender-monitoring activities devoid of any rehabilitative components; that persons hired to provide this monitoring will not have the education, training, or skills necessary to assist offenders. A balanced approach to probation and parole requires that the goal remain protection of the community, but with the recognition that this is best accomplished by rehabilitating offenders.

REVIEW QUESTIONS

1. What has research into the effectiveness of "intensive supervision" found?
2. What are the shortcomings of shock probation/parole?
3. What are the shortcomings of shock incarceration/boot camp?
4. Why is it difficult to provide a definition of recidivism for statistical purposes?
5. What are the variables over which a probation/parole agency has no control and which can affect case outcome?
6. Why is it so difficult to determine whether probation or parole is a success or failure?

References

(NOTE: Much of the material in this book has been derived from agency sources. See *Acknowledgments* in the frontmatter.)

ABADINSKY, HOWARD
    1975   "Should Parole Officers Make Arrests and Carry Firearms?" *Division of Criminal Justice Services Newsletter* (October).

    1976   "The Status Offense Dilemma: Coercion and Treatment." *Crime and Delinquency* 22 (October).

    1983   *The Criminal Elite: Professional and Organized Crime.* Westport, CT: Greenwood Press.

    1989   *Drug Abuse: An Introduction.* Chicago: Nelson-Hall.

    1990   *Organized Crime,* 3rd ed. Chicago: Nelson-Hall.

    1991   *Law and Justice,* 2nd ed. Chicago: Nelson-Hall.

ADMINISTRATIVE OFFICE OF THE COURTS
    n.d.   *Standards for Community Service Programs in New Jersey.* Trenton: Office of the Courts.

AICHHORN, AUGUST
    1963   *Wayward Youth.* New York: Viking Press.

ALBANESE, JAY S., BERNADETTE A. FIORE, JERIE H. POWELL, AND JANET R. STORTI
    1981   *Is Probation Working?* Washington, DC: University Press of America.

ALEXANDER, FRANZ AND HUGO STAUB
    1956   *The Criminal, the Judge, and the Public.* Glencoe, IL: Free Press.

ALLEN, HARRY, ERIC CARLSON, AND EVALYN PARKS
    1979   *Critical Issues in Probation.* Washington, DC: U.S. Government Printing Office.

AMERICAN BAR ASSOCIATION (ABA)
    1970   *Standards Relating to Probation.* Chicago: ABA.

AMERICAN FRIENDS SERVICE COMMITTEE
    1971   *Struggle For Justice.* New York: Hill and Wang.

AMERICAN JUSTICE INSTITUTE
    1981   *Presentence Investigation Report Program.* Sacramento, CA: American Justice Institute.

AMERICAN PSYCHIATRIC ASSOCIATION
    1974   *Behavior Therapy in Psychiatry.* New York: Jason Aronson.

ANSPACH, DONALD F. AND S. HENRY MONSEN
    1989   "Indeterminate Sentencing, Formal Rationality, and Khadi Justice in Maine: An Application of Weber's Typology." *Journal of Criminal Justice* 17: 471–85.

ARCAYA, JOSE
    1973   "The Multiple Realities Inherent in Probation Counseling." *Federal Probation* 37 (December).

ASHFORD, JOSE B. AND CRAIG WINSTON LeCROY
    1988   "Predicting Recidivism: An Evaluation of the Wisconsin Juvenile Probation and Aftercare Risk Instrument." *Criminal Justice and Behavior* 15 (June): 141–49.

ATHERTON, ALEXINE L.
    1987   "Journal Retrospective, 1845–1986: 200 Years of Prison Society History as Reflected in the *Prison Journal.*" *Prison Journal* (Spring-Summer): 1–37.

ATTICA COMMISSION, *See* New York State Special Commission on Attica.

AUERBACH, BARBARA J., GEORGE E. SEXTON, FRANKLIN C. FARROW, AND ROBERT H. LAWSON
    1988   *Work in American Prisons: The Private Sector Gets Involved.* Washington, DC: U.S. Government Printing Office.

AUGUSTUS, JOHN
    1972   *John Augustus, First Probation Officer.* Montclair, NJ: Patterson Smith.

BAIRD, S. CHRISTOPHER AND DENNIS WAGNER
    1990   "Measuring Diversion: The Florida Community Control Program." *Crime and Delinquency* 36 (January): 112–25.

BAIRD, S. CHRISTOPHER, RICHARD C. HEINZ, AND BRIAN J. BEMUS
    1982   "The Wisconsin Case Classification/Staff Deployment Project: A Two-Year Follow-Up Report," in *Classification: American Correctional Association* Monographs. College Park, MD: American Correctional Association.

BALL, RICHARD A., C. RONALD HUFF, AND J. ROBERT LILLY
    1988   *House Arrest and Correctional Policy: Doing Time at Home.* Beverly Hills, CA: Sage.

BANDURA, ALBERT
    1974   "Behavior Theory and the Models of Man." *American Psychologist* 29 (December).

BARNES, CAROLE WOLFF AND RANDAL S. FRANZ
    1989   "Questionably Adult: Determinants and Effects of the Juvenile Waiver Decision." *Justice Quarterly* 6 (March): 117–35.

BEAUMONT, GUSTAVE DE AND ALEXIS DE TOCQUEVILLE
    1964   *On the Penitentiary System in the United States and Its Application in France.* Carbondale, IL: Southern Illinois University Press. Originally published in 1833.

BENNETT, LAWRENCE A.
1988 "Practice in Search of Theory: The Case of Intensive Supervision—An Extension of an Old Practice." *American Journal of Criminal Justice* 12: 293–310.

BERK, RICHARD A., KENNETH J. LENIHAN, AND PETER ROSSI
1980 "Crime and Poverty: Some Experimental Evidence From Ex-Offenders." *American Sociological Review* 45 (October).

BERSANI, CARL A.
1989 "Reality Therapy: Issues and a Review of Research." Pages 177–95 in *Correctional Counseling and Treatment,* 2nd Ed., edited by Peter C. Kratcoski. Prospect Heights, IL: Waveland Press.

"B.F. SKINNER INSISTS IT'S JUST MATTER OVER MIND."
1987 *New York Times* (September 13): E6.

BISHOP, DONNA M., CHARLES F. FRAZIER, AND JOHN C. HENRETTA
1989 "Prosecutorial Waiver: Case Study of a Questionable Reform." *Crime and Delinquency* 35 (April): 179–201.

BLUMBERG, ABRAHAM
1970 *Criminal Justice.* Chicago: Quadrangle Books.

BLUMENSTEIN, ALFRED
1984 "Sentencing Reforms: Impacts and Implications." *Judicature* 68 (October-November).

BOHLEN, CELESTINE
1989 "Expansion Sought for 'Shock' Prison." *New York Times* (June 8): 14.

BOOTZIN, RICHARD R.
1975 *Behavior Modification and Therapy: An Introduction.* Cambridge, MA: Winthrop Publishers.

BOSWELL, JOHN
1989 *The Kindness of Strangers: The Abandonment of Children in Western Europe From Antiquity to the Renaissance.* New York: Pantheon.

BOWERS, SWITHUN
1950 "The Nature and Definition of Social Casework." Pages 97–127 in *Principles and Techniques in Social Casework: Selected Articles, 1940–1950,* edited by Cora Kasius. New York: Family Service Association of America.

BRENNAN, THOMAS P., AMY E. GEDRICH, SUSAN E. JACOBY, MICHAEL J. TARDY, AND KATHERINE B. TYSON
1986 "Forensic Social Work: Practice and Vision." *Social Casework* 67: 340–50.

BROWN, ALLAN G.
1986 *Group Work,* 2nd ed. Brookfield, VT: Gower.

BROWN, MARJORIE
1984 *Executive Summary of Research Findings from the Massachusetts Risk/Need Classification System, Report 5.* Boston: Office of the Commission of Probation.

BUCK, GERALD S.
1989 "Effectiveness of the New Intensive Supervision Programs." *Research in Corrections* 2 (September): 64–75.

BUREAU OF JUSTICE ASSISTANCE
1989 *Electronic Monitoring in Intensive Probation and Parole Programs.* Washington, DC: U.S. Government Printing Office.

BURGESS, ROBERT L. AND RONALD L. AKERS
  1969   "Differential Association-Reinforcement Theory of Criminal Behavior," in *Behavioral Sociology,* edited by Robert L. Burgess and Don Bushell, Jr. New York: Columbia University Press.

BURKE, PEGGY B.
  1988   *Current Issues in Parole Decisionmaking: Understanding the Past; Shaping the Future.* Washington, DC: National Institute of Corrections.

BYRNE, JAMES M.
  1990   "The Future of Intensive Probation Supervision and the New Intermediate Sanction." *Crime and Delinquency* 36 (January): 6–41.

BYRNE, JAMES M. AND LINDA KELLY
  1989   "Restructuring Probation as an Intermediate Sanction: An Evaluation of the Massachusetts Intensive Supervision Program." Final report to the National Institute of Justice Research Program on the Punishment and Control of Offenders.

BYRNE, JAMES M., ARTHUR J. LURIGIO, S. CHRISTOPHER BAIRD
  1989   "The Effectiveness of New Intensive Probation Supervision Programs." *Research in Corrections* 2 (September): 1–48.

CAHALAN, MARGARET WERNER
  1986   *Historical Corrections Statistics in the United States, 1850–1984.* Washington, DC: U.S. Government Printing Office.

CARLSON, ERIC AND EVALYN PARKS
  1979   *Critical Issues in Adult Probation: Issues in Probation Management.* Washington, DC: U.S. Government Printing Office.

CARTER, ROBERT M.
  1966   "It Is Respectfully Recommended . . ." *Federal Probation* 30 (June).

  1978   *Presentence Report Handbook.* Washington, DC: U.S. Government Printing Office.

CARTER, STEPHEN A. AND ANN CHADWELL HUMPHRIES
  1987   *Inmates Build Prisons in South Carolina.* Washington, DC: National Institute of Justice.

CHAMPION, DEAN J.
  1988   "Felony Plea Bargaining and Probation: A Growing Judicial and Prosecutorial Dilemma." *Journal of Criminal Justice* 16: 291–301.

  1988b   *Felony Probation: Problems and Prospects.* New York: Praeger.

CHAPIN, BRADLEY
  1983   *Criminal Justice in Colonial America: 1600–1660.* Athens, GA: University of Georgia Press.

CHARLES, MICHAEL T.
  1989   "Electronic Monitoring For Juveniles." *Journal of Crime and Justice.* 12: 147–69.

CHESNEY, STEVEN L.
  n.d.   "The Assessment of Restitution in the Minnesota Probation Services," in *Restitution in Criminal Justice,* edited by Joe Hudson. St. Paul, MN: Minnesota Department of Corrections.

CHESNEY-LIND, MEDA
  1988   "Girls in Jail." *Crime and Delinquency* 34 (April): 150–68.

CHODOROW, NANCY J.
  1990   *Feminism and Psychoanalytic Theory.* New Haven, CT: Yale University Press.

CITIZEN'S INQUIRY ON PAROLE AND CRIMINAL JUSTICE
1973   *Survey Report on New York State Parole.* New York: Citizen's Inquiry.

CLARKE, STEVENS H., YUAN-HUEI W. LIN, AND W. LEANN WALLACE
1988   *Probationer Recidivism in North Carolina: Measurement and Classification of Risk.* Chapel Hill, NC: University of North Carolina Institute of Government.

CLEAR, TODD R.
1988   "Statistical Prediction in Corrections." *Research in Corrections* 1 (March): 1–39.

CLEAR, TODD R. AND EDWARD J. LATTESA
1989   "Intensive Supervision: Surveillance Vs. Treatment." Paper presented at the annual meeting of the Academy of Criminal Justice Sciences, Washington, DC, March 30.

CLEAR, TODD R. AND PATRICIA R. HARDYMAN
1990   "The New Intensive Supervision Movement." *Crime and Delinquency* 36 (January): 42–60.

CLEAR, TODD R., SUZANNE FLYNN, AND CAROL SHAPIRO
1987   "Intensive Supervision in Probation: A Comparison of Three Projects." Pages 31–50 in *Intermediate Punishments: Intensive Supervision, Home Confinement and Electronic Surveillance,* edited by Belinda R. McCarthy. Monsey, NY: Criminal Justice Press.

CLEMMER, DONALD
1958   *The Prison Community.* New York: Holt, Rinehart and Winston.

CLINARD, MARSHALL B., ED.
1964   *Anomie and Deviant Behavior.* New York: Free Press.

CLINARD, MARSHALL B., PETER C. YEAGER, JEANNE BRISSETTE, DAVID PETRASHEK AND ELIZABETH HARRIES
1979   *Illegal Corporate Behavior.* Washington, DC: U.S. Government Printing Office.

CLOWARD, RICHARD A. AND LLOYD E. OHLIN
1960   *Delinquency and Opportunity.* New York: Free Press.

COHEN, ALBERT K.
1965   *Delinquent Boys.* New York: Free Press.

COHEN, HAROLD L. AND JAMES FILIPCZAK
1971   *A New Learning Environment.* San Francisco: Jossey-Bass.

COLLIER, WALTER V.
1980   *Summary of First Year Evaluation of the Special Parole Supervision for Violent Felony Offenders.* Albany: New York State Division of Parole.

COMPTROLLER GENERAL OF THE UNITED STATES
1979   *Correctional Institutions Can Do More to Improve the Employability of Offenders.* Washington, DC: U.S. Government Printing Office.

CONRAD, JOHN P.
1985   *The Dangerous and the Endangered.* Lexington, MA: D.C. Heath.

COOPER, IRVING BEN
1977   *"United States v. Unterman:* The Role of Counsel at Sentencing." *Criminal Law Bulletin* 13.

COOPRIDER, KEITH W. AND JUDITH KERBY
1990   "A Practical Application of Electronic Monitoring at the Pretrial Stage." *Federal Probation* 54 (March): 28–35.

COVEY, HERBERT C. AND MARY MANDE
1985   "Determinate Sentencing in Colorado." *Justice Quarterly* 2 (June).

CRAWFORD, WILLIAM B., JR.
1988   "Inmates Suing Over Gangs Lose Case." *Chicago Tribune* (March 8): Section 2: 3.

CRESSEY, DONALD R.
1955   "Changing Criminals: The Application of the Theory of Differential Association." *American Journal of Sociology* 61 (September): 116–20.

CRIPE, CLAIRE A.
1977   "Religious Freedom in Prisons." *Federal Probation* 41 (March).

CROMWELL, PAUL F., JR.
1978   "The Halfway House and Offender Reintegration," in *Corrections in the Community,* 2nd ed., edited by George C. Killinger and Paul F. Cromwell, Jr. St. Paul, MN: West.

CROMWELL, PAUL F., JR., GEORGE C. KILLINGER, HAZEL B. KERPER, AND CHARLS WALKER
1985   *Probation and Parole in the Criminal Justice System.* 2nd ed. St. Paul, MN: West.

CULLEN, FRANCIS T. AND KAREN E. GILBERT
1982   *Reaffirming Rehabilitation.* Cincinnati: Anderson.

CURRAN, DANIEL J.
1988   "Destructuring Privatization and the Promise of Juvenile Diversion: Compromising Community-Based Corrections." *Crime and Delinquency* 34 (October): 363–78.

CZAJKOSKI, EUGENE H.
1973   "Exposing the Quasi-Judicial Role of the Probation Officer." *Federal Probation* 37 (September).

DARROW, CLARENCE
1975   *Address to the Prisoners in the Cook County Jail,* 1902. Chicago: Charles H. Kerr.

DAVIDOFF-KROOP, JOY
1983   *An Initial Assessment of the Division of Parole's Employment Services.* Albany: New York State Division of Parole.

DAWSON, ROBERT O.
1969   *Sentencing.* Boston: Little, Brown.

1983   *Texas Adult Probation Law Manual and Supplement.* Austin: Texas Adult Probation Commission.

DEL CARMEN, ROLANDO V.
1985   "Legal Issues and Liabilities in Community Corrections." Pages 47–70 in *Probation, Parole, and Community Corrections: A Reader,* edited by Lawrence F. Travis III. Prospect Heights, IL: Waveland Press.

DEL CARMEN, ROLANDO V. AND PAUL T. LOUIS
1988   *Civil Liabilities of Parole Personnel for Release, Non-Release, Supervision, and Revocation.* Washington, DC: National Institute of Corrections.

DELL'APPA, FRANK W., TOM ADAMS, JAMES D. JORGENSEN, AND HERBERT R. SIGURDSON
1976   "Advisory, Brokerage, Community: The ABC's of Probation and Parole." *Federal Probation* 40 (March).

DEPARTMENT OF CORRECTIONAL SERVICES
1970   *Corrections in New York State.* Albany: Department of Correctional Services.

DICKEY, WALTER
1979   "The Lawyer and the Accuracy of Presentence Report." *Federal Probation* 43 (June).

DIETRICH, SHELLE
1979   "The Probation Officer as Therapist: Examination of Three Major Problem Areas." *Federal Probation* 43 (June).

DIVISION OF PAROLE OF THE STATE OF NEW YORK
1984   *1982-83 Annual Report.* Albany: Division of Parole.

DIVISION OF PROBATION
1974   "The Selective Presentence Investigation." *Federal Probation* 38 (December).

DODGE, CALVIN
1975   *A Nation Without Prisons.* Lexington, MA: D.C. Heath.

DOLAN, EDWARD J., RICHARD LUNDEN, AND ROSEMARY BARBERET
1987   "Prison Behavior and Parole Outcome in Massachusetts." Paper presented at the annual meeting of the American Society of Criminology, November 11-14, Montreal.

DOOM, ANDREW E., CONNIE M. ROERICH, AND THOMAS H. ZOEY
1988   "Sentencing Guidelines in Minnesota: The View From the Trenches." *Federal Probation* 52 (December): 34-38.

DRESSLER, DAVID
1951   *Parole Chief.* New York: Viking.

1989   "Drug Offenders Push Population Estimates Higher" *Illinois Department of Corrections Perspectives* 12 (August): 5.

DUMM, THOMAS L.
1987   *Democracy and Punishment: Disciplinary Origins of the United States.* Madison, WI: University of Wisconsin Press.

DURHAM, ALEXIS M., III
1989   "Origins of Interest in the Privatization of Punishment: The Nineteenth and Twentieth Century American Experience." *Criminology* 27 (February): 107-139.

1989b   "Rehabilitation and Correctional Privatization: Observation on the 19th Century Experience and Implications for Modern Corrections." *Federal Probation* 53 (March): 43-52.

1989c   "Newgate of Connecticut: Origins and Early Days of an Early American Prison." *Justice Quarterly* 6 (March): 89-116.

DURKHEIM, EMILE
1951   *Suicide.* New York: Free Press.

1966   *The Rules of the Sociological Method.* New York. Free Press.

EDMUNDS, PALMER D.
1959   *Law and Civilization.* Washington, DC: Public Affairs Press.

EMPEY, LAMAR T., ED.
1979   *Juvenile Justice: The Progressive Legacy and Current Reforms.* Charlottesville VA: University Press of Virginia.

EREZ, EDNA
1990   "Victim Participation in Sentencing: Rhetoric and Reality. *Journal of Criminal Justice* 18: 19-31.

ERIKKSON, TORSTEN
 1976 *The Reformers: An Historical Survey of Pioneer Experiments in the Treatment of Criminals.* New York: Elsevier.

ERWIN, BILLIE S.
 1984 *Evaluation of Intensive Supervision in Georgia.* Atlanta: Georgia Department of Offender Rehabilitation.

ERWIN, BILLIE S. AND LAWRENCE A. BENNETT
 1987 *New Dimensions in Probation: Georgia's Experience with Intensive Probation Supervision.* Washington, DC: National Institute of Justice.

ESKRIDGE, CHRIS W. AND ERIC W. CARLSON
 1979 "The Use of Volunteers in Probation: A National Synthesis." *Journal of Offender Counseling Services and Rehabilitation* 4 (Winter).

FABRICANT, MICHAEL
 1983 *Juveniles in the Family Courts.* Lexington, MA: D.C. Heath.

FALK, GERHARD
 1966 "The Psychoanalytic Theories of Crime Causation." *Criminologica* 4 (May).

FALLEN, DAVID L., CRAIG D. APPERSON, JOAN HALL-MILLIGAN, AND STEVEN AOS
 1981 *Intensive Parole Supervision.* Olympia, WA: Washington Department of Social and Health Services.

FEELEY, MALCOLM M.
 1979 *The Process is Punishment: Handling Cases in a Lower Court.* New York: Russell Sage Foundation.

FELD, BARRY C.
 1988 "In Re Gault Revisted: A Cross-State Comparison of the Right to Counsel in Juvenile Court." *Crime and Delinquency* 34 (October): 393–424.

FEMALE OFFENDER RESOURCE CENTER
 1979 *Little Sisters and the Law.* Washington, DC: U.S. Government Printing Office.

FINKENAUER, JAMES O.
 1984 *Juvenile Delinquency and Corrections: The Gap Between Theory and Practice.* New York: Academic Press.

FOGEL, DAVID
 1975 *We Are the Living Proof.* Cincinnati: Anderson.

 1984 "The Emergence of Probation as a Profession in the Service of Public Safety: The Next Ten Years," in *Probation and Justice: Reconsideration of Mission,* edited by Patrick D. McAnany, Doug Thompson and David Fogel. Cambridge, MA: Oelgeschlager, Gunn and Hain.

FONG, ROBERT S.
 1990 "The Organizational Structure of Prison Gangs: A Texas Case Study." *Federal Probation* 54 (March): 36–43.

FORD, DANIEL AND ANNESLEY K. SCHMIDT
 1985 *Electronically Monitored Home Confinement.* Washington, DC: National Institute of Justice.

FOX, VERNON
 1977 *Community-Based Corrections.* Englewood Cliffs, NJ: Prentice-Hall.

FREUD, SIGMUND
 1933 *New Introductory Lectures on Psychoanalysis.* New York: Norton.

FRIEDLANDER, KATE
1947   *The Psychoanalytic Approach to Juvenile Delinquency.* New York: International Universities Press.

FRIEDLANDER, WALTER A.
1958   *Concepts and Methods of Social Work.* Englewood Cliffs, NJ: Prentice-Hall.

FRIEDMAN, LAWRENCE M.
1973   *A History of American Law.* New York: Simon and Schuster.

GAYLIN, WILLARD
1974   *Partial Justice: A Study of Bias in Sentencing.* New York: Knopf.

GENDREAU, PAUL AND ROBERT R. ROSS
1987   "Revivification of Rehabilitation: Evidence From the 1980s." *Justice Quarterly* 4 (September): 350–407.

GILLIN, JOHN T.
1931   *Taming the Criminal.* New York: Macmillan.

GLASER, DANIEL
1969   *The Effectiveness of a Prison and Parole System.* Indianapolis: Bobbs-Merrill.

GLASSER, WILLIAM
1975   *Reality Therapy.* New York: Harper and Row.

1976   *The Identity Society.* New York: Harper and Row.

1980   "Reality Therapy: An Explanation of the Steps of Reality Therapy," in *What Are You Doing? How People Are Helped Through Reality Therapy,* edited by Namoi Glasser. New York: Harper and Row.

GLUECK, SHELDON, ED.
1933   *Probation and Criminal Justice.* New York: Macmillan.

GOETTING, VICTOR L.
1974   "Some Pragmatic Aspects of Opening a Halfway House." *Federal Probation* 38 (December).

GOFFMAN, ERVING
1961   *Asylums: Essays on the Social Situation of Mental Patients and Other Inmates.* Garden City, NY: Doubleday.

GOLEMAN, DANIEL
1987   "Embattled Giant of Psychology Speaks His Mind." *New York Times* (August 25): 17, 18.

GOODSTEIN, LYNNE AND JOHN HEPBURN
1985   *Determinate Sentencing and Imprisonment: A Failure of Reform.* Cincinatti: Anderson.

GOTTFREDSON, DONALD M., JAMES D. FINKENHAUER, JOHN J. GIBBS, AND CAROL RAUH
1980   *The Improved Correctional Field Services Project: Final Report.* Newark, NJ: Rutgers University School of Criminal Justice.

GREENBERG, DAVID F.
1975   "Problems in Community Corrections." *Issues in Criminology* 10 (Spring).

GREENBERG, DAVID F. AND DREW HUMPHRIES
1980   "The Cooptation of Fixed Sentencing Reform." *Crime and Delinquency* 26 (April).

GREENBERG, JAY R. AND STEPHEN A. MITCHELL
1983 *Object Relations in Psychoanalytic Theory.* Cambridge, MA: Harvard University Press.

GRIGGS, BERTRAM S. AND GARY R. McCUNE
1972 "Community-Based Correctional Programs: A Survey and Analysis." *Federal Probation* 36 (June).

GRISWOLD, DAVID B.
1989 "Florida's Sentencing Guidelines: Six Years Later." *Federal Probation* 53 (December): 46–50.

GROGGER, JEFFREY
1989 *Employment and Crime.* Sacramento, CA: Bureau of Criminal Statistics and Special Services.

HAGERTY, J.E.
1934 *Twentieth Century Crime, Eighteenth Century Methods of Control.* Boston: Stratford.

HAHN, PAUL H.
1976 *Community Based Corrections and the Criminal Justice System.* Santa Cruz, CA: Davis.

HALL, ANDY
1987 *Systemwide Strategies to Alleviate Jail Crowding.* Washington, DC: National Institute of Justice.

HALL, JEROME
1952 *Theft, Law and Society.* Indianapolis: Bobbs-Merrill.

HAMILTON, GORDON
1967 *Theory and Practice of Social Casework.* New York: Columbia University Press.

HAMMETT, THEODORE M.
1989 *1988 Update: AIDS in Correctional Facilities.* Washington, DC: U.S. Government Printing Office.

HAMPARIAN, DONNA M., LINDA K. ESTEP, SUSAN M. MUNTEAN, RAMON R. PRESTINO, ROBERT G. SWISHER, PAUL L. WALLACE, AND JOSEPH L. WHITE
1982 *Youth in Adult Courts: Between Two Worlds.* Columbus, OH: Academy for Contemporary Problems.

HARDMAN, DALE G.
1960 "Constructive Use of Authority." *Crime and Delinquency* 6 (July).

HARRIS, GEORGE A. AND DAVID WATKINS
1987 *Counseling the Involuntary and Resistant Client.* College Park, MD: American Correctional Association.

HARRIS, PATRICIA M. AND LISA GRAFF
1988 "A Critique of Juvenile Sentence Reform." *Federal Probation* 52 (September): 66–71.

HASENFIELD, YEHESKEL
1987 "Power in Social Work Practice." *Social Service Review* 61 (September):469–83.

HAWAII PAROLING AUTHORITY
1987 *Annual Report.* Honolulu.

HEALY, WILLIAM, AUGUSTA F. BRONNER, AND ANNA MAE BOWERS
1930 *The Structure and Meaning of Psychoanalysis.* New York: Knopf.

HILTS, PHILIP J.
1974 *Behavior Mod.* New York: Harpers Magazine Press.

HIRSCHI, TRAVIS
1969   *Causes of Delinquency.* Berkeley: University of California Press.

HOLLIN, CLIVE R.
1990   *Cognitive-Behavioral Interventions With Young Offenders.* New York: Pergamon.

HOLLIS, FLORENCE
1950   "The Techniques of Casework." Pages 412–26 in *Principles and Techniques of Social Casework: Selected Articles, 1940–1950,* edited by Cora Kasius. New York: Family Service Association of America.

HUGHES, ROBERT
1987   *The Fatal Shore: The Epic of Australia's Founding.* New York: Knopf.

HUNT, DANA ESER, WITH SAIRA MOINI, AND SUSAN McWHAN
1989   *AIDS in Probation and Parole.* Washington, DC: U.S. Government Printing Office.

HUNT, JAMES W., JAMES E. BOWERS, AND NEAL MILLER
1974   *Law, Licenses and the Offender's Right to Work.* Washington, DC: American Bar Association.

HUTCHINSON, ELIZABETH D.
1987   "Use of Authority in Direct Social Work Practice With Mandated Clients." *Social Service Review* 61 (December): 581–98.

IGNATIEFF, MICHAEL
1978   *A Just Measure of Pain: The Penitentiary in the Industrial Revolution.* New York: Pantheon.

INFORMATION FOR VICTIMS AND WITNESSES OF JUVENILE CRIME
1984   Las Vegas: Clark County Juvenile Court.

INVESTIGATION AND SURVEILLANCE IN PAROLE SUPERVISION: AN EVALUATION OF THE HIGH CONTROL PROJECT, RESEARCH REPORT NO. 63.
1981   Sacramento: California Department of Corrections.

IRWIN, JOHN
1980   *Prisons in Turmoil.* Boston, Little, Brown.

JACOBS, JAMES B.
1980   "The Prisoners' Rights Movement and Its Impacts, 1960–1980." Pages 429–70 in *Crime and Justice: Volume 2,* edited by Norval Morris and Michael Tonry. Chicago: University of Chicago Press.

JEFFREY, C. RAY
1971   *Crime Prevention Through Environmental Design.* Beverly Hills, CA: Sage.

JOHNSON, KIRK
1989   "U.S. Sues Town Over Rights of Retarded." *New York Times* (June 27): 7.
1989b   "Long Terms Hit Barrier in Connecticut: Early Releases by Crowded Jails." *New York Times* (July 25): 24.

JONES, JUSTIN AND CAROL ROBINSON
1989   "Keeping the Piece: Probation and Parole Officers' Right to Bear Arms." *Corrections Today* (February): 88, 90.

KANFER, FREDERICK H.
1975   "Self-Management Methods." Pages 309–356 in *Helping People Change: A Textbook of Methods,* edited by Frederick H. Kanfer and Arnold P. Goldstein. New York: Pergamon.

KANFER, FREDERICK H. AND ARNOLD P. GOLDSTEIN.
1975   "Introduction." Pages 1–14 in *Helping People Change: A Textbook of Methods,* edited by Frederick H. Kanfer and Arnold P. Goldstein. New York: Pergamon.

KASIUS, CORA, ED.
 1950   *Principles and Techniques in Social Casework.* New York: Family Service Association of America.

KELMAN, MARK
 1987   *A Guide to Critical Legal Studies.* Cambridge, MA: Harvard University Press.

KENNEDY, THOMAS D.
 1988   "Determinate Sentencing: Real or Symbolic Effects?" *Crime and Justice* 11: 1–42.

KEVE, PAUL
 1979   "No Farewell to Arms." *Crime and Delinquency* 25 (October).

KINGSNORTH, RODNEY AND LOUIS RIZZO
 1979   "Decision-Making in the Criminal Court: Continuities and Discontinuities." *Criminology* 17 (May).

KLEINIG, JOHN AND CHARLES LINDNER
 1989   "AIDS on Parole: Dilemma in Decision Making." *Criminal Justice Policy Review* 3 (March): 1–27.

KOLBERT, ELIZABETH
 1989   "Court Awards $1.3 Million to Inmates Injured at Attica. *New York Times* (October 26): 14.

KONOPKA, GISELA
 1983   *Social Group Work: A Helping Process,* 3rd ed. Englewood Cliffs, NJ: Prentice-Hall.

KRAJICK, KEVIN
 1978   "Parole: Discretion is Out, Guidelines Are In." *Corrections Magazine* 4 (December).
 1979   "The Quality of Mercy." *Corrections Magazine* 5 (June).

KRAUTH, BARBARA
 1987   "Parole: Controversial Component of the Criminal Justice System." Pages 51–57 in *Observations on Parole: A Collection of Readings From Western Europe, Canada and the United States,* edited by Edward E. Rhine and Ronald W. Jackson. Washington, DC: U.S. Government Printing Office.

KRISBERG, BARRY
 1988   *The Juvenile Court: Reclaiming the Vision.* San Francisco: National Council on Crime and Delinquency.

KUTCHER, JUDD D.
 1977   "The Legal Responsibility of Probation Officers in Supervision." *Federal Probation* 41 (March).

LAGOY, STEPHEN P., FREDERICK A. HUSSEY, AND JOHN H. KRAMER
 1978   "A Comparative Assessment of Determinate Sentencing Structures." *Crime and Delinquency* 24 (October).

LARKINS, NORM
 1972   "Presentence Investigation Report Disclosure in Alberta." *Federal Probation* 36 (December).

LATESSA, EDWARD J. AND GENNARO F. VITO
 1988   "The Effects of Intensive Supervision on Shock Probationers." *Journal of Criminal Justice* 16: 319–30.

LAW ENFORCEMENT ASSISTANCE ADMINISTRATION
 1973   *Reintegration of the Offender Into the Community.* Washington, DC: U.S. Government Printing Office.

LEARNER, MARK JAY
1977 "The Effectiveness of a Definite Sentence Parole Program." *Criminology* 15 (August).

LEFCOURT, ROBERT, ED.
1971 *Law Against the People.* New York: Random House.

LEMERT, EDWIN M.
1951 *Social Pathology.* New York: McGraw-Hill.

LENROOT, KATHERINE F. AND EMMA O. LUNDBERG
1925 *Juvenile Courts at Work.* Washington, DC: U.S. Government Printing Office.

LEWIS, W. DAVID
1965 *From Newgate to Dannemora.* Ithaca, NY: Cornell University Press.

LIBERTON, MICHAEL, MITCHELL SILVERMAN, AND WILLIAM R. BLOUNT
1990 "An Analysis Used to Predict Success of First-Time Offenders While Under Probation Supervision." Paper presented at the annual meeting of the Academy of Criminal Justice Sciences, Denver, April.

LILLY, J. ROBERT AND RICHARD A. BALL
1987 "A Brief History of House Arrest and Electronic Monitoring." *Northern Kentucky Law Review* 13: 343–74.

LINDER, CHARLES AND MARGARET R. SAVARESE
1984 "The Evolution of Probation." *Federal Probation* 48 (December).

LIPTON, DOUGLAS, ROBERT MARTINSON, AND JUDITH WILKS
1975 *The Effectiveness of Correctional Treatment: A Survey of Treatment Evaluation Studies.* New York: Praeger.

LOMBROSO, CESARE
1968 *Crime: Its Causes and Remedies.* Montclair, NJ: Patterson Smith. Originally published in 1911.

LONDON, PERRY
1964 *The Modes and Morals of Psychotherapy.* New York: Holt, Rinehart and Winston.

LOU, HERBERT H.
1972 *Juvenile Courts in the United States.* New York: Arno Press. Originally published in 1925.

MACKENZIE, DORIS LAYTON
1989 "The Parole Performance of Offenders Released From Shock Incarceration (Boot Camp Prisons): A Survival Time Analysis." Paper presented at the Annual Training Institute of the American Probation and Parole Association, Milwaukee, August.

MACNAMARA, DONAL E.J.
1977 "The Medical Model in Corrections: Requiescat in Pace." *Criminology* 14 (February).

MAESTRO, MARCELLO
1973 *Cesare Beccaria and the Origins of Penal Reform.* Philadelphia: Temple University Press.

MALCOLM, ANDREW H.
1989 "Florida's Jammed Prisons: More in Means More Out." *New York Times* (July 3): 1, 7.

1989b "More and More, Prison is America's Answer to Crime." *New York Times* (November 26): E1, 4.

1989c   "Explosive Drug Use in Prisons Is Creating a New Underworld." *New York Times* (December 30): 1, 10.

MALTZ, MICHAEL D.
1984   *Recidivism.* Orlando, FL: Academic Press.

MANDE, MARY
1987   *Getting Tough on Crime in Colorado.* Denver: Colorado Division of Criminal Justice.

MANGRUM, CLAUDE
1972   "The Humanity of Probation Officers." *Federal Probation* 36 (June).

MANN, DALE
1976   *Intervening With Convicted Serious Juvenile Offenders.* Washington, DC: U.S. Government Printing Office.

MARSHALL, FRANKLIN H.
1989   "Diversion and Probation Under the New Sentencing Guidelines: One Officer's Observations." Paper presented at the annual meeting of the Academy of Criminal Justice Sciences, Washington, DC, March 30.

MARTIN, DOUGLAS
1988   "New York Tests Inmates' Boot Camp." *New York Times* (March 4): 15.

MARTINSON, ROBERT
1974   "What Works? — Questions and Answers About Prison Reform." *The Public Interest* 35 (Spring).

MARTINSON, ROBERT AND JUDITH WILKS
1975   "A Static-Descriptive Model of Field Supervision." *Criminology* 13 (May).

MATZA, DAVID
1964   *Delinquency and Drift.* New York: Wiley.

MCANANY, PATRICK D., DOUG THOMPSON, AND DAVID FOGEL, EDS.
1984   *Probation and Justice: Reconsideration of a Mission.* Cambridge, MA: Oelgeschlager, Gunn and Hain.

MCCARTHY, BELINDA R.
1987   "Introduction." Pages 1–12 in *Intermediate Punishments: Intensive Supervision, Home Confinement and Electronic Surveillance,* edited by Belinda R. McCarthy. Monsey, NY: Criminal Justice Press.

MCCARTHY, BELINDA ROGERS AND BERNARD J. MCCARTHY
1984   *Community-Based Corrections.* Monterey, CA: Brooks/Cole.

MCDONALD, DOUGLAS C.
1989   "The Cost of Corrections: In Search of the Bottom Line." *Research in Corrections* 2 (February): 1–25.

1988   *Restitution and Community Service.* Washington, DC: National Institute of Justice.

MCGAHA, JOHNNY, MICHAEL FICHTER, AND PETER HIRSCHBURG
1987   "Felony Probation: A Re-Examination of Public Risk." *American Journal of Criminal Justice* 11: 1–9.

MCKELVEY, BLAKE
1972   *American Prisons: A Study in American Social History Prior to 1815.* Montclair, NJ: Patterson Smith.

1977   *American Prisons: A History of Good Intentions.* Montclair, NJ: Patterson Smith.

MCSHANE, MARILYN D. AND FRANK P. WILLIAMS III
1989   "The Prison Adjustment of Juvenile Offenders." *Crime and Delinquency* 35 (April): 254–69.

MELOSSI, DARIO AND MASSIMO PAVARINI
1981   *The Prison and the Factory: Origins of the Penitentiary System.* Totowa, NJ: Barnes and Noble.

MENNEL, ROBERT M.
1973   *Thorns and Thistles: Juvenile Delinquents in the United States, 1825–1940.* Hanover, NH: University Press of New England.

MERTON, ROBERT K.
1938   "Social Structure and Anomie." *American Sociological Review* 3.

1964   "Anomie, Anomia, and Social Interaction," in *Anomie and Deviant Behavior,* edited by Marshall B. Clinard. New York. Free Press.

MILLER, WALTER B.
1958   "Lower Class Culture as a Generating Milieu of Gang Delinquency." *Journal of Social Issues* 14.

MOHLER, HENRY CALVIN
1925   "Convict Labor Policies." *Journal of Criminal Law, Criminology and Police Science:* 15: 530–97.

MOORE, KATHLEEN DEAN
1989   *Pardons: Justice, Mercy, and the Public Interest.* New York: Oxford University Press.

MORASH, MERRY AND LILA RUCKER
1990   "A Critical Look at the Idea of Boot Camp as a Correctional Reform." *Crime and Delinquency* 36 (April): 204–22.

MULLANEY, FAHY G.
1988   *Economic Sanctions in Community Corrections.* Washington, DC: National Institute of Corrections.

MULLEN, JOAN
1974   *The Dilemma of Diversion.* Washington, DC: U.S. Government Printing Office.

1985   "Corrections and the Private Sector." *NIJ Reports* (May).

NADER, RALPH
1985   "America's Crime Without Criminals." *New York Times* (May 19): F3.

NATIONAL ADVISORY COMMISSION ON CRIMINAL JUSTICE STANDARDS AND GOALS
1973   *Corrections.* Washington, DC: U.S. Government Printing Office.

1975   *A National Strategy to Reduce Crime.* New York: Avon.

NATIONAL COMMISSION ON LAW OBSERVANCE AND LAW ENFORCEMENT
1931   *Report on Penal Institutions.* Washington, DC: U.S. Government Printing Office.

NATIONAL GOVERNORS' ASSOCIATION
1988   *Guide to Executive Clemency Among the American States.* Washington, DC: National Institute of Corrections.

NEITHERCUTT, MICHAEL G. AND DONALD M. GOTTFREDSON
1974   *Caseload Size Variation and Differences in Probation/Parole Performances.* Washington, DC: U.S. Government Printing Office.

NELSON, E. KIM, HOWARD OHMART AND NORA HARLOW
1978   *Promising Strategies in Probation and Parole.* Washington, DC: U.S. Government Printing Office.

NEWMAN, CHARLES L.
  1961   "Concepts of Treatment in Probation and Parole." *Federal Probation* 25 (March).

NEW YORK STATE SPECIAL COMMISSION ON ATTICA
  1972   *Attica.* New York: Praeger.

NIETZEL, MICHAEL T. AND MELISSA J. HIMELEIN
  1987   "Probation and Parole." Pages 109–133 in *Behavioral Approaches to Crime and Delinquency: A Handbook of Application, Research, and Concepts,* edited by Edward K. Morris and Curtis J. Braukmann. New York: Plenum.

NOONAN, SUSAN B. AND EDWARD J. LATESSA
  1987   "Intensive Probation: An Examination of Recidivism and Social Adjustment." *American Journal of Criminal Justice* 11: 45–61.

NORTHERN, HELEN
  1988   *Social Work with Groups,* 2nd ed. New York: Columbia University Press.

  1969   *Social Work with Groups.* New York: Columbia University Press.

OFFICE OF POLICY ANALYSIS AND INFORMATION
  1989   *Shock Incarceration: One Year Out.* Albany: New York State Division of Parole.

O'LEARY, K. DANIEL AND G. TERRANCE WILSON
  1975   *Behavior Therapy: Application and Outcome.* Englewood Cliffs, NJ: Prentice-Hall.

OMER, HAIM AND PERRY LONDON
  1988   "Metamorphosis in Psychotherapy: End of the Systems Era." *Psychotherapy* 25 (Summer): 171–80.

OSTROWER, ROLAND
  1962   "Study, Diagnosis, and Treatment: A Conceptual Structure." *Social Work* 7 (October).

OVERVIEW STUDY OF EMPLOYMENT OF PARAPROFESSIONALS
  1974   Washington, DC: U.S. Government Printing Office.

PALMER, TED
  1974   "The Youth Authority's Community Treatment Project." *Federal Probation* 38 (March).

  1975   "Martinson Revisted." *Journal of Research in Crime and Delinquency* 12 (July).

PARENT, DALE G.
  1989   "Probation Supervision Fee Collection in Texas." *Perspectives* 13 (Winter): 9–12.

  1989b   *Shock Incarceration: An Overview of Existing Programs.* Washington, DC: U.S. Government Printing Office.

  1988   "Overview: Shock-Incarceration Programs." *Perspectives* 12 (July): 9–15.

PARKER, WILLIAM
  1975   *Parole.* College Park, MD: American Correctional Association.

PAROLE OFFICER'S MANUAL
  1953   Albany, NY: New York State Division of Parole.

PARSONAGE, WILLIAM H. AND W. CONWAY BUSHEY
  1989   "The Victimization of Probation and Parole Workers in the Line of Duty: An Exploratory Study." Paper presented at the annual meeting of the Academy of Criminal Justice Sciences, March, Washington, DC. Forthcoming in *Criminal Justice Policy Review.*

PEARSON, FRANK S.
1988   "Evaluation of New Jersey's Intensive Supervision Program." *Crime and Delinquency* 34 (October): 437–48.

PERLMAN, HELEN HARRIS
1957   *Perspectives on Social Casework.* Philadelphia: Temple University Press.

1971   *Perspectives on Social Casework: A Problem Solving Process.* Chicago: University of Chicago Press.

PETERSILIA, JOAN M.
1990   "When Probation Becomes More Dreaded Than Prison." *Federal Probation* 54 (March): 23–27.

1988a   "Georgia's Intensive Probation: Will the Model Work Elsewhere?" Pages 15–30 in *Intermediate Punishments: Intensive Supervision, Home Confinement and Electronic Surveillance.* Monsey, NY: Criminal Justice Press.

1988b   *House Arrest.* Washington, DC: National Institute of Justice.

1987   *Expanding Options for Criminal Sentencing.* Santa Monica, CA: Rand Corporation.

PETERSILIA, JOAN AND SUSAN TURNER
1990   "Comparing Intensive and Regular Supervision for High-Risk Probationers: Early Results from an Experiment in California." *Crime and Delinquency* 36 (January): 87–111.

PETERSILIA, JOAN, SUSAN TURNER, JAMES KAHAN, AND JOYCE PETERSON
1985   *Granting Felons Probation: Public Risks and Alternatives.* Santa Monica, CA: Rand Corporation.

PLATT, ANTHONY M.
1974   *The Childsavers: The Invention of Delinquency.* Chicago: University of Chicago Press.

POLAKOW, ROBERT L. AND RONALD M. DOCKTOR
1974   "A Behavioral Modification Program for Adult Drug Offenders." *Journal of Research in Crime and Delinquency* 11 (January) 63–69.

POLLOCK-BYRNE, JOYCELYN M.
1990   *Women, Prison, and Crime.* Pacific Grove, CA: Brooks/Cole.

PRESIDENT'S COMMISSION ON LAW ENFORCEMENT AND ADMINISTRATION OF JUSTICE
1972   *The Challenge of Crime in a Free Society.* New York: Avon.

PRESIDENT'S COMMISSION ON ORGANIZED CRIME
1986   *The Impact: Organized Crime Today.* Washington, DC: U.S. Government Printing Office.

PRISON ASSOCIATION OF NEW YORK
1936   *The Ninety-First Annual Report.* Albany: J.B. Lyon.

PROGRAM SERVICES OFFICE
1983   *Probation Classification and Service Delivery Approach.* Los Angeles County Probation Department.

PRZYBYLSKI, ROGER
1988   *Electronically Monitored Home Confinement in Illinois.* Chicago: Illinois Criminal Justice Information Authority.

QUADAGNO, JILL S. AND ROBERT J. ANTONIO
1975   "Labeling Theory as an Oversocialized Conception of Man: The Case of Mental Illness." *Sociology and Social Research* 60 (October).

RAAB, SELWYN
    1989   "Youthful Offenders: 3 'Secure Center' Inmates Tell of Murder and Prison." *New York Times* (June 3): 9.

RACHIN, RICHARD
    1974   "Reality Therapy: Helping People Help Themselves." *Crime and Delinquency* 20 (January).

REED, JOHN AND DALE NANCE
    1972   "Society Perpetuates the Stigma of a Conviction." *Federal Probation* 36 (June).

REIFF, PHILLIP, ED.
    1963   *Freud, Therapy and Techniques.* New York: Crowell-Collier.

REIMAN, JEFFREY
    1990   *The Rich Get Richer and the Poor Get Prison,* 3rd ed. New York: Macmillan.

REMINGTON, BOB AND MARINA REMINGTON
    1987   "Behavior Modification in Probation Work." *Criminal Justice and Behavior* 14 (June): 156–74.

REYNA, L.J.
    1964   "Conditioning Therapies, Learning Theory, and Research." Pages 169–179 in *The Conditioning Therapies,* edited by Joseph Wolpe, Andrew Salter and L.J. Reyna. New York: Holt, Rinehart and Winston.

ROBBINS, IRA P.
    1988   *The Legal Dimensions of Private Incarceration.* Washington, DC: American Bar Association.

ROBBINS, WILLIAM
    1989   "Seeing a Prison Project as Economic Freedom." *New York Times* (May 25): 11.

ROBERTSON, JOHN A.
    1974   *Rough Justice: Perspectives on Lower Courts.* Boston: Little, Brown.

ROBITSCHER, JONAS
    1980   *The Power of Psychiatry.* Boston: Houghton Mifflin.

    1985   *Perspectives* 9 (Spring).

ROOT, LAWRENCE P.
    1972   "Work Release Legislation." *Federal Probation* 36 (March).

ROSE, SHELDON D.
    1977   *Group Therapy: A Behavioral Approach.* Englewood Cliffs, NJ: Prentice-Hall.

ROSENBLUM, ROBERT, AND DEBRA WHITCOMB
    1978   *Montgomery County Work Release/Pre-Release Program.* Washington, DC: U.S. Government Printing Office.

ROSS, BERNARD AND CHARLES SHIREMAN
    1972   *Social Work and Social Justice.* Washington, DC: National Association of Social Workers.

ROTHMAN, DAVID
    1971   *The Discovery of the Asylum.* Boston: Little, Brown.

ROUSSEAU, JEAN JACQUES
    1954   *The Social Contract.* Chicago: Henry Regnery.

RUBIN, H. TED
1980   "The Emerging Prosecutor Dominance of the Juvenile Court Intake Process." *Crime and Delinquency* 26 (July).

RUBIN, SOL
1974   "The Impact of Court Decisions in the Correctional Process." *Crime and Delinquency* 20 (April).

RUSH, GEORGE E.
1988   "Electronic Surveillance: An Alternative to Incarceration (An Overview of the San Diego County Program)." *American Journal of Criminal Justice* 12: 219–42.

SACHS, HOWARD AND CHARLES LOGAN
1979   *Does Parole Make a Difference?* West Hartford, CT: University of Connecticut Law School.

SAGAN, ELI
1988   *Freud, Women, and Morality.* New York: Basic Books.

SAGATUN, INGER, LORETTA McCOLLUM, AND MICHAEL EDWARDS
1985   "The Effect of Transfers From Juvenile to Criminal Court: A Loglinear Analysis." *Journal of Crime and Justice* 8: 65–92.

SALTER, ANDREW
1964   "The Theory and Practice of Conditioned Reflex Therapy." Pages 21–37 in *The Conditioning Therapies,* edited by Joseph Wolpe, Andrew Salter and L.J. Reyna. New York: Holt, Rinehart and Winston.

SANDHU, HARJIT S. AND RICHARD A. DODDER
1986   "Community-Based Alternatives to Incarceration: A Comparison of Their In-Progress Success or Failure." Paper presented at the Annual Meeting of the American Society of Criminology, November, Atlanta, GA.

SCHLOSSMAN, STEVEN L.
1977   *Love and the American Delinquent: The Theory and Practice of "Progressive" Juvenile Justice, 1825–1920.* Chicago: University of Chicago Press.

SCHMIDEBERG, MELITTA
1975   "Some Basic Principles of Offender Therapy: Two." *International Journal of Offender Therapy and Comparative Criminology* 1.

SCHMIDT, ANNESLEY K.
1989   "Electronic Monitoring of Offenders Increases." *NIJ Reports* (January/February): 2–5.

SCHRAM, DONNA D., JILL G. McKELVY, ANNE L. SCHNEIDER, AND DAVID B. GRISWOLD
1981   *Preliminary Findings: Assessment of the Juvenile Code.* State of Washington mimeo.

SCHULTZ, J. LAWRENCE
1973   "The Cycle of Juvenile Court History." *Crime and Delinquency* 19 (October).

SCHUMAN, ALAN M.
1989   "The Cost of Correctional Services: Exploring a Poorly Charted Terrain." *Research in Corrections* 2 (February): 27–33.

SCHUR, EDWIN M.
1973   *Radical Non-Intervention: Rethinking the Delinquency Problem.* Englewood Cliffs, NJ: Prentice-Hall.

SCHWARTZ, IRA M., LINDA HARRIS AND LAURIE LEVI
1988   "The Jailing of Juveniles in Minnesota: A Case Study: *Crime and Delinquency* 34 (April): 133–49.

SCHWARTZ, RICHARD AND JEROME H. SKOLNICK
1962   "Two Studies in Legal Stigma." *Social Problems* 10: 133–42.

SCHWARTZ, WILLIAM
1966   "Some Notes on the Use of Groups in Social Work Practice." Address delivered to the Annual Workshop for Field Instructors and Faculty of the Columbia School of Social Work, mimeo.

1976   "Between Client and System: The Mediating Function." Pages 171–97 in *Theories of Social Work With Groups,* edited by Robert W. Roberts and Helen Northern. New York: Columbia University Press.

SCHWITZGEBEL, RALPH K.
1969a   "Issues in the Use of an Electronic Rehabilitation System With Chronic Recidivists." *Law and Society Review* 3: 597–611.

1969b   "Development of an Electronic Rehabilitation System for Parolees." *Law and Computer Technology* 2: 9–12.

1968   "Electronic Alternatives to Imprisonment." *Lex et Scientia* 5 (3): 99–104.

SCULL, ANDREW T.
1977   *Decarceration.* Englewood Cliffs, NJ: Prentice-Hall.

SECHREST, DALE K.
1989   "Prison 'Boot Camps' Do Not Measure Up." *Federal Probation* 53 (September): 15–20.

SECHCREST, LEE, SUSAN O. WHITE, AND ELIZABETH D. BROWN
1979   *The Rehabilitation of Criminal Offenders: Problems and Prospects.* Washington, DC: National Academy of Sciences.

SELIGMAN, JOEL
1978   *The High Citadel: The Influence of Harvard Law School.* Boston: Houghton Mifflin.

SELLIN, THORSTON
1967   "A Look at Prison History." *Federal Probation* 31 (September).

SHAFFER, JOHN AND M. DAVID GALINSKY
1989   *Models of Group Therapy,* 2nd ed. Englewood Cliffs, NJ: Prentice-Hall.

SHELDON, RANDALL G., JOHN A. HORVATH, AND SHARON TRACY
1989   "Do Status Offenders Get Worse? Some Clarifications on the Question of Escalation." *Crime and Delinquency* 35 (April): 202–216.

SHENON, PHILIP
1985   "Data Sought on SmithKline Inquiry." *New York Times* (September 14): 8.

1985   "Drug Case Divided Officials at F.D.A. and Justice Department." *New York Times* (September 19): 1, 14.

SHICHOR, DAVID AND CLEMENS BARTOLLAS
1990   "Private and Public Juvenile Placements: Is There a Difference?" *Crime and Delinquency* 36 (April): 286–99.

SHORT, JAMES R., JR.
1968   *Gang Delinquency and Delinquent Subcultures.* New York: Harper and Row.

SKIDMORE, REX A., MILTON G. THACKERAY, AND O. WILLIAM FARLEY
1988   *Introduction to Social Work.* 4th ed. Englewood Cliffs, NJ: Prentice-Hall.

SKINNER, B.F.
1972   *Beyond Freedom and Dignity.* New York: Knopf.

SMITH, ALEXANDER AND LOUIS BERLIN
1974   "Self-Determination in Welfare and Corrections: Is There a Limit? *Federal Probation* 38 (December).

SMITH, RICHARD AUSTIN
1961   "The Incredible Electrical Conspiracy." *Fortune* (April). 161–64, 210, 212, 217–218; 221–24.

1961   "The Incredible Electrical Conspiracy." *Fortune* (May). 132–37, 170, 175–176, 179–80.

SPENCER, JIM
1987   " 'Kock 'em Out, Trainee.' " *Chicago Tribune* (July 26): Sec. 3: 1, 2.

STAMPFL, THOMAS G.
1970   "Comment" [on token economies] in *Learning Approaches to Therapeutic Behavior Change,* edited by Donald H. Levis. Chicago: Aldine.

STANLEY, DAVID T.
1976   *Prisoners Among Us: The Problem of Parole.* Washington, DC: Brookings Institution.

STAR, DEBORAH
1979   *Summary Parole: A Six and Twelve Month Follow-Up Evaluation.* Sacramento: California Department of Corrections.

STOLZ, STEPHANIE B., LOUIS A. WIENCKOWSKI, AND BERTRAM S. BROWN
1975   "Behavior Modification: A Perspective on Critical Issues." *American Psychologist* 30 (November).

STRONG, ANN
1981   *Case Classification Manual, Module One: Technical Aspects of Interviewing.* Austin: Texas Adult Probation Commission.

SULLIVAN, MICHAEL P.
1987   "Parole Guidelines: An Effective Prison Population Management Tool." Pages 83–85 in *Observations on Parole: A Collection of Readings From Western Europe, Canada and the United States,* edited by Edward E. Rhine and Ronald W. Jackson. Washington, DC: U.S. Government Printing Office.

SULZER, BETH AND G. ROY MAYER
1972   *Behavior Modification Procedures for School Personnel.* Hinsdale, IL: Dryden.

SUTHERLAND, EDWIN H.
1972   *The Professional Thief.* Chicago: University of Chicago Press.

1973   *Edwin Sutherland: On Analyzing Crime.* Edited by Karl Schuessler. Chicago: University of Chicago Press.

SUTHERLAND, EDWIN H. AND DONALD R. CRESSEY
1966   *Principles of Criminology.* New York: Lippincott.

SUTTON, JOHN R.
1988   *Stubborn Children: Controlling Delinquency in the United States, 1649–1981.* Berkeley, CA: University of California Press.

SWANGER, HARRY F.
1988   "Hendrickson v. Griggs: A Review of the Legal and Policy Implications for Juvenile Justice Policymakers." *Crime and Delinquency* 34 (April): 209–27.

SYKES, GRESHAM M. AND DAVID MATZA
1957   "Techniques of Neutralization: A Theory of Delinquency." *American Sociological Review* 22 (December).

TAKAGI, PAUL
1975   "The Walnut Street Jail: A Penal Reform to Centralize the Powers of the State." *Federal Probation* 39 (December): 18–26.

TAKAS, MARRIANNE AND THEODORE M. HAMMETT
1989   *Legal Issues Affecting Offenders and Staff.* Washington, DC: U.S. Government Printing Office.

TASK FORCE ON CORRECTIONS
1966   *Task Force Report: Corrections.* Washington, DC: U.S. Government Printing Office.

TAYLOR, IAN, PAUL WALTON AND JOCK YOUNG
1973   *The New Criminology.* New York: Harper and Row.

TEETERS, NEGLEY K.
1970   "The Passing of Cherry Hill: Most Famous Prison in the World." *Prison Journal* 50 (Spring-Summer): 1–12.

1985   "Tennessee Inmates Riot Over Uniforms." *New York Times* (July 3): 11.

TEXAS ADULT PROBATION COMMISSION (TAPC)
1988   *A Comparison of Special Program Probationers and Prison Inmates.* Austin: TAPC.

THALHEIMER, DONALD J.
1975   *Halfway Houses. Vol. 2.* Washington, DC: U.S. Government Printing Office.

THE AMERICAN RESPONSE TO CRIME
1983   Washington, DC: U.S. Bureau of Justice Statistics.

THOMPSON, JAMES W., MICHELLE SVIRIDOFF, JEROME E. MCELROY, RICHARD MCGAHEY AND ORLANDO RODIRIGUEZ
1981   *Employment and Crime: A Review of Theories and Research.* Washington, DC: U.S. Government Printing Office.

THORNE, GAYLORD L., ROLAND G. THARP, AND RALPH J. WETZEL
1967   "Behavior Modification Technique: New Tools for Probation Officers." *Federal Probation* 31 (June): 21–27.

TOBORG, MARY A., LAWRENCE J. CARTER, RAYMOND H. MILKMAN AND DENNIS W. DAVIS
1978   *The Transition From Prison to Employment: An Assessment of Community-Based Programs.* Washington, DC: U.S. Government Printing Office.

TOLCHIN, MARTIN
1985   "As Privately-Owned Prisons Increase, So Do Their Critics." *New York Times* (February 11): 1, 12.

TONRY, MICHAEL AND RICHARD WILL
1988   "Intermediate Sanctions." Preliminary report to the National Institute of Justice.

TORGERSON, FERNANDO G.
1962   "Differentiating and Defining Casework and Psychotherapy." *Social Casework* 43 (April).

TRAVIS, LAWRENCE F., III AND EDWARD J. LATESSA
1984 " 'A Summary of Parole Rules—Thirteen Years Later': Revisited Thirteen Years Later." *Journal of Criminal Justice* 12.

TWENTIETH CENTURY FUND TASK FORCE ON SENTENCING
1976 *Fair and Certain Punishment.* New York: McGraw-Hill.

VELIE, LESTER AND JEROME G. MILLER
1985 "More Prisons Aren't the Answer." *New York Times* (July 30): 31.

VINTER, ROBERT D.
1985 "The Essential Components of Group Work Practice." Pages 11–34 in *Individual Change Through Small Groups,* edited by Martin Sundel, Paul Glasser, Rosemary Sarri, and Robert Vinter. New York: Free Press.

VITO, GENNARO F.
1986 "Felony Probation and Recidivism: Replication and Response." *Federal Probation* 50 (December): 17–25.

"VOCATIONAL COUNSELING WITH THE OFFENDER"
1965 New York State Employment Services Vocational Rehabilitation Service mimeo.

VOLD, GEORGE B. AND THOMAS J. BERNARD
1986 *Theoretical Criminology,* 3rd ed. New York: Oxford University Press.

VON HIRSCH, ANDREW
1976 *Doing Justice: The Choice of Punishments.* New York: Hill and Wang.

VON HIRSCH, ANDREW AND KATHLEEN J. HANRAHAN
1978 *Abolish Parole?* Washington, DC: U.S. Government Printing Office.

WAGNER, DENNIS
1989 "An Evaluation of the High Risk Offender Intensive Supervision Project." *Perspectives* 13 (Summer): 22–27.

WALDO, GORDON AND DAVID GRISWOLD
1979 "Issues in the Measurement of Recidivism," in *The Rehabilitation of Criminal Offenders: Problems and Prospects,* edited by Lee Sechrest, Susan O. White and Elizabeth D. Brown. Washington, DC: National Academy of Sciences.

WALKER, SAMUEL
1980 *Popular Justice: A History of American Criminal Justice.* New York: Oxford University Press.

"WASHINGTON TALK"
1985 *New York Times* (August 15): 12.

WEBER, MAX
1958 *Protestant Ethic and the Spirit of Capitalism.* New York: Scribner's.

WEISHEIT, RALPH H. AND DIANE M. ALEXANDER
1988 "Juvenile Justice and the Demise of Parens Patriae." *Federal Probation* 52 (December): 56–63.

WHEELER, GERALD R., RODNEY V. HISSONG, THERESE M. MACAN, AND MORGAN P. SLUSHER
1989 "The Effects of Probation Service Fees on Case Management Strategy and Sanctions." *Journal of Criminal Justice* 17: 15–24.

WHEELER, HARVEY, ED.
1973 *Beyond the Punitive Society.* San Francisco: W.H. Freeman.

WHITE, JOSEPH L.
1987   "The Waiver Decision: A Judicial, Prosecutorial or Legislative Responsibility?" *Justice for Children* 2 (No. 1-2): 28-30.

WHITEHEAD, JOHN T.
1989   "The Effectiveness of Felony Probation: A Replication and Extension of Three Studies." Paper presented at the Annual Meeting of the American Society of Criminology, Reno, November.

WICKER, TOM
1975   *A Time to Die.* New York: Quadrangle.

WIEDERANDERS, MARK R.
1983   *Success on Parole.* Sacramento: California Department of Corrections.

WILENSKY, HAROLD L. AND CHARLES N. LEBEAUX
1958   *Industrial Society and Social Welfare.* New York: Russell Sage Foundation.

WILSON, ROB
1978   "Probation/Parole Officers as 'Resource Brokers.' " *Corrections Magazine* 4 (June).

WINES, FREDERICK HOWARD
1975   *Punishment and Reformation: A Study of the Penitentiary System.* New York: Thomas Y. Crowell.

WIZNER, STEPHEN
1984   "Discretionary Waiver of Juvenile Court Jurisdiction: An Invitation to Procedural Arbitariness." *Criminal Justice Ethics* 3 (Summer-Fall).

WOLPE, JOSEPH, ANDREW SALTER, AND L.H. REYNA, EDS.
1964   *The Conditioning Therapies.* New York: Holt, Rinehart and Winston.

YELLOLY, MARGARET
1980   *Social Work Theory and Psychoanalysis.* New York: Van Nostrand Reinhold.

ZAWITZ, MARIANNE W., ED.
1988   *Report to the Nation on Crime and Justice.* Washington, DC: U.S. Government Printing Office.

ZEVITZ, RICHARD G. AND SUSAN R. TAKATA
1988   "Paroling Prisoners Sentenced to County Jail: An Analysis of 75 Years of Misdemeanor Parole Legislation." *Journal of Criminal Justice* 11: 61-86.

ZINGRAFF, MATTHEW T. AND MICHAEL J. BELYEA
1986   "Child Abuse and Violent Crime." Pages 49-63 in *The Dilemmas of Punishment,* edited by Kenneth C. Haas and Geoffrey P. Alpert. Prospect Heights, IL: Waveland Press.

Author Index

Subject Index